## A student guide to
# Clinical Legal Education
# and Pro Bono

*The College of Law*
*of England and Wales*

**LIBRARY SERVICES**

Birmingham ● Bristol ● Chester ● Guildford ● London ● Manchester ● York

A student guide to

# Clinical Legal Education and Pro Bono

Edited by

**Kevin Kerrigan and
Victoria Murray**

First published 2011 by PALGRAVE MACMILLAN

Palgrave Macmillan in the UK is an imprint of Macmillan Publishers Limited, registered in England, company number 785998, of Houndmills, Basingstoke, Hampshire RG21 6XS.

Palgrave Macmillan in the US is a division of St Martin's Press LLC, 175 Fifth Avenue, New York, NY 10010.

Palgrave Macmillan is the global academic imprint of the above companies and has companies and representatives throughout the world.

Palgrave® and Macmillan® are registered trademarks in the United States, the United Kingdom, Europe and other countries

ISBN 978–0–230–24963–9  paperback

This book is printed on paper suitable for recycling and made from fully managed and sustained forest sources. Logging, pulping and manufacturing processes are expected to conform to the environmental regulations of the country of origin.

A catalogue record for this book is available from the British Library.

10  9  8  7  6  5  4  3  2  1
20 19 18 17 16 15 14 13 12 11

Printed and bound in Great Britain by Thomson Litho, East Kilbride.

# Contents

**7**    Legal writing and drafting                                            **126**
*Carol Boothby*

**8**    Practical legal research                                              **148**
*Jonny Hall*

**9**    Organising and strategising                                          **171**
*Caroline Foster*

## 10    Advocacy                                                          187
*Judith Gowland*

## 11    Presentations                                                     213
*Victoria Murray*

# Preface

This is the first ever handbook of clinical and pro bono learning aimed at students. This exciting, interactive and engaging way of learning the law appears in one form or another in the vast majority of UK law schools, having expanded dramatically in recent years. It is part of a global phenomenon which has its roots in social justice education projects in the USA, Australia, South Africa and elsewhere. It also reflects the desire of law societies around the world to promote the pro bono ethic to existing and future members of the legal profession.

This book offers essential guidance and advice if you are currently learning in a law clinic or pro bono project. It also assists you to prepare for future participation in such initiatives. If your law school does not yet offer opportunities to become involved, this book helps you to work with your lecturers to develop new projects.

Clinical legal education and pro bono are related but distinct concepts. This book addresses both areas while retaining common themes where appropriate. The book covers broad areas of legal education and legal practice. It introduces you to the concepts of clinical legal education and pro bono, advises on the establishment of new projects, addresses key strategic planning issues and provides individual guidance on your personal development, performance and reflection in clinic and pro bono schemes.

Key features of the book include accessible and practical advice to help you survive the challenging experience of clinical learning; expert guidance and tips on how to maximise your performance; and helpful checklists and activities to improve your core clinical skills. It has not been possible to include everything we would have wished to within these pages. You will therefore find a wealth of additional material available on our Companion Website at www.palgrave.com/law/lawclinic.

We hope that you find this book both informative and motivating and that it enriches your clinical and pro bono activities, which are likely to be the highlight of your university experience.

# Foreword

This book is written at a time when the need for pro bono legal services has never been greater. Far reaching governmental cuts during 2010 and 2011 will mean that many more vulnerable people may be unable to access vital legal services they will need in order to seek recompense following devastating events in their lives.

Some say that law and justice are two different things which should never be confused. Yet, every good lawyer knows that the skill is using the former in order to deliver the latter. Within our meritocratic society, it is essential for lawyers to bridge the gap between the 'haves' and the 'have-nots'. The 'haves' are those who can access and afford legal services. The 'have-nots' are the disadvantaged, the vulnerable and the disenfranchised; not just because of their finances but because the legal services they need just do not exist within their area.

Clinical legal education and pro bono service are a powerful force for good. I do not need to explain the ethical meaning and implications of the words *pro bono publico*; this book is testament to that. However, I would urge practitioners to take note of the framework set out within this book and breathe life into it to enable pro bono services to grow and underpin legal services for all, and not just for the privileged few.

To students who will pick up this book as part of their reading list, or in passing: I hope you use this to take the first step towards helping people in ways they could never have imagined. Use the experience you gain as part of your clinical legal education to hone the skills you will need: independence of mind, sound judgement, integrity, honesty and trustworthiness. These values will carry your name far and wide, for all of the right reasons. I believe pro bono is part of every good lawyer's DNA and the thirst to deliver justice for those who need it lies at its root.

Saving the best until last, I commend authors of this book: Kevin Kerrigan, Victoria Murray, Carol Boothby, Caroline Foster, Jonny Hall, Judith Gowland, Paul McKeown and all of the members and students at The Student Law Office at Northumbria University. Your work to document a vital area of our practice has provided an immovable stepping stone towards universal access to justice for all.

Best wishes,

The Rt Hon the Baroness Scotland of Asthal QC PC

*The Baroness Scotland of Asthal QC PC was the Attorney General between 2007–2010 and the first woman to hold the post since its creation in 1315.*

To all our families and colleagues

# Acknowledgements

We would like to acknowledge first the dedication and commitment of our fellow authors, Carol Boothby, Caroline Foster, Judith Gowland, Jonny Hall and Paul McKeown, whose expertise and wisdom have helped make this book a reality. We are all clinical supervisors at Northumbria University's award-winning Student Law Office. This is an inspirational learning and scholarly environment which pushes students to achieve their best and engenders a lifelong commitment to learning and public service.

The editors would also like to thank the brilliant LawWorks student team, particularly Martin Curtis and Richard Harrison, for their valuable assistance and comments on earlier drafts of this work. Their tireless work and enthusiasm in promoting the ideal of pro bono in law schools is greatly valued by students, clients and the profession.

We would further like to express our gratitude to all at Palgrave Macmillan who have supported the production of this book so professionally. We would like to thank in particular Rob Gibson, our commissioning editor, and Jasmin Naim, who encouraged us during the initial stages of the book. We found the comments of anonymous reviewers to be highly constructive in improving the quality of the finished product. We take full responsibility for any remaining errors and omissions.

Finally, this work would not have been possible without our students and clients, who have enriched our understanding of clinical legal education with all of its joys and challenges.

The editors and publishers wish to thank the following for permission to use copyright material: Princeton University Press for the quote from Einstein, Albert, *The Collected Papers of Albert Einstein*, 1987–2011, Hebrew University and Princeton University Press; The United Nations for extracts from the Havana Declaration on the Role of the Lawyer 1990; Graham Gibbs for Gibbs' Model of Reflection; Pearson Education, Inc for Kolb's Learning Cycle from Kolb, David A, *Experiential Learning: Experience as a Source of Learning and Development*, 1st edn (1984); Taylor & Francis

Group for 'Promoting Reflection in Learning: A Model' from Boud, D, Keogh, R and Walker, D (eds), *Reflection: Turning experience into learning* (pp 18–40) (London: Kogan Page). Every effort has been made to trace all copyright holders but if any have been inadvertently overlooked the publishers will be pleased to make the necessary arrangements at the first opportunity.

# About the authors

The authors are all employed by Northumbria University and supervise cases in the School of Law's award-winning legal clinic, the Student Law Office.

### Kevin Kerrigan

Kevin is Associate Dean for Undergraduate and Clinical Programmes and is a National Teaching Fellow. He is also a practising solicitor and Human Rights Act consultant with experience of conducting criminal and human rights cases in courts at all levels. He runs a criminal appeal clinic in the Student Law Office, is a co-ordinator of the Clinical Legal Education Organisation and is on the Advisory Board of the United Kingdom Centre for Legal Education. He is the editor of the International Journal of Clinical Legal Education and organises an annual international clinical conference.

### Victoria Murray

Victoria is a Senior Lecturer and Deputy Programme Leader of the M Law/ Exempting Degree. Her experience of clinical legal education dates back to her student days and she now supervises employment cases in the Student Law Office. Victoria is also responsible for the compulsory clinical module in year 3, which prepares students for the full representation clinic. Victoria was a finalist in the Law Teacher of the Year 2010 and she was highly commended at the Junior Lawyer Division 2008 Pro Bono awards in the 'Solicitor Team' category.

### Carol Boothby

Carol is a Principal Lecturer and Director of the Student Law Office. After several years in private practice working in the areas of family law, housing and civil litigation, Carol joined Northumbria University as a Solicitor Tutor. She supervises civil and housing cases and is also a member of the local Duty Possession Scheme, representing defendants in housing matters at Newcastle County Court. She is also a part-time tribunal judge with the Appeals Service, hearing social security cases.

## Caroline Foster

Caroline is employed as a Solicitor Tutor working exclusively in the Student Law Office. She supervises students conducting employment and civil cases including Criminal Injuries Compensation Appeal matters. Caroline was highly commended at the Junior Lawyers Division 2008 Pro Bono awards in the 'Solicitor Team' category. Before joining Northumbria she worked as a specialist employment solicitor at a national law firm undertaking work on behalf of trade unions.

## Jonny Hall

Jonny is a Principal Lecturer and is the Programme Leader of the M Law/LLB Exempting degree. He is a qualified solicitor with over ten years' experience of acting in civil and personal injury claims and actions against the police. Jonny continues to practise both through his role as a supervisor in the Student Law Office and as a consultant to a leading North East legal aid firm. Jonny was a commended finalist in the Law Teacher of the Year Award 2004.

## Judith Gowland

Judith is employed as a Senior Lecturer and is Programme Leader for the Graduate Diploma in Law. Judith qualified as a solicitor and spent the following seven years in private practice dealing primarily with criminal litigation. Judith's area of expertise is criminal defence work, although she also has experience in prosecuting for the CPS and various private bodies. She successfully passed the accreditation process for both police station and magistrates' court work and was a duty solicitor on both rotas. She supervises criminal cases in the Student Law Office.

## Paul McKeown

Paul trained as a solicitor at Carlisle Community Law Centre under the Legal Services Commission Training Contract Grants Scheme. Following qualification, Paul worked at Gateshead Law Centre before joining Northumbria University as a Solicitor Tutor, working in the Student Law Office. Paul specialises in housing, employment and welfare benefits. He also undertakes small claims work where legal aid is not available. Paul represents clients via the Duty Possession Scheme at Newcastle County Court. He was highly commended at the Junior Lawyers Division 2008 Pro Bono awards in the 'Solicitor Team' category.

# ① What is clinical legal education and pro bono?

> 'I shall not attempt to define hard core pornography but I know it when I see it ...'
>
> Justice Potter Stewart, *Jacobellis v Ohio* 378 US 184 (1964)

## ⓵ What is in a name?

This book is about clinical legal education and pro bono activities. Although these are conceptually distinct, there is significant overlap in law school-based projects, and this is why they have been brought together for the purposes of this book. Often participants will not be concerned about whether a particular project is clinical or pro bono or both – you will be more interested in what learning or other opportunities it gives rise to. Nevertheless, sometimes categories are important and, given that this book professes to be a guide to clinical legal education and pro bono, you can legitimately expect it to provide workable definitions. Unsurprisingly, like many educational concepts, it is very difficult to pin down one all-encompassing definition that will meet with the approval of everyone. Nevertheless, this chapter will attempt to give you a coherent explanation that will help to set the parameters for the remainder of the book.

## ⓶ Types of clinical schemes

Before moving on to definitions, it may be helpful to look at some common types of clinical and pro bono schemes:

### In-house advice and representation clinics

These are often viewed as the gold standard of law clinics as they seek to replicate in the law school the type of service clients could expect if they went to a firm of solicitors. You provide a full legal service to the public under the supervision of academic practitioners. These clinics may be general (covering a number of different areas of law) or may specialise in one or two areas (for example a housing law clinic specialising in landlord and tenant disputes). These clinics are often established only with significant backing from within the law school because they require sustained investment in staffing, premises and other resources (see **Chapter 2**).

## Advice-only/gateway clinics

These provide initial advice and/or referral to other legal services. This is a more limited version of the in-house advice and representation clinic. The key distinction tends to be that the clinic's involvement with the client is limited to initial or other specific tasks so that there is no open-ended retainer. These clinics cover a very wide range of different activities, such as a drop-in advice clinic where you will provide a type of triage service to make clients aware of other sources of help, a telephone advice line where you never meet the client, or an email research service where clients can ask you specific questions to help them with their legal problems. These types of clinics often work with external lawyers or other agencies, either referring clients on, or assisting the law firm/agency with its case work.

## Placement or externship schemes

These involve you going out of the law school to work (on a paid or unpaid basis) with law firms or other external agencies. This has the advantage of giving you an authentic experience in that you participate in a real-world organisation. It does this without the need to create a legal services infrastructure within the law school itself. A characteristic of this type of scheme is that the law school does not have day-to-day control or oversight of your learning experience. This can lead to quality control problems. There may also be challenges for assessment of learning outcomes if the clinic is part of an assessed module. Successful schemes therefore depend on good relationships between academic staff, external supervisors and you, the students.

## Streetlaw projects

In this type of project you work as a member of a team to educate community groups about an area of law or legal rights relevant to members of the group. You work with a university-based and/or external supervisor to prepare a presentation or briefing for a group or organisation such as a school, residents' association, prison and so on. As will be seen, there is some doubt over whether this type of activity counts as clinical legal education. Streetlaw has been included within this book as the authors think that it does fall within a broad notion of clinical activity and is often the type of venture that a law school will introduce initially before deciding whether to proceed with more ambitious clinical schemes.

## Simulation activities

You act in roles as lawyers performing realistic but standardised tasks set by your tutor. A major difference from other types of clinical project is that the clients and cases are hypothetical. This means that the academic coordinator/lecturer retains control of the experience and can to a significant extent dictate the tasks that you will need to perform and the learning outcomes to be achieved. Again, some have doubted whether such activities count as clinical legal education. This book will explain later that these activities clearly do count, albeit that your experience will often differ significantly from live client models.

### Voluntary pro bono activities

There are a significant number of pro bono schemes that take place as part of or as an adjunct to study at law schools. These include legal letter clinics, coordination of pro bono activity by local lawyers, legal literacy projects, court buddy activity, prison rights workshops, helping bodies such as the Citizens Advice Bureau or the Free Representation Unit and many others. Students may often not secure academic credit for such activities, but it ought to inform and contextualise your wider learning about law and the legal process.

### Specialist clinical projects

There is a wide range of other clinical projects which do not fall clearly into one of the above categories. These may include niche areas of law or provision of particular skills. Examples are Innocence Projects where students (possibly including non-law students) assist a criminal lawyer to investigate suspected miscarriages of justice, advocacy services such as the Free Representation Unit, or policy/law reform clinics which identify areas where the law operates unsatisfactorily and work with campaign or interest groups to try to change the law or procedure.

## **1.3** Definitions – what is pro bono?

Starting off with the more straightforward of the two concepts, pro bono is a shortened version of the Latin 'pro bono publico' which means 'for the public good'. It can be applied to any service provided for free for public benefit, but is most often referred to in a professional and more specifically legal context when lawyers provide their services for free, normally to people who could not otherwise afford to pay.

For many, a commitment to pro bono is part of a lawyer's ethical duty as a professional – given that lawyers make a living through the justice system, it is important that they give something back to benefit people who might otherwise not have access to justice. In some countries there is a professional expectation of pro bono, for example the American Bar Association requires US lawyers to provide a minimum of 50 hours of pro bono service each year (see ABA Model Rules of Professional Conduct, Rule 6.1). Some law societies have gone further and actually require lawyers to perform pro bono work, for instance, in South Africa, the Cape Law Society Rules, Rule 21 states: 'Practising members who have practised for less than 40 years and who are less than 60 years of age, shall, subject to being asked to do so, perform pro bono services of not less than 24 hours per calendar year.'

In most common law jurisdictions, provision of pro bono services is a voluntary activity but one that is strongly encouraged by solicitor or bar associations and governments. In England and Wales, each of the representative bodies of solicitors, barristers and legal executives has created charities specifically designed to foster a culture of pro bono. LawWorks, formerly the Solicitors Pro Bono Group, is the charity established by the Law Society of England and Wales to promote pro bono. The Bar Pro Bono Unit and the ILEX Pro Bono Forum are the bar and legal executive equivalent bodies. In summer 2010 the respective organisations joined together to create the National Pro Bono Centre with premises in Chancery Lane, London, to act as a unified national clearing house for pro bono legal services.

LawWorks and the Bar Pro Bono Unit jointly created the Pro Bono Protocol which has been approved by the Attorney General. It does not specify the amount of pro bono work that signatories will provide, but seeks to set the standard of work as equivalent to that provided to a paying client. It also includes a useful elaboration on the definition of pro bono.

---

**Extract from the Pro Bono Protocol**

**1   What is Pro Bono Legal Work?**

1.1   When we refer to Pro Bono Legal Work we mean legal advice or representation provided by lawyers in the public interest including to individuals, charities and community groups who cannot afford to pay for that advice or representation and where public funding is not available.

1.2   Legal work is Pro Bono Legal Work only if it is free to the client, without payment to the lawyer or law firm (regardless of the outcome) and provided voluntarily either by the lawyer or his or her firm.

1.3   Pro Bono Legal Work is always only an adjunct to, and not a substitute for, a proper system of publicly funded legal services.

---

There are a number of issues arising from this. First, pro bono is said to be provided in the public interest. At a basic level this will be satisfied whenever lawyers provide free legal services as they will be securing access to justice. However, it goes further in that it suggests this will be for the benefit of individuals or groups who could not otherwise access the services through private payment or public funding. This goes to the basic rationale for pro bono work. It is generally seen as a way for the legal profession to enhance access to justice. This would be less likely to be achieved if it were routinely provided to clients who would secure advice and representation anyway via personal payment or external funding (such as insurance or legal aid). Thus, although the Protocol does not impose a strict means test approach, the expectation is that pro bono services will be targeted at those who cannot afford to pay.

Secondly, the legal work must be free to the client regardless of the outcome. This prevents 'no win, no fee' conditional fee or contingency arrangements falling within the Protocol's definition of pro bono. It also rules out the 'first 30 minutes free' initiatives that some law firms offer to attract potential paying clients.

Thirdly, the Protocol emphasises that pro bono is not intended to replace the legal aid scheme. This reveals a tension in this jurisdiction and elsewhere about the balance between state-funded and voluntary legal services. Some fear that the more extensive and effective pro bono services become, the less committed the government is likely to be to funding legal aid schemes. Indeed legal aid lawyers are sometimes sceptical about pro bono initiatives given that their own commitment to access to justice requires them to work in an uncertain and often inadequate funding environment.

### Pro bono in law schools

In light of the definition set out above, the focus of pro bono is provision of a service as opposed to student education. This begs the question why pro bono activity would take place in law schools which are by their nature in the business of educating students. As has been said, there is a lot of overlap between clinic and pro bono. Thus, many clinical legal education activities may also be pro bono services. Nevertheless, there are also many pro bono projects in law schools where the focus is primarily service provision as opposed to education. Why is this? The reasons are diverse but include the following:

- Awareness about the ethics and practice of pro bono can be seen as part of the broad education of future lawyers. In the USA the American Bar Association accreditation standards for law schools states that schools 'should encourage and provide opportunities for student participation in pro bono activities' (Standard 302(e) (1999)).
- If you are a law student, particularly on a professional course, although you are not a full member of the legal profession, you are probably on the path to qualification and should therefore develop established professional habits including pro bono service.
- As a student in higher education you have opportunities not open to all. Many consequently feel a moral obligation to help those less privileged in society.
- You may welcome the opportunity to enhance your CV/resume by participation in professional-type activities.
- Academic lawyers working in higher education often have a commitment to pro bono and create pro bono projects as a means of utilising your time and enthusiasm to help provide a free community service. Similarly, law firms might be willing to support pro bono projects in law schools as part of the firm's pro bono provision and/or to enhance the firm's reputation among the student body.
- Many universities have mission statement or other commitments to community engagement. Pro bono projects are seen as excellent ways of universities interacting in a positive way with their surrounding communities.

## **1.4** Definitions – what is clinical legal education?

Clinical legal education is a phrase that has been used to describe a multitude of different learning activities involving law students. As previously mentioned, there is no universal definition of the concept. This book defines clinical legal education as learning through participation in real or realistic legal interactions coupled with reflection on this experience. Set out below are the characteristics which, taken together, make an activity clinical legal education.

### You learn by doing

Confucius, a Chinese philosopher who lived from 551 BC–479 BC, has had the following saying attributed to him: 'I hear and I forget. I see and I remember. I do and I understand.'

Whatever the provenance of the quotation, it has been used by advocates of clinical legal education to identify the shortcomings of learning based only on reading or listening to the wisdom of others. It suggests that practical wisdom should also be developed through personal experience. Modern theories about the way adults learn have provided further support for experience to play an important part in the development of knowledge and understanding. See, for example, David Kolb's development of the experiential learning cycle (Kolb, 1984), explored in more detail in **Chapter 12**. There is still significant debate about the process of adult learning, but it is widely accepted that performance can be a valuable vehicle for learning. Thus, experiential learning has become a major aspect of modern thinking about effective learning methods. Clinical legal education is a good example of experiential learning.

It is important to note that it has never been seriously suggested that all legal education can be achieved through experiential learning alone. Clinical legal education provides one additional method to sit alongside other learning opportunities.

### You learn through interacting in-role as a lawyer or other participant in the legal system

Learning by doing is a rather vague notion, so there is a need to be more specific. For example, pulling a statute book from a shelf and finding a particular statute could be described as 'doing' in a broad sense. Similarly, putting your hand up and answering a thorny question posed by the professor during a lecture is 'doing' as opposed to not doing. But this is insufficient. The 'clinical' aspect of the notion requires a context-specific approach towards the experience. As the name suggests, clinical legal education finds its origins in approaches towards learning in medical schools. For many years, medical students have developed their understanding of medicine and treatment, not just through study of biology or anatomy but through observation of and participation in clinical interactions with patients and other medical professionals. This pushes experiential learning into the specific context of personal interaction in the professional arenas of medicine (for example, patient consultation, ward round or operating theatre). In a legal context, 'clinic' requires that you act as participants in the professional arenas of the law (such as client interview, case strategy meeting and court hearing). This also means that clinic students are exposed to notions of professional ethics and the obligations of lawyers.

This criterion is not intended to be too limiting. Clinical legal education is broad enough to encompass a wide range of participation. The purest example is where you act as a legal advisor in the provision of legal services. However, it could also be met by you acting as a client, witness, investigator, opponent, judge, juror and so on in a simulated exercise. This could provide the necessary experience of professional arenas of the law but from a range of different but important perspectives.

Moreover, there are not always clear boundaries between clinical and non-clinical activity. So far, this chapter has suggested that some form of participation is required, but as part of this there may well be scope for significant observation or modelling activities. For example, as part of a free representation clinic, you might spend a lot of time visiting courts or tribunals to observe professional advocates at work and to reflect on the skills and behaviours you observe. Alternatively, you might observe your supervisor conduct a complex client interview and afterwards analyse the interaction, hoping to learn lessons about your own approach towards client interviews. The observation so closely impacts on your experience to count as part of your participation.

There are some activities that at first glance may appear so far removed from the traditional notions of lawyering that they fall outside the definition. One example is Streetlaw or other public legal education projects which involve a broad notion of community service in a legal context. These activities can constitute clinical legal education, as although they may not address case or dispute-based advice, they do involve you working to a specific brief and interacting with the public in relation to real legal rights and responsibilities. Modern ideas of community lawyering embrace a much broader role for lawyers, which encompasses legal education, leadership and activism (Levy-Pounds and Tyner, 2008).

### You learn by reflecting on your experience

Clinical *experience* is not the same thing as clinical *education*. The concept of 'learning *by* doing' suggests that the activity or experience is a means to an end and the end is education. Thus, an essential component of any clinical legal education project is that it has your learning at its heart. This requires those establishing such projects to think carefully about the type of learning they want to arise from your activities and to build opportunities for this into the scheme. Almost all legal experience provides the opportunity for a rich learning experience to take place. Learning outcomes might be quite modest or fairly broadly drafted, such as 'awareness-raising' or 'context-setting'. Nevertheless, this does mean that a clinical legal education project will be predicated on student learning as opposed to service provision per se. Clearly, there will often be a blurring of these distinct aims and a single activity may serve both educational and service purposes. For example, a drop-in clinic offering advice about entitlement to welfare benefits may provide a valuable community resource, while at the same time helping you to learn about welfare law, develop legal skills and appreciate some of the problems caused by poverty.

There is a further, more sophisticated (and difficult) distinction to consider between education and training. It has been argued that clinical learning offers the potential to provide much more than enhanced skills – it enables a richer understanding of legal rules, legal processes, the role of the legal professional and the impact of the legal system on people and organisations. This had led some to suggest that, in order to fully count as clinical legal education, an activity should achieve more than mere skills development or other technical how-to-do competencies, which can safely be left to the training stage of qualification as a lawyer. For example, Brayne, Duncan and Grimes in their book, *Clinical Legal Education, Active Learning in Your Law School*, state as follows:

> '... through clinical techniques students are capable of learning far more than skills, and can develop critical and contextual understanding of the law as it affects

people in society. Thus clinical education is defined as that which aims to achieve these intellectual and educational goals. The use of similar techniques with nothing other than skill development in mind would be seen as practical training, but not clinical in its true sense.' (Brayne et al, 1998, at xiii–xiv)

One difficulty is that the supposed distinction between education and training is sometimes vanishingly small. Take client interviewing as an example. All future lawyers need to be technically competent in interviewing skills; they must know the importance of clarity and precision, how and when to use open and closed questions, how to listen and take effective notes, how to recap and summarise and so on. Yet these aspects of interviewing are not 'mere' how-to-do technical skills. They also help you understand the relationship between lawyer and client, the power imbalance inherent in an interview situation, the fact that interviews are as much creative as deductive interactions and the central importance of communication in the law. Some teachers are therefore sceptical of attempts to exclude certain activities from the notion of clinic on the basis that the learning is merely technical; rather it should be seen as a continuum. Some clinical activities will focus on skill competencies, whereas others will address broader learning outcomes. Indeed you will often achieve different learning outcomes from the same activity.

Nevertheless, it should be recognised that, in England and Wales, law is still partly an apprenticeship profession. Solicitors must complete a two-year training contract, while barristers undertake a one-year pupillage post-university. This training stage of legal education is largely outside the influence of law schools. It appears counter-productive to merely replicate at university the experience you will have if you commence the training stage in the profession. To do so would be repetitive, potentially confusing and would not take advantage of the learning environment offered by the academic context in which the activity takes place. Moreover, it would be a reductive view of clinical legal education as a mere precursor to professional training. It can be much more than this. Indeed, its aims and objectives should have validity irrespective of whether you intend to enter the legal profession once you graduate.

This is where reflection comes in as a necessary part of the notion of clinical legal education. Reflection can help to make the difference between doing and *learning from* doing. Reflection is dealt with in a chapter of its own (see **Chapter 12**) and you will see that it is a challenging but rewarding activity. For present purposes, reflection is the process of reviewing and analysing experience so that you can identify and absorb the elements of learning arising from it.

Clinical learning offers you the unique opportunity of time and expectation to reflect on your experience of legal practice which will not arise in the same way again once you enter the world of work. So, to count as clinical legal education, a programme must include reflection. If there is no opportunity or expectation to reflect then an activity is likely to be a valuable pro bono experience but it will not amount to clinic. A good example of the difference reflection makes is the Portsmouth University CAB project. In a collaboration between the law school and the Citizens Advice Bureau, students are trained to perform the role of a CAB adviser and are placed in the CAB, dealing with members of the public. This is a good example of a pro bono partnership where students help to deliver a valuable voluntary legal service. However, it is transformed into clinical legal education by the educational aims of the academic module that is built around the project, and in particular by the reflective diary and essay undertaken by the students (Sparrow, 2009).

### You address real or realistic legal issues

In this chapter it has already been suggested that clinical legal education requires participation in the legal system. It will now discuss an important and difficult question: can simulated legal issues count as clinical legal education? Some lecturers think the answer is clearly yes. Although the focus of this book will be about your involvement with real cases, it is important to recognise that clinical methodology can be used without a real client or real problems. It is possible to design simulated schemes that seek to achieve broadly equivalent learning outcomes and adopt similar teaching and learning methods as live client clinics. These can still count as clinical learning so long as they meet the other parts of the definition outlined above (learn by doing, participate in the legal system and reflect on the experience).

Clearly there will be major differences between live client and simulation clinics, and many people believe that a live client clinic is the best example of clinical legal education. Indeed, live client clinics do offer opportunities for learning that are simply not possible with simulated activity, such as spontaneity, authentic emotion, personal commitment etc. But there is no logical reason to exclude simulated activities from the definition of clinical learning. This is reinforced by the fact that many law courses use simulation as a preparatory, parallel or integrated activity alongside live client work. If a law school established a wholly simulated clinic with no possibility of live client interaction, it might be open to the challenge that it did not realise the full potential of clinical learning (and might be pressed to develop it further), but this would not stop the simulated scheme from counting as clinical legal education.

If a clinic does adopt simulated activities, these should be as realistic as possible. Examples of how this can be achieved are through the use of properly briefed actors or standardised clients (Barton et al, 2006), use of adapted/anonymised real case documentation, use of realistic or real courtrooms for mock hearings, and the introduction of unexpected events or requests.

## 1.5 A brief history of clinical legal education

Clinical legal education is now firmly established in higher education worldwide, but the origins of modern clinical legal education are relatively recent. In the early part of the twentieth century, only a handful of law schools in the USA offered community law clinics, although no academic credit was awarded and students offered their time voluntarily. Practical work was seen as outside the academic realm, and law schools mainly focused their efforts on developing the case method based on analysis of appeal court decisions. From the 1930s to the 1950s there were intermittent critiques of the lack of attention to practical lawyering but no significant response from law school hierarchies. Towards the end of the 1950s, there was sporadic but significant growth of courses covering skills such as legal writing, research and advocacy. These courses began to adopt clinical methodology, but there was a lack of a common rationale and no academic clinical community as such.

The social problems, civil rights movement and political unrest of the 1960s and 1970s helped to provide a catalyst for student demand and a coherent purpose for the developing clinical movement. The focus shifted from skills development to service provision, particularly addressing social injustice by the creation of clinics aimed at providing access to justice for the poor and dispossessed. Another significant factor was that, for the first time, law schools were able to access funding (from the Council on Legal Education and Professional Responsibility) to establish or develop clinics. By the end of the 1970s, the modern American clinical structure was in place and has continued to grow since then with extensive clinical programmes in almost all law schools and a nationwide network of clinicians through the Clinical Legal Education Association (CLEA) and the Association of American Law Schools Clinical Section. There has been some concern that clinical method has not been embraced throughout law schools and that clinics are seen as separate from the main doctrinal purpose of the academy (Barry, Dubin and Joy, 2000).

In England and Wales clinics began to develop in the early 1970s, partly as awareness and interest in what was happening in the USA grew and partly as a consequence of greater commitment by academics and students to social justice issues in the time following the university unrest of 1968. Clinics were established in the then 'new' universities, such as the University of Kent and Warwick University, and in some polytechnics. Early clinics tended to offer advice to fellow students, but some, such as the one at Kent, were established as a fully fledged legal practice offering a wide range of advice and representation to the public. The majority of early clinics were extracurricular, so students did not receive any academic credit for their efforts. This fitted with the access to justice imperative of the original pioneers, although early adopters did see opportunities for changing the way law students learned.

Throughout the 1980s and 1990s there was sporadic development of clinical legal education, and a wide variety of clinical schemes came and went but with little coherence. In the late 1990s the establishment of the Clinical Legal Education Organisation saw the development of a small clinical community which offered mutual support and generated further interest. Former polytechnics, such as Northumbria University and Sheffield Hallam University, developed extensive credit bearing clinical programmes, the former being integrated into its curriculum as a mandatory part of undergraduate studies. The professional law schools, such as BPP and the College of Law, developed innovative clinical modules and extracurricular pro bono activities. Research done by LawWorks in 2008 suggests that 68% of law schools currently offer some form of clinical or pro bono activity to students (Curtis, 2008).

**Some key questions about clinical legal education and pro bono**

### Are clinic and pro bono schemes part of law student education elsewhere in the world?

No comprehensive study has been completed, but clinical legal education is now firmly established in law schools right throughout the world. By far the most extensive network of clinical projects is in the USA, where almost all law schools offer clinical modules. There is well-developed coordination by academic faculty members committed to clinical methodology. The Clinical Legal Education Association is the interest group that promotes clinical learning and encourages scholarship in the field. The Clinical Law Review is a peer-reviewed journal devoted entirely to research and scholarship about the clinical approach to legal education.

Other countries where clinical legal education is very common include Australia, Canada, South Africa, Nigeria and Poland. There are also expanding opportunities in China and India and in many of the countries of the former Soviet Union. Western Europe (apart from England and Wales) has not embraced clinical methodology extensively, although in recent years a number of clinical schemes have been established in Ireland, Spain, Italy and the Netherlands.

There are clinical legal education associations in many countries, and the Global Alliance for Justice Education (GAJE) provides a loose network for those working in clinical legal education schemes worldwide. GAJE organises a bi-annual conference at different locations around the world. There is also an annual international conference organised by the International Journal of Clinical Legal Education. The Public Interest Law Institute, based in New York and Budapest, is a non-governmental organisation which seeks to advance human rights around the world by stimulating public interest advocacy and pro bono. It organises an annual European Pro Bono Forum.

The book, *The Global Clinical Movement: Educating Lawyers for Social Justice*, by Frank Bloch (Bloch, 2010), provides an excellent overview of the issues facing clinical legal education throughout the world, looking at the development of clinic in different regions and the problems faced and also addressing themes such as the relationship between clinic and social justice, legal ethics, public interest law and legal aid.

### Are clinic and pro bono schemes carried out as part of the curriculum or as extracurricular activities?

There is a rich tapestry of clinical projects in law schools throughout the country. The relationship between the clinic or project and your other studies is important, not only because it will affect how much time you might have available to devote to it, but also because it will determine whether your performance is assessed and credited towards your overall degree classification. It will also affect the resources that your law school is willing to devote to the project.

Set out below are the typical models you will find for clinic projects in law schools. There is a separate chapter dealing with assessment (see **Chapter 13**), but outlined here is the possible relationship between your participation and your performance on the programme:

### Extracurricular

If an activity is extracurricular, it does not constitute a formal part of your studies, and the law school will not be obliged to provide or continue to provide resources. The activity might not have detailed learning outcomes and will be viewed by the law school as an added value activity. It may be that other course commitments will be seen as taking priority, but if the project involves commitments to clients or others then there may be moral or professional duties to finish what has been started. It is essentially a voluntary activity that you will do alongside your studies. You will have the satisfaction of helping to provide a pro bono service and will also gather useful experience and enhance your profile. The activity may be:

- student-organised – the law school permits the activity but has little or no commitment to it. The onus is on you to generate interest, organise the activity and secure funding;
- law school-organised – the law school puts some (perhaps significant) resources into the programme, sometimes including a member of staff with responsibility for coordinating the activity. However, the activity is not assessed and does not count towards your overall performance on your course. Some law schools may not credit your performance towards your degree classification but will provide other benefits, such as a special prize, award or certificate for participants.

### Intracurricular

Clinic or pro bono may feature within your curriculum as either a compulsory or optional module. All modules organised by your institution will have been through the law school's or university's quality control procedures. There is likely to be a list of learning outcomes associated with the module so that you can see what you are expected to achieve during your time in the clinic activity. You can also expect appropriate resources to be spent on the project as it is a formal part of your course of study. It is becoming increasingly common for clinic modules to count as formal modules. One reason is that students have requested this. Many students want their hard work, commitment and high level of performance to be appropriately recognised by credit on their programme of study. Clinical supervisors also see formal credit as a means of encouraging students to participate, spend more time and effort on the clinical project and as a way of embedding the project into the curriculum so as to make it sustainable.

Clinic and pro bono modules tend to be offered as options. Compulsory clinic schemes are rare if the project involves advising and representing clients. There are a number of reasons for this, including the high cost of providing such a service and the fact that clinical learning is not required as part of the qualifying law degree or professional courses. However, there are a large number of compulsory modules or activities on undergraduate and vocational courses which involve simulated clinical legal education. Examples are required participation in a court visit scheme, mock trials, mooting projects and skills modules.

The module may or may not be assessed. **Chapter 13** deals with assessment issues in more detail.

### I am doing a law degree but do not want to qualify as a lawyer – is clinic and pro bono relevant to me?

An obvious characteristic of learning via clinic or pro bono is that it relates to legal practice. This begs the question of its relevance to the significant proportion of law students who do not enter the legal profession. In other words, if law is studied as an academic inquiry, is there any place for clinical methodology? It is the contention of this book that clinic and pro bono has relevance through all aspects of the study of law, including the academic stage.

Clinical legal education is essentially a method of learning as opposed to a subject or discipline in its own right. The method can be utilised for a variety of different purposes. It can certainly be used to develop professional awareness and legal skills that will be of value for future lawyers, but it can also be deployed to develop knowledge and general or intellectual skills that are required for undergraduate legal study. Similarly, participation in pro bono activities provides a valuable platform for the achievement of graduate level outcomes. To illustrate this, outlined below are the key attributes that the Quality Assurance Agency expects from law graduates (Quality Assurance Agency, Benchmark Statements for Law, QAA 2010) and suggestion of how clinical methodology can help to achieve these. It is not suggested that clinic can achieve all this on its own but rather that it can contribute as part of a varied learning and teaching strategy.

### Knowledge

The QAA requires that law students develop a broad knowledge of the legal system including legal concepts, values, principles and rules. Clinical methods cannot deliver all of this, but they can clearly contribute. In particular, you are required to demonstrate the study in depth and in context of some substantive areas of the legal system. A clinic or pro bono project can be an ideal vehicle for developing in-depth, contextualised knowledge because you tend to work on a specific area of law on behalf of a client and need to understand that area in great detail in order to be able to advise or otherwise advance the client's cause. You do this in a real or realistic context of the legal system in which the legal issue will be resolved.

### Application and problem-solving

You must be able to demonstrate the ability to apply knowledge and provide arguable conclusions for actual or hypothetical problems. Clinical methodology is clearly appropriate for developing these abilities because it is built around the application of legal rules and principles to particular situations and involves exploration of authentic legal problems and their potential resolution.

## Sources and research

The QAA requires that you demonstrate the ability to identify issues which need to be researched, and retrieve up-to-date legal information, using a variety of sources including relevant primary and secondary legal sources. Clinical methodology lends itself to the development of factual and legal research skills. In particular, the problem to be addressed is often not precise or coherently expressed (for example by the client during an interview) so you may need to explore and clarify the issues before embarking on the research. In order to be able to advise or otherwise advance your client's case, you need to explore the area of law in depth and find legal authorities that help or hinder the client's interests. Given that you are likely to be considering a fairly precise question, there is a risk that your research will be myopic in that some sources that are broadly relevant to the area of law will not be relevant to the particular issue. However, this does not undermine clinical methodology as a whole; it merely confirms that it should be part of a range of learning methods available to students.

## Analysis, synthesis, critical judgement and evaluation

These are some of the core intellectual skills that you are required to develop and demonstrate through your legal studies. You should have the ability to recognise and rank the relevance and importance of issues; bring together material from a variety of sources; synthesise doctrinal and policy issues; make critical judgements; and present a reasoned choice between alternative solutions. Alongside other learning opportunities, clinical legal education can help you acquire and develop these attributes, but clearly you will require expert help. The clinical activity will need to be designed in order to address these areas, and your supervisor will need to encourage and assist you to undertake the tasks required in order to achieve these outcomes. These are quite high-level intellectual skills and are unlikely to arise automatically by participation in real or realistic scenarios. Guidance and reflection are essential components of the learning journey.

## Autonomy and ability to learn

The QAA believes these are the key attributes of graduateness. You must be able to act independently when planning and undertaking tasks in areas of law you have already studied. You should also have the ability to research independently in areas you have not previously studied. You must also be able to reflect on your own learning and use feedback. Clinical projects tend to require you to act not only under instruction and supervision but also independently, using your initiative to explore problems in areas of law that you may or may not have encountered previously. As made clear earlier, reflection is an essential part of clinical learning and is what helps to distinguish it from mere legal experience.

## Communication and literacy

The QAA requires you to demonstrate oral and written communications skills by understanding and using English language appropriately, presenting knowledge or arguments comprehensibly and reading and discussing technical and complex legal materials. Clinical learning requires you to act as a participant in the legal system and thus necessarily involves extensive communication. Most clinical projects provide a wealth of opportunities to develop oral and written communication skills. In particular, where a clinic requires you to interact with a lay person about the law, you need to communicate about the law in an accessible manner which is targeted to the needs of the non-lawyer. This will often require you to translate technical and complex legal materials into plain English that can be more readily understood by the public.

### Numeracy, information technology and teamwork

You must be able to use, present and evaluate numerical or statistical information, create word-processed documents, use information and communication technology, such as the Web and email, and be able to contribute effectively to group tasks. You may or may not have to work with numbers, but it is likely that all of the other requirements will be developed in the clinic or pro bono project. In particular, clinical learning tends to be collaborative. You will normally work with a variety of other people, including your fellow students and your supervisor, as part of a team and with common objectives. This is particularly the case if you are working with fellow students on behalf of a client.

### Is clinic and pro bono relevant to me if I want to become a barrister?

In England and Wales there is a split profession, in that lawyers may practise either as a solicitor or a barrister but not as both at the same time. The professional bodies for solicitors and barristers specify certain requirements for the academic stage of legal education set out in the Joint Statement on the Academic Stage of Legal Education (Joint Academic Stage Board, 2002). These can be achieved either through a Qualifying Law Degree or a Common Professional Examination/Graduate Diploma in Law. Thereafter the qualification route diverges, in that intending solicitors study the Legal Practice Course while would-be barristers do the Bar Professional Training Course. There follows a two-year training contract for solicitors or a one-year pupillage for barristers.

The question about the relevance of clinic to future barristers tends to arise because clinic projects are often (but not always) designed so that the services offered or the experience gained is similar to that offered by solicitors. For example, a number of in-house law clinics are modelled on law firms, so that instructions are received directly from members of the public and case files are opened. Indeed, cases are often supervised by practising solicitors, and students carry out the tasks that would normally be performed by a solicitor. Is this experience and the learning arising from it helpful if you do not want to become a solicitor? The answer is yes, for a number of reasons. First, it is important to appreciate that clinic learning is not merely preparation for a particular profession. In the previous section it was explained that clinic can play an important part in developing the knowledge and general and intellectual skills you require as part of your legal education, irrespective of career choice. Secondly, awareness and experience of the role and duties of a solicitor is of significant value to future barristers. Remember that almost all barristers' work comes from solicitors. Thirdly, knowledge and skills learned in a solicitor context are often transferrable to a barrister context. For example, the skills necessary for successful client interviewing by a solicitor are likely to be of real value for a barrister's ability to conduct effective conferencing.

## Should clinic and pro bono schemes include a commitment to social justice?

The relationship between clinical legal education, pro bono and social justice is intimate and complex. For many clinical scholars educating students about and tackling the problems of poverty and other social injustice is a fundamental part of the purpose of clinical legal education. Indeed, as has been seen, the early development of clinical teaching and the struggle for social justice went hand-in-hand. The twin aims of educating students in practical lawyering while securing access to justice for dispossessed groups are seen as inseparable aspects of clinical endeavour. It has been argued that the social justice imperative of clinical legal education and pro bono helps students to understand essential values of the legal profession such as promotion of justice, fairness, and morality (Barry et al, 2000). Others have argued that a value of legal education lies in encouraging students to nurture their 'capacity for moral indignation at injustice in the world, or to challenge and inspire them as lawyers to use what they have learned to work for social justice' (Wizner, 2001). See also Aiken, 1997.

This view has been reinforced by the tendency of law school education in general to neglect social justice issues. Thus law students may fail to grasp the reality that legal rules and legal processes are not separate from social, political and economic relationships, but are an intrinsic part of the unequal distribution of power and resources in society. The clinic is seen as an opportunity to raise student consciousness to the social context of the law which they may not obtain elsewhere.

The relationship between clinic and social justice is thus long-standing and deeply entrenched. Clinical commentators sometimes debate whether the priority of clinic should be student education or meeting unmet legal need (see eg Nicolson, 2006), but the reality for most clinics is that the client base will be those at the margins of society or bodies representing such groups. The educational and service imperatives tend to go together.

In light of this, why does this chapter not include social justice as a core part of the definition of clinical legal education? Although it is acknowledged that most clinical programmes have education for social justice as a goal, it is argued that this should be viewed as part of the culture of clinical legal education as opposed to its meaning. Moreover, the emphasis on social justice will be to an extent context-specific. The greater the social problems and inequality in a society, and the greater the legal need that is not addressed by traditional legal services, the more likely it is that clinical education will focus on social issues. A law clinic that neglected social justice issues would be open to criticism that it was not fulfilling its potential, but it would still amount to clinical education. Ultimately, clinical legal education in law schools should reflect the educational needs of law students. A rounded legal education is bound to include some appreciation of the social context for the creation and resolution of legal disputes and the role of lawyers within this. Clinical methodology provides an ideal but not exclusive means for addressing this context.

### Should services offered by law clinics be means-tested?

This is linked to the social justice imperative of most law clinics and it touches on the relationship between clinical legal education and pro bono. Clinics that provide a legal service to clients do so without charging clients a fee. An equivalent paid-for service may cost many hundreds or even thousands of pounds. On what basis should these extremely valuable resources be allocated? One obvious basis is to allocate the service only to those who would not otherwise be able to access justice due to an inability to pay or secure external funding.

There is no common approach to the question of whether to means-test potential clients. Some clinics do so; others allocate their resources in different ways, eg by targeting services that are more likely to be relevant to poorer clients, such as welfare rights advice, without imposing a prior test of a client's ability to pay. Other clinics adopt an 'educational value' test to deciding whether to enter into a retainer, and may end up taking on clients who could afford to pay but prefer to use a free service. These matters are often the subject of ongoing debate within clinics because demand is almost always going to outstrip the ability of the clinic to supply the service, so there needs to be some means of deciding how to deploy scarce resources. Some of these issues are explored further in **Chapter 3**.

## 1.7  Summary

Clinical legal education and pro bono has been undertaken by law students in the United Kingdom since the 1970s and continues to expand in popularity amongst law teachers and law students. There is now a huge range of projects taking place in law schools in this country and throughout the world. Defining clinical legal education and pro bono is not straightforward, but this chapter has identified essential themes as follows: learning by doing; real or realistic participation in the legal system; and reflection on your experience. Although they are not the same thing, it is clear that there is significant overlap of clinic and pro bono, and the social justice origins and connections of the clinical movement have been noted. There is no reason at all why clinical methodology cannot be utilised at all levels of legal education and can help students develop a more holistic view, not just of legal skills but also of the role of the law in society, legal ethics, and doctrinal legal rules and principles. Moreover, general and intellectual skills can readily be developed and enhanced by involvement with clinical learning.

 Further reading

## Introductory

**Bloch, F, *The Global Clinical Movement: Educating Lawyers for Social Justice* (Oxford University Press, 2010)**

This ambitious work is the first book to build a global picture of developments in clinical legal education and social justice initiatives. It draws on leading thinkers from all over the world and is edited by one of the founding members of GAJE, the Global Alliance for Justice Education.

**Brayne, H, Duncan, N and Grimes, R, *Clinical Legal Education, Active Learning in Your Law School* (Blackstone Press, 1998)**

This text is aimed primarily at law teachers. It provides an overview of the history and development of clinical legal education, expounds the advantages of this approach and explores the learning and teaching methodology in detail.

**Curtis, M, 'Public Interest and Human Rights in Law Schools: Ideals and Realities – The UK Student Pro Bono Experience', unpublished paper, 2008. A copy is on file with the authors.**

This paper provides an overview of pro bono activity in UK law schools drawing on LawWorks research into current projects.

**Nicholson, D, 'Legal education or community service? The extra-curricular student law clinic' [2006] 3 Web JCLI**

http://webjcli.ncl.ac.uk/2006/issue3/nicolson3.html

This article argues that the primary goal of clinics should be provision of legal services to the needy and that the prioritising of educational needs risks treating clients unethically as means to educational ends.

**Sparrow, C, 'Reflective Student Practitioner – an example integrating clinical experience into the curriculum' [2009] IJCLE 70**

This article summarises a partnership between Portsmouth Law School and Portsmouth Citizens Advice Bureau which created a clinical legal education project involving placement at the CAB and reflective analysis by students of their development.

## Intermediate

**Aiken, J, 'Striving to Teach Justice, Fairness and Morality' (1997) 4 Clinical L Rev 4**

This article explores the role of the supervisor in the delivery of a justice education. It underlines an important point, 'Everything we do as law teachers suggests something about justice', and argues that law schools traditionally fail to explicitly teach justice, thereby undermining the potential of student learning.

**Barton, K, Cunningham, C, Jones, G and Maharg, P, 'Valuing What Clients Think: Standardized Clients and the Assessment of Communicative Competence' (2006) 13 Clinical L Rev 1**

This article reports on research conducted into the effectiveness of standardised clients (trained actors briefed to perform the role of a client) for providing feedback and assessment of student performance in client interviewing.

**Barry, M, Dubin, J and Joy, P, 'Clinical Education for This Millennium: The Third Wave' (2000) 7 Clinical L Rev 1**

This important article provides a detailed overview of the growth, development, challenges and future opportunities for clinical legal education in this century. It focuses on the normalisation of clinical legal education as a routine method of delivery of legal knowledge, skills and awareness.

**Levy-Pounds, N and Tyner, A, 'The principles of Ubuntu: Using the legal clinical model to train agents of social change' [2008] IJCLE 7**

This article explains an ambitious notion of what clinical legal education and pro bono lawyering can achieve in terms of empowering communities and enabling students to become legal activists who can help to educate, enthuse and emancipate oppressed people.

**Wizner, S, 'Beyond Skills Training' (2001) 7 Clinical L Rev 2**

The author argues that clinical legal education has a moral and political purpose rooted in a social justice mission. He suggests that clinics should teach not only knowledge and skills but also the ethical value of pursuing social justice.

## Advanced

**Kolb, D, *Experiential learning: Experience as the source of learning and development* (Prentice Hall, 1984)**

This is one of many publications by leading modern educational theorist, David A Kolb, exploring the value of practical experience and reflection as a learning tool.

 Activities

### Activity 1: The value of pro bono

This exercise can be run as a simple group discussion activity or as a series of mini-presentations or debates.

**Group size:** 4–20

**Materials:** access to the Internet

**Instructions:** your group should be divided into four small teams. Each team is allocated one of the following statements:

- Pro bono is part of the moral commitment all lawyers should make to access to justice.
- Pro bono should only be given to those who cannot afford to pay and are not eligible for external funding.
- Pro bono is dangerous because it undermines the state's commitment to publicly funded legal services.
- Pro bono is so important that all lawyers should be required to provide a minimum number of hours each year.

The teams should conduct some basic Internet-based research into the issues arising from their statement. Each team should then prepare a short (approximately 5 minutes) submission arguing in favour of its statement. You should deliver this presentation to the other members of the group who will ask questions. This should lead to a general discussion about the value and problems associated with pro bono.

### Activity 2: Clinical legal education and pro bono balloon game

This exercise involves sorting and ranking of characteristics making up clinical legal education projects. It works best if you are contemplating a specific clinical scheme that you know something about, rather than considering the issues in the abstract.

**Group size:** 4–20

**Materials:** A3 paper, post-it notes and a marker pen (or alternatively the exercise can be done using a word processor)

**Instructions:** your group should be divided into four individuals or small teams. Each team should be given a sheet of A3 paper, 15 post-its and a marker pen. At the top of the A3 sheet you should write, 'Reasons for doing clinic or pro bono project'. On 10 of the post-its you should write the following with the marker pen:

- Work as a team.
- Reflect on student experience.
- Serve the community.
- Improve legal skills.
- Understand legal rules.
- Appreciate the law in context.
- Comprehend the role of the lawyer.
- Enhance employability.
- 'Hit the ground running' in your career.
- Improve exam grades.

You should then discuss within your team and attempt to rank the post-its as a hierarchy, with the most important reason at the top and the least important at the bottom. It is permissible to put two or more post-its side by side if they are deemed to be of equal rank.

Your team should then attach the sheet of paper to the wall or a flip chart and be prepared to justify your findings and identify any areas of disagreement within your team. You also have the opportunity to add up to five further post-its with additional reasons you believe ought to motivate students to participate in a clinic or pro bono project.

## Activity 3: Social justice or education?

This is a group discussion exercise that will require you to read an article about clinical legal education and then discuss your thoughts about the issues it raises.

**Group size:** 4–20

**Materials:** you require prior access to the Internet.

**Instructions:** read the article by Professor Donald Nicolson, 'Legal Education or Community Service? The Extra-Curricular Student Law Clinic' [2006] 3 Web JCLI. You can access this by going to http://webjcli.ncl.ac.uk/index.html and searching under 'Nicolson'.

The article describes clinics where the priority is the education of law students as 'educationally-oriented' (EO) clinics and suggests there are three disadvantages with such clinics relating to (a) service to the community, (b) clinic ethics and (c) student ethics. Within your group discuss whether you think Nicolson's criticisms of EO clinics are valid, and if so whether the suggested alternative of the extracurricular in-house clinic (EIC) provides a suitable answer. What do you think ought to be the criteria for deciding whether to take on and/or continue with a client's case if you do not use educational priority?

# 2 Setting up a clinical legal education or pro bono project

> 'And everyone that heareth these words of mine,
> and doeth them not, shall be likened unto a
> foolish man, who built his house upon the sand.'
>
> The Bible, King James Version, Matthew 7:26

## 2.1 Introduction

This chapter provides guidance and practical advice about the key issues you need to address when contemplating a new clinical project or developing existing schemes. It is aimed at students and academic staff because successful clinical and pro bono schemes are almost always partnerships between these two groups. By its nature, the chapter is quite general, but it does provide specific guidance about setting up a live client in-house clinic. Parts of this guidance are also relevant for readers who have a different clinical model in mind, for example an advice-only clinic, Streetlaw, simulation model and so forth. This chapter also explores the tactical considerations and practical steps that should be addressed if you wish to establish a sustainable clinical or pro bono project in your institution.

## 2.2 Building support for a clinic or pro bono project

The first point to note is that establishing a project will not always be straightforward. Depending on the model adopted, it may be a complex, time-consuming and lengthy process. It may also be expensive and controversial. Support for such a project should not be taken for granted, and you should develop a broad and informed coalition carefully and over a significant period of time. Conversely, some clinical and pro bono schemes are very simple and work well without complex layers of bureaucracy. As with many things, the investment of time and resources will depend on the project you have in mind. It is a case of horses for courses.

In addition to reading this chapter and the suggested further reading, you should consider attending relevant conferences or meetings to learn from others who have been through the process, and perhaps visit established clinics to view the premises and facilities for yourself and question those responsible about the issues they have encountered. Many clinics and pro bono schemes are more than willing to assist those hoping to establish their own projects.

Wheels tend to turn slowly in academia. Depending on the type of clinical or pro bono project you intend to establish, you should expect at least one academic year of planning. This could be significantly more if the project is ambitious in scale, involves services to real clients or if you intend to offer it as part of the academic credit towards a law degree or other course. If you are lucky and have the support of key people, it may be possible to get a simple project off the ground quite quickly. For example, an agreement for law students to work in conjunction with an external advice agency such as a Citizens Advice Bureau might be capable of swift implementation. In all cases you need to make sure that you have thought through how the scheme will operate and how it will be sustainable in the medium to long term.

## **2.3** Identifying your target audience

The active promoters of clinical projects are likely to be law school students and/or staff. However, there are a range of other stakeholders that you should consider as part of your plan to generate support for the project:

- University/college management – a clinic project is unlikely to get off the ground without at least tacit support from the Head of your faculty, school or department. He or she may also wish to consult with higher university or college management to make sure that the proposal fits with the wider institutional plan and mission. You should try to make sure that your ideas are well formed and costed, as far as possible, and that you already have a degree of informal support from existing teaching staff before approaching the Head.

- Teaching staff – even if the clinic project is intended to be operated by students, you should speak to academic staff at your institution to seek feedback about the idea and to establish whether they would be willing to support and offer assistance with the project. If the clinic is intended to be linked in any formal way to the curriculum (for example by being offered as an optional module on a programme of study) then it is essential that academic staff are involved from a very early stage, as the project will have to be designed to fit into the existing teaching and learning structures, and there will be teaching resource implications.

    A further relevant consideration is that many academic staff will be unfamiliar with clinical legal education and potentially concerned about the prospect of a clinical project being established in the law school. Some academic staff are not legally qualified and may have little knowledge of or interest in legal practice. There could be significant debate among faculty members about the necessity for, or the value of, clinical legal education. Not everyone is convinced of the benefits of such methods for educating law students. You may need to tread carefully and with sensitivity to the concerns of others. It will also be useful if you are able to articulate the potential wider relevance of clinical methods in developing general and intellectual skills (see **Chapter 1**).

    One way of ensuring that non-clinical academic staff have a better understanding of the clinic or pro bono service and can see for themselves the way that students engage with the law is to invite them to become academic consultants for areas of law that coincide with their teaching and research interests. This co-opting of academic staff can provide the service with a valuable additional consultancy facility and create influential advocates within the law school.

- Student representatives – students are going to be the main participants in any clinical or pro bono scheme, so you need to be confident that there is sufficient demand for such learning opportunities to make it worthwhile establishing. The fact that there is widespread support among students is likely to be an important factor in helping to persuade the university or college management that a scheme is worthwhile investing in. You should consider talking to student representatives in the law school and perhaps in the wider institution. If you have an active students' union, you may wish to speak to the relevant executive officers to see if they would be willing to support the project. Furthermore, if you are considering setting up a live client clinic, you could ascertain what demand there might be from students for legal assistance from the clinic, for example by speaking to the students' union advice centre. Students often form a significant proportion of the client base for law clinics. Indeed, clinics are sometimes established exclusively as a service for other students, at least initially.

- Community/client groups – if your clinic intends to offer any type of community service (advice clinic, Streetlaw, representation service etc), you should find out information about local needs and how these are currently addressed. A service will be more welcomed by the community if it addresses an unmet need. For example, if there is an acute local need for more housing advice for public and private sector tenants, this may suggest that a landlord and tenant clinic would be particularly useful. Similarly, it would be unwise to jump into offering a service where there is little community need or where the demand is currently met adequately without a clinical project. For example, if you intend to set up an asylum seeker advice clinic, but there is already a well-established and effective charitable service operating in the locality, you may wish to rethink your plans or at least talk to the charity to see if there is some way of working together for mutual and community benefit.

  Talking to community groups has the added benefit of making it more likely that the clinic will be understood and welcomed by local people rather than seen as an externally imposed or elitist experiment.

---

**Finding out about local services**

It is a good idea to find out about the services that are currently available in your local community so that (a) you do not replicate projects that are already in place, and (b) you can find potential partners to work with. Here are some good places to start.

Contact Advice UK (www.adviceuk.org.uk). This is the membership network for advice agencies throughout the country and may be able to help put you in touch with local organisations. Note that these organisations will not necessarily be legal advice providers but address a broad range of different community needs.

▸

> Find your local council for voluntary service (CVS). The National Association for Volunteer and Community Action (www.navca.org.uk) is the voice of local support and development organisations whose members work with over 160,000 local charities and community groups. Larger towns and cities are likely to have a local network organisation that you should be able to find using the interactive map on the website. These organisations will be able to offer crucial information about local needs and priorities.
>
> Speak to the local Citizens Advice Bureau (see www.citizensadvice.org.uk which has a local bureau finder facility) or Law Centre (www.lawcentres.org.uk). These organisations often require volunteers or may wish to become involved in some other way with your proposed scheme.
>
> Search the Community Legal Advice Directory (www.communitylegaladvice.org.uk). This provides access to a huge database of local and national organisations offering advice and assistance under the Community Legal Service. You can search this database by town/postcode or by area of law.

- Law firms, chambers and other legal services providers – this is a potentially tricky constituency to persuade of the benefits of a clinical or pro bono project, particularly if it seeks to offer free legal assistance to the community. Apart from the obvious concerns about a free service attracting clients who may otherwise pay a lawyer, there may also be legitimate concern about the quality of the service that is offered and the type of skills and experience participants will develop. Lawyers are rightly sensitive of the reputational damage that can be done to the profession if legal services are of poor quality or if the client experience is bad. They are also recipients of the skills and attributes of law school graduates who become paralegals, trainee solicitors or pupil barristers so are bound to have a keen interest in the learning outcomes of the clinic. Creating a good relationship and mutual understanding with local Law Society and Bar Circuit representatives is very important. LawWorks, the pro bono charity, may be able facilitate links with members it may have in your area (www.lawworks.org.uk).

  A further important consideration is that local lawyers are often key supporters, sponsors and participants in clinical projects. They may act as consultants, sources of client referrals, partners in service provision, placement/externship providers, sponsors of activities etc. As you will see, it is often extremely valuable to create an advisory forum that can ensure the concerns of the profession are aired and the wisdom and enthusiasm of local lawyers nurtured.

- Judiciary/tribunal – if the clinic project is likely to conduct any advocacy (undertaken either by the students themselves, their supervisors or lawyers they have instructed) then local judges and tribunal members will have a legitimate interest in the training given by the clinic and the standard of representation that is offered to litigants. Statements made from the bench about the standard of advocacy are powerful public pronouncements. Everyone wants to hear judges extol the excellence of the representation they have witnessed and wants to avoid at all costs the critical exposure of substandard work. The better informed the judiciary are about the purpose and context of the service, the more likely they are to provide constructive comments and feedback.

Furthermore, judges and tribunal chairs can provide valuable support to law clinic projects in numerous ways. For example, judges may be willing to permit student marshalling in court, or permit groups of students to observe cases and discuss the issues with the judge afterwards. Alternatively, they may be willing to participate in simulated exercises, such as judging a mock trial, or enhance practical understanding by giving guest lectures or seminars.

- Professional regulators – the Legal Services Board (LSB) is tasked with ensuring that regulation of legal services is carried out in the public interest and particularly that the interests of consumers are placed at the heart of the system (Legal Services Board, 2010). The relevant regulators for clinical purposes are likely to be the Solicitors Regulation Authority, the Bar Standards Board and perhaps the Institute of Legal Executives Professional Standards Board.

It is important to note that there is currently no requirement for all law clinics to be subject to professional regulation. If the clinic is not conducting work that is reserved for practising lawyers and does not employ qualified lawyers then it is unlikely to have any formal relationship with an approved regulator. However, if you do carry out any form of legal advice or representation service, or if qualified lawyers (even if they are not practising lawyers) work in the clinic or supervise students, you need to check very carefully whether you fall to be regulated by a professional body. For example, any law clinic that holds out a supervisor as a solicitor must ensure that the solicitor has a current practising certificate and complies with any further regulatory requirements. Moreover, it is possible that the Legal Services Board will in the future require regulation of not-for-profit legal services offered to the public as 'alternative business structures'.

##  Setting up a new clinic or pro bono project – fundamental questions

Later in this chapter there is guidance on the practical steps you need to take once you have decided to create a new project. However, before you get to that stage, there are a number of key strategic issues to grapple with. These fundamental questions will help you to decide whether you wish to go ahead with your initial intention to set up a clinic or pro bono project and, if so, what type of project it will be.

### What type of clinic or pro bono project do you want?

**Chapter 1** provided an overview of different types of project. Before you embark on a detailed planning process, you need to decide the general model you are interested in developing. For example, if your primary motivation is to give future students an opportunity to make a voluntary contribution to the local community by using their legal skills then it makes sense to establish a clinic or pro bono project that is an extracurricular activity. Alternatively, you may be responding to a particular local issue (eg if you have a prison near the law school and have an interest in providing prison rights advice), in which case you will consider a specialist advice clinic, possibly based off campus. If there are few resources available, you may wish to consider a simulation clinic or a project run in conjunction with a local advice agency so that you do not have to establish a legal office infrastructure in your own institution.

Another approach may be to establish a placement or externship scheme where students can be placed with organisations outside the university where they will gain first-hand experience and insight into the work of the partner organisation and provide free time and skills.

If you do intend to set up an in-house model, there are still a number of potential variations, in particular as to whether you opt for a specialist clinic covering one or two areas of law or a more general clinic which covers a wide range of client problems. The type of clinic that is realistic will always depend on a combination of interest, time, resources, demand, expertise, contacts and opportunity, and there may be a significant degree of compromise. There are over 200 examples of different pro bono projects on the public database at www.studentprobono.net. You should peruse these examples to give you ideas and inspiration for your own project.

### What is your educational rationale for having a clinical project?

Your law faculty is likely to require a clearly articulated justification for investing time and resources in a new clinical project. Even if the clinic is intended to be resource light or resource neutral, if your faculty is being asked to put its name and reputation behind the idea then it will want convincing that it is justified and that it complements the existing learning and teaching strategy. It is not possible in a book such as this to provide a rationale that will be appropriate for all purposes – clearly each institutional environment will differ. However, a summary of potential reasons for clinic is set out on the Companion Website for you to consider and adapt to your own context.

### Will the clinic deal with real cases, simulated cases or both?

This is clearly a hugely important decision. It will affect the whole nature of the clinical enterprise including, importantly, the learning experience of the students and the outcomes they can expect to achieve. **Chapter 1** suggested that simulation clinics lack certain valuable characteristics of live client clinics, such as real-life experience, authentic emotion, spontaneity, unpredictability and the personal satisfaction of serving others. However, these characteristics can also be problematic, and simulation schemes therefore tend to be simpler to establish and operate. They also have the advantage of enabling a standardised learning experience for a significant number of students with planned, achievable learning outcomes. For many students, the reassurance that they will have parity of experience with their peers is an important guarantor or fairness and equality of opportunity.

Most of the benefits of clinical legal education set out the previous section can, with some adjustment, also be attributed to simulated clinical experience if it is well designed and implemented. As you will see, many of the problems and costs associated with clinical projects are incurred because they engage in some real service provision and thus have to provide quality control and risk management mechanisms that would not arise in a simulated environment. So what might motivate you to undertake a live client model? There are three related reasons outlined below.

1   If authenticity of experience is crucial to you then some live client aspect to the clinic is probably required. With creative planning it is possible to build unexpected and challenging events into simulation activities in ways that can stretch students and retain their attention and interest. Nevertheless, even the best-designed simulations cannot replicate reality. A good simulation may provide a realistic representation of law in practice, but there is bound to be a gulf between this artificial construct and the law as experienced in the real world.

2   Similarly, if student engagement and motivation is a primary requirement then a live client scheme will be preferable. The reality of having your own client for the first time engenders a new sense of personal responsibility and motivates you to perform. The energy and vitality that this often gives rise to in a live client clinic is palpable. A simulated experience can foster personal satisfaction and a team ethic, but ultimately students know that there is no external imperative or achievement beyond the learning experience.

3   Finally, if service provision is an essential component of your desire to establish a clinic then a simulated clinic will not suffice. The provision of legal advice or representation to serve a community need is a key distinguishing feature of live client clinics. Simulation clinics can replicate the types of problems, issues and cases that such clients generate but, by their nature, do not actually address this need in a direct way. Nevertheless, you should be careful not to overplay the contribution to public service that can be provided by a clinic project. Given the lack of experience of the student participants, the necessity for expert supervision of work, the need to learn from and reflect on experience, and the other demands on student time, most clinics can only conduct a relatively small number of cases. They are highly unlikely to become a major provider of legal services in a community and will certainly not be able to help *all* clients in need.

If you intend to establish a live client clinic but do not feel confident doing this immediately then it may be sensible to start with a simulation clinic as a stepping stone. This can help the academic staff to develop case management, supervision and assessment strategies that can be utilised in a live client context at a later stage. Alternatively, a clinic project might be designed as a hybrid live/simulated experience across two years or two semesters so that students commence their clinical work using simulated activities to help them develop the skills, professional awareness and coping mechanisms they will need for the live client experience that will follow.

One major challenge when establishing a simulated project is the creation of realistic but manageable scenarios and associated documents. This is something that requires expert input. A significant number of simulations are adaptations of real cases that academic lawyers have had experience of when practising law. Clearly not all cases are suitable for adaptation. It depends on the learning that you intend to achieve from the experience, but a case will normally be sufficiently evidentially and legally complex as to raise a range of different procedural and substantive issues. It will also be flexible so that it can be adjusted for different groups of students, for example by the insertion of professional dilemmas or unexpected changes of instructions.

For further information on use of simulated projects, see the range of freely accessible material on simulations on the Simshare website, which includes a video analysing the use of simulations for law degree students at the University of Glamorgan (www.simshare.org.uk). See also the extensive work on the SIMulated Professional Learning Environment (SIMPLE), a digital platform and toolkit for simulated learning funded by the United Kingdom Centre for Legal Education and JISC, including the Final Report on the project (Hughes et al, 2008).

### Will the clinic be intracurricular or extracurricular?

**Chapter 1** has already set out the different approaches to whether clinic should be part of a programme of study, credit bearing, optional or mandatory. These will not be repeated here other than to emphasise that this decision will impact extensively on a number of other key issues such as: available student time to devote to clinic; student motivation; staff and other resources; assessment and so on. It is important for the law school to discuss this issue with students to establish what their views are.

### How will your clinic or pro bono project survive after you have gone?

One of your first and most important considerations should be how the clinic or pro bono project will remain sustainable in the long term. You will be highly committed to the project and may drive it forward with enthusiasm. If the project becomes over-reliant on a small group of dedicated people, there is a risk that it will flounder if and when these people leave. Students, no matter how committed, will eventually graduate and leave the law school. Even academic staff may move on to other duties or leave the institution. Thus you must start with succession. You should try to ensure that the management of the project is diverse and inclusive so that other people can take over in the event of unexpected departures. Furthermore, you should undertake an evaluation each year and ensure that, at student level, the project is formally handed over to the next year group. If possible it is good to involve more than one year of students in the project to enable the future leaders of the project to become involved at an early stage.

 **2.5**    In-house live client clinics – a checklist of practical considerations

Models of clinic vary from institution to institution and not everything set out in this section will be appropriate for each new live client clinic. Indeed, it is possible to establish a basic live client clinic with far less resources – see the 'Clinic on a shoe-string' section below for further information. If you intend to establish something short of a full live client model then you need to be selective. Pick and choose between aspects that are applicable to your local circumstances and needs and those that are not.

This is an outline checklist – in the pages that follow you will find more detailed information on each of these points.

---

- ✔ Do background research and networking
- ✔ Consult widely
- ✔ Prepare and approve a clinic business plan
- ✔ Identify your implementation team
- ✔ Identify your target client group
- ✔ Find premises
      Location
      Facilities
          Reception area                    Library
          Interview room(s)                 Telephones
          Meeting room                      Other equipment
          Student work space                Stationery etc
          Storage
- ✔ Consider funding options
      Funding the clinic
      Funding cases
      Insurance
- ✔ Agree a management structure
- ✔ Agree a learning and teaching structure
      Group size
      Teaching sessions
      Reflection
- ✔ Agree your standard office procedure
      Office opening hours
      Initial client contact
      Client rejection/referral
      Dealing with correspondence/messages
      Student and supervisor availability
      File review process
      Managing holiday and summer cover
- ✔ Writing policies/information sheets
      Retainer letter
      Information for clients leaflet
      IT policy
      Confidentiality
      Client care and complaints
      Risk assessment
      Environmental policy ▶

---

▸ - - - - - - - - - - - - - - - - - - - - - - - - - - - - - - - - - - - - - - - - - - - - - - - - - - - - - - - - - - - - - - - - - -

   ✅ External relations/marketing
      Knowledge of your service
      Website
      Information leaflet/brochure
      Newsletter
      Annual report
      Press releases/media appearances
      Awards
      Community liaison
      Receptions/clinic launch
      Links with other clinics

An in-house live client clinic can be a major investment of time and resources for any law school, so you need to be confident that this is the right model for your institution. This type of clinic tends to operate just like a firm of solicitors and should provide a similar level of client care and representation. It needs to employ at least one practising solicitor, barrister or legal executive to take responsibility for the office and to conduct litigation or other reserved areas, as appropriate. It is possible to run an in-house clinic without employing a qualified lawyer, but the clinic will not then be permitted to do areas of work that are reserved activities under s 12 of the Legal Services Act 2007.

## Do background research and networking

As mentioned earlier, you can learn a lot about clinic design, planning and implementation by reading the existing literature and talking to others. You will find some useful literature listed at the end of this chapter. An article by Alwyn Jones summarises the crucial early decisions that need to be taken when designing a clinical project, as discussed at the Clinical Legal Education Organisation conference, themed 'Starting, sustaining and growing a law clinic'. His article can be found in issue 13 of the UKCLE Directions Newsletter at www.ukcle.ac.uk/resources/directions/previous/issue13/cleo/

There are also regular conferences which normally have sessions devoted to the practical and tactical decisions involved in clinic start-up. A list can be found on the Companion Website.

## Consult widely

Once you have a good idea of what you want to do, you should consult locally on your ideas and refine them as you receive feedback. Keep a list of all the people and bodies that you talk to and any significant points arising from their feedback. Consultation will both inform your plans and make local stakeholders feel valued. It makes sense to start in your law department, then move to the wider university/college and then to the community and legal profession. See the list of consultees at the beginning of this chapter for suggested key people, and give serious consideration to the establishment of an advisory committee to offer assistance prior to and during the early life of the clinic.

## Prepare and approve a clinic business plan

You will need to secure the support of your university/college management in order to commence a clinic project. You have the best opportunity to do this if you have a clear, concise and well-thought-out plan to present to the powers that be. See the sample outline business plan at **2.6** for an example.

## Identify your implementation team

The implementation team will be responsible for the detailed work that is required prior to start-up of the clinic or pro bono project. This team needs to start work many months before the clinic opens its doors. For an in-house live client clinic, you will require a clinic director to drive the project forward. You will also need a supervising lawyer who may or may not be the clinic director, and you will need to decide who will pay for his or her practising certificate (reduced fees are available for solicitors depending on their earnings from the provision of legal services). Any other clinic teaching staff should also be on the implementation team, possibly along with the programme leader of the course which will utilise the clinic modules and the administrator, if he or she has been appointed. You need to decide whether any student representative should also be involved with the implementation team. This may in turn depend on the extent to which you envisage students being involved in the management of the clinic.

### Core clinic team

*Director of clinic* – overall responsibility for the clinic and any academic modules associated with it. You should consult the Solicitors Regulation Authority rules for the supervision and management of a firm or in-house practice (Solicitors' Code of Conduct, Rule 5) to establish whether your clinic director needs to conform to those requirements and, if so, the implications for the running of the clinic.

*Supervising lawyer* – may or may not be the clinic director – will have day-to-day responsibility for the office and the conduct of cases and client affairs. This is a key appointment and it is often beneficial to appoint someone with a wide experience of the different areas of practice that the clinic wishes to conduct.

*Supervisors* – may or may not be practising lawyers – if they are not practising lawyers then they must not be held out to be so and must not themselves conduct reserved legal activities.

*Administrator* – to help to run the office, assist students and administer file management systems. It may be helpful for this person to have previous legal secretarial experience.

*Academic consultants* – some clinics have an informal arrangement with non-clinic academic staff whereby they will offer guidance to students who are dealing with cases in their areas of teaching or research interest. This is a good way to involve the wider law school in the work of the clinic.

▶

> *External consultants* – some clinics work with external lawyers on an ad hoc or regular basis to provide additional support and supervision to students or expert input on particular cases. There are a number of potential advantages to this, including helping to cement relationships with the local legal profession, enhancing student employment prospects and expanding the range of work that can be undertaken by the clinic. You need to agree and confirm in writing who is responsible for paying for and insuring the work of the external consultant. Many firms are happy to give time as part of their pro bono commitments.
>
> *Student advisors* – the students normally work on the cases and they should expect to have most contact with clients and to manage cases in accordance with client instructions and supervisor guidance. Some clinics engage more senior students as mentors or student supervisors, perhaps on an informal basis, or on a credit-bearing module or even under a bursary arrangement. A few clinics employ their own trainee solicitors who may also be former students.

### Identify your target client group

Your consultation exercise will have helped you to assess which areas of law are likely to be most in demand in the local community. However, this will not necessarily be the deciding factor in relation to your target client group. Student interest will be a significant influence, but the main determinant is likely to be the expertise of the supervising lawyer(s). Under the Solicitors' Code of Conduct, a solicitor is professionally obliged to provide a good standard of service to clients and cannot take on a case where he or she has insufficient resources or lacks the competence to deal with the matter. The larger your clinic and the more supervisors you have, the more variety of work you are likely to be able to undertake, but it is often the case that clinics, particularly new ones, tend to specialise in a limited number of areas of law linked to the supervisors' areas of experience. Working in partnership with an external firm can expand the potential areas of law that can be offered. Make sure that you are clear about any practice limitations in all clinic literature and pronouncements as it is important not to raise false expectations or to mislead potential clients.

### Find clinic premises

Premises are important as they will be the working environment for a significant number of staff and students and will be part of the public face of the law school for visiting clients, witnesses, experts, lawyers and judges. It is obviously desirable to have as sizeable and attractive a space as possible, but you will have to work with what is available. An outline of some key considerations regarding premises is below:

### Location

Give careful thought to how your clients will access your clinic. There is little point setting up a law clinic to serve the public in your law school if it is located in an isolated campus site with poor public transport links. Even if your faculty is reasonably accessible, consider how prospective clients will find the clinic within the law school. Clients may often be vulnerable and/or intimidated by the prospect of seeking legal advice. Long or winding routes through poorly signed buildings are not conducive to good client experience. Ideally your clinic will be positioned prominently with ground floor or easy lift access, preferably with access to a building receptionist who is briefed to give clear directions, or with students to meet and greet clients and other visitors.

For law schools located in city centres or easily accessible parts of town and cities, it makes sense to use law school premises for the clinic. Nevertheless, some law schools that are not so well located or that seek a higher profile, 'shop-front' clinic can rent premises in central locations or share premises with other organisations such as Citizens Advice Bureaux or Law Centres, community centres, or other independent advice agencies which are members of AdviceUK. It is worthwhile exploring with your local authority the potential for low or no cost rental of premises. Particularly in times of economic recession or in deprived areas, councils are willing to consider permitting their shop or office premises to be occupied for the community good at nominal rents rather than stand empty. In addition, libraries and similar venues are often good locations, and local authorities are often attracted by the idea of a service that may increase footfall to an existing community resource.

If you do contemplate off-campus premises, you need to give careful thought to issues like security of premises, health and safety, staff and student travel etc. You will need to liaise with the university or college health and safety and/or security adviser regarding these issues, and your insurer will need to be informed of and approve the arrangement. As part of a higher education institution, the clinic will clearly need to comply with accessibility requirements for disabled staff, students and clients under the Equality Act 2010 and related regulations, including the requirement to make reasonable adjustments to accommodate disability and make premises and services more accessible. Student access to the clinic is another important issue.

## Facilities

A major point is that the area occupied by the clinic will effectively need to be given over exclusively to clinic use rather than used flexibly for other teaching purposes. The reason for this is the confidential nature of the material being discussed and documentation being stored and handled in the clinic. For confidentiality purposes you need to limit access only to those staff and students who are working in the clinic. It may not be feasible or desirable to issue everyone with a key. Alternatives include electronic security access pads operated via student and staff ID badges or having someone present in the clinic during office hours to police access to the premises. Unless the clinic is sufficiently large to employ a full-time administrator, this task is likely to fall to supervisors or trusted students.

This adds to the costs of the clinic project because it closes off part of the law school from other uses. Your clinic will need to have the following basic physical facilities. If possible, you should build sufficient flexibility into the design of the clinic to enable expansion at a later date.

- Reception area for clients who are waiting to be seen – this should be sufficiently separate from work areas so as to prevent confidential information being seen by waiting clients.

- Interview room(s) – these need to accommodate a minimum of four people (students often interview in pairs or are observed by their supervisor, and clients often bring a friend or relative with them to an interview) but ideally will be slightly larger so as to couple as a meeting room when not being used for interviewing. They should be fitted with comfortable seating and a table. It is helpful to have video recording facilities in the interview rooms so that, with the client's consent, it is possible to record the interview for review, reflection or assessment purposes. Some clinics have camera-monitoring facilities so that the supervisor can observe the interview from outside the interview room so as to monitor progress but not interfere unnecessarily with the dynamic of the interview.

   If appropriate, an interview room may be fitted with a personal attack alarm system that can be used by a student if he or she is faced with a risk of violence or intimidation by a client. The number of interview rooms needed will be dictated by the number of clients you expect to have. An interview room may need to be reserved for between 60 and 90 minutes for each interview. This permits around six to eight interviews to be conducted per day, per interview room assuming the clinic is open during normal office hours.

- Meeting room – you need sufficient meeting rooms to enable clinic meetings (variously known as clinical rounds, firm meetings, clinic business meetings, case strategy meetings, supervision seminars etc) to take place in accordance with your learning and teaching plan. The number of meetings rooms required will clearly be determined by the number of students using the clinic and the number of hours of meetings that are expected. As suggested, it is often possible to use dual-purpose interview and meeting rooms to maximise efficient use of space. As a minimum, you probably need at least one meeting room in addition to an interview room so that a meeting and an interview can take place at the same time.

- Student work space – the size and layout of this space will vary significantly, depending on the number of students using the clinic and the number of clients. Depending on the type of clinic, this could be a small office or a huge open-plan work area.

   Judging the amount of space and the number of computer terminals required is always difficult. The duration students can be expected to spend in the clinic will to an extent depend on the academic credit they are receiving for their clinic modules. For example, a student who is receiving 40 out of 120 credits can be expected to spend approximately 10–15 hours in the clinic each week. If a clinic had 100 such students then there would be 1,000–1,500 student hours in the clinic each week. If we take the top end of this estimate and assume the clinic is open for 40 hours per week, it suggests that at any one time there will be around 37 students in the clinic, meaning that this would be the optimum number of work stations. A similar type of calculation can be done to enable you to work out the size of work space and computer access you require for your clinic.

This calculation obviously does not take account of the reluctance of many students to get out of bed so as to be in the clinic at 9.00am. Neither does it take account of the peaks and troughs of clinic work and the tendency of many clinic students to put more hours into their cases than the academic credit suggests.

- Storage – you need sufficient lockable filing cabinets and/or storage room space to handle all of the confidential client material you will accumulate during the year. New clients may arrive with voluminous amounts of documentation, whilst others might have files held by previous lawyers that you will need to request. Some types of work tend to be more demanding on space, eg criminal appeal work tends to lead to large box files of trial material and exhibits such as tapes or video cassettes. You should also factor in the requirement to store files after they are closed. Files are normally kept for at least six years prior to confidential destruction, often longer if there are ongoing issues or potential future resuscitation, eg where prisoners are still in prison. You should consider the cost–benefit of using up space in the clinic or paying to store files off-site using a data storage company.

- Library – a major part of case work is legal research, so students will need access to a law library. If the clinic is based in the law school then students should have ready access to the library. However, if students are going to the library, there are clearly issues regarding the confidentiality of client material they may need to refer to during their research. You will need to develop a policy regarding student work on clinic cases outside the clinic. You may decide that files should not normally be removed from the clinic, in which case there will be difficulties for students conducting research in the library. They may be able to borrow the book and take it to the clinic, but many relevant books are reference only. In an ideal world there will be a library attached to the clinic so that students can collect the books they need and work on them in the clinic, but this is only really feasible if a clinic is built into the design of a new-build law school at an early stage.

  A further problem regarding library facilities is that some law collections may not include relevant practitioner texts necessary for clinical work. It is therefore sensible to build into the initial clinic plan a basic book collection that will be of particular relevance for the areas of work to be conducted by the clinic and that are not readily available in the law school library. This is likely to include practitioner texts or looseleaf collections, legislation handbooks and some skills manuals relevant to the clinical work the students will be doing. You should also contact the law librarian and ask him or her to inform you when replacement books mean that older editions will be discarded. If these editions are of value to the clinic, the library may be willing to donate them.

- Computers – in most clinics students are responsible for their own typing. They will draft various documents using a word processor and thus will need access to a computer. It may not be necessary to have one computer per student work station as student advisors will not always be working on a computer, but the reality is that they will need to use a computer for much of their work. If the premises have wireless capability then it may be possible to use laptop computers rather than fixed terminals. This will increase flexible use of space, but you will need to develop a clear IT policy for the clinic so as to preserve the security of data and the confidentiality of client material. Some, if not all, of the computers will need to have Internet access for legal research purposes and access to online legal research databases if feasible, such as Westlaw, LexisNexis and Lawtel. At the time of writing LawWorks has an arrangement with LexisNexis whereby the LexisPSL product is offered free of charge to all student clinics which are members of the LawWorks Clinics project (membership of this network is free). LexisPSL is the online resource aimed at practitioners and is an invaluable resource for student law clinics. See www.lexisnexis.org.uk/lexispsl.

You need to have sufficient storage space on a server or hard drive to enable clinic-related electronic data to be stored securely and accessed only by authorised people. Speak to your institution's IT manager about the most effective means of achieving this. Some clinics are given their own dedicated drive on the law school server for storage of material. Your IT policy will need to determine how electronic material is to be stored. For example, you may decide that there will be no use of memory sticks or other portable storage and that all material must be stored on the clinic server or hard drive. You may also wish to give consideration to the need for case management software to help you manage your client files. There is a wide range of different systems available on the commercial market and it may be possible to arrange a discounted rate as a not-for-profit organisation.

It is useful to have a clinic email address so that clients and others can contact the clinic by email, but it is important to ensure that the inbox is checked regularly and that you have an appropriate auto response activated to inform people of when they are likely to receive a response. Your IT policy will need to determine how email is to be used in the clinic (eg whether students may use their university email account, when clinic correspondence should be deleted, what the disclaimer should state at the bottom of the email etc). It is important to ensure that all electronic communication relating to client cases is checked and filed in the same way as postal communications.

- Telephones – your clinic will need to be equipped with sufficient telephones for student and staff use. Ideally you will have a dedicated external telephone number, which you can publish with the clinic opening hours, and a clear answer phone message for anyone calling outside office hours. Clinics are often busy and noisy places, so it is useful to have a quiet area where people can communicate effectively. A conference call function may also be useful. If this is not available already then there are several providers which provide very low cost solutions.

- Other equipment – you will need a photocopier, printers, a fax machine, a document scanner, a shredder, confidential waste disposal, a digital camera, a calculator, video and audio playback facilities and all of the routine equipment required for running a legal office (eg storage drawers, in-trays, hole punches, staplers, scissors etc).

- Stationery etc – you will need a clinic letterhead, leaflets with travel directions, file pro forma sheets such as client personal information sheets, blank attendance notes, retainer information, file dividers, time recording sheets, client questionnaires and possibly business cards. You need empty client files (it is helpful to have different colours for different areas of law), document clips, plastic document wallets, box files, coloured ribbon and cardboard document corners (for briefs to counsel and some court documents) and so on.

---

### Clinic on a shoestring

If you are intimidated by the huge amount of facilities and equipment indicated above, please remember that not all clinical or pro bono programmes will be the same. It is possible to set up the bare bones of a law school-based clinic by begging, borrowing (but not stealing) the basics as follows:

- Lockable room with basic office furniture.
- Space for interviewing clients – a separate room is much better, but it is possible to use the clinic room as a last resort or to borrow other private space on an ad hoc basis to see clients, eg an academic staff office.
- Filing cabinet.
- Telephone.
- Computer and printer.
- Law school stationery.

This basic infrastructure will get you started and then you can start eyeing up more attractive premises and agitating for more resources.

---

## Consider funding options

There are two main issues regarding funding: (a) how will the staffing and operating costs of the clinic be met; and (b) how will costs associated with client cases be met? The latter is dealt with separately in **Chapter 4**, 'Client funding'. In relation to the first issue, the core funding of any clinic is likely to come from the law school itself. The main expenditure is on staff, space and operating costs and may be quite substantial. In order to justify this type of investment, most in-house clinics tend to be linked to one or more academic modules. This enables the law school to devote teaching and related resources to the clinic. But running a clinic is much more expensive than a standard law module.

Given the current funding structures in higher education, the institution will only secure the lowest band of funding from the Higher Education Funding Council (HEFCE) despite the fact that clinical learning is as resource-intensive as many methods in subjects that attract much higher funding per student. Funding cuts are likely to mean that subjects such as law attract little or no state subsidy. This is a difficult issue and leads some law schools to conclude that, despite its attractiveness, an in-house clinic is too expensive and not justifiable. Others are persuaded that it is important to invest additional resources in a clinic as a showcase for student performance and as a contribution to the local community.

Some clinics have sought sponsorship from external bodies or applied for additional funding from research bodies or teaching and learning budgets. Clinics are certainly an attractive proposition for law firms or other potential employers as they are then associated with the law school in a positive way for the benefit of students and the community, and it is helpful for enhancing their reputation with future applicants for jobs.

In the USA and elsewhere, a number of clinics are named after sponsoring law firms or benefactors. There is nothing intrinsically problematic with this, but the clinic needs to be careful to ensure it retains its identity and independence. A further issue in relation to external funding is that by its nature it tends to be insecure over the long term, so that if such funding is a major part of the clinic resource then sustained commitment to ongoing fund-raising activities is required. You may wish to investigate the possibility of establishing a charitable trust for your clinic in order to be able to channel donations or sponsorship to ring-fence its use for clinic purposes. This will need to be discussed with your university/college finance director.

A further financial issue is insurance. A law clinic is not a firm for the purposes of the Solicitors' Indemnity Insurance Rules. Thus it does not need to secure insurance under those rules. Nevertheless, your institution will still be liable for any successful claim brought against the clinic by an aggrieved client. You therefore need to check that your institution's existing insurance policy has adequate professional indemnity provision to cover any claims that could be brought and, if not, seek an adjustment to the terms of the policy. It is sensible to seek cover that offers an equivalent amount per claim as required by the Solicitors' Indemnity Insurance Rules (currently £2 million, not including defence costs – read the rules in full on the Solicitors Regulation Authority website at www.sra.org.uk). The fact that your clinic may only take on cases that have significantly less value does not mean that you are at no risk of facing a high value claim. For example, a client who alleges that he had a high value claim but the clinic negligently advised him not to pursue it would potentially have a high value professional negligence claim against the clinic. It is vital that you explain to your institution's insurance officer the nature of the clinic project and seek written confirmation that you are appropriately insured.

### Agree a management structure

Irrespective of the size of your clinic, you need to have a clear decision-making process. Consider how you would deal with the following issues which could arise:

- A client wishes to make a formal complaint about the clinic's alleged failure to advise him about a pending deadline.
- A group of clinic students want to hold a protest meeting in the clinic against planned legal aid cuts.
- Part-time students have requested that the clinic open on evenings and/or weekends so that they can also work in the clinic.

- The Business School has approached the clinic about the possibility of a joint venture to offer legal and marketing advice to entrepreneurs and small businesses.
- The Dean of the law school thinks it might be a good idea for the clinic to apply for a national pro bono award.
- A student representative has argued that the module credit given to clinic does not adequately reflect the time and effort students have to put into it and this undermines their performance in other important subjects.

This selection of potential queries, requests and complaints reveals the wide variety of decisions that may need to be taken by clinic management. It is not the purpose of this book to suggest one particular structure, but here are some important considerations:

- Decide how much student input there should be into the management of the clinic – students are clearly central to the clinic and will be affected by its policies and direction. How much influence over the clinic should they have? At one extreme, students might effectively run the clinic themselves, or there might be full democratic decision-making with no management hierarchy. At the other end, students might be recipients of clinic learning but with no voice or influence over decisions that are taken. Most clinics have some sort of student consultative mechanism, such as student reps or a clinic liaison committee. They will normally have end-of-module questionnaires and/or feedback sessions. Some have gone further and have a student rep on the management committee or a student council to make or contribute to decisions about clinic policies. The more listened to students feel, the more satisfied they are likely to be and the more enthusiastic they will be about the clinic.
- Decide the appropriate level of decision-maker – many decisions will be taken by the clinic director, possibly with the help of a management committee if the size of the clinic merits this. Certain matters, such as dealing with complaints, should always be dealt with by the clinic director. However, a number of other matters can safely be left to individual supervisors (eg the student who wants a new partner) or to students themselves (the student could be told to speak to his or her partner and resolve their differences). Many matters will not be resolvable solely within the clinic and will require consultation or referral to others. The example of the potential joint venture with the Business School will probably need to be raised with the law school management as it affects inter-school collaborations. The request to increase module credit will need to be discussed with the relevant programme leader as it is bound to impact on other subjects and the overall learning strategy for the course. Opening times are normally something for the clinic to resolve, but it would be wrong to unilaterally open up the clinic to students on other courses without discussing it with the programme leaders first. Even something as basic as a request to eat food in the clinic may impact on, for example, institutional policies about IT spaces, so it is often advisable to consult on changes widely.

- Decide whether you need an ethics committee – some decisions may involve ethical considerations or give rise to reputational concerns. This had led some clinics to establish an ethics committee to offer advice and/or take such decisions. There is, of course, a risk of institutional and political pressure or interference with clinics, particularly where they undertake legal campaigns or litigation against powerful corporations or interests (see Joy, 2005). You should therefore be clear about your motivation for introducing such a committee and careful about the membership. For example, imagine a convicted paedophile is seeking compensation. Are you content for the decision about whether to take on this case to be left to the student advisors, the supervising lawyer, the director of the clinic, or do you think that a committee should decide, and, if so, should there be any external membership on the committee, eg the Head of the law school?

### Agree a learning and teaching strategy

The clinic is not merely a service to the community – it is a learning environment. Elsewhere in this book you will read about the relationship between students and supervisors, about collaborating with others in your learning and about reflecting on your experience. This section gives an overview of some key decisions you need to take regarding the structure of the learning. This section is of particular relevance to academic staff.

### Group size

Clinic works best when students are collaborating in small groups and also working individually where appropriate. If possible, the main clinic cohort should be divided into small 'firms', 'clinics' or 'teams', who will work together for the duration of the semester or academic year under the same supervisor. The optimum size of group is around 6–8 students. It is also helpful to enable students to work in pairs on cases, at least initially, as they are then able to assist each other, bounce ideas around and help each other reflect on their experience. It is possible for students to work in clinic in larger groups – see for example the attempts to introduce clinic to wider student audiences in the USA (Millemann, 2005: 441) – and resource limitations may dictate that class sizes need to be larger than suggested here, but if this is the case you will encounter additional difficulties of managing student expectations and ensuring everyone buys into the client's case given that they may have only peripheral involvement.

### Teaching sessions

Clinical legal education in a live client clinic obviously requires students to work on real cases, but some formal teaching/supervision sessions need to be built into the working week in order to provide structure, regular case reviews and opportunities for discussion, analysis and reflection. The main vehicle for this learning is generally a small group clinic discussion between students and supervisor, known by various names such as 'clinical round', 'firm meeting', 'case strategy session' and 'clinic debriefing'. The duration will vary from clinic to clinic but is likely to be between 1–3 hours and will tend to be fairly unstructured, reacting to developments on the cases, gauging student reaction and strategising about next steps.

Some clinics will hold a separate 'clinic seminar' or 'reflection session', which will not focus directly on the case work of the clinic but will seek to draw wider lessons about the law, justice, skills, ethics etc. These sessions may draw more extensively on academic commentaries and simulated or hypothetical scenarios and will tend to be more structured than the clinical round type of session, with advance preparation and clear learning outcomes emerging from a planned curriculum. Most clinics will also have a degree of one-to-one supervision sessions, which tend to be ad hoc and informal, when the student discusses his or her case with the supervisor and receives feedback about the steps taken.

Finally, most clinics will have a lecture programme aimed at the whole clinic group, which will address broad issues arising out of clinical work, such as access to justice, public funding, professional ethics, reflection, skills development, client care etc. Within these main teaching and learning structures, a wide variety of activities will take place, for example student presentations, video playback, debates, guest lectures, joint meetings (bringing together different clinic groups to share experience), simulated interviews, mock trials, court visits, masterclasses, reflection exercises, client feedback and so on.

### Making space for reflection: law in slow motion

Clinic is, or should be, 'law in slow motion'. At no other time in your life will you have the opportunity to think so much about the work you are doing, why you are doing it, how it could or should be done differently and what difference you can make. There is a separate chapter on reflection in this book (**Chapter 12**), which explains what reflection is and how vital it is for student development in clinical legal education.

There is a tendency when setting up a new clinic to overestimate the amount of cases that students can reasonably manage. This is probably due to the fact that some supervisors are measuring their expectations against what they themselves achieved when working as a lawyer in practice. If too many cases are taken on then students will struggle to complete the work that is needed to service the clients' needs, and they will not find the time to think deeply about the issues that the cases give rise to, their own attitudes to these issues, and how they should react as professionals. When deciding on your notional use of clinic time, try to build in a significant period for reading, discussing and reflecting outside the formal class sessions.

### Agree your standard office procedure

It is very important to have a good idea of how you want the clinic to operate right from the outset. Clearly you will need to adjust this in light of experience, but you need to give consideration and agree your approach in relation to some basic office processes so that the clinic operates smoothly and you do not have any nasty surprises as the academic year progresses.

## Office opening hours

Decide on how many hours per week and how many weeks per year the clinic will remain open. You may decide to have set times when the clinic will be open to clients and other times when it is only open to students and supervisors. Normal office hours are 9.00am–5.00pm, Monday to Friday, excluding bank holidays. However, there is no requirement that you open the clinic during normal office hours. Provided you clearly inform current and potential clients, it is perfectly legitimate to restrict your opening hours. For example, you may open in the afternoons only or three days per week. However, note that limitation periods, court deadlines and the like will continue to run irrespective of whether your office is open. Therefore, if you are conducting any work that is time sensitive, you will need to have a system for ensuring regular checking of correspondence. A particular issue is clinic opening hours outside of term time. The main periods of difficulty are Christmas, Easter and Summer. You should plan how you will cover these periods, and if you cannot cover them you will need to close your office. If you do close your office for significant periods of time, this could seriously restrict the type of work you can take on. Ideally you will have a system of holiday cover (see below).

## Initial client contact

You should have a clear procedure for when new clients contact the office by telephone, letter, email or in person. It is advisable to create a pro forma initial client contact sheet which records basic contact details and identifies the general area of concern. This information should be stored or copied into a readily accessible database of new queries that can then be viewed by students and supervisors to make decisions about whether the client should be offered an interview.

A standard response should be given to all new contacts which will give them clear information about what, if anything, will happen next. If it is clear from the initial contact that the clinic cannot help then the client should be informed immediately or as soon as possible and given some information about what else he or she might do (see below). If the clinic might be able to help then there need to be strict initial time limits for making decisions and contacting the client.

If clients contact the clinic when new cases are not being taken on, there should be a standard letter informing them of this. You need to decide if you wish to create a waiting list of cases for when the clinic does have capacity, and, if so, clients need to be informed and asked if they wish to wait but should be told that there is no guarantee that they will be taken on. If a case is accepted then you need to have clear file recording and case management procedures (see **Chapter 9**, 'Organising and strategising').

## Client rejection/referral

If it is decided not to take on a client then the client needs to be informed quickly so that he or she has the opportunity to seek help elsewhere, drop his or her case or proceed without legal assistance. You need to be clear about your reason for not taking on a case and this should comply with the Solicitors' Code of Conduct. You are likely to end up rejecting a large number of potential clients, so you may wish to create standardised rejection letters which can be tailored to the particular reasons in each case (eg lack of capacity, lack of expertise, end of academic year, case is too complex, case has insufficient educational value, case has no merit). Whenever you reject a client, you should try to provide some referral information so as not to leave him or her stranded. You may wish to develop reciprocal referral arrangements with local firms, Law Centres, CABs and pro bono organisations such as the Bar Pro Bono Unit and LawWorks, or at least provide the Community Legal Service telephone number so that the client can seek referral to another firm that practises in the area of law he or she is seeking help with.

Some clinics, when rejecting a case, will nonetheless distil the facts of the case and draft a letter, 'To whom it may concern', clearly setting out the client's case and hopefully making it more likely that the client's case is given fair consideration by the next organisation he or she approaches.

### Dealing with correspondence/messages

One essential office task is ensuring that correspondence in and out of the clinic is dealt with appropriately and within a reasonable time. You need to have systems for dealing with each method of communication: post, email, fax, telephone call, personal visit. The clinic needs to nominate one or more persons to check the incoming correspondence each day the clinic is open and allocate this to the relevant students/supervisors. This requires clearly labelled and regularly checked in-trays. It is also good practice for someone to check all outgoing correspondence. This will already have been checked by a supervisor, but a final check is often really useful for routine errors, such as letters not being signed, faulty pagination, missing enclosures, incomplete address and so on.

### Student and supervisor availability

There needs to be a clear understanding about the commitment students are taking on if they work on behalf of clients. Once a client is taken on then the clinic is obliged to act in his or her best interests, and this means that the essential tasks on the case must be performed diligently and expeditiously, irrespective of other commitments. This means that students and supervisors need to plan carefully and complete case work in good time so that there is less chance of a last minute rush to meet a deadline. You need to decide whether students should be released from other academic commitments, such as seminars and lectures, if absolutely necessary to secure the client's interests. If yes, you need to discuss this with the relevant programme leader and seek his or her agreement. If not, then you need to put in place a system to ensure that supervisors or others can step in to cover for absent students. Students should be strongly advised to get on with other academic commitments whenever there is quiet time in the clinic as the unpredictable nature of a real case means that it could flare up at any moment.

### File review process

You should have a system for ensuring that all open files are reviewed regularly and checked by a supervisor and that any defects or necessary action are identified and progressed. Obviously there will be regular discussion of progress on cases at clinical meetings. However, this is not always systematic and may not focus on every case, particularly if there is little movement on the case. Thus a formal check by students and supervisors at fixed intervals helps to ensure that files do not lie dormant, clients are not ignored and deadlines are met. It also acts as a quality control mechanism for the work done by the students. As a minimum, this should be at the point of a file being opened and at fixed points during the academic year.

## Managing holiday and summer cover

During term time, students will work on client cases, but what happens when they go home for two or three weeks at Christmas and Easter, and when they finish their studies to complete exams and have summer holidays? Given that client cases cannot be turned on and off like a tap, you need to have a plan for dealing with these periods. Many students will live locally and may be willing to continue working on cases during holiday periods, but this cannot be guaranteed, so it is likely that the clinic will need a system of holiday cover to ensure that essential steps can be taken and that there is continuity for clients.

Some cases will have come to a natural end by the end of the academic year, but there are bound to be cases which are still active at this time. It would be extremely prejudicial to those clients to arbitrarily close their files at this point, so it is going to be necessary to cover them over the summer period. There is no ideal solution, but there are a number of possibilities, such as employing a solicitor on a temporary basis to cover the office during the summer, with client consent agreeing with a local firm of solicitors that it will take responsibility for client files over the summer period, employing students to help cover the clinic over the summer period, or asking for student volunteers for the summer period. Most options will still require the clinic director to be present for a significant period over the summer. In all cases there is a need for clear and accurate file handover notes.

## Writing policies/information sheets

In due course, you will need to create a clinic office manual that gathers together all key policies, guidance, standard documents and so on. At this stage, you will probably wish to adopt a more flexible approach so that you can learn from experience before setting out written policies. Furthermore, each clinic will have a different approach to policy issues, so it is something you will wish to review with other stakeholders. Below is a list of policies and information sheets you will need to consider creating. A sample clinic handbook can be found on the 'Law Schools' section of the LawWorks website. LawWorks and many other clinics are often willing to share template documents. LawWorks also provides free consultancy to help review clinic documents and procedures.

## Retainer letter

A retainer letter sets out your agreement with the client and is thus of crucial importance. Although you are not charging the client for the work you do, there is a fiduciary relationship and you have professional obligations to the client. The retainer letter should set out the parameters of this relationship, including the steps you will and will not take on the client's behalf. For example, if you do not undertake advocacy in court or tribunals, this should be clearly stated in the retainer. It will also deal with any particular adjustments to the normal professional relationship arising from the fact that students are working on the case, for example if confidential client material may have to be disclosed to an external examiner as part of the assessment moderation process.

It is also important to set out any particular conditions or restrictions on the relationship, for example the fact that work may take longer than with a normal firm of solicitors due to the need for checking, or the fact that the case may not be able to be continued if it is too complex for students to deal with. You will also need to deal with costs and disbursements (as to which see **Chapter 4** and **7.5**). Although the retainer will be your agreement with the client, its terms will not displace any professional obligations the clinic has under the Solicitors' Code of Conduct (eg the requirement in Rule 2 to terminate the retainer only where there is good reason and on reasonable notice).

For further details regarding the retainer and a sample client care letter, see **7.5**.

### Client information leaflet

The retainer is likely to be quite technical and legalistic in nature. You may therefore find it helpful to prepare a summary of the clinic service in the form of an information leaflet which will be easy to read and readily understandable. You need to make sure that the information in this document and the retainer letter are compatible.

### IT policy

As previously mentioned, you will need an IT policy to govern a range of important matters such as digital storage and security of personal information (eg client contact and financial or medical details) and confidential case information (eg word-processed drafts and final versions of letters, court documents etc), use of email for communication within the clinic and with clients or external contacts, checking and filing of correspondence sent and received electronically, and so on. Given the confidential and sensitive nature of the information you hold, you should seek to create as secure a system as possible for the handling of electronic data. You should also consult with your institution's data protection officer to ensure compliance with the Data Protection Act.

### Confidentiality

You need to read and make sure that your systems comply with Rule 4 of the Solicitors' Code of Conduct: Confidentiality and Disclosure. This policy will address matters such as discussion of client affairs outside the clinic, whether and if so in what circumstances client files or other confidential material may be taken outside the clinic, steps to take if confidentiality has been or is at risk of being compromised, steps to take when it is necessary to disclose client information to a third party (including pro forma client disclosure agreements), how to deal with visitors to the clinic and any confidentiality agreements they may be required to sign. For further information on ethical responsibilities, see **Chapter 3**.

## Client care and complaints

You should develop a policy that ensures you comply with Rule 2 of the Solicitors' Code of Conduct: Client Relations. In particular, you should ensure that everyone is aware of the clinic's obligations to explain to the client your and the client's respective responsibilities, to explain the issues involved in the case and the options and next steps, and to keep the client informed of progress. You must also have a written complaints policy that can be given to the client on request, which sets out whom to contact in the event of a complaint, how it will be handled and the timescales involved.

## Risk assessment

You should discuss with your institution's health and safety officer whether you need to prepare a risk assessment policy for the clinic. There are certain matters that may be viewed as risks that are particular to the clinic, for example clients visiting the clinic premises, students interviewing clients in private, conducting site visits and visiting clients off campus. It may be appropriate to assess these risks and identify an appropriate response.

## Environmental policy

The clinic will use a significant amount of resources. Particular environmental issues could include electricity usage, consumption of paper and the amount of waste that is created, use of cars or public transport when travelling on clinic business, and so forth.

## External relations/marketing

It may seem unnecessary to worry about external relations and marketing when you have a free legal service to offer – it should sell itself. This may be the case, although even a free service needs to be publicised to those who may wish to take advantage of it. Moreover, your external relations are much wider than the need to attract potential clients. There is a large institutional, community and potentially national or international audience whom you will want to inform and enthuse about your project to help secure its success and sustainability. It is much more difficult to close down a well-respected, high-profile, award-winning clinic than one which has hidden its light under a bushel. You can read more about the main sources of external relations and marketing on the Companion Website.

##  Sample outline business plan for a new clinic project

**Name of project:** Newtown University Legal Advice Centre

**Outline rationale:** To enhance the legal skills, knowledge and employability of LLB students while providing a free community legal advice service to members of the public in Newtown.

**Project proposers:** Karen Foss (Senior Lecturer); Paramjit Singh (LLB year 2; law school rep)

▶

**Consultation:** Initial discussion with Law School Senior Management Group; Fact finding visit to Oldtown Student Law Office; Participation at LawWorks student pro bono conference; Meeting with Law School Student Forum and Student Union; Presentation to Newtown Law Society; Creation of Advisory Group including: District Judge Cross, Jonathan Head QC, Head of Station Chambers, Amir Hussain, senior partner of Hedleys LLP, Karen Knox, manager of Newtown Citizens' Advice Bureau and Jan Kapolski, head of legal department, Newtown Council (minutes annexed).

**Outline of service:** Initially we will offer a pro bono advice service on 3 afternoons per week (Monday, Wednesday and Friday) from 2.00pm–5.00pm plus one evening session on Thursday from 5.00pm–8.00pm. This will run from October to May. Clients will attend an initial interview and then receive a follow-up advice letter prepared by students under the supervision of qualified solicitors. The areas of law covered will be (i) Education Law, (ii) Community Care Law and (iii) Employment Law. These reflect the expertise and interests of the supervising lawyers. NB. At this stage the Legal Advice Centre will *not* be taking on clients on a representation basis. The service will be advice and referral only. In the future it may be possible to expand the service into a full representation service but this will depend on demand and future resourcing.

**Academic modules:** A 20 credit optional module at level 5 (Law in the Community) will be offered to year 2 students, and a 20 credit optional module at level 6 (Advanced Law in the Community) will be offered to year 3 students (module descriptors annexed). Numbers will be initially capped at 16 students per module (32 in total).

**Premises:** Office space including a meeting room, two interview rooms and use of a networked computer has been kindly donated by Hedleys LLP in its town centre premises. A secure office is also required in the Law School for the storage of client documentation and student work on client queries. This will need to be equipped with a minimum of 10 work stations, two networked PCs, a telephone and fax machine. It will also require two lockable filing cabinets, a lockable drawer set and modest shelf space for Legal Advice Centre books (a proposed purchase list of textbooks is annexed). Room 021 has been identified as suitable and the Estates Department estimate for fitting out the room is annexed. [In the future it is intended to convert the attached store room into an interview/meeting room so that the legal advice centre can be partly brought in-house.]

**Other resources:** Legal Advice Centre stationery, information leaflets, posters, business cards and file management materials (folders, document front sheets, pro forma information sheets etc) are required. Two reduced fee Solicitors Regulation Authority practising certificates will be required for Law School solicitor supervisors. A full costed list is attached.

**Staff resources:** The Legal Advice Centre will run for 10 weeks in the first semester and 10 weeks in the second semester (20 weeks). There will be 4 × 3-hour supervision sessions per week plus 4 × 1-hour debriefing sessions (16 hours per week). This is a total of 320 hours per academic year across the two new modules. 50% of the supervision will be conducted by Hedleys LLP staff on a voluntary basis. This leaves 160 hours of supervision by Law School staff. Karen Foss and John Webster have offered to share this commitment (80 hours each). Karen Foss is the proposed

Legal Advice Centre Director and Module Leader for both modules for which she will receive the normal administrative time allocation. A part-time secretary is required for the administration of the Legal Advice Centre.

**Hedleys LLP:** The Law School's relationship with Hedleys LLP is longstanding. The firm is a strong supporter of the School and of pro bono initiatives. It has made a generous and long-term commitment to supporting the new clinic project through the provision of premises at no cost, staff time and general advice and assistance. Hedley's staff will work for the Legal Advice Centre during their normal working week, under their own practising certificates and under the firm's insurance policy. They will not be employed by the University. The relationship between Hedleys LLP and the Law School is set out the Draft Memorandum of Understanding (annexed).

**Teaching/learning:** Students will be divided into 'firms' of eight. Following an intensive induction/training fortnight, each firm will participate in 1 × 3-hour advice session and 1 × 1-hour debrief per week. They will interview clients in pairs for 30 minutes, report their findings to the supervisor, conduct initial research and report back to the client. This will happen while the client waits wherever feasible. The debrief session will identify further areas for research and explore student reactions and learning. Students will then return to the Law School and continue their research and preparation of an advice letter.

**Assessment:** The learning outcomes and assessment strategies for the two new modules are set out in detail in the module descriptors. The level 5 module is assessed by way of a portfolio of material focusing on interviewing, legal research and legal writing issues plus a reflective diary. The level 6 module is assessed by way of a reflective diary and extended essay.

**Insurance:** The Legal Advice Centre is not a 'firm' for the purpose of the Solicitors' Indemnity Insurance Rules. It does not therefore require insurance in accordance with those Rules. Nevertheless, the University Insurer has confirmed that professional indemnity insurance equivalent to cover under the Rules is available (see letter annexed).

**Compensation fund:** The Legal Advice Centre will not have a client account and will not hold client monies. There is thus no requirement for a contribution to the Solicitors' Compensation Fund.

 ## Summary

It can be seen that the creation of a live client clinic project is (a) time consuming, (b) complex, and (c) a collaborative effort that involves a number of different stakeholders. However, there is a wide variety of clinic and pro bono projects that are more manageable in terms of size, management and resources. There is also a huge amount of advice, assistance and general goodwill in the clinic and pro bono community that you can draw on when you are working on your project. Whilst there is a lot of groundwork involved, the benefits to you, your law school and community are well worth the effort. Finally, remember that when you establish a clinic or pro bono project you need to address sustainability from the outset.

 Further reading

## Introductory

**LawWorks website**

The pro bono charity has an excellent student pro bono office and useful material on its website on setting up a student pro bono project (www.lawworks.org.uk/index.php?id=students) and funding such an initiative (www.lawworks.org.uk/?id=student-funding).

**Studentprobono.net**

A useful web resource with a searchable database of existing pro bono initiatives in law schools (www.studentprobono.net/).

**The United Kingdom Centre for Legal Education (UKCLE)**

This subject centre hosts clinic pages on its website and also a useful FAQ document prepared by Professor Julian Webb regarding the establishment of a law clinic (www.ukcle.ac.uk/resources/teaching-and-learning-practices/clinical-legal-education/). The resource also links to the Clinical Legal Education Organisation model standards for live client clinics which provide a potential template if you intend to establish a live client clinic (www.ukcle. ac.uk/resources/clinic/index.html).

## Intermediate

**Solicitors Regulation Authority, *Solicitors' Code of Conduct* (Law Society Publishing, 2007)**

The updated version is available at www.sra.org.uk/solicitors/code-of-conduct.page.

**Hughes et al, *SIMulated Professional Learning Environment (SIMPLE), Final Report*, 2008**

www.simplecommunity.org

**Millemann, M and Schwinn, S, 'Teaching legal research and writing with actual legal work – extending clinical education into the first year' (2005) 12 Clinical L Rev 441**

The authors describe two experimental courses with first-year legal research and writing (LWR) students at the University of Maryland. One utilised a criminal appeal case being conducted by more experienced upper-year students in the school's clinic. The LRW students had to evaluate the legal issues, understand the criminal process as it stood at the time of the appellant's trial and brief on and argue the points in class. Their conclusions were that actual legal work motivates students to learn the basic skills of LRW and begin to develop the use of facts and construction of legal arguments in response to indeterminate legal issues.

## Advanced

**Joy, P, 'Political interference in clinical programs: lessons from the US experience' [2005] IJCLE 83**

This article addresses the history and increasing problem of political interference and other attacks on law clinics in the USA with regard to student representation of poor people in legal challenges to powerful economic or political interests. It provides a warning against complacency in other jurisdictions about the freedom of clinics to represent the interests of vulnerable clients.

 Activities

### Activity 1: What sort of clinic do you want?

This exercise involves the sorting and ranking of attributes that might go to make up your desired clinic. It helps you to work out the priorities for a new clinic or for significant review of an existing clinic.

**Group size:** 4–20

**Materials:** A3 paper, post-it notes and a marker pen (or alternatively the exercise can be done using a word processor)

**Instructions:** your group should be divided into four individuals or small teams. Each team should be given a sheet of A3 paper, 15 post-its and a marker pen. At the top of the A3 sheet you should write, 'Our new clinic should …'. On 10 of the post-its you should write the following with the marker pen:

- Provide an excellent legal education for students.
- Develop the skills of future lawyers.
- Increase awareness of poverty and the legal problems this causes.
- Be organised by students rather than academic staff.
- Provide advice only and refer people to other agencies.
- Provoke students to think about the law and legal practice.
- Use simulations rather than real clients.
- Enhance the reputation of students and the law school.
- Only represent people who have no other source of legal funding and cannot pay themselves.
- Enable students to help others while gaining academic credit.

Use the remaining post-its to note down your own ideas. You should then discuss within your team and attempt to rank the post-its as a hierarchy, with the most important reason at the top and the least important at the bottom. It is permissible to put two or more post-its side by side if they are deemed to be of equal rank.

Your team should then attach your sheet of paper to the wall or a flip chart and be prepared to justify your findings and identify any areas of disagreement within your team.

## Activity 2: Pitching for a new clinic

This exercise is best run as a series of mini-presentations.

**Group size:** 4–20

**Materials:** access to this chapter

**Instructions:** your group should be divided into four small teams. Each team should read the following information:

Your law school has decided in principle to found a new law clinic project. It has established a student competition to come up with proposals for the new project. The following guidance has been issued:

- The school would like to partner with a local or national organisation if possible.
- Students in the clinic should have some contact with real people.
- Resources are tight – the proposal should not be a full representation, in-house law centre.
- Proposals should identify potential premises in the law school.
- The proposal should outline what is innovative or unique about the clinic.
- The proposal should outline how students will benefit from the new clinic.

Your group should prepare a plan based on your own knowledge of your institution and local community. Prepare a short (maximum 10 minute) presentation to deliver to the rest of the group. Following the presentations, the tutor or the whole group will decide on the winning proposal.

## Activity 3: Devising a clinic policy

This is a workshop session that requires you to brainstorm ideas for important clinic policies.

**Group size:** 4–20

**Materials:** access to this chapter, A3 paper and marker pens

**Instructions:** you should assume that you have set up a live client, in-house law clinic. You will be taking clients from members of the public, and students will work in small 'firms' supervised by practising solicitors employed by the university. Your group should be divided into four small teams. One of the following policies should be allocated to each team. For each policy area, you should assess the potential issues/problems and what rules and procedures you need to put in place to deal with these.

- IT policy
- Confidentiality policy
- Client care and complaints policy
- Environmental policy

In your small teams you should take a sheet of A3 paper and put a line down the middle. On the left-hand side you should compile a list of issues or problems; on the right-hand side you should compile a list of rules or procedures. Once you have completed this task you should present your findings to the rest of the group.

# 3 Ethics and professional conduct in clinic and pro bono

'God works wonders now and then;
behold a lawyer, an honest man.'

Benjamin Franklin

## 3.1 Introduction

As a law student you are likely to be collared at some point by a non-lawyer acquaintance. 'How can you represent someone who is guilty?', he or she will ask. 'How can you sleep at night?' In a rather inelegant way, that person is asking you to reflect on the ethics of your future profession, and it will serve you well to give some thought to your response both before and during your time conducting clinic and pro bono work.

This chapter is therefore about right and wrong and the often difficult-to-pin-down distinction between the two. The chapter recognises that the parameters of the civil and criminal law are not always sufficient and that you will often need to understand and apply moral reasoning even when acting within the law. As someone who works in a clinical or pro bono environment you are likely to encounter situations where the law does not provide an answer, and you will need to decide for yourself which is the proper or, to adopt the language of this chapter, ethical course of action. You will see that such judgements are not always clear cut and may lead to substantial differences of opinion.

The chapter introduces you to important concepts that set the landscape for ethical decision-making and underpin the relationship between lawyer and client. It also addresses the regulatory codes and guidance that have been formulated to provide an ethical framework for legal professionals and considers how these may be relevant to your work in clinic and pro bono.

Before proceeding further, you may find it useful to reflect on your current response to the questions posed above. *Could* you represent someone you believed to be guilty? *Could* you sleep at night? Do you already have a clear view about your role as a future lawyer and are you comfortable with the situations you will face and the decisions you are likely to have to make? As you will see, one of the potential benefits of clinical and pro bono learning is that you will have to face up to these types of question, not on a hypothetical level, but for real, where your answers truly shape the type of professional you may become. Moreover, you have the rare opportunity to examine and critique current ethical norms, subjecting them to fresh analysis and comparing them to your own ethical commitments. This chapter encourages you to question received wisdom and ask yourself not just which rules apply, but whether they are logically and morally sustainable. This will enrich your knowledge of conduct rules and your appreciation of professionalism. However, this should not be taken as encouraging a take it or leave it, relativist approach towards professional rules. There may be situations where you are obliged to conform, but you should mull over and discuss your reactions as part of reflection on your experience.

## 3.2  What are legal ethics?

Before addressing the notion of *legal* ethics, it is worthwhile considering the idea of the general meaning of ethics. The following extract from Simon Blackburn's excellent book, *Ethics: A Very Short Introduction*, reveals the ambition and breadth of the concept:

> '... the moral or ethical environment ... is the surrounding climate of ideas about how to live. It determines what we find acceptable or unacceptable, admirable or contemptible. It determines our conception of when things are going well and when they are going badly. It determines our conception of what is due to us and what is due from us, as we relate to others. It shapes our emotional responses, determining what is a cause of pride or shame, or anger or gratitude, or what can be forgiven and what cannot. It gives us our standards – our standards of behaviour. In the eyes of some thinkers ... it shapes our very identities.' (Blackburn, S, 2003: 1)

If this is true of ethics generally then the *legal* ethical environment may be taken as meaning the climate of ideas about how *lawyers* should live. It gives us our standards of behaviour *as lawyers*.

At some point during your legal studies you are likely to hear some variation on the jibe: 'legal ethics is a contradiction in terms!' In fact legal ethics is a fairly sophisticated branch of applied ethics. A great deal of intellectual and practical energy has been invested in many jurisdictions trying to understand and implement an appropriate standard of ethical behaviour among lawyers. At its broadest, legal ethics discourse seeks to identify what is good about the law and about lawyering, and to analyse and criticise the component values that make up the moral worth of the law. As such, the legal ethics debate draws on high-level philosophical concepts and may seem far removed from the day-to-day decisions of lawyers.

On a more practical level, legal ethics discussion focuses on the specific obligations that lawyers owe to clients and the situations where there should be exceptions or exclusions to these rules. From this dialogue arises a set of principles that often crystallise into rules or codes dictating the expected behaviour of lawyers, commonly referred to as professional conduct and client care. The process is not always straightforward and is often the result of vigorous disagreement, debate and compromise. The ethical front line is rarely peaceful for long as new problems surface and new perspectives emerge. Such a debate is currently taking place in the solicitors' profession on a number of levels.

---

**Current issues**

As the legal profession moves towards the implementation of the Alternative Business Structures model dictated by the Legal Services Act 2007, the Solicitors Regulation Authority (SRA) intends to reform the current code of conduct and move towards 'outcomes-focused regulation' as set out in the strategy paper, *Achieving the right outcomes* (SRA, January 2010) and in the consultation paper, *Outcomes-Focused Regulation – Transforming the SRA's regulation of legal services* (SRA, April 2010). The stated objective is to 'put public protection at the heart' of regulation by 'achieving a common standard of client protection across all types of firm and improving standards ...', and this will be achieved by the creation of a new set of principles that define the fundamental ethical and professional standards expected, a new code of conduct which illustrates the practical application of the principles in particular contexts, and a new comprehensive regulatory handbook (see SRA consultation, *The architecture of change: the SRA's new Handbook,* July 2010).

There is also renewed focus on the way that future lawyers are educated about legal ethics and professional responsibility. The report, *Preparatory ethics training for future solicitors* (Economides and Rogers, 2009) challenges the status quo by arguing, among other things, for mandatory ethical training at the undergraduate stage prior to the Legal Practice Course and for a legal equivalent to the doctors' Hippocratic oath.

---

## 3.3 What are the professional conduct rules?

Most professions have written codes or guidelines that include ethical norms and expectations. Such codes underpin the relationship that a professional has with his or her clients and helps to form the basis of legitimate client expectations.

Professional conduct rules for solicitors and barristers are of relatively recent origin. The Guide to the Professional Conduct of Solicitors was first published in 1960 by the Law Society and gradually developed into a code of conduct, formalised in 2007, the Solicitors' Code of Conduct. At the time of writing the most recent hard copy version, along with guidance, is dated 2009 and is available from Law Society Publishing. However, the rules are regularly updated and therefore the most recent version of the Code is always available on the Solicitors Regulation Authority website at www.sra.org.uk.

The Bar code was implemented following a recommendation in the final report of the Royal Commission on Legal Services (the Benson Commission (1979) Cmnd 7648). The rules are found in the Code of Conduct of the Bar of England and Wales which is available, together with guidance, on the Bar Standards Board website at www.barstandardsboard.org.uk. Legal executives are governed by the ILEX Professional Standards Code of Conduct which can be viewed at www.ilex.org.uk.

Clearly, at this stage of your career you are not yet qualified. Perhaps you never intend to practise as a solicitor, barrister or legal executive. Thus detailed analysis of the professional conduct rules may seem to be premature or even irrelevant. However, as you will see, if you are engaging in clinical or pro bono activities as part of your education, you are performing in the role of a lawyer, and people will certainly expect you to act as a lawyer, including being aware of and capable of complying with relevant professional obligations. Thus you will need to develop a basic understanding of the key obligations under the rules. It is beyond the scope of this book to provide a detailed guide to professional conduct, but it underlines the importance of the core duties and indicates further sources to enable you to conduct your clinical or pro bono work in compliance with the rules. While acknowledging the relevance of other professional codes, given the likely structure of clinical and pro bono projects, this chapter focuses, where relevant, on the professional responsibilities of solicitors.

The professional conduct rules have been criticised as largely disciplinary, as opposed to offering a richer account of the positive aspects of professionalism. It is sometimes argued that this leads to a myopic and defensive view of what it means to be ethical. Sir Mark Potter lamented what he felt was a mechanistic approach in England and Wales: 'But ethics go far wider than this. Ethics are not simply regulatory: they are aspirational. They inform the moral dimension of a lawyer's role and work; the ideals and expectations which inform or ought to inform, the practice of his profession as well as his own view of himself and his function in society.' (Potter, 2005: 24) One difficulty is that there is little natural consensus on the core function of lawyers in society. This means that codes of conduct tend to be fairly limited in their outlook, focusing on prohibiting clear ethical wrongs as opposed to promoting wider, positive obligations. The SRA has been moving slowly towards more principles-based regulation of the profession, although arguably this leaves matters rather vague and conduct subject to subjective interpretation. In an effort to signal the key principles which should govern solicitors' conduct, the Code contains a set of 'Core duties'.

---

### Solicitors' Code of Conduct

**Rule 1: Core duties**

1.01 Justice and the rule of law
You must uphold the rule of law and the proper administration of justice.

1.02 Integrity
You must act with integrity.

1.03 Independence
You must not allow your independence to be compromised.

1.04 Best interests of clients
You must act in the best interests of each client.

1.05 Standard of service
You must provide a good standard of service to your clients.

1.06 Public confidence
You must not behave in a way that is likely to diminish the trust the public places in you or the legal profession.

These rules are mandatory and breach may lead to disciplinary action. The Code seeks to influence behaviour by defining values but permitting a balance between certainty of expected standards and flexibility for professionals. On 6 October 2011 the core duties will be incorporated into a new set of professional principles in the SRA's Handbook.

**3.4** How are legal ethics and professional conduct relevant to clinic and pro bono?

### Clinic/pro bono and learning about ethics

If you help someone with his or her legal problems as part of a clinical or pro bono project, you are in a stimulating environment for engaging with ethical thinking and the application of professional rules. Similarly, if you participate in simulated legal representation, you are likely to be presented with situations that require you to analyse professional obligations and make decisions about the proper course of conduct. The fact that the problem is real or realistic and calls for a response from you can be challenging. You may feel intimidated or unprepared for such decisions. In addition, often there is no obvious answer and you are unable to apply a traditional legal analysis to the problem as the rule may not be clear cut and there is a dearth of authoritative decisions.

Arguments about the benefits of learning ethics from experience are longstanding. Jerome Frank, back in 1933, argued: 'Professional ethics can be effectively taught only if the students while learning the canons of ethics have available some first-hand observation of the ways in which the ethical problems of the lawyer arise and of the actual habits (and 'mores') of the bar.' (Frank, 1933: 922) More recently, Peter Joy, in his article, 'The Ethics of Law School Clinic Students as Student Lawyers', proposed that: 'By interacting with clients, lawyers, and others in role as lawyers, clinic students begin the process of truly becoming lawyers. In no other course are law students able to confront their own behaviour and relationships with others. And, unlike other law school subjects, legal ethics or professional responsibility is about a lawyer's relationships with others.' (Joy, 2005: 836–7)

However, there are those who remain sceptical about the ability of clinic to generate high quality learning about ethics. For example, Robertson has argued that: '... the case for clinics as sites for deep, authentic learning experiences in legal ethics would always need to be demonstrated conclusively. Unfortunately, some of the literature that celebrates the contributions of particular clinics to "deep learning" in ethics provides little in the way of hard evidence to back the claims.' (Robertson, 2005: 233) Steven Hartwell did investigate the impact of simulated case work on ethical awareness in students and found extensive improvements for students undertaking the simulation. Interestingly, he decided not to conduct the same research in relation to live client work as he did not think that live experience would significantly improve students' moral reasoning: 'Although moral questions certainly do arise spontaneously in clinic work, they do not arise with the same frequency as they arise by design in a professional responsibility course.' (Hartwell, 1994: 535)

While acknowledging the limited amount of research in this area, intuitively, clinical and pro bono opportunities provide at least the potential for in-depth engagement with ethical reasoning. Uniquely, your learning of ethics is placed in the context of real-life practice. It provides you with the opportunity to grapple with the laws, rules, principles and values of the legal profession, not as an external observer, but as a participant and stakeholder. Particularly with live client work, you are socialised in the professional environment and exposed to ethical issues in your role as a lawyer (see Joy, 2005: 837). Participating in clinical and pro bono activities enables you to descend into the 'swamp'.

> 'The practitioner must choose. Shall he remain on the high ground where he can solve relatively unimportant problems according to prevailing standards of rigor, or shall he descend to the swamp of important problems and non-rigorous inquiry?' (Schön, 1987: 4)

The realism of clinic exposes you to the messy, uncertain and non-technical aspects of lawyering that are rarely found in appellate cases. 'Swampy' notions such as fear, anger, confusion, imprecision, obfuscation, untruth, cost, enforceability and so on impinge on the legal rules learned in textbooks so as to make a legal problem multi-faceted (see Maughan and Webb, 2005, Chapter 1). The human interactions presented by clinical and pro bono experience can create particularly unclear and complex situations regarding values and ethics. Deciding what the appropriate course of action is when your notions of professional conduct are challenged can pose acute difficulties and tell you a lot about your values as a lawyer and as a human being (see Webb, 2002).

> 'Once they encounter a client, the blind faith that there is a "truth" or a "law" that can be applied must give way to a more sophisticated understanding. Clients' cases rarely present simple facts that lend themselves to right and wrong answers. It is the complexity and unpredictability of working with real people that makes clinical legal education so rich.' (Aitken, 2001: 292)

## Do I need to learn about ethics?

If you are undertaking a law degree or Common Professional Examination/Graduate Diploma in Law, there are very few requirements for ethical dimensions in your studies. In relation to degree studies, the Joint Statement on the Academic Stage of Legal Education (Joint Academic Stage Board, 2002) contains no explicit requirement for any ethics component as such. Although the Quality Assurance Agency National Benchmark Standards for Law require some understanding of, inter alia, the ethical context in which law operates, there is no clear requirement for courses to address the ethical rules or the moral foundations of the law or lawyering. Your course might include optional or compulsory subjects addressing ethical dimensions, but they are not currently required by the academic or professional regulatory bodies.

At the 'vocational' stage of legal education, the professional bodies are much more prescriptive as to what students should be taught and assessed. Professional conduct and regulation is a required part of the Legal Practice Course (LPC) and the Bar Professional Training Course (BPTC). In relation to the LPC, successful students should 'understand where the rules of professional conduct may impact and be able to apply them in context ... be able to identify and act in accordance with the core duties of professional conduct and professional ethics ... be familiar with the Solicitors' Code of Conduct [and] understand the organisation, regulation and ethics of the profession' (Solicitors Regulation Authority Legal Practice Course Outcomes, 2007). The course must address core duties under Rule 1 of the Code and in particular matters such as competency, conflicts of interest, confidentiality, undertakings and duties to the court.

Nevertheless, the vision of professional conduct contemplated is rather narrow, largely rules-oriented and entirely client-centred. It presents very much as a technical 'can do' approach which requires no consideration of wider values of the legal profession identified in the ACLEC First Report: 'a commitment to the rule of law, to justice, fairness and high ethical standards, to acquiring and improving professional skills, to representing clients without fear or favour, to promoting equality of opportunity, and to ensuring that adequate legal services are provided to those who cannot afford to pay for them.' (ACLEC, 1996: para. 2.4, adapted from the MacCrate report)

Students on the BPTC are, at least on paper, expected to address ethical issues in more depth and more detail (see Bar Standards Board, Bar Professional Training Course, Handbook, 2010–2011, July 2009, para 2.2.4). Students must develop knowledge and understanding of the core principles underpinning the Code of Conduct, including professional independence, integrity, duty to the court, loyalty to the lay client, conflicts of interest, non-discrimination and commitment to the rule of law.

In summary, there is very little required ethical content at the academic stage of legal education, but more at the vocational stage. The solicitor route requires knowledge and application but no real depth or analysis. The Bar route, at least in theory, requires exploration of underlying principles and, indeed, commitment to the professional conduct rules. Clinical and pro bono experience is not compulsory at any stage of legal education, but it is argued that this type of experience provides a valuable opportunity for developing ethical awareness in a realistic context, and for reflecting on the underlying principles and on the merits and problems thrown up by applying the current rules.

## Is pro bono an ethical obligation in itself?

As was seen in **Chapter 1**, the professional bodies in England and Wales do not oblige solicitors or barristers to perform pro bono work. Neither is there a minimum suggested amount of time that ought to be spent on pro bono activity. Rather, the approach is to encourage, facilitate and celebrate the provision of pro bono activity by willing lawyers. Initiatives such as LawWorks, the Bar Pro Bono Unit, National Pro Bono Week, the Attorney General's Pro Bono Committee and Protocol and various awards schemes seek to educate and enthuse the profession and the public about pro bono activity.

### Extracts from the Havana Declaration on the Role of the Lawyer, 1990

4. Governments and professional associations of lawyers shall promote programmes to inform the public about their rights and duties under the law and the important role of lawyers in protecting their fundamental freedoms. Special attention should be given to assisting the poor and other disadvantaged persons so as to enable them to assert their rights and where necessary call upon the assistance of lawyers.

14. Lawyers, in protecting the rights of their clients and in promoting the cause of justice, shall seek to uphold human rights and fundamental freedoms recognized by national and international law and shall at all times act freely and diligently in accordance with the law and recognized standards and ethics of the legal profession.

25. Professional associations of lawyers shall cooperate with Governments to ensure that everyone has effective and equal access to legal services and that lawyers are able, without improper interference, to counsel and assist their clients in accordance with the law and recognized professional standards and ethics.

*Adopted by the Eighth United Nations Congress on the Prevention of Crime and the Treatment of Offenders, Havana, Cuba 27 August to 7 September 1990.*

Most lawyers tend to agree in principle that pro bono is a good thing, although there is often disagreement over whether provision of services for free is an ethical *obligation* potentially enforceable by a professional body, or an act of charity given *voluntarily* according to the individual lawyer's own commitments. This is a somewhat intractable debate and will not be inquired into further here, other than to identify some of the reasons why lawyers often feel an ethical commitment to pro bono (for more detailed analysis, see Sossin, L, 'Professionalism and Pro Bono Publico' in Tranter, K, *Reaffirming Legal Ethics* (Tranter, 2010: 143)).

A key reason is that lawyers are in a very privileged position: educated, articulate and informed. They make their living from securing the legal rights of those who can afford to pay. This can be seen as giving rise to an expectation that they will contribute towards access to justice for those who cannot pay. Secondly, law is not just a business, it is about helping people, and many lawyers take great personal satisfaction from their pro bono work. Thirdly, lawyers have a monopoly of access to the courts to represent clients. This is seen as entailing a commensurate responsibility to help ensure access to the courts of those who would otherwise have no access. Finally, lawyers are in a powerful economic position as a result of their status as professionals and feel a need to help disadvantaged groups by voluntarily offering their expertise. There is a spectrum of reasons why lawyers do pro bono work, including the assuaging of guilt and the enhancement of personal reputations. Nevertheless, many lawyers have a serious and sustained commitment to pro bono work.

### Why should clinic and pro bono students focus on the ethics of lawyering?

'Neither reason, nor love, nor even terror, seems to have worked to make us "good," and worse than that, there is no reason why anything should. Only if ethics were something unspeakable by us, could law be unnatural, and therefore unchallengeable. As things now stand, everything is up for grabs. Nevertheless: Napalming babies is bad. Starving the poor is wicked. Buying and selling each other is depraved. Those who stood up to and died resisting Hitler, Stalin, Amin, and Pol Pot – and General Custer too – have earned salvation. Those who acquiesced deserve to be damned. There is in the world such a thing as evil. [All together now:] Sez who? God help us.' (Leff, AA, *'Unspeakable Ethics, Unnatural Law'* [1979] Duke Law Review 1229 at 1249)

This book does not suggest that there is some omnipotent supernatural force clearly indicating the correct approach towards ethical standards. Rather, it suggests that you should explore the notion of professional ethics, understand the rules and limitations thereon and reflect on how these fit with your own developing ideas about the law. Also, before you are tempted by Leff's somewhat depressing moral relativism, there are a number of sound practical and pragmatic reasons for complying with the current ethical standards, so please read to the end of this chapter before you decide to devise your own conduct rules.

This section sets out some of the reasons why you should engage with ethical concerns in clinic and pro bono activities.

### Acting professionally

If you intend to enter the legal profession, you need to be aware of the ethical responsibilities of lawyers. By providing a professional service in your clinic and pro bono activity, you are preparing for your future career and building a bank of experience about how to treat clients, fellow professionals and other people you will encounter in the law.

### Providing a good service

A crucial aspect of ethical responsibilities is client care and this is also the factor that most influences the attitude of clients to the service provided. Clients are in fact entitled to a good level of service from solicitors (Solicitors' Code of Conduct, Rule 1). If your clinic or pro bono activity is supervised by or run in partnership with solicitors, they will have this responsibility, and your work will determine whether they meet their obligation.

### Meeting expectations

Your client (whether this is a real person or simulated client) will come to you expecting to be treated with care, respect and sensitivity. He or she is also entitled to expect that you will treat him or her in a professional manner because you are in the role of providing legal services. The client should not have to lower his or her expectations merely because you are a student.

### Enhancing reputation

On an personal level, it is satisfying if people are happy and grateful with the service you have given them. They are more likely to think good of you if you have acted in an ethical manner towards them. Moreover, it is not just your personal reputation on the line. The reputation of your supervisor and institution is extremely important and you are acting as an ambassador when you act as a clinic/pro bono adviser. Furthermore, the reputation of the legal profession itself is to an extent in your hands. Clients who receive a professional service are likely to view all lawyers in a better light, and the converse is equally true.

## Complying with legal duties

Ethical rules often correspond with legal duties and you are much less likely to fall foul of the law if you have complied with the professional code of conduct. A good example is the ethical duty of confidentiality. There is a corresponding equitable tort of breach of confidence which gives rise to a cause of action if there is improper disclosure of information held in confidence.

## Reducing complaints

If you conform to the current ethical standards, you are likely to reduce the risk of clients complaining about the service you have provided and, if they do complain, of their grievance being found to be substantiated.

## Avoiding sanctions

There are two main types of sanction you could face if you fail to comply with the code of conduct. First, you could face academic sanctions, most likely a reduced or failed mark if your clinic or pro bono work is assessed. For serious breaches, it is possible that you could be required to leave the clinic or pro bono project or even face formal disciplinary action by your institution. Secondly, you could potentially face professional sanctions. If you are an LPC or BPTC student, you will have already joined as a student member of the Solicitors Regulation Authority or an Inn of Court. Serious breaches of the relevant code, even pre-qualification, could give rise to disciplinary proceedings before the professional body. Even if you are on the academic stage and have not yet registered as a student member of the profession, your conduct can be taken into account by the professional bodies in deciding whether you are a fit and proper person to permit you to join in the future. Serious defects in your approach towards professional conduct prior to application could potentially prejudice your future career.

## Enriching your learning

The more you think about how the professional rules affect the service you provide, the better informed you will be about the role of the lawyer. Reflecting on your ethical responsibilities can help you squeeze a lot of learning opportunities from even very modest cases. This reason is fairly prominent in law teachers' motivations for including ethical discourse within a clinical environment. The following extracts are from research into the attitudes towards ethics teaching of clinical law teachers in UK law schools.

### Why do you teach ethics in your law clinic?

'to protect our clients, students, supervisors and the reputation of the Law School; as an educational resource, a tool for reflection on the process of lawyering.'

'... because of the virtual silence in the curriculum on the issues.'

'Important as part of expanding our knowledge of law and society.'

> 'For obvious reasons this is important in ensuring a high level of service and that the clinic and solicitors and students working in it do not breach professional conduct rules. ... Students are encouraged to reflect upon their interaction with clients and their feelings about their work for those clients, the impact that that work has upon themselves and their clients ... It is important that work in clinic not be seen as simply mechanistic ie that lawyers should only be interested in ensuring they act in the best interests of their clients. If work students do in clinic is not reflected upon in this way there is very little chance of students doing so as practitioners.'
>
> 'It is important because if we don't teach ethics then students lose part of the opportunity to reflect and to develop.'
>
> (Kerrigan, 2007: 16)

## Benefits of ethics arising in a clinical context

The uncertain and dynamic nature of a real or simulated case adds to the authenticity of the ethical environment you are working in. Where you are working with live clients, there is the added dimension of actual consequences which adds a sense of urgency and responsibility; ethical issues cannot be timetabled into the teaching session, so when they emerge they have a freshness and vitality about them. Below are further comments from UK clinical teachers.

**What do you consider to be the advantages of law clinics for teaching legal ethics?**

'The complexities of actual (and developing) situations challenge students in a manner different from that of lecture/seminar teaching ...'

'Issues are raised contextually and require resolution rather than just discussion in the abstract. Issues thus come across as "real" to students.'

'Immediacy: these are not abstract issues; they have immediate relevance. Breadth: covers ethics in its widest sense, from professional conduct to Aristotle.'

'Problems are real. The student is not being asked in the abstract whether they can act for a particular client who they feel is lying to them, it is real and this makes the decision much more difficult and engaging.'

'... reflect critically on the nature of lawyer–client relationships and other processes of lawyering'

'... to introduce students to and to develop their critical understanding of law in an applied context.'

'A wider appreciation of the lawyer's role, pressures and dilemmas for lawyers and the social, political and economic impact of the law on individuals and groups in society.'

(Kerrigan, 2007: 16)

Below are some questions you might ask yourself on a regular basis while conducting clinic or pro bono work. Perhaps you could add to this or come up with your own list and post it on the wall of your clinic or pro bono premises.

### Extract from the Pro Bono Protocol

- What is my function as a lawyer?
- How can I help to achieve justice within the legal system?
- How can I improve access to justice?
- Does what I do contribute to the upholding of the rule of law?
- Where is the balance of power between the individual and the state; how can I protect human rights in my work?
- Are there any circumstances when I should ignore the requirements of the Code of Conduct?
- How do my own preconceptions and ignorance affect my conduct of a case?
- Can and should the law be reformed and how can I be creative to achieve this?
- What are the obstacles to the independence of my profession and how can I overcome them?

## 3.5 Some core ethical concepts

It is not possible to find clear consensus over the proper role of the lawyer and this is perhaps not surprising. Ethical norms are moral and philosophical constructs and are thus open to a variety of viewpoints and differing interpretations. This section summarises some basic ideas about the relationship of the lawyer with the client and others but does not attempt to offer a full account. For further analysis, see Boon and Levin, *The ethics and conduct of lawyers in England and Wales* (2008) and Nicolson and Webb, *Professional legal ethics, critical interrogations* (1999).

### The concept of partisanship

One of the core duties in the Solicitors' Code of Conduct 2007 is that you must act in the best interests of your client (Rule 1.04). This appears to arise from the ethical notion of partisanship, which is a standard view of the lawyer's role, at least in adversarial legal systems. This is about taking sides – advocating for clients' interests above any competing interests – sometimes referred to as 'zealous advocacy'. Thus the lawyer's only duty is to protect and advance the legal rights of his client, regardless of the consequences to the lawyer and others. As Lord Reid stated in the House of Lords case of *Rondel v Worsley* [1969] 1 AC 191 at 227, 'Every counsel has a duty to his client fearlessly to raise every issue, advance every argument, and ask every question, however distasteful, which he thinks will help his client's case'. Unlike many other professions, a lawyer has no duties towards other people or interests. Thus, for example, he has no duty to protect vulnerable people, to ensure equality of arms or to secure a fair trial.

### Neutrality

The principle of neutrality seeks to enable a lawyer to act with the zeal of the partisan without being personally associated with the morality of his or her client's goals or means of attaining them. This is sometimes called professional detachment and asserts that the case belongs to the client, not the lawyer, so if there is moral obloquy attaching to a legal strategy, this should be aimed at the client. This 'role morality' seeks to insulate the lawyer from the cause of the client and for many lawyers provides a strong and sufficient moral justification for their conduct. It also enables, and at times obliges, the lawyer not to make a moral judgment of the client when deciding whether to take on or continue with a case. This is said to arise most potently with the 'cab rank' principle for barristers, who may not refuse instructions on the basis that the nature of the case is objectionable or the conduct, beliefs or opinions of the client are unacceptable (Bar Code of Conduct, para 601). An equivalent rule applies to solicitors contemplating instructions to act as an advocate (Solicitors' Code of Conduct, Rule 11.04). The situation for solicitors deciding whether to accept instructions initially is somewhat different; a solicitor is 'generally free to decide whether or not to take on a particular client' (Rule 2.01) and so may at this stage apply some moral judgment about the client or the case that is contemplated.

Taken together, these concepts create the powerful notion of 'neutral partisanship'. Arguably, this constitutes the ethical foundation of a wide range of other lawyer obligations such as the duty of confidentiality, the duty of disclosure of information, the duty not to act if there is a conflict of interests, the duty not to permit one's independence to be impaired and so on. For some it also gives rise to the caricature of lawyers as amoral 'hired guns' who 'regard their role as the zealous representatives of clients irrespective of moral, political or justice considerations' (Nicolson and Webb, 1999: 165).

## Competing duties

It is rarely argued now that neutral partisanship is an absolute principle. Thus, for example, the guidance to the Solicitors' Code of Conduct, Rule 4 (paras 13–14) states that it is permissible to act against a client's interests by disclosing confidential information where necessary to prevent a criminal act likely to result in serious bodily harm or where a child is at risk of continuing sexual or other abuse. Moreover, the duty to the client is said to be counterbalanced by a wider duty to the administration of justice in general. Lord Reid tempered his defence of partisanship with a firm indication that there were limits (*Rondel v Worsley* [1969] 1 AC 191 at 227):

> 'But, as an officer of the court concerned in the administration of justice, he has an overriding duty to the court, to the standards of his profession, and to the public, which may and often does lead to a conflict with his client's wishes or with what the client thinks are his personal interests. Counsel must not mislead the court, he must not lend himself to casting aspersions on the other party or witnesses for which there is no sufficient basis in the information in his possession, he must not withhold authorities or documents which may tell against his clients but which the law or the standards of his profession require him to produce.'

Indeed the Solicitors' Code of Conduct guidance now states that where there is a conflict between core duties, the factor determining precedence must be 'the public interest, and especially the public interest in the administration of justice' (Guidance to Rule 1, para 3). Moreover, there may be legal obligations that override the lawyer's duty to the client in some circumstances, eg duties to make disclosures under money laundering and terrorism legislation.

These considerations suggest that the role of the lawyer is ethically complex. Particularly when conducting litigation, but also in other situations, the lawyer is likely to be called on to balance the interests of the client against a range of potentially conflicting duties. It will rarely be as simple as the lawyer blindly following the desires of the client.

## 3.6 Identifying and dealing with ethical dilemmas and professional obligations

You may encounter a whole range of ethical issues, some more obvious than others.

| **10 examples of ethical considerations you may encounter in clinic/pro bono work** |
| --- |
| 1  'Should we take on this client?' |
| 2  'Do we believe this client?' |
| 3  'Do we like this client?' |
| 4  'Is the client's case a worthy one?' |
| 5  'How far should we go to comply with the client's desires?' |
| 6  'Do we have a good reason to stop working on this client's case?' |
| 7  'Is the client culpable?' |
| 8  'Has the client been badly treated by the law?' |
| 9  'Should we aim to be competent or passionate in our work?' |
| 10  'Should we be working for this client when there are other, more deserving cases out there?' |

### Worked examples of professional conduct issues in clinic and pro bono

The following examples are intended to illustrate the operation of important aspects of the Solicitors' Code of Conduct. For all of these scenarios and any others that involve application of the Code of Conduct, you should discuss your response in detail with your supervisor before taking any action.

### Conflict of interests 1

You are instructed by a student in relation to the loss of an expensive coat during a music gig at the Students' Union. He claims this was due to the negligence of the people staffing the cloakroom. The next day, a university porter who was staffing the cloakroom comes to the office seeking advice about the same matter.

On the face of it this is simple. Rule 3.01(1) states that you must not act if there is a conflict of interests. Such a conflict would arise if 'you owe, or your firm owes, separate duties to act in the best interests of two or more clients in relation to the same or related matters, and those duties conflict, or there is a significant risk that those duties may conflict'. Given that you have taken instructions from the student, it would not be possible also to take on the porter in relation to the same case. Their interests undoubtedly conflict in relation to this case. There is a further consideration, though. Rule 1 obliges you not to allow your independence to be compromised. Given that the potential defendant in this case is an employee of your university, there may be a risk that your independence of action on behalf of the student would be compromised due to your commitment to the university. Indeed, if university teaching staff supervise the clinic or pro bono project, they may well be colleagues of the potential defendant and may even end up suing their own employer vicariously. This is why many clinics or pro bono projects adopt rules that they will not deal with any matter that is or could potentially lead to a dispute with their own institution.

## Conflict of interests 2

You interview a new potential client and take details of her case. She is seeking compensation from a shop owner for a broken wrist she sustained when she slipped on some spilled orange juice while shopping. When you check your records, you notice that last year some other students represented the shop owner during his divorce.

You no longer act for the shop owner, so the conflict is not as obvious as in the previous scenario, but you do have access to information about his assets and financial circumstances that may well be useful to the claimant in her case for compensation. It is in the new client's interests to access this information. Thus your duty to act in the best interests of the claimant would conflict with your duty to keep confidential the affairs of the former client. This view is reinforced by Rule 4.03, which sets out the duty not to put confidentiality at risk by acting.

This case also illustrates the need to have a reliable system for ascertaining who the clinic or pro bono project has previously acted for or against. The conflict of interests database must be checked and updated for each new case you deal with.

## Confidentiality 1

You take instructions from your client (who has learning difficulties) in relation to a divorce, and he tells you that he sometimes sleeps with his three-year-old daughter because she gets cold and that he is tempted to touch her private parts but manages to stop himself.

This scenario presents a classic conflict between the solicitor's duty of confidentiality and competing public interest considerations. The duty is clear: a solicitor has a duty to 'keep the affairs of clients and former clients confidential except where disclosure is required or permitted by law or by your client (or former client)'. If disclosure *is* permitted by law (and it seems clear that the common law would permit the disclosure of this type of information), the Code gives little concrete indication as to whether a lawyer *should* disclose the information. The closest it comes is in the Guidance to Rule 4, para 13, which states: 'There may be exceptional circumstances involving children where you should consider revealing confidential information to an appropriate authority. This may be where ... an adult discloses abuse ... but refuses to allow disclosure. You must consider whether the threat to the child's life or health, both mental and physical, is sufficiently serious to justify a breach of the duty of confidentiality.'

You should make a very careful note of any situation in which you do decide to breach confidentiality as you may be required to justify your conduct at a later date.

## Confidentiality 2

A new client comes to see you for advice regarding a 'road traffic matter'. When you see the client he bursts into tears and tells you that he was involved in an accident two nights ago where he hit somebody who was crossing the road. He panicked and left the scene because he had had a couple of glasses of wine at lunch time and feared he was over the alcohol limit. He later discovered that he had knocked down a nine-year-old child who had subsequently died. He is desperately sorry for what he has done but does not want to go to the police because he is too frightened.

This may seem similar to the previous situation, but the potentially crucial difference is that there is no apparent ongoing risk of serious harm. The client has come for advice about this matter which is clearly playing on his mind. However, he appears unwilling to confess his conduct to the police. The information is clearly confidential and it is difficult to see an obvious legal justification for disclosure in the absence of the client's consent. The guidance states that confidential information may be disclosed 'to the extent that you believe necessary to prevent the client or a third party committing a criminal act that you reasonably believe is likely to result in serious bodily harm' (Guidance to Rule 4, para 12), but this is prospective, whereas the harm in the client's case has already occurred. There could be good reasons for the client to confess, for example to secure a lighter sentence if convicted and to address his personal guilt, but, in the absence of evidence linking him to the offence, it appears to be contrary to his best interests, so you would be breaching a core duty by disclosing.

This is perhaps one of those hypotheticals that you hope will never arise and that might test your resolve to abide by the professional conduct rules. One related issue is the extent to which you ought to use whatever influence you do have to try to persuade the client to confess himself. Some lawyers would take the view that it is part of their role to try to get their clients to face up to their wrongdoing, whereas others think such considerations are wholly outside their professional role.

## Entering into a retainer 1

You receive a request for help from a client who is a member of the British National Party. He has been banned from holding a meeting in the Town Hall and wishes to challenge the decision.

You may find the policies of the BNP offensive, but to what extent should you allow your view to affect your decision about whether to take a case on? The Code of Conduct states, 'You are generally free to decide whether or not to take on a particular client' (Rule 2.01(1)). This gives you a very wide discretion as to what criteria to impose, subject to the core duties in Rule 1 and the equality and diversity requirements in Rule 6. Thus you need to work out some basis to decide which cases you will take on. There are a variety of potential approaches such as: a legal needs assessment which seeks to ascertain how acute the potential client's legal circumstances are; a moral value assessment which makes a judgment about the moral worth of the client or the client's case; a social justice/human rights assessment which tries to assess how important the client's case is in terms of addressing poverty and social injustice/human rights concerns; or an educational value assessment which tries to anticipate whether the student advisers will learn from the case and be able to offer a useful service. None of these are perfect and all are likely to be tested, as normally demand will outstrip your ability to provide a service, so you will have to work out some way of rationing your time.

## Entering into a retainer 2

You discuss a client's complaint against the police. You decide that there are no prospects of success. However, your supervisor suggests that there is some useful further research that could be done and it would be useful experience to draft the complaint. Your client is keen to complain.

This scenario raises the prospect of exploitation of a client's case for educational reasons. You need to be cautious that your zeal for learning does not blind you to your client's best interests and does not lead you to behave in a way that could diminish public trust in the profession. In this particular scenario, the client is not at any costs risk from pursuing a complaint and is clearly keen to do so. If he has been clearly advised that he has no prospects of success, arguably it is permissible to pursue the claim in order to at least air his grievance, although you should also consider your justification for putting the police to the expense of an investigation that you consider to be doomed to failure.

## Terminating the retainer

You have represented a client for the past year. He has been seeking advice regarding the way the council tax system operates in his local authority area. You conducted research into his case and provided advice that the council was acting within its legal powers. He then requested that you negotiate with the council to see if it would be willing to change the operation of the rules. You did so and the council declined to change its approach. The client then asked you to submit several Freedom of Information Act 2000 requests to the council to access information about its council tax policies and statistics. You did so. He now wants you to prepare a judicial review of the council's policy and to find a barrister to conduct the representation pro bono.

This raises the question of when, if at all, it is appropriate to stop acting for someone who wants your help. Once you have taken on a client, you may only terminate the retainer on reasonable notice and for good reason (Rule 2.01(2)). With any free service there is always a risk of a client wishing to take advantage of the available assistance beyond that which you consider to be reasonable. You need to have some way of judging when this point has been met and, if you do decide to stop acting for a client, of justifying your decision. The grounds for you ceasing to act for someone should ideally be written into your retainer information and shared with clients. An example of termination of a retainer arose in the case of *Richard Buxton (a firm) v Mills-Owens* [2010] 1 WLR 1997 where the Court of Appeal ruled that a firm of solicitors had 'good reason' for terminating a retainer for a client who insisted on pursuing a claim that the firm judged to be unarguable. This was not a situation where the solicitor was being instructed to do something improper, but neverthe-less the duty not to advance contentions that were not properly arguable entitled the firm to withdraw from the case. This provides a clear basis for a clinic or pro bono project to refuse to keep flogging the proverbial dead horse.

## Gifts from clients

You win an employment tribunal case on behalf of your client who was unfairly dismissed from her job as a bus driver. She is awarded £3,000 compensation and is absolutely delighted. After the hearing she gives you a thank-you card. Inside is a cheque for £500 made out to you.

This sort of situation arises a lot in clinic and pro bono projects, although the gifts are normally much smaller. The basic Code of Conduct rules are contained in Rule 1.02 (integrity) and 1.06 (public confidence): a solicitor must not act in such a way as to diminish public trust in the profession. A conflict of interests can arise when a client proposes to offer a gift to his or her legal representative. Rule 3.04 states that where a proposed gift is a significant amount (either on its own or having regard to the assets of the client), you must advise the client to take independent advice about the gift. If the client does this, there is no rule against accepting gifts, but clearly it puts a significant barrier between you and the gift. In any event, you should pause to reflect on whether it would be appropriate for you to accept such a gift. The client received your help ostensibly as part of a clinical legal education or pro bono service. She is now proposing to give you one-sixth of her compensation and it may well not be in her best interests to do so. For these reasons, many clinics and pro bono projects develop their own policies about what type of gifts or donations, if any, it is appropriate to accept from clients.

## Litigation 1

You represent a client in a personal injury action. His instructions are that he has constant back pain and has limited mobility. This is backed up by a medical report which states he cannot bend, run or sit for long periods. You are out for a stroll on Saturday in a local park. You see your client playing football for a local pub team and you see him running freely and leaping to score a headed goal.

This scenario directs you to Rule 11 of the Code of Conduct and the duties in relation to litigation and advocacy. You must never deceive or knowingly or reck-lessly mislead the court (Rule 11.01(1)). Examples offered in the guidance include where you submit inaccurate information or permit another person to do so, indicate agreement with information that you know is false, or call a witness whose evidence you know is untrue. A key section reads: 'Only where it is clear that the client is attempting to put forward false evidence to the court should you stop acting. In other circumstances it would be for the court, and not for you, to assess the truth or otherwise of the client's statement' (guidance to Rule 11, para 17). The informa-tion you now have appears to suggest that the medical evidence is inaccurate. If you called your client to give evidence about his limited mobility, you would now be clear that the client was attempting to put forward false evidence. Thus, unless your client is willing to alter his instructions, you should seriously consider terminating your retainer, while of course respecting your client's confidentiality.

## Litigation 2

You are representing your client in the housing possession court. You are arguing that a possession order would violate your client's human rights. While conducting your research, you come across a case that suggests the court is not obliged to apply a European Convention on Human Rights, Article 8 balancing exercise where there is a legal right of possession. This case significantly undermines your arguments, but your opponent has not spotted the case.

Rule 11.01(2) requires you to draw to the court's attention any relevant cases or statutory provisions. Guidance to Rule 11, para 18 confirms that if the other side omits a case or provision or makes an incorrect reference to it, you must draw attention to it even if it assists the opponent's case. Thus you are required to disclose the authority unless your client refuses to permit you to do so, in which case you would need to stop acting.

## Litigation 3

You have just won a case for your client following a hearing at the county court, at which he gave evidence. Your client says to you as he is leaving the court building, 'Ha! I can't believe we won that – I was lying through my back teeth!'

This situation requires you to consider whether you have any overriding duty to the court when clients disclose they have perjured themselves. You have a core duty in Rule 1 to uphold the rule of law and the proper administration of justice. In this case it appears that this does not give rise to any power or duty to take any immediate steps contrary to your client's interests, such as reporting his disclosure. Rule 11.01 prevents you from deceiving or misleading the court, but you have not knowingly or recklessly done so. Guidance to Rule 11, para 16 states that if a client admits to having committed perjury in relation to an ongoing matter, you must not act further unless the client agrees to disclose the truth to the court. However, in this case the proceedings are at an end. But you may well decide that you will terminate your retainer immediately on the basis that your relationship with the client has broken down. This would amount to a 'good reason' under Rule 2.01(2). You may also decide that you will not take instructions from this client in the future, as you are free to decide under Rule 2.01(1).

## Litigation 4

You are representing a client in the employment tribunal against a former boss who sacked her for allegedly stealing from the till. She asks you to 'make mincemeat' out of her ex-boss to give him a taste of his own medicine.

This scenario addresses the limits of permissible advocacy. Rule 11.05 prevents a solicitor from saying anything as an advocate that is merely scandalous or intended only to insult a witness or any other person. Nor is it permissible to suggest a witness is guilty of crime, fraud or misconduct unless this goes to a matter in issue and is supported by reasonable grounds. The client here does appear to be using the hearing as a means of exacting personal revenge. Thus, although you can be extremely forceful on behalf of clients where appropriate, you do not have to accede to every request they make about the conduct of a case.

### Advice and best interests

Your client has just purchased a small specialist paint factory. She wants advice on how much effluent she can pump into the local river as it is costing her a lot of money to dispose of the factory waste. You conduct some research and discover that although there is a limit beyond which it is illegal to pollute, the local enforcement policy is not to prosecute where offenders exceed the limit by up to 25%.

This is the sort of advice dilemma that is likely to face many lawyers in their careers. You may feel uncomfortable with giving the client the advice because she is likely to use if to pollute more of the river than she would otherwise do. But are you permitted to withhold the advice or present it in such a fashion that the client will comply with the law? A duty that is related to the duty of confidence is the duty of disclosure in Rule 4.02. In this case you must disclose to the client all information which is material to her case except where this is prohibited by law or would cause serious physical or mental injury. You may feel able to justify your conduct ethically by reference to the principle of neutrality; alternatively you may feel that the rules in such a case enable the lawyer to be used as the means of breaking the law and getting away with it, and that they diminish the autonomy of the lawyer.

 ## Ethical decision-making

You should give some thought to how you will make ethical decisions in your clinic or pro bono project. This need not be a particularly sophisticated process, but you should have some means of flagging up and discussing ethical matters, and you should try to develop an environment where people are willing to talk about their ethical concerns. It is suggested that any case that requires interpretation and application of the Code of Conduct should be raised with your supervisor prior to any action being taken. In addition, you should make an accurate record of the issue.

As mentioned in **Chapter 2**, some clinics have established committees to deal with significant ethical policies and/or cases that give rise to ethical dilemmas. The SRA has a professional ethics guidance service which is available for solicitors, so will only be applicable if your work is supervised by a solicitor. You should check with your supervisor whether it is appropriate to refer matters to the service. If the answer is yes, the contact details are as follows:

professional.ethics@sra.org.uk; Ethics guidance helpline 0870 606 2577

If and when things do go wrong, for example you think that you have breached the professional conduct rules in some way, the best course of action is to report the matter immediately to your supervisor and agree what remedial steps can be taken. Never try to hide breaches of the professional conduct rules.

## 3.8   Summary

This chapter has provided an overview of the concept of legal ethics, including some key ethical concepts such as the traditional notion of neutral partisanship and the limitations of this principle. It has explored the relevance and value of ethics learning within a clinic or pro bono environment, identifying the opportunities you will have for exploring ethical norms in depth and in an authentic manner. Ethics and professional conduct matters are not always clear cut, but the practical guidance within the chapter should hopefully help you to deal with such issues in your own clinical or pro bono environments.

 Further reading

### Introductory

Blackburn, S, *Ethics: A Very Short Introduction* (Oxford University Press, 2003)

This little gem of a book provides an overview of general ethical issues and is a great starting point for your thinking about morality in lawyering.

Frank, J, 'Why Not a Clinical Lawyer-School?' (1993) 81 U PA L Rev 907

This was one of the earliest calls for the introduction of experiential learning in US law schools. Jerome Frank criticised the prevailing Langdell/Harvard case method of legal instruction and argued that students would flourish in a system that mixed rigorous theoretical and substantive content with hands-on experience: 'But is it not plain that, without giving up entirely the case-book system or the growing and valuable alliance with the so-called social sciences, the law schools should once more get in intimate contact with what clients need and with what courts and lawyers actually do?' (at 913)

Kerrigan, 'How do you feel about this client? A commentary on the clinical model as a vehicle for teaching ethics to law students' [2007] IJCLE 7

This article reviews the current approach towards the teaching of ethics in UK law schools and reports on research conducted in UK law clinics as to the rationale and value of learning about legal ethics in a law clinic environment.

Leff, AA, 'Unspeakable Ethics, Unnatural Law' [1979] Duke Law Review 1229

This polemical article really makes you think about the basis for morality in law. It adopts a provocative morally relative approach.

Nicholson, D, 'Legal education or community service? The extra-curricular student law clinic' [2006] 3 Web JCLI (http://webjcli.ncl.ac.uk/2006/issue3/nicolson3.html)

This article posits two types of law clinic: the educational-oriented clinic and the social justice-oriented clinic. It argues that the primary goal of clinics should be provision of legal services to the needy and that the prioritising of educational needs risks treating clients unethically as means to educational ends.

### Intermediate

ACLEC (the Lord Chancellor's Advisory Committee on Legal Education and Conduct), *First report on legal education and training*, 1996

This is the UK equivalent of the MacCrate report (see below) and provides a starting point for modern debate about the role of higher education in relation to law and the legal profession.

**Aitken, J, '*Provocateurs for Justice*' (2001) 7 Clinical L Rev 287 at 292**

This article focuses on the social justice imperatives of clinical legal education and argues that supervisors should act in the role of provocateurs to inculcate a desire within students to do justice on behalf of clients.

**Boon, A and Levin, J, *The Ethics and Conduct of Lawyers in England and Wales*, 2nd edn (Hart, 2008)**

This is the main textbook on legal ethics in the UK. It undertakes a socio-legal analysis of the professional codes of conduct of the legal profession and covers key areas of professional conduct such as confidentiality, conflicts of interest, client relations, costs and so on.

**Hartwell, S, 'Promoting Moral Development Through Experiential Teaching' (1994–1995) 1 Clinical L Rev 505**

This article reported on 6 years of applied teaching research into the effectiveness of a semester-long simulated experiential learning course for developing moral reasoning in law students.

**Joy, P, 'The Ethics of Law School Clinic Students as Student Lawyers' (2004) 45 South Texas L Rev 815 at 836–7**

This article relates to the position in the USA, but provides a comprehensive overview of the ethical position of law students acting in a clinical or pro bono environment. It addresses questions such as: What do practice rules ethically require of students? Do ethical rules apply to student lawyers in the same way as they apply to lawyers? How should supervisors structure programmes to reinforce the ethical obligations of students? What role does clinical legal education play in the ethical development of students? Clearly the material will be primarily of comparative value but provides a useful platform for prompting discussion of the approach in the UK.

**MacCrate Report, especially Chapter 5: www.abanet.org/legaled/publications/online-pubs/maccrate.html**

This is the seminal report of the American Bar Association task force on the regulation, values and education of the legal profession. Part II contains a much-debated statement on the skills and values new lawyers should seek to acquire.

**Potter, M, 'The ethical challenges facing lawyers in the twenty-first century' (2001) 4 Legal Ethics 23**

In this article Lord Justice Potter paused to reconsider the pressures affecting the legal profession and the consequent tensions for maintaining a clear ethical role.

**Robertson, 'Challenges in the Design of Legal Ethics Learning Systems: An Educational Perspective' [2005] Legal Ethics 222**

This article draws on the learning theory of John Biggs to ask questions about the design and implementation of ethical learning in the law curriculum. Of particular interest is Robertson's discussion of whether clinical experience can provide the sustained exposure to ethical issues that he considers necessary. He thinks that this method may provide the best opportunity for such learning but believes the case needs to be made through clear pedagogic research.

**Singer, P, *Applied Ethics* (Oxford University Press, 1986)**

Singer's classic introduction to ethics provides a thorough and detailed explanation of core ethical concepts, particularly in relation to life and death but also more generally, for example Chapter 12 asks the ambitious question, 'Why act ethically?'

## Advanced

**Nicolson, D and Webb, J, *Professional legal ethics – Critical interrogations* (Oxford University Press, 1999)**

This scholarly book is perhaps the first philosophical and moral analysis of the role of the legal professional in the UK. It addresses the theoretical underpinnings of legal ethics and challenges traditional approaches towards the notion of the ethical lawyer.

**Webb, J, 'Being a Lawyer/Being a Human Being' (2002) 5 Legal Ethics 130**

This article addresses the question, 'who am I being as a lawyer?' Do not be put off by the apparent complexity of the narrative in places (the second paragraph raises the 'dispute between aretaic and deontic constructions of ethics'). If you persevere, this article provides a rich analysis of the moral role of the lawyer and the extent to which the lawyer's own humanity and autonomy can be preserved within the lawyer–client relationship.

 Activities

### Activity 1: Whose core values?

Re-read the 'Core duties' in the box at **3.3** above. There are six core duties according to the Solicitors Regulation Authority. Write out these duties on post-it notes and then discuss how you would rank these in terms of priorities if you had a choice.

Are there any further duties you would like to add to the SRA's core duties? Try to identify two or three additional duties that you think properly reflect the ethical obligations of solicitors.

### Activity 2: A moral role for lawyers?

This activity operates as a debate. In advance of the session, read Chapters 6, 7 and 8 of Nicolson and Webb, *Professional Legal Ethics – Critical Interrogations* (1999). Divide into two groups.

Group 1 will argue the following proposition: *'The proper role of the professional lawyer is that of the neutral partisan.'*

Group 2 will argue against this proposition. At the end of the debate, try to write half a page on the following question: *'Am I a neutral partisan?'*

### Activity 3: Confidentiality – a matter of life and death?

This exercise encourages you to think about the moral reasoning underlying the rules relating to client confidentiality and your own attitude towards the application of these rules. It works best when conducted as part of a group meeting, but you can conduct this exercise alone should you wish to.

### Preparation

Read the following articles which can be found at www.heinonline.org:

*Symposium Problem – the Wrong Man is about to be Executed for a Crime he did not Commit* (1995–1996) Loy LA L Rev, Vol 29, pp 1543–1546

*Damned and Damnable: A Lawyer's Moral Duties with Life on the Line*, Robert P Lawry (1995–1996) Loy LA L Rev, Vol 29, pp 1641–1658

*An Ethical Fairy Tale*, Gerald F Uelmen (1995–1996) Loy LA L Rev, Vol 29, pp 1685–1690

Having read the articles, consider the questions posed below:

## Questions

**1** When you read about the Public Defender, Claire Hopewell's dilemma, what was your initial response – did you think that she ought to disclose the information she had received from Ben Jones? Why did you feel the way you did?

**2** In Lawry's article the author suggests that Hopewell should begin her moral journey by following the example of Socrates. What do you think this would involve and why might it be useful? How would you follow the example of Socrates if you were in her shoes?

**3** Lawry discusses 'role-differentiated morality'. What do you take this to mean and do you agree with his rejection of the notion that lawyers are not morally responsible for the decisions their clients make?

**4** Lawry suggests that part of Hopewell's role when discussing the case with her client should be to help him become a 'better person'. How do you feel about this?

**5** Assuming for a moment that Hopewell was not a lawyer – do you think she would have a moral duty to disclose Jones' confession to the authorities? If so, why?

**6** Now, recognising that Hopewell is a lawyer, what additional moral imperatives come into play?

**7** Try to identify and list some of the interests that are at stake:
  • Interests in favour of disclosure:
  • Interests in favour of non-disclosure:

**8** Lawry suggests that, if he were in Hopewell's shoes, he would disclose the confession to the authorities even if the professional conduct rules forbade him from doing so. He would do this in the spirit of civil disobedience. Do you think such a course of action would be morally justified?

**9** In Uelman's article the author recounts a conversation between Claire Hopewell and her client. Do you think Hopewell was acting appropriately as a professional lawyer?

**10** Obviously we do not have the death penalty in the United Kingdom, so the issues are not the same, but please assume that you have a confession from your client to a murder for which an innocent person is about to stand trial. Please find out what the rules of professional conduct suggest you should do. How do you feel about the answer?

## Follow up

Find one confidentiality issue within your own case files or relevant pro bono activity (obviously it need not be as dramatic as Claire Hopewell's) and write a one-side reflection incorporating some of the issues you discussed at this meeting. See **Chapter 12** for information relating to reflection.

For a UK-based analysis of similar issues, read Dr Eileen Fry, 'Justice or Confidentiality' (1997) New Law Journal, Vol 147, No 6774, p 30.

# 4 Client funding

'There can be no equal justice where the kind of trial a man gets depends on the amount of money he has.'

Justice Hugo Black, US Supreme Court,
*Griffin v Illinois, 373 U.S. 12 (1964)*

## 4.1 Introduction

Whilst clinical work is generally undertaken on a pro bono basis, it is important to understand the different forms of funding that are available to clients. Although this sounds counterintuitive, despite being 'free', pro bono assistance might not necessarily be in the client's best interests financially. In some cases, your institution may not be able to assist the client, and you may need to refer him or her to another organisation which offers a better method of funding the client's case.

It is therefore important to remember that, whilst pro bono means that the client will not be required to pay your legal fees, there may be other expenses that the client is liable to pay and therefore other forms of funding may assist. You should also remember that some forms of litigation involve a costs risk for clients. This chapter will explore the main funding options available to clients and offer advice as to when each option may be appropriate. It also highlights the consequences of not investigating funding options for both your organisation and the client.

## 4.2 The importance of funding

Providing your client with funding information is one of the key obligations imposed under Rule 2.03 of the Solicitors' Code of Conduct 2007. It is your duty to provide the best possible information about the likely total cost at the outset and as the matter progresses. Amongst other matters, this involves informing your client of any likely disbursements, considering your client's eligibility for public funding and whether they have legal expenses insurance. All costs information should be confirmed in writing and updated regularly (Rule 2.03(5)). Whilst it is good practice to provide your clients with relevant funding information, Rule 2.03(7) recognises that in some circumstances it will not be appropriate to inform them of some or all of the matters stipulated under 2.03.

Just because your clinic or pro bono project does not charge the client for your services does not mean that you can ignore funding options. If a client is eligible for external funding but you fail to ascertain this, he may incur significant additional expense and may be deprived of available expertise. For example, if you conducted a disability discrimination claim for a client, you may not charge him, but he may have to pay for expert reports, counsel's opinion, postage and copying costs, travel costs etc. If you failed to spot that he was a member of a trade union with a good members' legal service, he may be significantly out of pocket. Moreover, his union may have been willing to pay for an experienced solicitor or barrister to represent him at the tribunal hearing. The failure to assess his eligibility for financial assistance could have prejudiced his interests considerably.

Funding can seem complicated at first, so when you begin advising on financing cases, you may find it helpful to use the checklist below to ensure you have considered all of the possibilities. An explanation of the methods mentioned in the checklist is set out later in the chapter.

### Funding Information Checklist

**Client Name:**                    **File Reference No:**

- Does the client have before the event (BTE) insurance? This is often contained within household insurance policies but also in other types of insurance policy. If the client is unsure, explain that you can check the policy.
  - ○ Yes            ○ No                  ○ Client to confirm
- Is the client a member of a trade union?
  - ○ Yes            ○ No
- Might the client be eligible for public funding? To assess eligibility, detailed financial information is required and the case must be of the type covered by public funding.
  - ○ Yes        ○ No          ○ Need to check financial information
- Will the case involve disbursements (eg expert report or court fees)?
  - ○ Yes            ○ No
- Is the matter contentious with the possibility of litigation and therefore cost risks?
  - ○ Yes            ○ No

*Possible* methods of funding are:
- ○ BTE insurance
- ○ trade union
- ○ public funding (CLS/CDS)
- ○ CFA
- ○ contingency fee arrangement
- ○ pro bono
- ○ private

The *most appropriate* method of funding is:
- ○ BTE insurance
- ○ trade union
- ○ public funding (CLS/CDS)
- ○ CFA
- ○ contingency fee arrangement
- ○ pro bono

Signature of student(s):

Date:

## 4.3  Pro bono

Working on a pro bono basis means that your clients will not pay for the legal work that you undertake on their behalf. However, whilst *your* services may be free, there may still be costs that you need to bring to your client's attention.

### Disbursements

Disbursements are fees payable to third parties and you may be required to incur these expenses in order to progress your client's case. For example, if you are representing a client in a claim for disability discrimination, you may be required to obtain a medical report to help establish whether your client is disabled. Similarly, if you are required to issue proceedings at court, there will usually be a court fee to pay. Most clinics and pro bono institutions do not have the means to cover the costs of these disbursements, and therefore clients will be required to pay these expenses out of their own pocket. If your client has a low income then he or she may not be able to afford to pay these costs.

### Avoiding disbursement costs

You may not be able to avoid the disbursement, but in some circumstances you may be able to circumvent or reduce the fee.

- Expert reports – some experts may provide a report free of charge, although it has to be said this is the exception rather than the rule. It is always worthwhile enquiring whether the person in question is amenable to waiving or reducing his or her normal fee. Where you do this, it is a good idea to explain that you are assisting the client pro bono as this is more likely to persuade the expert also to contribute some pro bono time. A useful source of pro bono expert advice is, of course, universities. Academics are often leading experts in their field, and if they know that students from other departments of the university or from other institutions are working on a case pro bono, they are often willing to assist.

---

**Suggested wording for letter seeking expert assistance**

We act for Mr Brown in respect of an appeal to withdraw his Disability Living Allowance. We need to present evidence to the Tribunal which sets out his medical condition and how it impacts on his day to day living. Mr Brown requires a report based upon any clinical examinations which you may have performed and any consultations you have had with our client.

We understand that preparing this report may involve a fee. However, it would be much appreciated, given Mr Brown's financial circumstances, if the report could be provided free of charge. Kindly note that we are not charging Mr Brown for the legal work which we are carrying out on his behalf, and therefore it would be particularly appreciated if you could provide a medical report either free of charge or at a reduced rate.

Should a fee be payable, please contact us to confirm the proposed charge *in advance* so that we are able to check our client's financial position and, if appropriate, obtain his consent *prior* to this fee being incurred.

- Court fees – if your client is in receipt of means-tested benefits or his or her income falls below the prescribed threshold, the client should be exempt from paying civil court fees. Alternatively, if by paying the fee your client would suffer financial hardship, the court may agree to a reduced rate. If you think the above applies to your client, you should apply for a fee remission using Form EX160, and guidance is provided in leaflet EX160A, available at www.hmcourts-service. gov.uk.
- Counsel's opinion – **Chapter 15** includes the contact details for the Bar Pro Bono Unit. It may be possible for you to secure pro bono assistance from a barrister via this scheme if your client is eligible. In addition, you should develop links with local sets of chambers. Clerks are often willing to check whether barristers would be willing to take instructions pro bono. If you do this, please ensure that you clearly mark your instructions 'pro bono' and mention this prominently in your covering letter so as to avoid any misunderstanding about the financial arrangements.

## Cost risks

A further matter to consider when acting pro bono is the cost risk associated with litigation.

If your client's opponent has retained the services of a solicitor, it is almost certain that the solicitor will be charging for the work that he or she carries out on the case. In many areas of litigation, the usual rule is that the loser pays the winner's legal costs. There may also be cost consequences if a party is deemed to have acted unreasonably within the course of the litigation, even if that party is ultimately successful. This means that there will often be a risk that your client may have to pay the opponent's legal costs. It is therefore important that your client is warned of this risk before commencing any form of litigation.

Rule 2.03(6) of the Code of Conduct requires you to consider and discuss with your client whether the risk and expense justifies any benefit which might be obtained from the outcome of the case. You must therefore weigh up the cost and risk on one hand against the benefit to be obtained on the other. You need to think carefully about the implications of this for your work. It certainly means that you need to be cautious about the types of case you take on. Some clinics have taken a policy decision to refrain from representing clients involved in litigation or to offer advice only as they do not wish to expose their clients to the risk of extensive legal costs.

## Protective Costs Orders (PCOs)

Courts have the jurisdiction to award costs under s 51 of the Senior Courts Act 1981 and Part 44 of the Civil Procedure Rules. Although the general rule is that the losing party must pay the winning party's costs, the courts have developed the practice of making Protective Costs Orders (PCOs) or Costs Capping Orders (CCOs) in certain circumstances. Although the conditions for the granting of such orders are quite restrictive (they apply only in public law litigation where there is some exceptional public interest reason to protect the claimant from the normal cost consequences – see *R (Corner House Research) v Secretary of State for Trade & Industry* [2005] 1 WLR 2600), they can be extremely helpful in enabling challenges to decisions that affect broad community interests but where otherwise the cost risk would make a claim untenable. A Protective Costs Order can be made at any stage of the proceedings and may include an order preventing the defendant claiming costs if it wins, or an order restricting the amount of costs the defendant is able to claim if it wins (a Costs Capping Order). Such orders can provide sufficient security regarding likely costs liability so as to make it viable to conduct the litigation. Normally a litigant must have no private interest in the outcome of the case, so the orders tend to be applicable to NGOs, charities or pressure groups which are seeking to challenge the conduct of public bodies. Of particular relevance for this book, the courts have taken the view that if the claimant is being represented pro bono, this is likely to enhance the prospects of securing a PCO.

## Pro bono cost orders

For many years, a party that was being represented on a pro bono basis was at a disadvantage. As the pro bono party did not incur any legal costs, courts and tribunals could not make a costs order in his or her favour. This meant that the opponent was in the more luxurious position of being able to fight the litigation knowing that he or she would not be at risk of paying further costs if he or she lost. In essence, the only cost risk the opponent faced was his or her own legal costs.

It is arguable that this placed the pro bono party at a tactical disadvantage, as costs are an important factor in negotiating any settlement. Where a party is faced with the risk of not only paying compensation but also a large legal bill, he or she may be more inclined to reach an agreement.

Section 194 of the Legal Services Act 2007 (which came into force on 1 October 2008) allows the courts to make costs orders in favour of a party who has been assisted on a pro bono basis. However, the costs are paid to the Access to Justice Foundation rather than the organisation that acted for the client. Pro bono cost orders are available in the county court, High Court and Court of Appeal. They are also available where settlements or orders have been agreed.

However, pro bono cost orders are not available where the *opponent* has been in receipt of Legal Services Commission funding or has also been represented on a pro bono basis (Legal Services Act 2007, s 194(5) and (6)).

The procedure for claiming these costs is similar to that for claiming costs where the representation was not free and is set out in Rule 44.3C of the Civil Procedure Rules. The pro bono assisted party is entitled to claim the same costs that he or she would have been entitled to claim had the representation not been free. You should therefore file and serve a summary statement of costs (Form N260) in advance of the hearing. The court can assess your costs either by summary assessment or detailed assessment, if deemed appropriate to do so.

The Bar Pro Bono Unit has suggested wording for a draft order, which can be found at www.barprobono.org.uk.

Note, however, that this is merely suggested wording and may be subject to change in each particular case. A copy of the court order should be sent to the Access to Justice Foundation within seven days of receipt.

An important difference between pro bono cost orders and normal cost orders is that normal costs cannot be set off against sums ordered under s 194 of the Legal Services Act 2007, and any payments made to the Access to Justice Foundation cannot be returned. You must therefore be careful if the case is likely to have subsequent stages, such as a final hearing (if costs are determined at an earlier stage) or an appeal. You may therefore want to ask the court to reserve any decision on costs at an interim stage so a single decision can be made on costs. The court can then consider who should be awarded what level of costs reflecting any earlier decisions that have been made.

## 4.4 Public funding

Public funding, or legal aid as it is more commonly known, is available to members of the public who are financially eligible and where their case has sufficient merit to justify public expense. Public funding is available for both civil and criminal matters. The rules which govern eligibility for public funding, and the application procedures, are quite complex. However, that does not mean this method of funding can be ignored. It is important that you are familiar with public funding as solicitors have a professional obligation to advise clients where public funding may be available (Rule 2.03(1)(d)).

### Civil cases

Public funding for civil matters is known as Community Legal Service (CLS) funding and is administered by the Legal Services Commission (LSC). Not all civil cases attract public funding and therefore it is important to consider the type of case and the area of law involved. For example, most personal injury cases will not attract public funding.

Applicants for CLS funding must pass both a merits test and a financial test. In determining whether a case has sufficient merit, regard must be had to the prospects of success and outcome to be achieved. A simple method of determining whether a case has merit is to ask whether a client of reasonable means would pay to fund the case. It is not as straightforward as querying whether your client is likely to be successful as a case could have high prospects of success but be worth very little. In this scenario, it is unlikely the case would pass the sufficient merit test. Alternatively, a case may have low prospects of success but the client may be at risk of losing his or her home. In this example, the case may pass the sufficient merit test as the outcome has an overwhelming importance to the client in maintaining a roof over his or her head.

The financial limits which determine eligibility change on an annual basis. The test considers the client's capital assets, such as savings or valuable property, as well as his or her disposable income to determine eligibility. The LSC publishes a Keycard which sets out the financial limits together with step-by-step guidance on assessing eligibility. If an applicant is in receipt of certain benefits, he or she will automatically pass the financial test. This is known as being in receipt of a passporting benefit.

There are two forms of public funding available, Legal Help and Legal Representation.

## Legal Help

The LSC contracts with various solicitors' firms and advice agencies to provide Legal Help in specific areas of law. Some clinics may have a CLS franchise to provide advice and assistance and therefore you should check whether your clinic is able to offer this form of funding.

Legal Help is a lower level of funding that provides clients with legal advice and assistance. However, it will not usually cover the costs of representation at a court or tribunal hearing unless the LSC allows it as Help at Court.

Organisations will contract with the LSC to provide an agreed number of matter starts (number of cases) within a particular area of law. You must therefore locate an appropriate organisation if you are considering referring a client elsewhere. You can find suitable organisations on the Community Legal Advice website at www.communitylegaladvice.org.uk/en/directory/directorysearch.jsp.

It is important to note that, under Legal Help, you will not usually be named as formally representing the client within the proceedings.

The individual organisation is responsible for the administration of Legal Help and will be required to correctly complete a Legal Help form (usually a CW1 form). It will also be responsible for ensuring that the client is financially eligible and obtain appropriate evidence such as bank statements and pay slips.

Whilst Legal Help means that the LSC will pay for many disbursements, including expert reports, the organisation is responsible for ensuring that the disbursement was reasonably incurred. This means that disbursements should not be paid at an excessive level and must be reasonably necessary for the conduct of the case. You should also note that, under Legal Help, court fees cannot be paid as a disbursement as you are not formally representing your client.

## Legal Representation

Legal Representation is a higher level of funding where, if granted, you will formally be representing your client within the legal proceedings to undertake all work that is necessary within the litigation and advocate on the client's behalf if necessary. You must complete an application and means assessment form, and send them to the LSC, to obtain Legal Representation. If granted, the LSC will send the organisation and the client a Legal Representation Certificate which sets out the limits on the funding. For example, the LSC may limit the stage of proceedings or the costs which may be incurred under the certificate. You can apply to extend these limitations if it is appropriate within the proceedings.

The LSC will pay disbursements, including court fees, although you must ensure that they are reasonably incurred to progress the case. However, in some circumstances, you may be required to obtain prior authority before incurring a significant expense.

It is important to note that whilst the client will not have to pay for his or her legal advice under Legal Help, he or she may be required to make a contribution for Legal Representation. This may be the case if your client is in employment. The contributions are a set monthly sum calculated on the basis of the client's disposable income. If he or she fails to make this payment, the client will lose the funding and may be liable for some or all of your legal costs.

As with pro bono assistance, your client may be liable for his or her opponent's legal costs in the event that your client loses or has acted unreasonably. However, clients in receipt of Legal Representation are afforded a significant degree of protection by s 11 of the Access to Justice Act 1999. If a cost order is made against such a client, the order shall not exceed a level that is reasonable for him or her to pay having regard to all the circumstances, including the financial resources of the parties and their conduct in connection with the dispute. This means that clients on relatively low incomes may be protected from adverse cost orders in the event that they lose their case.

However, where a client, with the benefit of Legal Representation, wins and preserves some money or property, he or she may be susceptible to the Statutory Charge. This allows the LSC to recover any legal costs to which it was liable from any money or property the client has gained or preserved. It is therefore important to try to recover all your legal costs from the opponent. However, if no order is made in respect of costs, or the opponent is unable to pay, the client may lose some of his or her winnings.

## Criminal cases

Criminal legal aid, otherwise known as Criminal Defence Service (CDS) funding, is also administered by the LSC. It is available to clients who are facing criminal charges or are under police investigation. Given that a person's liberty may be at stake, the assistance offered under CDS is quite extensive. For example, it provides free legal advice at the police station by a duty solicitor and representation for criminal defendants at all court levels.

Following some controversial cases involving highly paid sports stars receiving public funding, the decision was made to apply means testing to CDS funding for magistrates' court cases. This move ensures that public funding is only available to those individuals who would not otherwise be in a position to pay for legal advice and representation. As well as being financially eligible, applicants must pass the Interests of Justice test, which, like CLS funding, ensures the case has sufficient merit to justify public funding being granted.

In order to apply for criminal legal aid, Form CDS 14 must be submitted to the magistrates' court. If the applicant is not in receipt of a passporting benefit, Form CDS 15 must also be completed with supporting evidence of finances. Full guidance and the relevant forms can be obtained on the LSC website.

In order to conduct CDS work, your firm must be contracted with the CDS. Given the high volume of work that must be undertaken, it is unlikely that this will apply to a clinical or pro bono organisation. You should still be aware of this scheme, however, as if your client is eligible for CDS representation, it is almost certainly in his or her interests for you to refer him or her to a firm that can offer such assistance.

Note that in criminal cases, where a defendant is convicted, it is normal for the court, in addition to any fine, compensation or other order it makes, to make an order requiring the defendant to pay some or all of the prosecution costs. Clients should be advised about these consequences if they are facing a criminal trial.

**4.5**   Trade union funding

You should check whether your client is a member of a trade union as the union may pay all of his or her legal costs. Many people think that a union will only support employment law claims although, in practice, the support may be significantly wider and include such matters as consumer disputes.

If your client is a trade union member, he or she should be advised to check whether it is a matter that the union will support. There is significant benefit for clients with trade union support as they are likely to get all their legal costs and disbursements paid. The union is also likely to provide representation at any hearing that may occur, something that often pro bono organisations are unable to guarantee.

In the event that the union will fund a particular matter, it will usually offer the client an initial interview with an approved solicitor. The solicitor will determine whether the case has reasonable prospects of success, usually over 50%. If the case does have reasonable prospects, the union will usually support the client through to the conclusion of his or her case.

**4.6**   Before the event insurance

Many clients will have legal expenses insurance, often without realising it. Legal expenses insurance is often contained within policies such as those for household insurance and car insurance. You should therefore ask whether the client has relevant insurance. If your client is not sure, you could check the insurance policy on his or her behalf and advise your client accordingly.

It is important that your client contacts the insurance company promptly, as many policies contain a clause requiring it to be notified of a claim within a specified time limit.

If your client's claim is covered, the insurance company may refer your client to a solicitor on its own panel to determine whether the claim has prospects of succeeding; usually this means at least 51%. If the claim does have sufficient prospects of success, the insurance company is likely to pay all the necessary costs in pursuing the claim.

##  Conditional fee agreements

Commonly referred to as 'no win, no fee', these funding arrangements are often used in fast track and multi-track litigation. Over recent years, conditional fee agreements have become particularly prevalent within the area of personal injury.

Under this arrangement, your client will sign an agreement whereby he or she will not be liable for your costs in the event that the case is unsuccessful. However, if the client is successful, the solicitor will charge his or her fees plus a success fee determined upon the difficulty of the case. In some types of claim there are fixed percentage uplifts, for example in employers' liability claims. Clients will usually not be liable for their solicitor's costs, as these will normally be recovered from the opponent.

It should be noted that clients may be liable for their opponent's legal costs in the event that they lose their claim. It is therefore standard practice to insure the claim in the event that any adverse cost orders are made. This insurance is known as 'after the event (ATE) insurance'. The premium payable on the insurance can be recovered in the event that the claim is successful under s 29 of the Access to Justice Act 1999.

It is important to check for BTE insurance, considered above, as failure to use BTE insurance might prevent the successful party's solicitor recovering the cost of the ATE insurance premium (see *Sarwar v Alam* [2001] EWCA Civ 1401).

## Contingency fee agreements

Contingency fee agreements are an alternative form of no win, no fee funding available in non-contentious matters. However, under this form of arrangement, the costs are determined as an agreed percentage of any compensation awarded. These have become common in employment and criminal injury compensation matters, which, due to the limited circumstances in which costs can be recovered, render conditional fee agreements unsuitable.

All costs of representation and pursuing the claim are likely to be met under the contingency fee, although the client is likely to pay a significant proportion of his or her compensation, up to a maximum of 35%, if the client is successful. For this reason, only high value claims tend to benefit from contingency fee agreements as a funding option. Contingency fee agreements are not always an appropriate source of funding due to the proportion of their compensation which the client may ultimately be required to pay in respect of his or her legal fees. However, they do offer an alternative if the client is unable to secure pro bono representation or is unable to pay for assistance.

Contingency fee agreements are regulated by the Damages-Based Agreements Regulations 2010 which prescribe the maximum percentage fee which can be charged and the information which must be given to clients prior to entering such an agreement. Failure to adhere to these Regulations renders the agreement unenforceable.

## 4.9 Private payment

Finally, another option available to clients is to pay for their solicitor or legal advisor to carry out work on their case. It is important to remember that not all legal work is litigious, and in such cases clients will not be able to recover their legal costs or compensation. Indeed, not all litigation will lead to costs orders being made (eg small claims track cases in the county court). Transactional cases, such as conveyancing and wills, usually require clients to pay an agreed rate for the work carried out.

Clients will be liable for the costs of all the legal work undertaken and any disbursements that may be incurred. If the matter is litigious, they may also be liable for their opponent's legal costs if they lose, and after the event insurance may be taken out.

Clients should be advised as to the level of costs which may be incurred in any particular case so they can make a decision whether or not they wish to pursue the case.

### Summary table

| | Client's legal costs | Disbursements | Opponent's legal costs |
|---|---|---|---|
| **Pro bono** | Free | Client usually liable | Client may be liable |
| **Public funding – Legal Help** | Paid by LSC | Most reasonable disbursements paid by LSC. Client may be liable for court fees | Client may be liable |
| **Public funding – Legal Representation** | Paid in full by LSC or client may pay contribution based on disposable income | Reasonable disbursements paid by LSC | Court must consider client's means of paying any cost order having regard to all the circumstances |
| **Before the event insurance** | Covered by insurance | Covered by insurance | Usually insured |
| **Trade union** | Paid by union | Paid by union | Trade union usually liable, not client |
| **Conditional fee agreement** | No win, no fee | Dependent on firm of solicitors – client might be liable or firm might pay | Usually insured |
| **Contingency fee agreement** | Percentage of damages recovered | Client may be liable | Usually used in non-cost jurisdiction although client potentially liable |
| **Privately paying** | Client liable | Client liable | Client liable |

## 4.10 Summary

How a case will be funded is a primary concern of every client. Even though acting on a pro bono basis means your client does not have to pay any legal costs, this is not always the best method of running a client's case. It is a complex but necessary consideration and there can be serious consequences if you fail to act in your client's best interests in respect of costs and funding. To aid your understanding of the variety of funding methods, refer to the funding checklist and table above.

 Further reading

### Introductory

**Solicitors' Code of Conduct 2007 (Law Society)**
Rule 2.03 and the accompanying guidance is essential reading to ensure you are aware of the funding information with which a client should be provided.

### Intermediate

*Blackstone's Criminal Practice/Blackstone's Civil Practice* (Oxford University Press)
Both of these texts cover funding and are regularly updated.

### Advanced

**Legal Services Commission**
The LSC website (www.legalservices.gov.uk) is not the easiest to navigate, but it contains all you need to know about public funding. You can access the relevant forms, guidance and the rules governing legal aid (contained within the Legal Services Commission Manual).

 Activities

### Activity 1: To fund or not to fund?

Consider the scenarios below and determine which funding methods are available, and which appears to be the preferred method:

1 Lucy, 20, has been dismissed from her employment and wants to lodge a claim for unfair dismissal at the employment tribunal. She lives at home with her parents. She is not a member of a trade union and she has no insurance policies in her name.
2 Mr Hughes has an ongoing dispute with his neighbour, Mrs Johnson, in respect of the position of her hedge which runs along the boundary to their properties. After trying to resolve the matter informally, Mr Hughes has decided to litigate. Both Mr Hughes and Mrs Johnson are retired with a state pension as their only source of income.
3 James has recently been involved in a car accident in which he sustained several injuries. His motor insurance has declined to cover his legal expenses and he has no other insurance available. His injuries are likely to attract damages in the region of £5,000 to £7,000.

### Activity 2: Do you qualify?

To practise determining eligibility for CLS funding, input your own financial details into the eligibility calculator (www.legalservices.gov.uk/civil/guidance/eligibility_calculator.asp) to determine whether you qualify for Legal Representation and Legal Help. Remember any student loan (despite the fact it is a loan, which is repayable, it counts as income).

# 5 Working with your supervisor and others

'A boat does not go forward if each
one is rowing their own way.'

Swahili proverb

## 5.1 Introduction

One of the most challenging aspects of clinic is adjusting from working on your own to working with others. Years of academic study may have left you reluctant even to speak to another student about assessed work, let alone work together, for fear of being accused of collusion or academic misconduct. All of a sudden, that is turned on its head and you are being positively encouraged to share your thoughts and ideas with others before deciding on an agreed course of action. This can be quite unsettling but it is a vital aspect of clinical learning. Clinic tends to replicate the professional working environment, where you will rarely work in isolation. Most organisations have teams which work together on cases or projects as this is often the most efficient way to get the job done.

Working in a group does not necessarily mean that you are working as a team (Levin, 2005). Therefore this chapter will look at the relationships you will experience during your clinic and pro bono activities and consider the best ways to work together effectively. The chapter is divided into the vertical experience, ie your relationship with your supervisor, and the horizontal relationship, meaning your interaction with fellow students and other people you may encounter. It will provide helpful hints that should smooth the way for a peaceful supervisor/supervisee relationship and advice on how to work effectively with your colleagues.

## 5.2 Working with your supervisor

Wherever you undertake your clinical or pro bono experience, whether it is within your institution's law clinic, on placement, or as part of a Streetlaw programme, you will be supervised in some capacity. Thus, a great deal about what you get out of your clinical experience will depend on the relationship you develop with your supervisor. If you undertake clinic or pro bono at your institution, you may already know your supervisor. In the context of placements and work within external organisations, it is very unlikely that you will have had much contact, if any, with your supervisor or coordinator.

Regardless of whether you have had prior contact with your supervisor, you will very quickly need to learn how to develop an effective working relationship with that individual.

## What will your supervisor be like?

A supervisor has a multifaceted role. According to McAllister et al (1997) some of the key functions are:

- Role model – someone who models professional behaviour.
- Colleague – someone with whom you will develop a professional relationship.
- Teacher – someone who assists your development and maximises your learning experience.
- Assessor – someone who may be called on to evaluate your work.
- Manager – someone who ensures you comply with any relevant policies and procedures, and manages the client relationship.
- Counsellor – someone who deals with personal issues and emotional responses to clinical interactions.

It is important to remember that your supervisor has to balance these responsibilities, which may at times conflict, and this may impact on your interactions.

In many clinics, your supervisor will be a qualified lawyer who may be employed purely to supervise clinical students, in which case you may not have met him or her before, or he or she may be an academic member of staff who supervises students in addition to teaching more traditional, academic subjects. It is also possible that you will be supervised by someone who is not a practising lawyer but is involved in teaching the clinical programme.

Although your supervisor is a professional teacher, dedicated to helping you achieve your potential, there are sometimes obstacles that can prevent this objective from being achieved. It is vital that you bond with your supervisor from the outset and that you develop a trusting relationship. If you feel comfortable with your supervisor then you will be able to communicate freely with him or her, and this can only benefit you and your clients.

## How can you work effectively with your supervisor?

It is essential to form a positive relationship with your supervisor. During your time in clinic you are likely to have more contact with your supervisor, both in person and via telephone/email, than you will have had with any other member of staff during your time at university. Unlike your previous tutors who have *taught you law*, often in a very dry academic setting, your supervisor will be working with you as you *apply the law* in a very real setting. As a result, you will find yourself talking to your supervisor on a completely different level, more as colleagues rather than as teacher and student. Your supervisor will adopt a range of different techniques when interacting with you in the clinic. These will be different to what you are used to and can be strange or frustrating at first. Most clinical teachers try to adopt what is referred to as non-directive supervision. This is a method where the onus will be placed on you to think through planned actions, strategies, problems, etc and to reflect on your performance, without your supervisor immediately telling you what the answer is or instructing you to do something a particular way, or showing you how to do it. There is a possibility that you will feel a little lost or bewildered as your supervisor sits back and requires you to play a more significant part in the discussion. However, as you become more confident at offering your opinion, and more willing to participate, you will see significant advantages and feel a more mature and professional relationship develop. Non-directive supervision can result in the following advantages: enhanced student autonomy; more coherent, structured decision-making; more rigorous reasoning process; better solutions may emerge; both you and your supervisor may learn something. 'The non-directive approach also enables the relationship between clinical student and faculty to evolve into a more collegial or peer-like relationship, with the faculty member taking on the role of mentor-coach rather than supervisor.' (Dunlap and Joy, 2004/05)

An important point to remember is that, however positive your working relationship, this person is still your supervisor, and a certain degree of professionalism and formality is still required. Therefore, when it comes to your work, your supervisor will remain objective and will not be swayed by your personal relationship. Humorous emails with smiley faces attached and text speak are best avoided. On a similar note, when you speak to your supervisor, by all means speak openly but maintain respect and save your banter for your friends.

Another key point to bear in mind when working with your supervisor is that, although you are the person directly working on the file, you are working under his or her supervision and therefore as a team. For the team to function effectively, you must keep your supervisor fully up to speed with what is happening on the file; otherwise he or she will not be able properly to supervise you. This means routinely updating your supervisor as to what is happening on the file and not just assuming that, by checking letters, he or she should have a sufficient knowledge of what is happening. So, for example, every time a letter or telephone call comes in, summarise the content to your supervisor or, if he or she has just approved a letter, send him or her an email to confirm that it has been sent out. Similarly, if you have just undertaken an interview, send your supervisor a copy of the attendance note. This not only keeps your supervisor 'in the loop', but it is common courtesy to keep him or her informed when it is that person's practising certificate or reputation you are working under.

## First meeting – what can you expect?

Most supervisors will organise a short, introductory meeting with their students or firm at the start of the academic year or module. This is an opportunity for you to introduce yourself to your supervisor and the other students in the group. This can feel a little awkward and there may be a sense that everyone is 'sizing each other up', but, as you will discover, clinic is not a competition; it is a learning journey. So instead of obsessing about how much smarter your colleagues may be, focus instead on yourself and take this opportunity to impress your supervisor with your enthusiasm for what lies ahead and your willingness to work hard.

You are likely to be asked to introduce yourself. Although you might feel anxious about doing this, particularly if you are not familiar with the other members of your group or your supervisor, try not to allow your nerves to get the better of you. Remember that you are all in the same position; everyone is new to clinic and unsure of what to expect. You will not be expected to provide your life history, but you should be prepared to explain why you chose to undertake clinical or pro bono work (if it is an optional part of your programme) and what you hope to gain from the experience.

Remember that, at this first meeting, your supervisor is looking to gauge your personality and what sort of experience you are looking for. It will help your supervisor decide which case or task he or she is going to allocate to you, so appear enthusiastic despite any shyness or nerves.

### Team meetings – what can you expect?

You are likely to have regular meetings with your supervisor and fellow students. In some institutions, meetings usually take place on a weekly basis. At your first meeting, your supervisor is likely to fix a regular day and time that suits everyone in your group. It is very important that you attend your meetings, as failing to turn up means that you will lose touch with what is going on with the cases. If an emergency situation arises and you are unable to attend a meeting then, as a matter of courtesy, you should give your supervisor as much notice as possible.

The content of meetings can vary widely. Sometimes your supervisor will expect you to provide a presentation, discuss and reflect, analyse an article or perhaps role-play, and at other times it may be a more routine case round-up. These typical activities are examined below.

### Case rounds

Case rounds or updates tend to be the steady diet of firm meetings. This is an opportunity for you to provide an update on recent developments and to share ideas about your cases with your colleagues. Far too often, students eagerly explain the developments in their own case and then sit back, mute, once their turn has passed. This will not impress your supervisor and it does nothing for the dynamics of the meeting. You must actively listen to what others are saying about their cases and show an interest. Can you see a parallel to your own case? Can you offer a different way of looking at the problem? Do you have some knowledge that may be of assistance? Have you read something about this type of case? Have you seen something in the news about this that might be helpful? If you chip in with your ideas, others will follow suit, and a lively discussion should ensue. This sort of dynamism will please your supervisor, and it will bond your group together. It does not matter if your contributions are not fully thought through, or indeed if they are off the wall. The key is to participate and get discussion going, which will provide a much more interesting session for all parties.

If the spotlight is turned on you, and you need to describe one of your cases, remember to be thorough in your explanation. In order for your supervisor and other team members to engage with the case, you need to give a full overview. You need to briefly summarise what the case is about and then explain the issues that it has brought up. It is important to be thorough at this point, as although you might think a point is fairly insignificant, somebody else might pick up on it and give you some new insight that could help the case. You then need to describe how you approached the issues and the steps that you propose in order to move the case on.

## Discussions

Sometimes your supervisor will come along to a firm meeting with a topic for discussion. If you are lucky, you might have been forewarned of the topic so that you can think about if beforehand, but sometimes the topic will be sprung on you. Again, this is not designed to cause you stress; it is simply a way to get you to 'think on your feet', a crucial skill to develop for your future career, particularly if you hope to become an advocate.

Just about anything can form the basis of a discussion; it could be something topical such as a recent case that has been in the news, or it could be a conversation about your sense of justice or morality, or it could be about reflection, absolutely anything. The topic is not the central issue; it is the process of discussion that matters. When you debate an issue, you express and advance your own thoughts and ideas and then you listen to what others have to say on the same topic. You then reflect on your original thoughts and, having heard another perspective, you can consider whether your thoughts still stand, or whether your ideas have changed and if so how. You can then express your further thoughts, perhaps reaffirming your ideas or advancing a new argument in the light of what you have heard. It seems obvious, but this exchange of ideas and re-evaluation of your own thoughts is another key skill that you need to acquire. Good professionals will always invite opinion and discussion as it will enable them to assess all of the strengths and weaknesses of the matter at hand, including those that were not perhaps immediately apparent.

In the light of the above, you can see why it is so important to become involved in discussions. They will enable you start thinking like a professional, and they will also help you develop the confidence to express your ideas and convey them to others in a persuasive manner.

## Presentations

You may be asked to prepare a presentation about an aspect of a case that you are working on, or a topical issue that is relevant to your group. It is vital that you take these tasks seriously. It can be tempting, particularly when other subjects are competing for your time, to allow non-client based tasks to take a back seat, knowing that, at a push, you can always wing it in front of your fellow colleagues and supervisor. The temptation can be all the greater if you know that the presentation is not something that will be formally assessed. If you start to find yourself thinking along these lines then you need to stop and consider what impression this creates for your supervisor. He or she is very likely to think that if you cannot be bothered adequately to prepare a presentation, then you are lacking in professional commitment. If you are idle when it comes to presentations, are you also lazy with your cases? This could lead to your supervisor questioning your ability to run a case, and it may mean that the next juicy case or task goes to another, more enthusiastic and committed student. Do not put yourself in this situation. If you are given a task or presentation to prepare, do it to the best of your ability. If you find yourself pushed for time, speak to your supervisor before the appointed date and explain the situation; you are likely to receive a much more sympathetic ear this way than if you battle on and produce work that does not do you justice.

If you are undertaking a presentation, feel free to use props. If the meeting room has a whiteboard, or a projector, would it help to make use of it? If you do not have access to such facilities, could you produce a handout summarising what you have to say, perhaps using a diagram or flowchart. Be creative. If there are two or more of you presenting, could your presentation involve a debate or a line of questioning? Try to make it as interesting and engaging as possible for your colleagues and your supervisor.

Remember that when your supervisor asks you to prepare a presentation, there is a good reason for it; he or she is not setting the task with the intention of making you feel self-conscious in front of your peers. Delivering a presentation is an exercise that encapsulates research, organisational skills, drafting and advocacy, all valuable skills that you need to acquire during your clinic and pro bono experience. Imagine that one of your cases which you thought was going to settle out of court unexpectedly blows up, and an urgent court application has to be made. All of a sudden, you are faced with the prospect of having to file an application, on time, and in the correct form, and possibly having to explain it before a District Judge. If you think about it, this is no different to giving a presentation. Both situations involve researching the issue within a set time limit, drafting what you want to say and then delivering it in person. So if you have survived a presentation, you can be confident that you can survive a hearing.

You can read about presentations in more depth in **Chapter 11**.

## Supervisor/supervisee relationship pitfalls

Having outlined what makes for a positive relationship with your supervisor, it would be remiss if we did not consider what may sour the relationship.

### The big cover-up

It is the moment that every student dreads, that awful, sinking feeling when you realise that you have missed a hearing date, or failed to file a document in time, or your client has told you that he or she is going to seek advice from a 'proper' solicitor instead. It happens. Although it may be embarrassing, and you may feel a little foolish if it was an avoidable mistake, you will survive and you will learn from your mistake. You need to remember that you are still a student and not yet the finished article; you are still learning.

Happily, the vast majority of problems are averted by a vigilant supervisor who should be closely monitoring every step you take, but accidents can and do happen.

The important thing to remember is to alert your supervisor as quickly as possible. Do not try to cover up your mistake, or try to remedy it before anyone notices, or, worse still, ignore it. Go to your supervisor and explain what has happened immediately. Most supervisors will be understanding, but do not be overly surprised if your supervisor is a little displeased; remember that any mistake will ultimately be attributable to your supervisor and therefore his or her livelihood and professional reputation. Your supervisor will want to know how the mistake has occurred before deciding on the best way to recover the situation.

The vast majority of mistakes occur due to a breakdown in communication. It is all too easy for students to fail to communicate the case properly to their supervisor, and as a result there follows some form of oversight. Sometimes, wrong information has led your supervisor to approve something that he or she would not otherwise have approved. Perhaps your supervisor has told the student to do one thing, but the student has misunderstood and has done something quite different. There is always a lesson to be learned in these situations; the lesson is, if in doubt, check with your supervisor.

Ask any supervisor which they would prefer: a student who asks questions and gets it right, or a student who stoically battles on and gets it wrong. The answer is obvious.

## Personal problems

It would be great if all students could sail through their clinical or pro bono experience without any personal problems to contend with so that they could give their full, undivided attention to their work and clients. Unfortunately, this is not always the case. Your time at university can be very challenging and you may not make it through without encountering a few problems along the way.

Be assured that, whatever the issue, you will not be the first student to have that personal problem, be it stress, bereavement, disability, pregnancy, family issues; it has all been seen before. Just because you are undertaking clinic or pro bono work, the most relevant and exciting part of your course and the one that you may have been looking forward to for years, there is no reason to suffer in silence. If you have a problem, you must talk to someone about it.

Ideally, you should feel able to talk to your supervisor, but if for any reason you do not feel comfortable with that then speak to another member of staff. If your supervisor or tutor is unable to help with the problem then he or she will most certainly be able to refer you to someone who can. In any event, your supervisor will need to be made aware that you are experiencing personal issues in case it impacts upon your ability to carry out your clinical or pro bono work.

Your supervisor may need to organise cover for your cases, or reduce your workload to help you through the problem. If the matter is sufficiently serious, it may be worth discussing the possibility of deferring your clinical experience to a later date. So on a practical as well as emotional level, you can see how important it is that you do not ignore the problem and hope that it goes away.

## Clash of personalities

Working in a clinical or pro bono setting can prove to be a testing time, particularly when you have other academic modules to contend with. When your supposedly straightforward, two-paragraph letter has come back to you for amendments for the fourth time that day, you might feel exasperated and that your efforts are not being appreciated. Before you storm off to have a showdown with your pernickety supervisor, stop for a moment and consider how he or she must be feeling. Your supervisor has other matters to deal with and has probably spent as much time checking your letter and making amendments as you have in drafting it, and of course he or she may be equally frustrated that it has taken four attempts.

A meeting with your supervisor when you are angry and frustrated could lead to an uncomfortable exchange that sours the relationship. Try to calm down and ask yourself why you are feeling the way you are. Are you annoyed with yourself? Is it because you have too much to deal with it? Is it because you feel the feedback is entirely negative? Try to pinpoint what the source of the upset is and then ask to see your supervisor in private. If you then explain the matter to your supervisor in a calm and level-headed manner, you can expect a response in the same style.

If you feel that there is just a basic personality clash with your supervisor then you essentially have three options. You can either say nothing, you can ask to move firms, or you can explain the problem to your supervisor and hope that you can work around the problem. The third option is clearly the most preferable. Quite clearly, nobody wants to work in an awkward atmosphere as it will further damage your relationship with your supervisor and also affect the dynamics of the firm. Remember that, at the end of your clinical experience, your supervisor will not only have to grade your performance, but he or she is also likely to be your best prospect when it comes to providing a reference for a training contract, pupillage or other postgraduate employment.

Sometimes, a clash of personalities between two students who have to work together may result in some resentment being felt towards the supervisor who brought them together. Rest assured that your supervisor will never have intended to create such friction. It is commonplace for students to be paired up to work on cases, particularly in the early days of clinic. If your supervisor is not familiar with the other students in your firm then this will be a random allocation that may or may not work out. If you find yourself clashing with another student, do not blame your supervisor; instead, look upon it as a challenge. You should make efforts to work out your differences with the other student as far as you are able. If the situation seems impossible to reconcile then speak to your supervisor, who may be able to iron out the problem, or, alternatively, you might be asked to work with another student.

Too often, students demand to work alone on a case, often hiding behind the pretext that they want an opportunity to shine, but in reality it is because they do not want to work as a pair. Your supervisor will see through this and recognise, rather than conveying individualism and enthusiasm, that it shows a lack of team-spirit and an inability to work with others. The ability to work with others is a vital skill for any profession. When you start work, you will not be working in a bubble; you will be working in a busy office having to deal with everyone from the cleaner to the director, and you must find a way of communicating with people at all levels, regardless of your personality differences or styles of working. So if you find yourself clashing with your supervisor or another student, try to find a way of working together that accommodates both of your personalities.

---

**Extracts from student responses to questionnaires about the relationships developed between students and supervisors**

'You feel more at ease and the session is more like a chat.'

'I found it much easier to talk to my supervisor than any other member of staff on my four-year course.'

'I felt a stronger rapport with my clinic tutor.'

'A student can raise issues more personal to him/her and the teacher may develop an understanding of how that student thinks and behaves based on the 'off-topic' issues raised.'

'It is a continuous working relationship that develops outside of firm meetings as much as in.'

'More approachable due to having contact through the week.'

'I have a stronger bond with my clinic tutor as I worked with him every day and he is aware of my capabilities and weaknesses and I am also more aware of what he requires.'

'You spend more time with them discussing personal things such as how you felt doing this, what it would be like doing this, how did you handle that etc.'

'Seminars had a more rigid structure, and less scope for little conversations and observations. Most firm meetings had discussions about personal aspects ... it would be hard to open up and be honest in a formal environment.'

'The relationship between a tutor and student is more horizontal than I originally perceived it would be, you are more team members than teacher pupil in the non-clinical sense, because you are running cases together. You are on the same side of the fence rather than being on opposite sides.'

(Kerrigan, 2006)

---

## 5.3 Working with other students

Your clinical or pro bono experience will be very different from your other academic studies, not least because you are often positively encouraged to collaborate and work as part of a team with your fellow firm members. Whilst this is usually a rewarding experience, problems can arise whilst working together.

### What makes a good team player?

Whilst life as a professional may appear to be about the ability to work alone and getting the job done, in reality you need be a team player. This is the case whether you find yourself in a large commercial environment putting together that big deal, or in a small firm helping out a colleague. You should use your clinical experience to harness and develop these skills, which will stand you in good stead. So, what makes a good team player?

### Strong communication skills

The vital characteristic which marks out a good team player is the skill of being a good communicator. Without clear communication, there will be endless misunderstandings as to who is meant to be doing what, and this can cause frustration and annoyance. If, however, everyone communicates, so that the team has a clear understanding of what the other team members are doing then you are free to get on with your tasks. To improve your communication skills, you may want to try Activity 3, at the end of this chapter.

### Dividing the tasks

Your clinical or pro bono experience is likely to be part of a wider academic programme. When finding your feet, you may want to work together for reassurance. However, you may also have commitments outside of the university which mean that it is unlikely you can be in the office all of the time to do everything required. Sharing out the various tasks can therefore prove to be an invaluable method of getting the job done, and once you are more confident with the work, you may want to work independently.

There are various aspects of the case work which can be divided between those running the case. At the outset, you may need to interview your client to discover the factual background of the problem and find out what your client actually wants. You can divide the different parts of the initial interview between you. However, you should ensure that you both agree prior to the interview who is doing what. If you fail to do so, you run the risk of stepping on each other's toes, and the interview will not look very professional, which would create a bad first impression for your client. You can easily attend to this by printing out two copies of the interview plan and highlighting your respective sections.

After the interview, you will need to research and analyse your client's problem so that you can offer practical advice. Whilst there are some cases which have discreet legal issues, it is usual for a case to have a range of legal issues. Once you have identified these, it would be best to divide the issues between you to carry out the research. This means that you will not be duplicating each other's research and it is likely that you will achieve a conclusion more quickly. You should remember that you will still have to collate your research cohesively and therefore it is important that you agree timescales to complete the research together. Upon completion, you could check each other's work and see if you agree with the outcome, and collectively you may come up with a range of options available for your client.

Similarly, you can share the various tasks involved in the case management. You can agree who will write the various letters that need to be drafted, for example one person can draft the advice letter, whilst the other can write the letter before action. Again, this will save valuable time as work is not being duplicated. However, you need to remember the importance of good file management to ensure your partner knows what is happening on the case.

Even if you are not involved in case work, it is probable that you can divide up the component tasks which make up the project as a whole.

Working together but apart is quite a difficult skill to master and requires quite sophisticated techniques. You each need to be clear who is expected to do which task and provide updates on your progress. If you cannot be in the office at the same time, because of timetable clashes for example, consider leaving your partner a note on the file or sending him or her an email to let that person know of any developments which have happened whilst you have been working on the case.

## Debating the issues

Everybody knows that lawyers like to argue and take issue with each other, even if they are working on the same case. This is seen in every courtroom and every legal office. Whilst this is often viewed negatively, particularly by clients who simply want a definitive answer, it is also very much a positive quality. After all, if we all agreed on one interpretation of the law, there would be no need for lawyers.

In every office, legal or otherwise, colleagues will be asking each other their thoughts on a particular matter. This is a useful technique to ensure that the issue has been explored thoroughly, and possibilities and consequences have been fully identified. It is far better to have a fellow worker spot the flaws in your argument rather than your client, opponent or a judge, so that you then have the opportunity to remedy those flaws in advance.

However, you should not be afraid to stand your ground provided your argument is well reasoned and logical. Remember that the aim of the exercise is to bring consensus on an appropriate course of action. You should therefore aim to persuade the other members of the team that your idea is the appropriate course of action in a polite and controlled manner.

## Working together professionally

It is essential that the professional image is maintained. Whilst disagreements may occur within the team, the outside world, including your client, must not be made aware of the differences. If your client were aware of differences of opinion within the team, they might lose confidence with the service that they are receiving. If your opponent became aware of any disagreement, this could be potentially fatal for the case.

It is important therefore that you agree a plan of action before speaking to your client and third parties so that you are in agreement as to what you are going to say. It is also essential that all members of the team understand the legal position of the case. If people have a different understanding, your client may not be advised correctly or you may act incorrectly on your client's instructions. This again goes back to the need for clear communication.

## Curbing competitiveness

Competitiveness is natural, particularly in a legal environment, as you strive to be the best. However, this invariably obstructs good teamwork. It is a particular problem if your work is assessed, as you may feel that your partner is domineering or making you appear lacking in some aspect to your supervisor. This is not always a deliberate act on the other student's behalf, as often competitive students may be trying so hard to impress their supervisor that they fail to consider the effect of this on their partner. If you feel that your partner is seizing all of the opportunities and taking all of the credit then speak to him or her about it and suggest a fairer allocation of work.

If, however, you find yourself guilty of stealing the limelight then stop and think about the impression you are creating. There is no need for you to dominate the relationship in an effort to prove how good you are. Rest assured that your supervisor will be able to gauge your ability from your share of the work. If you continue to stomp all over your colleague in an effort to impress your supervisor then all you are proving is your own insecurity and inability to work as a team player. Experienced supervisors can easily spot disharmony amongst partners and groups.

---

**Extracts from research into student attitudes which offer some insight into students' perceptions of their involvement in clinical teaching sessions**

'In the other teaching sessions you were less interactive with other students and everything was more theoretical.'

'Much more of an opportunity for students to address issues specifically relevant to what they are doing and compare experiences.'

'Seminars just seem to be very predictable. The teacher will go round the class from left to right as we progress through each question. There is often little deviation from the direct topic at issue and often little time at the end to raise anything as the seminars are designed to end on 50 minutes. Clinical sessions however allow the student more freedom to raise issues that may concern him, yet not necessarily be directly related to the topic at issue. I think this is a major benefit and one of the real areas that allows students to develop.'

'It is the students themselves who decide the direction of the meeting.'

'Because you discuss your own case in firm meetings you must participate. In seminars it is easy to sit at the back and not participate.'

'In a firm meeting it was possible to say, 'can we talk about y' and we would do that.'

'Students can raise any point and direct the session in a direction more suited to their problem even if it is a deviation.'

(Kerrigan, 2006)

---

### Problems you may encounter when working with other students

Throughout your clinical experience, it is likely that issues will arise whilst working as part of a team; what matters is how you then go on to resolve them.

The starting point should always be identifying the problem. Until this is achieved, you stand no chance of actually addressing the issue and settling it. As stated above, often problems arise through poor communication or misinterpretation. This means the problem could be rectified simply by speaking to your partner about your concerns.

### Stalemate

Maybe your problem is a genuine disagreement and you simply cannot reach a mutually acceptable decision on the same point. If it is a legal issue then your supervisor may have to step in and cast the deciding vote. If it is disagreement as to a more practical matter, for example an opportunity to undertake advocacy has arisen and you both want to do it but only one student is required, then you need to find a solution. Again, this may be resolved by speaking to one another and sharing your thoughts. It may be possible to reach a compromise so, in the advocacy example, there may be two hearings and you can each take a turn. Alternatively, if there is just the single opportunity, one of you will have to concede but perhaps on the basis that you will be allowed to take the lead in the next noteworthy experience that comes along, such as an interview or a conference.

Always try to take a step back and view that matter objectively, putting your client's best interests first.

### Different approaches to work/different abilities

As previously mentioned, working in a clinic or pro bono environment is different to any other form of academic study as it actively encourages teamwork. Disputes can therefore arise where one person is extremely enthusiastic and energetic and wants all of the tasks undertaken straight away, whilst the other student wants to take a more considered approach to the work. Similarly, one student might have a natural flair for letter-writing whilst the other struggles to pull together a coherent paragraph. In such situations, it can be difficult to work together, but you must find a way forward. For example, you may agree that the 'raring to go' student could prepare a rough draft which the other student might then mull over, suggest amendments to, and rephrase in places before you both meet up to agree a final version. Although you may feel that you have to make concessions and perhaps resent having to help out another student, this is all part of teamwork. Remember that, although you might be the gifted one when it comes to letter-writing, you might need your partner's help when it comes to interviewing or research.

### Working with friends and strangers

As mentioned above, you may be paired with a friend or a student with whom you are not so familiar, and both of these possibilities have pros and cons.

You might think that working with a friend is the more desirable option as you already know each other quite well. This can actually be an impediment. Friendship does not always make for a successful working relationship. Common issues which friends encounter include not wanting to disagree, criticise, highlight mistakes or point out when the other is not pulling his or her weight, for fear of ruining the relationship. This eagerness to please can often result in work which neither of you is happy with. No matter how well you know each other and get along on a social level, working together is very different. Establishing some basic ground rules before you start working together should prevent any conflict, leaving your relationship intact.

Working with unfamiliar people can be equally challenging. Whereas friends are reluctant to point out errors, it is easier to do so with someone you do not know. However, the risk is that he or she may take it personally, whilst a friend would accept the criticism with good humour. Whilst you may both be itching to get started on your work, it is highly advisable that you take some time out to get to know one another first. Spend half an hour chatting over coffee or have a working lunch where you discuss your expectations, standards and working practices. Just make sure you allow time to talk about non-work matters too. Once you have broken the ice, you can then agree how you intend to work together.

## You just do not get along

This is just a fact of life that needs to be accepted. We all encounter some people we just do not get along with and yet have to work with every day. During your career, you are unlikely to have the luxury of hand-picking your colleagues, and in clinic it is equally unlikely that you will be able to choose your supervisor, let alone your partner or firm members. However, despite this, you must continue to work with people to get the job done.

In the event of a personality clash with another student, you have several options. As with personality clashes with your supervisor, you can do nothing, ask to be re-partnered or deal with the problem. The latter is the most appropriate option as suffering in silence can be destructive not only to the team but also for you.

## Your supervisor, the peacemaker

There are going to be occasions when it is just not possible to compromise and it is necessary to bring in your supervisor to help resolve the situation. You should remember that your supervisor is not there to take sides in the dispute, and whatever he or she decides will not be a reflection on you personally. Ultimately, there is also a professional obligation to protect your clients' interests and these will not be served if you do not get along with your colleagues.

Your supervisor is likely to want to speak to both of you, either together or separately, to understand the nature of the dispute. It is possible that your supervisor may be able to find a compromise to ensure that both of you are satisfied with the outcome. However, if that is not possible, your supervisor must make a decision based upon the best interests of all concerned, primarily those of your client. You should therefore not take any decision personally.

---

**Further extracts from research into student attitudes to clinical teaching, which illustrate student attitudes to teamwork**

'There is more of a team spirit that does not exist in seminars.'

'Without the partner performing their side of the task the whole task may fail.'

'You feel connected to the students … you know each one is in the same boat as you.'

'There is much more scope for group activity.'

'Academic learning is largely independent study – in clinical learning you rely upon your firm.'

'You help others, receive help from others and you get a real feeling of team spirit. I became great friends with all the firm members.'

(Kerrigan, 2006)

## 5.4 Working with others

Aside from other students and supervisors, you will interact with a variety of people, in person, by telephone and by letter. How you communicate with these people will be considered in detail in **Chapters 6** and **7**, but this section will briefly consider the practicalities of working with others.

### Clients

Clinical work brings you into direct contact with members of the public. For the vast majority of students who have embarked upon their legal studies directly from school, this is the first time you will ever be acting in a professional capacity. Your clients will look to you for advice on matters that affect them personally, emotionally and often financially. They will put their faith and trust in you. It is a huge responsibility and not to be taken lightly.

It is therefore understandable that the one quality clients can legitimately expect of you is professionalism. This does not mean acting like a lawyer, as this can lead to, at best, a slight awkwardness as you are not yet a lawyer and, at worst, arrogance. The key to acting professionally is respect. You must respect the fact that your client has come to you for help and you must appreciate the position of trust you are in.

If you follow these basic rules then you are unlikely to give your client any cause for complaint:

- Keep your client's affairs confidential. Although you will share information with your group and your supervisor, it must go no further, however exciting the case may be.
- Deal promptly with any query your client raises. Do not ignore his or her letters or telephone calls. If you are unable to provide an instant answer, at least let your client know that you are looking into the problem.
- Mind your manners. When you meet your client, greet him or her with a smile, shake hands and offer him or her a seat. If you are providing advice, make sure that the client feels able to ask questions if he or she is unclear about anything you have said. When you have finished your meeting, thank the client for coming in and ensure that he or she is escorted from the office.
- Keep it formal. Do not use slang phrases or swear words, even if your client chooses to speak in this manner.
- Keep your distance. Do not agree to see your client on a more informal basis. Do not provide your personal telephone number or email address to your client. Be careful about what you disclose on your social networking public profile and do not join clients as 'friends'.
- Dress professionally. This shows that you are taking your client seriously and it also helps you to feel more professional. You should make the effort to dress smartly for all meetings with your client, even if he or she is simply dropping off some documents.

Remember that being professional, well mannered and formal does not mean that you need to act in an uninvolved manner. Your client needs to trust you so that he or she can open up to you and tell you his or her problem. You therefore need to show some empathy and understanding of his or her situation. This can be tricky as some clients can seize on this and start to treat you as some sort of personal counsellor, so remember that you are there for legal advice, not life coaching.

### Other members of your clinic

Aside from your supervisor, the office in which you work may be staffed by administrators, for example secretaries or receptionists. Larger clinics may also have trainee solicitors, bursary students or other professionals working there. It is important to treat everyone with respect, however 'lowly' you perceive their status, as you never know when you might need their help. Administrators know the office and its procedures inside out. You are likely to need their assistance when the photocopier inevitably jams or the fax machine runs out of paper. They can also be your supervisor's eyes and ears when your supervisor is out of the office, so maintain a professional attitude at all times.

### Judges, tribunals and professional panels

These are the people who have the power to make decisions that can directly impact upon your client's life. It could be something as simple as awarding compensation for a faulty toaster, but it could be as serious as awarding a disability benefit for life, or having your client's sentence for life imprisonment overturned.

Given the power that these people exercise, you must treat them with absolute respect at all times. In **Chapter 10**, you can read about how you should address judges/panels, the sort of language you should use and how you should conduct yourself in court, but there will be other occasions when you make contact other than in the courtroom setting, and in these situations it is always important to be respectful.

### Barristers

Certain types of case can involve you seeking the assistance of counsel, perhaps simply by way of written advice or opinion, but sometimes it can involve a conference or even full representation. As clinical work is usually pro bono, you will find that most of the barristers who agree to help out are usually very pleasant and easy to deal with, as they would not give up their free time if they did not have a genuine interest in assisting. There are still, however, certain formal practices that you will need to observe, such as preparing briefs and instructions in the correct form. You can find a sample brief in any of the standard advocacy guides available. It is also usual practice when writing to counsel to refer to him or her in the third person, for example 'Would counsel please find enclosed herewith the case papers'.

Remember that if you do 'instruct' counsel, it does not mean that counsel takes over your responsibilities. You will still be responsible for running the case and you may have to attend court to take notes, lodge any papers that need to be filed, track down witnesses and so forth.

## Your opponent

Your opponent could be anyone; it could be the Crown Prosecution Service, the Prison Service, a trade union, a solicitor, a paralegal, another pro bono organisation or perhaps members of the public representing themselves. What you need to do is avoid seeing them as 'the enemy' as this inevitably results in you adopting a hostile attitude, which rarely helps the situation. An awful lot of litigation and stress can be avoided by both sides showing each other respect and a willingness to negotiate. It is therefore vital to keep your dealings with your opposite number polite if you wish to leave the door open for resolution.

If, however, you and your opponent are completely entrenched and there is no hope for an amicable solution, then you can adopt a more forthright and business-like approach. That is not to say that you should be abrupt or abrasive; just be professional. If you treat people this way, they should return the courtesy. If, however, you receive an irate telephone call or an angry letter from your opponent, do not bite back as this reduces you to the same level. Instead, keep calm and consider the point he or she is trying to make. You can then respond to the point, but not the emotion.

## Intermediaries

If you are involved with contentious matters, you may have contact with intermediaries, for example ACAS, the Criminal Cases Review Commission and mediators. Whilst the purpose of these organisations may be to assist your client, that does not mean that they are on your side. You should remain professional and careful when discussing your client's case. Remember not to say anything that you would not want the organisation to relay to your opponent. Occasionally your client may have provided instructions or decided on a course of action which you do not agree with, but under no circumstances should this be conveyed to the intermediary, either directly or implicitly.

## 5.5 Summary

Entering a clinic or pro bono setting involves stepping out of your comfort zone. Instead of learning the law by means of lectures and seminars, you will be learning by experience and this can be a real shock to the system. In order to make the most of this new form of learning, you must adapt and learn to work with others, chiefly your supervisor and your fellow students.

You must learn to see your supervisor as a trusted guide to your learning journey. If you cultivate a positive relationship, you can expect to receive valuable feedback and insight that will help you make the difficult transition from student to professional.

In relation to your colleagues, you will need to foster team spirit. They are a rich source of learning, so do not overlook them. They can inspire you, they can support you, they can help you out with the little things you ought to know but do not and are too afraid to ask. On a more practical level, your time in clinic is limited, and you are unlikely to be able to achieve all that is required on your files or tasks without sharing some responsibility with your fellow students, so if you can learn to share the workload everyone will benefit.

Finally, remember that working in a legal environment is a precious opportunity. You will never again have the chance to 'practise' being a professional under the watchful eye of your supervisor. So, make the most of this opportunity as the next time will be in the 'real world' where there is a lot more at stake than your final grade.

#  Further reading

## Introductory

Levin, P, *Successful Teamwork! For Undergraduates and Taught Postgraduates Working on Group Projects* (OUP, 2005)
> A 20-minute skim-read of this engaging text will provide excellent practical advice on how to work effectively as a team. It offers guidance on common issues, including working with strangers and people you dislike. The book also sets out basic theories to help you understand the underlying principles of teamwork.

Kerrigan, K, *But you must know the answer: Clinical learning and the myth of the omniscient law teacher,* unpublished conference paper delivered at the International Journal of Clinical Legal Education conference, London, 2006, available from the author
> This paper analyses the working relationship between students and supervisors in a clinical learning environment and reports on research into student and supervisor attitudes towards this relationship.

## Intermediate

Barnhizer, 'The clinical method of legal instruction: its theory and implementation', 30 J Legal Educ 67, 145
> This perceptive article makes the following critique of the traditional power relationships in legal education, at least in the USA: 'The major part of the educational life of almost every student has been filled with the rigidity of formal instruction. ... With few exceptions their education has been in a rigidly structured, authoritarian mould ... creating intense pressures to conform. The roles of student and teacher are very well defined and, with the power available to the law teacher, are generally quite carefully maintained. An authoritarian model requires a substantial element of interpersonal distance to function effectively.'

Dunlap and Joy, 'Reflection in Action – Designing New Clinical Teacher Training By Using Lessons Learned From New Clinicians', 11 Clinical L Rev 49, 84 (2004–05)
> This is a wide-ranging article which includes consideration of the relationship between students and supervisors in clinical legal education: 'Non-directive supervision may be viewed as the manifestation of the Socratic method within clinical teaching. The questions that the teacher asks the student – guiding the student to explore issues, angles, facts, and theories the student may have left unconsidered and untested – is the measure of directiveness. On the more directive end of the scale, the teacher asks fewer questions and gives more instructions. At the opposite end, the teacher gives virtually no instruction but rather asks the student questions such as "what do you think"?'

Healey, J and Spencer, M, *Surviving Your Placement in Health and Social Care: A Student Handbook* (OUP, 2007)
> Do not be put off by the title; this book contains information which is equally applicable to law students on placement. It contains useful guidance on how to keep motivated during

your placement, dealing with difficulties, time management and professional development. Chapter 8 deals with supervision.

**Katz, H,** *Collaboration and Modeling: Reconsidering 'Non-Directive' Orthodoxy in Clinical Legal Education,* **Bepress Legal Series, Working Paper 775, 14 September 2005**
    law.bepress.com/expresso/eps/775

**Lomax, R et al,** *Surviving Your Social Work Placement* **(Palgrave Macmillan, 2010)**
    Again, do not assume that, just because this is primarily aimed at social work students, it should be ignored. It contains valuable guidance and practical advice on matters including adapting to life on placements, the power dynamics within supervision, managing stress and assessment. Chapter 8 is particularly useful as it troubleshoots common issues experienced on placement including workload and lack of support. A recommended read for anyone undertaking a placement.

## Advanced

**Avery, C,** *Teamwork is an Individual Skill – Getting Your Work Done When Sharing Responsibility* **(Berrett-Koehler Publishers Inc, 2001)**
    This book presents information on the skills and behaviour that will help you attain both your personal goals and team success, covering issues including powerful partnerships, trust and collaboration.

**McAllister, L et al,** *Facilitating Learning in Clinical Settings* **(Stanley Thornes (Publishers) Ltd, 1997)**
    This book provides a good overview of the aspects of clinic, but pp 53–59 are particularly helpful in understanding the roles and responsibilities of clinical supervisors.

 Activities

### Activity 1: Team scoreboard

As a group, rank the following teamwork characteristics in order of importance, with 1 being the most important and 10 being the least important. There is only one rule – you must be unanimous in your decisions.

- Communication
- Cooperation
- Listening
- Tolerance
- Trust
- Responsible
- Understanding
- Commitment
- Motivation
- Focused

### Activity 2: There's no 'i' in team

Take the above characteristics and rate how highly developed your skills are in respect of each attribute. Use the following grading scale:

1: Not at all    2: Poor    3: Satisfactory    4: Good    5: Excellent

Once you have completed the self-assessment, consider what action you can take to develop these essential teamwork skills.

### Activity 3: Say what you see

The purpose of this exercise is to improve your communication skills. Choose a picture, something relatively simple, perhaps taken from a magazine or something similar. Working in pairs, you need to describe the picture to your partner without telling him or her what the picture actually is. Your partner then has to draw the image you have described. If the picture is way off the mark then your communication skills need some attention.

# **6** Interviewing and advising

> 'I always pass on good advice.
> It's the only thing to do with it. It
> is never any use to oneself.'

> Oscar Wilde, *An Ideal Husband* (1895),
> Lord Goring to Mabel Chiltern

## **6.1** Introduction

One of the most important skills in clinic and pro bono is interviewing, as it tends to be the main forum for obtaining instructions and information about your client's case. The information gathered during your interviews will be used when performing every other subsequent legal skill, be it research or case planning. Therefore, developing effective interviewing skills will help you to understand your client's instructions and objectives and allow you to perform effectively.

The interview is also the point at which you will truly engage your client in the legal process and therefore the stage when your relationship with your client will be formed. The success of your student–client relationship can turn on your first interaction, and it is for this reason that interviewing skills are so important. There is much more to an effective interview than simply turning up and asking questions. This chapter considers how to conduct an effective interview and examines some common problems that can arise.

This chapter assumes that you will be the person conducting the interview. Several clinics and pro bono schemes involve students observing their supervisor or lawyer interviewing the client. If you are part of such a scheme you may still find this chapter informative, and when you next watch an interview you can see whether the principles below are followed. If your clinic or pro bono activities do not involve interviewing, you may want to consider entering one of several interviewing competitions which are held annually. A list of these competitions can be found on the Companion Website.

## **6.2** Practical preparation

It is important that you prepare thoroughly for any interview you undertake. Your interview preparation begins even before you first make contact with your client.

## Arranging interviews

If your institution does not have set interview blocks or drop-in sessions, you will need to consider how to arrange your interview.

Interviews can be conducted both face-to-face and by telephone, so you will need first to consider the most appropriate method. If you are conducting your interview by telephone, you will need to ensure that your client has time to speak and that he or she is in an appropriate setting. For example, a client is unlikely to want to discuss a delicate legal matter whilst he or she is in a busy shopping centre. It is therefore advisable to call your client in advance to arrange a telephone interview at a mutually convenient time.

When contacting your client to arrange the interview, you need to have your (and your partner's) availability to hand together with a proposed interview time. Make sure you leave enough time between arranging the interview and the interview itself to allow you to prepare properly and to have work checked, where applicable.

## Location

Most interviews will probably be conducted in the office where you carry out your clinical and pro bono work. If this is the case, you should ensure that your client knows the location of the office and how to get there. It is usually a good idea to send your client a map showing your location. If your client does not know where your office is located, he or she may be late for the interview or, worse still, may fail to turn up. You should also specify where and to whom your client should report on arrival.

Some clients may be unable to travel to your office; therefore it may be necessary to conduct the interview elsewhere. For example, if your client is in custody, the interview will need to be conducted at the prison. Alternatively, your client may have mobility problems. Before arranging interviews out of the office, you should speak to your supervisor and ensure that you have authority to visit your client. This is important as your institution may need to carry out a risk assessment to make certain your visit is conducted as safely as possible. Common precautions include the following:

- considering any particular risks, if any, posed by an individual client;
- not conducting a visit alone;
- letting someone know where you are going and what time you expect to be back;
- notifying someone when you have safely left the premises you are visiting.

Once you have complied with your institution's risk assessment procedure, you should then ensure you know exactly where you are going and how you are going to get there.

## Timing and duration

You should advise your client how long you expect the interview to last and therefore be able to work out a suitable time to conduct it. If your institution has a room-booking procedure, ensure that you reserve the interview room for the appropriate length of time. This will avoid the risk of having to end the interview prematurely because your time is up and someone else is waiting to use the room immediately after you. As a precaution, you may want to book the room for an additional half an hour in case of any unforeseen problems, such as your client arriving late.

As soon as you have agreed the practical arrangements with your client, it is sensible to confirm them in writing.

### Template appointment letter

[Client name]
[Address]
[Date]

Dear [name],

**Appointment confirmation**

Following our telephone conversation, I am writing to confirm your appointment on [day and date] at [time]. The interview will take place at [venue] and is expected to last [timescale]. Please report to the ground floor reception on entering the building. A map is attached for your convenience.

[As discussed, this interview is to obtain further details about your enquiry. Unfortunately, I will not be able to give you any advice at this interview as further research will need to be undertaken before I am in a position to offer advice.]

If you have any queries, or cannot attend the appointment, please contact me on [contact details] as soon as possible.

I look forward to meeting you.

Yours sincerely,

[Your name]
[Your organisation]

##  Types of interview

Before you can begin planning for the interview itself, you need to ascertain the type of interview you are about to conduct. There are two broad categories: initial interviews and advice interviews. Their purpose differs substantially and you need to be aware of the objectives of each so you can conduct the interview effectively. Many clinic and pro bono projects adopt a pattern whereby you will gather the factual account in the first interview and give advice only after you have been able to conduct research. You will not normally have sufficient expertise to be able to offer advice in the first interview and, in any event, will need to check your proposed advice with your supervisor.

## Initial interviews

These tend to be fact-finding interviews designed to obtain detailed information about your client's legal problem. However, because they are likely to be your first major interaction with your client, they have the additional objective of establishing a good working relationship which will last for the duration of the case. There are several stages to an initial interview, which are considered below:

### Welcome

You should remember that, whilst you may be nervous, it is likely that your client will also be nervous. After all, many people do not encounter the legal profession very often. It is therefore sensible to greet your client warmly and engage in some form of small talk or icebreaker. It is not essential to shake hands, but this can add a sense of professionalism. This type of introduction should put you and your client at ease. First impressions are important, so make sure your welcome has the desired impact.

### Introduction

You should then briefly (re)introduce yourself (you may have spoken previously on the telephone) and confirm your status as a student adviser. If the interview is to be recorded, ask your client's permission to tape it. At this stage you should explain the structure of the interview. This sets out the parameters and ensures your client knows how the interview will progress. Clients are often desperate to get their problem off their chest, which means that, until they have done so, they will not really be listening to you. You should therefore keep your introduction brief.

### Eliciting information

This is perhaps the most important part of the initial interview. You must ensure that you obtain sufficient information for several reasons. The information you acquire will help determine the following:

- The area(s) of law – on the face of it, the problem may seem like an employment matter, but is it really concerned with personal injury, or both? Does your organisation advise on these areas?

- The urgency and complexity – it is not always apparent from any information you are given prior to the interview whether a case is too urgent or complex for you to deal with.
- The limitation date – has it passed, is it quickly approaching, have you got some breathing space?
- How far advanced the matter is – are there any deadlines looming, or has the case not yet commenced?
- The merits of your client's case – whether the case has good or poor prospects of success.

Your client should be allowed to explain the problem in his or her own words. Clients need to feel relaxed and comfortable in order to be as open as you require them to be to obtain full and frank instructions. Hopefully your welcome will have reassured your client and created the right environment in order for him or her to do this.

## Questioning techniques

Obtaining detailed and accurate information can be achieved through effective questioning. Proficient questioning relies on understanding the different sorts of questions and when to use them. Regardless of the type of question asked, it should:

- be clear and concise;
- deal with one thing at a time; and
- be worded in a way which your client will understand.

Open questions invite a broad or long answer. Such questions are generally used at the beginning of an interview when the full extent of the problem is not yet clear.

### Examples of open questions

- Can you tell me in general terms about your problem?
- What happened next?
- When did you first notice there was a problem?
- Why do you think your employer responded in this way?

If you have been given some basic details prior to the interview, you can invite your client to start speaking with an open question or statement such as, 'So, I understand you are having problems at work. Can you please tell me a little bit more about that ...' If you have no information at all, you might want to begin by saying, 'Could you please briefly tell us about the matter you want our help with ...' You will note the wording uses the terms 'a little' and 'briefly.' You want to allow your client the opportunity to tell his or her story, but at the same time you do not want to give your client free rein to recount every single detail, as not everything will be factually or legally relevant. At the beginning of the interview, it is good to allow your client some room to tell his or her story, so you should avoid interjecting with lots of questions – this will only disrupt your client's flow. If you think of a question to ask when your client is speaking, note it down and ask it at an appropriate juncture.

When allowing your client to explain his or her problem, you should be prepared for an account which is not necessarily ordered or chronological. Take a look at the account below from an initial interview:

---

**Nicola Ridley's problem**

**Excerpt from initial interview**

Nicola: 'I've got a problem with my landlord. I live in this really nice area of the city and the rent's very cheap. To be honest I'm really worried about him evicting me. He's been really abusive. The next-door neighbour is like something out of a soap opera, a real drunk, and she's leaving such mess about that rats are in the yard and I've even seen one in my kitchen. I've asked her to tidy up but she just starts swearing at me and tells me her boyfriend is "into martial arts". Also, one of my windows is rotten and the flat's damp and draughty in winter, my sofa's wrecked by mould. I went round to the landlord but he was really nasty and told me I could leave. I do not want to have to go and live in the West End where the rent's cheaper but there's a lot of crime. I've got no written tenancy agreement but I've been living there and paying rent monthly since April 1996. He can't just throw me out can he?'

---

It is your job to work with clients to help them provide a coherent account of their problem. This is likely to require more focused questions and may require you to take more control over the type of information sought and the way it is presented. Thus you may adopt closed questions which encourage a brief and specific answer. These are best used when you want to focus on a particular point or clarify an issue. In interviews they can be used once you have identified the relevant points or narrowed the issues.

---

**Examples of closed questions**

- How much rent do you pay per month?
- What is your neighbour called?
- What is your full address?
- What exactly did she say to you?
- Can you provide an example of your landlord's abusive behaviour?

---

To avoid your client providing information in a disorganised manner, once you have a fair understanding of the nature of the problem, you may want to guide your client with focused questions. You may be able to plan many of these questions in advance if you have been provided with some basic information prior to your interview. If not, you will need to listen carefully and plan your questions as you go.

Once you have finished asking your questions, take a moment to review your interview plan to check whether your client has answered all the questions you had previously considered relevant. If there is anything missing then you can go through this with your client.

Clients will often refer to people or places, not realising that you do not know who or where they are. Do not be afraid or embarrassed to ask, as these details could be important to the case.

## Clarification

It is important to summarise your understanding of your client's problem at appropriate points during the interview. Alternatively, you may wish to do this once you have finished asking your questions.

'So, as I understand it, the facts of your case are …'

It is important at this stage to clarify any inconsistencies in your client's instructions or resolve anything you are not sure about. Do not be afraid to query any inconsistencies. You may not feel comfortable doing this in your early initial interviews, but it is better you do this from the outset rather than waiting until a later date. Whatever you do, do not let inconsistencies go unchallenged as you can guarantee that your opponent or a judge will spot them. If you are aware of the problems in your case at an early stage then these can be addressed to minimise any adverse impact. Often, inconsistencies are due to confusion on your client's part and, therefore, when your client is forced to focus on the facts, he or she will remember what happened.

If your client is unclear about any facts, it is important that you do not lead him or her. Some clients' instructions may be influenced by the impact of your advice on their case. For example, in a criminal case, a client may ask whether it is better if he or she were already holding the knife, or went to get the knife, when the victim was stabbed following an argument. In this scenario, the facts may have a huge impact on potential defences available to your client. It is therefore important that the client provides you with his or her version of the facts, and that you do not suggest a version of the facts for your client to adopt.

You should ensure that you know your client's objectives by the end of the interview, as this will be the focus of your subsequent work. If your client has not made this clear during the course of the interview, ask your client what he or she wants to achieve. Some clients present you with a long factual background to a case but do not know what they actually want. Some clients may just want an apology, whilst others want compensation. If you know what your client wants, you may be able to save yourself hours of needless work.

## Explaining procedure and client care

Once you have obtained all the factual information from your client, you should then discuss any important procedural matters and deal with issues such as client care. You may choose to do this at the start of the interview, but clients are often keen to discuss their problem, which is why it is advisable to leave this information to this stage.

Your client should be given basic information about how your service works. You should also explain the limits of your involvement with the case, and funding options available to the client. Clients are more likely to retain the information that you provide at this stage, as they are no longer concerned about getting the problem off their chest.

Remember that this may be the first time your client has sought legal assistance, so you should explain matters in an accessible way. Do not feel that this is just a formality and can therefore be rushed. Client care is very important and you are required to explain certain matters for good reason. See **7.5** for further details on client care information.

## Closing

You should close the interview by giving a clear indication of what will happen next so your client is not left in limbo. Remind your client what you have said you will do (if anything), what is expected of the client (for example, he or she may need to provide certain documents) and give a timescale for your next contact.

## Dealing with documents

Before your client leaves, you may wish to copy any relevant documents he or she has brought in so you can return the originals there and then. Ideally this should only be done if the amount of documentation is manageable, otherwise your client may be waiting for an unduly long time. If your client has brought in copious documentation, you may want to arrange a further appointment when your client can return to collect the paperwork once you have finished copying it.

## 6.5 Advice interviews

As the title suggests, the objective of this type of interview is to advise clients of their legal rights and the options available to them. As with initial interviews, there are distinct stages:

## Welcome

Even though you have already met your client at the initial interview, you should build on the rapport that has already been established. It is also possible, of course, that you are picking a case up from a fellow student and that the advice interview is your first contact with the client, in which case all that was said above about first contact will be relevant.

## Introduction

You should outline the proposed structure of the interview and what you intend to cover. As part of the interview, it can also be useful to explain what action you have taken since your last contact with your client.

Given that you are providing advice tailored to your client's situation, you should be confident that the facts on which your advice is based are correct, having confirmed them with your client after the initial interview. Before explaining your advice, it can be useful to recap the facts on which you have based your advice.

At this stage, it is not unusual for clients to provide new information or modify their initial instructions. If this happens, you may need to speak to your supervisor. Alternatively, you may decide to continue with the interview but make it clear that the advice is based on your initial understanding of the facts. If you opt for the latter option, you should revise your advice as necessary when confirming it in writing.

## Providing information

This is perhaps the section of the interview about which you will be most nervous. It will involve you doing most of the talking and you may be required to explain complex points at length.

### What should you advise on?

Your client will want you to explain his or her legal position and so you should avoid providing statements of the law in general. Having set out his or her legal rights, your client will then want to know what options are available and the pros and cons of each. When advising your client of the courses of action, you should also explain the potential consequences of the alternatives, including the likely benefits, prospects of success, costs and risks. Without this information, your client will not be in a position to make an informed decision as to how he or she wishes to proceed.

### Providing complex advice

Explaining complex legal issues can be difficult. If the advice or area of law is very complex, you may want to set out the advice in a letter and send this to your client prior to your meeting. You can then use the interview to discuss and clarify the finer points.

### Giving clients advice that they do not want to hear

Every legal advisor at some point must tell a client that he or she does not have a case or is unlikely to succeed. Whilst this may not be what the client wants to hear, he or she must be appropriately advised to avoid wasting time and incurring considerable expense in pursuing a case which has no realistic prospects of success.

However, you must also balance this against the fact that you are providing an opinion, not an absolute statement of fact. Many people have been told that they are unlikely to be successful and have gone on to succeed at court or tribunal. You must therefore exercise caution in your advice. Solicitors will therefore usually adopt phrases such as 'reasonable prospects of success' or 'low prospects of success'. These phrases provide your client with your opinion as to the likely outcome of your case, whilst leaving room for you to be wrong. Ultimately it is up to your client whether to pursue a case, even if it is hopeless. However, your client will at least pursue the matter with his or her eyes open. There is also a great sense of satisfaction if you achieve a result for a client who had limited prospects of success.

When providing your advice to your client, you should ensure that you explain the rationale for your opinion. For example, if there is adverse case law or legislation, you should explain the law and why it may have a negative impact on your client's case.

You can temper unfavourable advice by carefully managing the tone with which it is conveyed. See the section on empathy at **6.7** below.

### A note on language

If you are providing your client with advice during the interview, you should remember that your client may not understand legal terminology and therefore you will need to use appropriate language. It is important to gauge your client's level of understanding and to use tailored language, as you do not want to patronise your client at one level and you do not want to appear pompous at another level. You should also ask your client whether he or she understands what you have told him or her. However, you may want to exercise some caution as clients may tell you that they understand, when in fact they do not.

Whilst you should avoid using legalisms as much as possible, sometimes it is unavoidable. If you use any legal terminology, you should explain the meaning to your client.

### Clarification

Allow time for your client to digest, question and clarify any of the information you have provided.

### Obtaining instructions

Having listened to the information, your client may or may not be in a position to confirm what he or she wants to happen next or the preferred course of action. This stage of the interview may feel more like a conversation where you discuss and weigh up the legal and practical aspects.

You should not force your client into making a decision at this point. Many clients will need time to consider their options and may wish to discuss matters with family or friends. If your client is unable to provide instructions, you should indicate a timescale by which they should contact you with instructions. Sometimes clients will make a snap decision and you may wish to encourage them to go away and think about the matter where you feel they have reacted hastily.

Once you have provided your client with advice on his or her case, the decision as to how to proceed must be your client's decision. It is not your role to tell clients what they must do; it is your role to advise them of their options. If your client chooses a particular course of action then you should comply with his or her instructions, even if you do not agree. The only circumstance in which you do not need to follow an instruction is where this would conflict with an overriding professional or legal obligation, or where the instructions are outside the scope of your retainer. In such cases, your client should be advised why you cannot take a particular course of conduct and be allowed to proceed on his or her own or with alternative representation.

### Closing/next steps

When bringing the meeting to an end, you should confirm the next steps. This will usually involve explaining that you will confirm the advice in a letter. At other times, you may need to reassure your client that you will be in touch having conducted any further research required. Alternatively it may be case of waiting for further instructions before you can progress the case.

## 6.6 Planning your interview

Whilst it is perfectly natural to feel nervous prior to your first interview, planning and preparing properly can help you approach the interview with a certain degree of confidence.

Having established the purpose of the interview, you can begin to prepare a plan which will ensure that you know how to guide the interview and cover all of the necessary points. It is very easy, particularly during your early interviews, to miss out vital information or to forget to ask an important question. The plan is also useful for your supervisor as he or she can check what you will be saying throughout the course of the interview. A template interview plan can be found overleaf.

Your plan should set out the main points that must be addressed during the course of the interview. For example, during an initial interview, you are likely to provide your client with some basic information about your clinic or pro bono scheme and explain the basis upon which you will be acting. You should also note the appropriate questions you will need to ask your client. This assists in ensuring that you obtain all the relevant information during the interview. If you are providing your client with advice during the interview, you should outline the advice on the plan.

Many students who prepare interview plans fall into the trap of preparing a script which results in the interview sounding artificial. It can also give the impression that you lack confidence, which is not the best start to the relationship. If the interview is scripted, you may fall into difficulty if your client is unwilling to stick to the order of your script. Worse still, your client may just read the script from the other side of the table and not listen to you.

Your interview plan should therefore constitute a list of the important matters that need to be raised. This ensures that these points are mentioned, whilst allowing the interview to flow naturally. Where you are interviewing with another student, your plan should be clearly divided and you may wish to highlight who is to say what. You may want to conduct a practice interview to become adept at using your plan prior to the real thing. This is particularly advisable if you are conducting the interview with a fellow student, so that your handovers are seamless and you do not inadvertently cover each other's parts.

## Interview plan

Client name:                                           Date of Interview:         Time:

**1 Introductions/icebreaker**

**2 Purpose of the interview**
- Explain the aim of the interview [find out the facts of the problem/provide advice/ discuss the forthcoming court hearing]
- Set out any limitations [cannot provide advice/cannot confirm that you can take on the case at this stage, etc]

**3 Structure of the interview**
- Outline structure
- Obtain information about the problem
- Provide information about the clinic
- Go through any relevant documentation
- Answer any questions or queries

**4 Obtain information about problem**
- Ask client to outline the problem in his or her own words
- Questions:
  - [Insert specific questions relevant to your client's case]
  - Establish date of cause of action
  - Events leading up to the cause of action
  - Time, dates, places, names and addresses of parties and any third parties clearly recorded
  - What was said and by whom. Where and when?
  - Name and address of proposed defendant
  - Details of witnesses? Names, addresses, contact telephone numbers
  - What your client wants to achieve – refund, compensation, apology?
  - Has your client already instructed a solicitor?

**5 Clinic information**
- Basic information
  [Obtain client's basic details – name, address, contact details, etc]
- Clinic procedures and policies
  [Go through the information about your clinic and how it operates]
- Funding
  Explain funding, including disbursements
  [Go through funding information checklist]
- Complaints procedure
  Explain that you have a written complaints procedure available on request. Explain that, in first instance, the client should speak to [student or supervisor]. After that, any complaints should be directed to clinical director

**6 Retainer**
- This is the document that confirms that the clinic will act for the client and that the client agrees to it acting for him or her ▶

- Highlight key terms of retainer

**7 Evidential documents/ID**
- Explain that you need to take a photocopy of the documents for file

**8 Next steps**
- Explain what will happen next
[For example that you will discuss the matter with your supervisor/you will be in touch to confirm whether the case can be taken on/confirm you will write a letter of advice, etc]

**9 Questions and clarification**
- Invite client to ask any questions

**10 Closing**
- Thank client for attending and confirm the next steps to be taken and timescale for next contact

## 6.7 Rapport building, body language and other subtleties

Asking the right questions and following your plan are not the only ingredients to a successful interview. Your interviews should serve to build and maintain a professional relationship and establish a good rapport with your client. To this end, there are a range of other non-tangible aspects to master:

### Listening skills

It is important that your client knows that you are listening to what he or she is saying. It is very difficult to open up to someone who looks disinterested, and therefore it is unlikely that you will receive full instructions if you are not seen as paying attention to your client. You can demonstrate this with gestures, such as nodding, and reassuring comments, such as 'yes' and 'I understand'. At the end of the interview, you should also clarify your understanding of the facts or instructions received.

Similarly, you need ensure your client is listening to you. It is a good idea to check your client has understood what you have said at appropriate intervals during the interview. On occasions, clients may state that they have understood the information or advice you have provided, but it is clear from their body language or tone of voice that this is not the case. If you find yourself in this position, you may wish to remind clients that it is important that they have understood so that they can make informed decisions, and you should provide a carefully worded summary at the end when wrapping up the interview.

## Empathy

It is also an essential skill to empathise with your client. This should be distinguished from sympathy, as you must keep a professional relationship. Empathy is about understanding your client's issues and concerns, which will assist you in forming a good relationship. It is not necessary to like your client, or even to agree with his or her point of view, but you must be able to act in your client's best interests, and to do this you must understand your client. Be careful how you convey empathy – it should not sound patronising.

## Eye contact and note taking

You may be anxious to ensure that you make a note of everything your client says. This can result in your head dropping down over your notes. This may give your client the impression, albeit wrong, that you are not listening. Therefore, whilst you obviously need to look down to make notes, you should still maintain a good level of eye contact throughout the meeting.

 **Top tip**

If your client is speaking too fast, ask him or her to slow down; you may think you will be able to remember what was said, but in long interviews it is unlikely and risky.

Effective note taking is a skill in itself. However, it is necessary to accurately record the interview. It is useful to develop a form of shorthand so you can note down the key points that have been made. Remember that you are unlikely to be able to make verbatim notes and engage with your client. If interviewing as a pair, agree a note-taking procedure.

 **Top tip**

A sensible arrangement when interviewing in pairs is to take turns at note taking. When not speaking, take notes so that your colleague can speak and maintain eye contact with your client. When it is your turn to speak, your colleague can assume note-taking duties.

## Control

You must keep control of the interview as clients have a tendency to digress and spend time telling you irrelevant things. This can often be attributed to the client not knowing what is relevant. A common mistake of students is to allow clients to deviate from the relevant material due to a fear of appearing rude. This does not help either you or your client, and there are various techniques for steering the interview back in the right direction. For example, you could say to your client that you understand but would like more information about something he or she has already discussed. This demonstrates that you are interested in your client's problem and you have been listening to him or her. Alternatively, you could ask your client questions about relevant pieces of information that will hopefully bring him or her back on track.

Another tactic is to use a summarising intervention. If a client is rambling, you could intervene and say, 'so, just to summarise, your concern is about ... now can I ask you to specifically deal with ...'. This stops your client talking for too long and focuses his or her mind on a particular matter.

It can be useful to state the duration of the interview at the outset and politely remind your client that the interview is time limited if he or she insists on deviating from the point.

It is quite rare, but sometimes you may have to explicitly ask a client to stop speaking and to answer specific questions. You need to deal with these situations sensitively, but you could say, 'Sorry, can I just stop you there for a moment?', 'I understand your overall concerns, but I have some specific questions I would like you to deal with so that my notes are complete ...', 'My first question is ...'

### Using pauses

In a conversation it is natural to have pauses. For some reason, in an interview setting, these pauses can seem like an age. However, both you and your client may need thinking time, or a period to digest the question or information. If there is a short pause, do not feel tempted to speak to fill the gap. Longer pauses may be an indication that your client has not understood or is unable to answer your question, and you may need to rephrase it.

### Managing client expectations

It is important that you are clear about what you can and cannot do for your client. This requires you to phrase your advice carefully and not raise your client's expectations. Whilst you may be eager to please, do not promise anything that you might not be able to deliver, or inadvertently mislead your client.

## (6.8)  Interview dos and don'ts

**Do**

- ✔ Appear confident (even if you are not)
- ✔ Smile and put the client at ease
- ✔ Be empathetic
- ✔ Show interest in your client's problem
- ✔ Listen carefully
- ✔ Vary your questioning technique
- ✔ Control the direction of the interview
- ✔ Take careful notes
- ✔ Ask for clarification if required
- ✔ Summarise where appropriate

**Don't**

- ✘ Don't ever go into an interview unprepared
- ✘ Don't be late or let the interview overrun
- ✘ Don't become too familiar – retain a professional attitude
- ✘ Don't just sit there and write notes – be proactive
- ✘ Don't doodle on your pad while your client is speaking – this indicates that you are not listening to what he or she is saying
- ✘ Don't let your client take over the interview
- ✘ Don't be afraid to ask awkward questions
- ✘ Don't be tempted to fill in the silent gaps
- ✘ Don't patronise or otherwise offend your client
- ✘ Don't go beyond your remit – know your advice, state your limits and stick to them

After the interview

If you have made notes throughout the course of the interview, it is likely that they will be very rough. It is therefore important to draft an attendance note, accurately recording what happened in the interview. The purpose of the note is to ensure that anyone picking it up will know what your client has said and has been advised. It is therefore important that the note is comprehensive. Attendance notes should also be typed if possible so that they can be easily read without the need to decipher handwriting. Further guidance on attendance notes can be found at **7.3**.

It is also good practice to write a letter following the interview, confirming your instructions and the advice that has been given. This avoids the risk of a misunderstanding between yourself and your client. Again, this is covered in more detail in **Chapter 7**.

 Reflecting on your interview

When you have completed the interview, you should reflect upon your performance.

Some clinics provide facilities to record the interview. It is useful, as a reflective process, to watch the interview and analyse your performance. You may pick up upon subconscious habits, such as playing with your pen or saying 'okay' after every sentence. People often have these habits, but it is only when you become aware of them that you can try to eradicate them from your performance. Equally, watching your interview could demonstrate that it was better than you thought it was.

---

**Suggested starter questions for interview reflections**

1 What was the best thing about this interview?
2 What was the worst thing about this interview?
3 What different types of questioning technique did you adopt and why?
4 What techniques did you adopt to establish a rapport with the client and how successful do you think these were?
5 What non-verbal forms of communication did you adopt and were you conscious of these at the time?
6 What comments do you have on the clarity of your questions and/or explanations?
7 Were there times when you felt your client took control? If so, why might this have happened and how can this be avoided in future?
8 Did you ramble on? If so, what was the cause of this?
9 Did you feel at ease; do you think your client did? What factors might have influenced how you and your client felt?
10 How do you think your client might have felt about his or her experience following the interview?

---

The skill of reflection is considered in detail in **Chapter 12**.

##  Common problems

Preparing for the unexpected should help you conduct your interview smoothly in the event of any unplanned questions or situations arising. You will find below some of the common issues that can occur.

### Your client has asked a question and you do not know the answer

There is a public perception that legal advisors should know the answer to every question and, if they do not, that they are not very good. If you do not know the answer to a question, advise your client that this is a complex area of law, or that the law is often evolving and therefore you need to check and get back to them. Your client is likely to appreciate the right answer after some research rather than the wrong answer immediately. You should never guess the answer and, in any event, you may not be permitted to discuss matters with your client which have not previously been approved by your supervisor.

### Your client wants a definite answer on the prospects of success

Clients are often frustrated that legal advisors are unable to state whether their case will succeed. You should advise clients that it is your role to advise them on the strengths and weaknesses of their case so that they can make an informed decision as to how they should proceed. As such, you can only advise on whether they have a strong case or a weak case. You must always frame your advice on prospects of success carefully. You may choose to use language such as 'reasonable' to convey the possible chances of success. For example, 'we think your case has reasonable prospects of success'. If your client pushes you for a definitive answer, you should gently point out that you simply do not know what the outcome of the case will be as you do not make the decision – that is the function of a judge.

### Your client is aggressive with you

Some clients can become aggressive, which can lead to you feeling intimidated. In most instances, this is due to frustration borne out of their problem and dissatisfaction with the legal system. Clients may view you as part of that system and therefore direct the frustration at you.

If you are faced with such frustration, you should attempt to pacify your client. Empathise and acknowledge that you understand his or her concerns or frustration. A useful technique is to remind your client that you are on his or her side and, whilst you understand the frustration, the legal system has procedures in place which must be followed. In advising your client of this, you should detach yourself from the system and be seen to be working on your client's behalf.

If your client becomes threatening, or you are worried that matters may escalate, you may need to leave the room and seek assistance from your supervisor.

### Your client uses inappropriate language

In the course of an interview, your client may use inappropriate language or make remarks that you find offensive. It is important that this behaviour is not tolerated, as you should not have to work in an uncomfortable environment. It may be a one-off, in which case you may let the matter go on the first occasion. If it continues, you may choose to discuss the matter with your supervisor or raise the issue with your client direct.

If the situation does not improve, you can advise your client that you may have to stop working on his or her case. This is usually sufficient to stop this conduct occurring in future.

### Your client becomes very upset

Legal problems can be very sensitive and frustrating. Clients inevitably become emotionally attached to their cases, as the outcome may have a significant impact on their lives. For example, in a family case, the result could deprive a parent of access to his or her child, or, in a criminal matter, the outcome may mean a period of imprisonment and loss of reputation. It is therefore understandable that clients at times become upset when discussing their cases. In some instances, this emotion can turn into tears. In an interview situation, you may find this awkward, unnerving and/or disconcerting.

If your client becomes emotional, there are several ways to handle the situation. You could decide to carry on regardless, glossing over the fact that your client is distressed. This is not necessarily the best course of action as your client is unlikely to listen fully to whatever you proceed to say. A preferable option would be to pause and allow your client time to compose him- or herself. If your client is too upset to continue, you may have to halt the interview and rearrange it for a later date. It is always useful to have some tissues with you in an interview.

## 6.12 Summary

Interviewing is a crucially important skill, with many components to balance. The interview sets the scene for the professional relationship to follow and is the basis of the client's version of events and his or her instructions to you. In a relatively short period of time, you need to ascertain and record a coherent factual account and (in advice interviews) give clear and accessible legal advice based on these facts. This is no easy task and is further complicated by the emotional impact of the case on the client and the intensity of having to explain often sensitive personal matters to a stranger. You need to deploy a wide range of technical skills and personal sensitivities in order successfully to conduct an interview. You may never become a perfect interviewer but, if you continually reflect on your performance and on how you interact with your client, you will always improve.

 Further reading

## Introductory

**Boyle, F et al,** *A Practical Guide to Lawyering Skills*, **3rd edn (Cavendish Publishing, 2005)**
　　Chapter 8 deals with interviewing and includes sample interview plans and self-assessment checklists. There is a useful self-assessment checklist at p 250 and sample interview plans relating to a personal injury matter and a plea before venue hearing.

**Webb, J et al,** *Lawyers' Skills* **2010–11 (Oxford University Press, 2010)**
　　A Legal Practice Course text that provides guidance on various legal skills including interviewing and advising in Chapter 2.

## Intermediate

**Maughan, C and Webb, J,** *Lawyering Skills and the Legal Process (Law in Context)* **(Cambridge University Press, 2005)**
　　Chapter 3 covers all aspects of communication including barriers to effective communication. Chapter 5 addresses interviewing in some detail.

## Advanced

**Law Society's Initial Interviews Practice Note**
　　In force from 20 May 2009, this Practice Note sets out good practice and the areas to be covered in an initial interview. Whilst aimed at practising solicitors, it is a useful guide to expected standards and content.
　　See www.lawsociety.org.uk/productsandservices/practicenotes/initialinterviews/2816.article.

**Solicitors Regulation Authority Legal Practice Course Outcomes**
　　Page 19 sets out the interviewing and advising standards expected on completion of the Legal Practice Course. These are a good benchmark even if you are not yet at the stage of postgraduate vocational study.
　　See www.sra.org.uk/documents/students/lpc/outcomes.pdf.

 Activities

## Activity 1: Fact-finding flair

The purpose of this exercise is to develop the skill of finding accurate information. As a group you should pick a general topic, such as holidays or films.

Pair up and spend 5 minutes obtaining as much relevant information about the topic from your partner as possible. You should then switch, so that the interviewer becomes the interviewee. At the conclusion of the interviews, the interviewer must present the findings of their interview to the rest of the group, who will be permitted to ask questions of the interviewer. The interviewee must then report on accuracy of the presentation.

## Activity 2: Advice acumen

Read **Chapters 7** and **8** and the practical legal research report on Nicola Ridley's housing dispute (available on the Companion Website). Prepare an advice interview plan for Nicola's case. Consider how you can effectively deal with the various aspects of her case and the pros and cons of the various courses of action available to her.

# 7 Legal writing and drafting

> 'Lawyers try to cover every contingency,
> but in doing so they get lost in obscurity.'

> Lord Denning (1982 Plain English Awards)

## 7.1 Introduction

Lord Denning's words perhaps explain why the language of lawyers is characterised as lengthy and convoluted. This perception of the typical lawyer, and lawyer-speak, colours student attitudes to legal writing, and many attempt to emulate that stilted, Dickensian style of prose when composing their first letters or statements of case.

However, the fundamental components of writing are clarity, precision and tailoring. Set aside any preconceptions you have of writing in a legalistic style and start with a blank sheet. Decide what you want to say, say it, then stop writing. Review, and cut out all extraneous words ruthlessly. These basic rules will take you a long way towards achieving a good writing style.

Communications in law tend to be categorised as either legal writing or drafting. Legal writing relates primarily to letters, whereas drafting relates to formal documents such as statements of case and contracts. You can read extensively on these two areas, but the aim of this chapter is to introduce the main types of written communication you may encounter in your clinical and pro bono activities. It also provides a brief reminder of the key writing conventions and rules.

This chapter will continue with the Nicola Ridley case study introduced in the previous chapter. You will recall that she is worried about being evicted, and her landlord is being abusive to her. Her next-door neighbour is leaving a mess in the yard, causing a rat infestation. Additionally, one of her windows is rotten, the flat is draughty and damp in winter and her sofa has been ruined by mould.

First, though, there is a need to address some fundamental principles.

## 7.2 Back to basics

You are probably already quite familiar with academic writing from your previous legal studies, eg essays, coursework, reports etc. This type of writing is very different from the techniques required in a clinic and pro bono context. However, the basic principles regarding grammar, layout and so on apply equally. Below is a brief reminder of the key conventions that you should bear in mind when composing any type of written document.

## Spelling, punctuation and grammar

Poor written standards reflect badly on the writer and the organisation from which the document originates. In a legal context, if a client receives a poorly drafted document, he or she may doubt your capabilities as an adviser if you have an inability to write basic English. It is therefore vital you adopt a good standard of writing. If you have a condition, for example dyslexia, which affects your literacy skills, then consult your supervisor for advice.

Accurate spelling is extremely important in legal writing. Modern word processing packages all have spell-checking facilities, which can certainly be used but cannot be relied on to identify all errors, so a careful proof-read is essential. It is poor practice to rely on your supervisor to check your spelling and grammar. When you send a draft letter to him or her, it should be the best you can produce and should have been carefully checked.

## Commas

The comma signifies a pause, but can also change the meaning:

'The barrister said the judge had made an error of judgement.'
'The barrister, said the judge, had made an error of judgement.'

Who made the error of judgement?

Often students use a comma where instead there should be a full stop or a conjunction. For example, 'We have taken a full statement from Miss Finn, she confirms she is prepared to attend court if necessary.'

This should be changed to either, 'We have taken a full statement from Miss Finn **and** she is prepared to attend court if necessary.' or 'We have taken a full statement from Miss Finn. She is prepared to attend court if necessary.'

## Capital letters

The rule is that proper nouns (individual titles or names) start with a capital letter (Newcastle County Court, Judge Jackson, Solicitor General) but common nouns do not (the county court, judge, solicitor).

## Apostrophes

These can cause no end of difficulty, so if you are not sure how and when to use them, make it a priority to find out. The most common error is inappropriate use of an apostrophe when signifying the plural, for example, *a firm of solicitor's* should be written as, *a firm of solicitors.*

Several texts deal with punctuation and grammar in detail, some of which are listed at the end of this chapter if you need a quick refresher in this area.

## Language

Language plays a vital role in written communication; the wrong word or unclear expression can have serious consequences. In clinic and pro bono work you will need to develop a different way of communicating; the style you have developed for academic essays is ill suited to letters, and to some extent practical legal research reports. You must therefore be mindful that what you write, and how you write it, needs to be carefully tailored to the reader. Your choice of language should enable the recipient to understand the information provided, not confuse him or her further.

## Ambiguity

You can easily understand what you have drafted; after all, you wrote it. However, do not assume that the reader will interpret your language and meaning in the same way.

You can avoid ambiguity by using the active instead of passive. For example: 'A claim will be filed at court.' Who is filing it? Which party? Why not say, 'I will file your claim at court.' Or better still, in case the person receiving the letter does not know what filing means, simply state, 'I will send your claim to the court.'

'You will be met at reception and brought to the office.' By whom? Why not, 'Our administrator, Laura, will meet you at reception and bring you to the office.'

Check carefully to ensure any ambiguity is eliminated so that there is no scope for misunderstanding. If in doubt, ask someone else to read over what you have written and check that his or her understanding matches your own. It is good practice to invite the recipient of your correspondence to contact you for clarification if anything is unclear. A simple 'Please do not hesitate to contact me if you would like me to clarify any matters raised in this letter' will suffice.

## Use of Latin

As a general rule, avoid using Latin words or phrases, and never use them when communicating with clients. Whilst Latin phrases can on occasions be adopted as a form of legal shorthand, such usage is often seen as elitist. Look at these example phrases. Would you ever need to use the Latin version?

*ab initio* – from the outset
*per se* – in each and every case
*in camera* – proceedings conducted in private
*inter alia* – among others

The same applies to legal jargon and words such as 'hereinafter', 'abovementioned', 'aforesaid', 'whosoever'. They rarely enhance meaning and can appear archaic and obscure.

## Avoid double negatives

Steer clear of double negatives as they can be confusing, as illustrated in the following sentence:

'No application will be approved unless the board reviews the application and finds that it is not lacking any requisite materials.'

This could be amended to make the meaning clearer:

'Applications will only be approved once the board has reviewed the application and finds that it contains all requisite materials.'

## Tone

Tone is perhaps one of the most difficult aspects to master when you first begin legal writing. It is important to realise that the way in which you convey information depends very much on the purpose and type of document you are preparing. Your tone and language will need to be tailored according to the objective to be achieved. It is therefore pertinent to determine the purpose of the document before you begin drafting it. For example, is the letter intended to advise, persuade or merely inform?

Letters to clients have a very different tone to correspondence with an opponent. The former will generally be warm (to enhance client relations) whilst the latter will be formal and firm, yet polite (given the need to defend your client's interests).

## Style

Everyone has their own style of writing including, where applicable, the person who approves your written communications. If you are working in a clinic or on placement, that organisation may have its own house style – a set of rules on how written work should be composed or presented. If your organisation has a house style, ensure you follow it.

Alternatively, you may need to adapt to the style of the person who is approving your work in order to reduce the number and extent of corrections required and ultimately to speed up the approval process. Some supervisors allow students to develop their own writing style but will still ensure the basic standards are met before approving written work, particularly if the document is being placed on file, or being sent to a client or third party.

As a general guide, you should avoid flowery language, not be overly wordy and ensure your expression remains professional at all times, even if you have developed a good working relationship with the recipient.

## Layout and presentation

It is important that the document is set out in such a way that it invites the recipient to read it. This is particularly important in respect of lengthy documents, such as reports and long, complex letters of advice. You could consider whether there is a ready-made template on your word processing software which can lend a professional appearance to your documents. For example, many packages have templates for memos and reports. There are several mechanisms you can employ to ensure your work is appealing to the eye, yet maintains a professional presentation.

- Use short sentences – long sentences can become complex and therefore confusing.
- One concept per paragraph – deal with each point in a separate paragraph to ensure it is understood, before moving on to the next issue.
- Leave lots of white space. Dense blocks of text are very hard to read. Use indentation, numbering, bullet points, line spacing and so forth to break up the content into digestible chunks.
- Headings – use headings and subheadings to guide the reader through the key points of the document.

### Proofreading and reviewing your work

You should take responsibility for proofreading your work, even if the document in question requires approval from your supervisor. This involves more than using the spell-checking facility or relying on your computer to underline any suspect grammar. You must read over the work, as not all errors will be highlighted by a spell-check. Common errors which escape your computer's software include 'compliant' (when you mean 'complaint'), 'trail' (instead of 'trial') and 'effect' (when it should be 'affect'). In addition, beware that many spell-checking facilities adopt American English as the default language.

- Take a break – proofreading your work immediately after you have completed drafting a document reduces the efficiency of your proofreading skills. Take a short break and review the document with a fresh pair of eyes.
- Even if you have checked the letter on your computer, review the final hard copy thoroughly to make sure the lay-out fits onto the letter head.
- Double-check all information such as figures and dates.
- Check attachments and make sure they *are* attached.
- Check the date, address and that the document is signed appropriately.

### 7.3 Types of documents

Below is an overview of the main written documents you may be asked to prepare as part of your clinic or pro bono activities. Letters will be dealt with separately. You have seen above that different organisations have different approaches to written communications; therefore the information below should be considered as a guide rather than as prescriptive.

### Attendance notes/action notes

As the name suggests, this document records any action which has been taken or any instructions received or information given during client meetings or interviews. They are used primarily for casework, but you may wish to keep a note of what has happened or been agreed for any projects you are undertaking. However, the usual format for this latter type of activity will be minutes of the meeting.

#### Why are attendance notes so important?

It is essential that anyone working on, or who has oversight of, the file can clearly see what action has been taken and the current state of play. Attendance notes achieve this objective, but only if they are detailed and kept in a well-ordered file. It may sound hard-hearted, but if you were knocked over by a bus, and one of your colleagues or your supervisor picked up your file, would they be able to tell at a glance what needs doing and what stage the case is at?

Attendance notes are a vital part of protective lawyering, a concept which involves you keeping a clear and accurate record of your actions to reduce the chance of a client successfully complaining about your work. At a later date (and it could be years later) your client may decide that he or she has not been properly advised. The file would then be retrieved from storage, and your attendance notes and letters reviewed. These can then be crucial in any negligence action. It is vital that attendance notes are detailed: it will be extremely difficult to recall exactly what you did or said some years previously.

Although it may not be as important in a clinic or pro bono environment, in a solicitors' practice your attendance note is likely to be used as a basis for recovering costs, either from your client or your opponent. Should a client seek to query or challenge the bill, your attendance note may need to be consulted as a means of justifying the work undertaken and the length of time spent on the matter.

### Preparing attendance notes

Usually, attendance notes start out as handwritten notes, which are then typed up into a formal and legible document. There is no hard and fast rule that all notes must be typed, but it goes without saying that they must be legible. It is a good idea to establish whether your organisation has a policy as to whether notes should be typed. If there is, you should aim to type these up as soon as possible while the interview is fresh in your mind; otherwise your detailed notes may be indecipherable when you come to type them up at a later date.

Attendance notes should record every action taken, be it a case discussion with your supervisor during which you have agreed on a course of action, the fact that you have undertaken research on the matter, or the details of a telephone conversation or interview. For example, if you see your client and advise him or her that there is a strong risk that he or she may lose the case, based on the evidence, but the client instructs you to proceed regardless, your file note should show this discussion and not just the outcome.

You should also write to your client confirming these instructions. Then, if your client should at a later date allege that you have misled him or her, or given him or her false hope as to the strength of the case, then the file will clearly show the true position.

The attendance note will need to include:

- the name of the client and any file reference number;
- the name of the person making the note;
- the person or body contacted (for example, the client, opposing solicitors, a witness, the court);
- the type of contact or action (telephone call in or out, interview, research, drafting, attendance at court etc);
- the date and time spent working on the matter;
- relevant details/information – these should be set out in a logical and coherent order.

The attendance note recording the initial interview with Nicola Ridley might look as follows:

---

**Attendance Note**

Client: Nicola Ridley     Action taken by: Sarah Parker & Ben Green

Date: 1/12/2010     Start time: 10.00     End time: 10.36

Time spent: 36 minutes (6 units)

Action taken: Interview

We welcomed the client (NR) and introduced ourselves. Advised NR of details of the clinic, the retainer, and client information including the complaints procedure.

The client has a problem with her landlord. She lives in a nice area and rent is very cheap. Her next-door neighbour is a problem – drinks and leaving a mess, there are rats in the yard and the client has seen one in her own kitchen. NR has asked the neighbour to tidy up but she swears and tells our client that her boyfriend is 'into martial arts'.

One of the windows is rotten and flat is damp and draughty in winter; sofa has been wrecked by mould. NR has approached landlord but he was unpleasant and told her to leave. Client does not want to move. She has no written tenancy agreement but has been living there and paying rent monthly since April 1996. Client wants to know if landlord can evict her.

Advised client that we will be back in contact within 7 days to confirm whether we can take on her case.

---

This is a very brief example, and in practice you should have obtained more detailed information, including dates, examples of the confrontations she has had and other key facts, such as contact details for the landlord.

### Proof of evidence

A proof of evidence is a summary of the main facts, written in the form of a statement. You can use the information from your handwritten notes or attendance note to prepare a draft proof of evidence, which should be sent to the client for approval and signature. This is a useful way to ensure that you and your client are 'singing from the same hymn sheet', and could assist you if your client changes his or her instructions at a later date, possibly alleging that you have misunderstood or misrepresented him or her.

If you include a statement of truth, as shown below, then it can potentially be helpful if that person is unable to make a statement at a later date, for example if he or she was to lose capacity or die.

In creating a proof, you will be ordering the information your client gave you into a chronological account. This is useful as it can help you start to see where you may require more information. From this you can develop a time line or chronology, which can be a very useful tool for examining your client's case.

---

**Proof of Evidence**

Name: Nicola Ridley
Address: 1, Avon Street, East End, Nicetown, NZ99 9ZZ
NI Number: WK 15 27 30 C
Occupation: sales representative
Date of Interview: 1 December 2010

I, Nicola Ridley, will state as follows;

1 I am 30 years old and my date of birth is 1/1/1981.

2 I have been living in a flat rented from my landlord, Mr Atkinson, since April 1996. It is in a good area, and the rent is relatively cheap, at £200 per month. There is no written tenancy agreement.

3 I am concerned about a problem with rats. I have seen a rat in my kitchen, and I believe this is a result of my next-door neighbour failing to clear up her yard. I have seen rats in her yard. I have approached her and asked her to tidy up but she drinks a lot, swears at me, and has told me that her boyfriend is 'into martial arts'.

4 I am also concerned about the condition of the property. One of the windows is rotten. The flat is damp and draughty in winter, and my sofa has been damaged by mould. The sofa was brand new when I moved in, and I have a receipt to show that it cost £850.

5 I have approached my landlord about these issues last month but he told me I could leave. I do not want to have to move out. I want to know my rights, and in particular whether my landlord can tell me to leave.

6 I believe the facts stated in this proof of evidence are true.

Signed: *N. Ridley*
Dated: 5 December 2010

---

If you have prepared a proof like this, your attendance note could be shorter and refer to the proof for the detail of what your client has said, without repeating it in the note itself. If you do this, you must ensure the proof is actually placed on the file with the attendance note.

## Witness statements

A witness statement is a comprehensive, chronological account of all of the relevant details pertaining to a case. They are often used during civil court proceedings as evidence in chief. Given it is a legal document which could affect the success of a case, it should be prepared carefully and checked several times by the witness to ensure it is accurate and complete. Witness statements should not include legal argument – the purpose is to present facts and the witness' version of events.

In theory, statements should be drafted using the words of the witness. However, in reality, it is the role of the legal advisor to prepare the statement; therefore it is inevitable that it will not be entirely in the witness' own words. Bear in mind that the witness may be required to read the statement aloud in court, so do not include words or phrases which they would not use themselves.

Witness statements must be carefully drafted – careless wording can leave the witness open to attack if the language is ambiguous or unclear. For example, 'I *would have* provided Ms Ridley with a copy of her tenancy agreement when she moved into the property' is not the same thing as 'I *provided* Ms Ridley with a copy of her tenancy agreement when she moved in.' Such phrasing suggests the landlord is unclear or cannot accurately recollect what actually happened and could be damaging to his defence if cross-examined on this point.

As with the proof of evidence, the statement should be well ordered. Use numbered paragraphs so that the witness can be directed quickly and easily to the relevant parts of his or her statement during questioning.

### What is the difference between a proof of evidence and a witness statement?

As the proceedings progress, you will collect more detail to flesh out the original proof of evidence. For example, you will gather more detail about the damp problem, which parts of the property are affected, and any consequences of that, such as effects on your client's health, damage to any property other than the sofa, increases in heating bills. There may also be parts of the original proof that do not go on to form part of the claim, which should then be excluded. For example, the comment by the neighbour about her boyfriend may turn out to be irrelevant, and may be cut out of the final witness statement.

##  General guidance for letters

Each letter will differ in content or purpose, but there are some general points to note.

### Letter layout

The layout may seem incidental, but it is worth using a template that you follow each time you write. Your organisation or supervisor may have a preference as to how your letters should be set out. If not, choose a font and use this consistently. Times New Roman or Arial, size 12 is normally suitable.

### Opening and closing

How should you address the person you are writing to?

If writing to a client, it is 'Dear Ms Brown' or 'Dear Jane', and the letter concludes 'Yours sincerely', followed by your name.

There are divergent views on this, but when writing to a third party, such as a solicitors' firm, you generally address them as 'Dear Sirs', and conclude the letter 'Yours faithfully' with the name of your organisation underneath. If you are writing to an individual such as an unrepresented opponent, 'Dear Sir' and 'Dear Madam' can be used, and these letters will also conclude 'Yours faithfully'.

Confusion can arise where you have telephone conversations with solicitors or individuals and know them by name. It is tempting then to use their name in correspondence, but it is preferable to continue to address them as 'Dear Sirs' (in that you are addressing their firm or company) and mark at the top of the address section, 'For the Attention of Miss X'.

It is normal to use a heading which identifies what the case is about, for example:

---

Dear Sirs,

**Re: Our Client – Nicola Ridley; Your Client Harry Atkinson; Tenancy at 1 Avon Street**

We are instructed ...

---

The first paragraph should set the context. For example, if you have had recent contact with the recipient about the case, you may start by referring to that, so that he or she realises that you are confirming that interaction.

Make sure that you have included any references for the person handling the case. This could be a file number, or initials, or a combination of both.

If the matter is urgent, make sure you mark the letter as 'urgent'.

The last sentence or paragraph should confirm the next steps so that the client is not left wondering what to do. For example, 'This letter is for information only and I will be in touch to update you of any further developments'. Or, 'Before I am able to progress this matter further I would be grateful if you would provide me with the documents requested above'.

## Enclosures

If you attach enclosures with your letter, in many cases it is useful to put copies on the file with the copy letter. This ensures that if you need to check what documents have been sent, this will be clear. It is common practice to put 'Enc'. after the final signature clause, to indicate to the reader that there is an enclosure attached.

## 7.5  Client care letters

Having obtained the factual background and ascertained what assistance your client is seeking, it is usual to write to your client. The first letter should set out the terms of the retainer, confirm the instructions received and deal with various client care issues, in accordance with Rule 2 of the Solicitors' Code of Conduct. This is known as a client care letter. In practice, virtually all firms will have a template with pre-prepared clauses covering the required areas, and your organisation may use an approved template. You will need to find out what the format is for your clinic, and use this, with any additional guidance provided by your supervisor.

The more common contents of a client care letter are set out below:

### Confirm the nature of your retainer

For example, a client may come to see you with more than one issue. You need to make it clear what you advising on and what action you are agreeing to undertake. If Nicola, in addition to her landlord problems, had also told you that she had a child who had been excluded then expelled from school, and she wanted advice on this area, you would have to indicate whether you could provide advice on this matter. If you cannot act, perhaps because this is not an area that your clinic can advise on, then this should be set out clearly. Similarly, you need to make it clear if you are unable to represent the client at court should the case proceed to the commencement of court proceedings and a hearing.

### Confirm who is dealing with the case and how your client can make contact with you

One of the most common client complaints is not being able to reach their advisor, and the failure of advisors to return clients' calls. If you are only available part of the time, it may be helpful to indicate the times at which you can be contacted.

### Explain funding issues

The letter should clearly set out how the case will be funded. This applies even if you are acting pro bono. Remember to address whether any expenses or disbursements are likely to be incurred and how they will be paid. In Nicola's case, it may be necessary to obtain a surveyor's report and, if the matter proceeds to court, there may be court fees, so you would need to cover these points in your letter.

### Explain the complaints procedure

This is another professional conduct matter which needs to be dealt with at the outset (see Rule 2.05 of the Solicitors' Code of Conduct). You are also now required to provide full details of the Legal Ombudsman service.

### Explain the next steps

Confirm what steps you will take, and the steps you need your client to take, such as providing further information, and what will happen next. For example, if you have sent a proof of evidence for client approval, the letter should clearly state that you need the client to check the statement and return a signed copy to you. Alternatively, you may not need the client to do anything at this stage other than wait for you to get in touch; if this is the case, let the client know that he or she just needs to sit tight.

An example client care letter is set out opposite:

Firm's name/letterhead

Ms N. Ridley
1 Avon Street
East End
Nicetown
NZ99 9ZZ

3 December 2010

Dear Ms Ridley,

### Your tenancy at 1 Avon Street

Thank you for coming to see us on 1$^{st}$ December 2010 to discuss the problems you have been having with your tenancy.

Your case is being dealt with by Sarah Parker and Ben Green. We are the law students who will carry out the work on your case. We are under the supervision of Susan Jones who is a qualified solicitor.

### Confirmation and extent of instructions

We have discussed your case with our supervisor and confirm that we are able to take on your case to the extent that we will research and give you initial advice but cannot commit to taking any further steps on your behalf.

The terms on which we operate are set out in the attached retainer form, which is enclosed for your information. Please read this document carefully and note that we do not undertake to represent you at any court or tribunal hearing which may arise in your case unless we confirm that we can do so in writing to you.

We are instructed to advise you in connection with your potential claims in relation to your tenancy and the problems you are experiencing with your neighbour. The facts of your case are set out in the enclosed proof of evidence. We would be grateful if you could read the enclosed statement which is based on the information obtained during your interview. Please check this carefully and let us know if there are any amendments to be made. If not, then sign and return in the self-addressed envelope included for your convenience.

We are currently researching the legal issues and will contact you within the next 14 days to arrange an interview at which we will advise you further.

### Costs

As explained at the interview, we do not charge for any of the work that we do on your behalf. However, in some cases there may be fees charged by third parties, for example court fees or experts' fees, or charges for medical reports. We are unable to cover the cost of any expenses and such fees would be payable by you. However, these expenses will not be incurred without your prior approval.

If your case cannot be resolved amicably, it may be necessary to take legal action and you may be required to pay for expenses such as court fees. We will inform you in advance of any fees which are likely to arise, as your case progresses.

> **Complaints**
>
> If you have any concerns about the way in which your case is conducted then please feel free to contact our supervisor. If you are still unhappy at that stage, we have a written complaints procedure, which is available on request.
>
> If there is anything you wish to discuss you can contact us on the telephone number above. If we are not available you can leave a message and we will contact you as soon as possible.
>
> Thank you for your instructions in this case and we look forward to receiving your signed statement.
>
> Yours sincerely,
>
>
>
> Sarah Parker and Ben Green

##  Advice letters

Once you have researched the legal issues relevant to your client's case, you will want to advise your client of your findings. This can be done in the form of an advice interview or by letter. If you provide advice by means of an interview, it is good practice to confirm that advice in writing.

If you are providing detailed advice, you could introduce by briefly outlining the facts. For example: 'You booked a holiday to Turkey but, due to adverse weather, your flight was cancelled. You are seeking advice on recovering the cost of the holiday, and whether you may be entitled to any compensation for the inconvenience.'

If it is a complex piece, perhaps advising a client on a number of possible options, or a complex legal claim, then it is worthwhile jotting down the key points that you want to get across. Use headings for each key area, and break the text into paragraphs.

Using the example of Nicola Ridley's case, you could look at:

- the status of the tenancy and how she can be evicted;
- staying in the flat and not being evicted, and the landlord's abusive behaviour;
- windows and damp/mould and draughts;
- rat infestation.

Firm's name/letterhead

Ms N. Ridley
1 Avon Street
East End
Nicetown
NZ99 9ZZ

16 December 2010

Dear Ms Ridley,

### Your tenancy at 1 Avon Street

We write following your appointment on 1st April. We have now researched the legal issues in your case, and our advice is set out below.

### Do I still have a tenancy even though there is no written tenancy agreement?

For tenancies of less than three years, it is not essential for the agreement to be in writing. Therefore, if the circumstances indicate that you have a tenancy, for example if you have been paying rent to your landlord, the court is likely to accept that you did have a tenancy.

### Can your landlord evict you?

The date on which your tenancy started is very important. You stated that your tenancy started in April 1996. If your landlord also served you with a valid notice, stating that your tenancy was an assured shorthold tenancy, then you have limited security and your landlord could evict you by serving a notice, as long as this notice complies with certain legal requirements.

If you were not served with one of these notices, then you may be an assured tenant. In this case you would have much more security, and your landlord would have to have specific grounds for evicting you, and follow the correct procedure. Before advising you further, we need you to confirm whether you received a notice at the start of your tenancy.

### Is my landlord responsible for carrying out repairs to the rotten window?

We understand that you are unhappy about the condition of the property, in that the one of the windows is rotten, the flat is damp and draughty and your sofa has been damaged by mould.

The law places some obligations on your landlord so that he is obliged to keep in repair the structure and exterior of the property. So if the window requires repair, you can ask your landlord to repair this. However your landlord's obligation only arises from when he has notice of the problem.

### Is my landlord responsible for the damp and draughts, and the damage to my sofa?

In relation to the damp and draughts, it depends on whether these are caused by disrepair. However, if the property has never had a damp proof course, and the other

▶

windows are letting in draughts but are not in a state of disrepair, it may be difficult for you to force your landlord to carry out work which essentially may be classed as 'improvements'.

**Is my landlord responsible for the damage to my sofa?**

In relation to any damage caused to you or your possessions, such as your sofa, you will only be able to recover compensation from your landlord if you are able to show that the damage is related to the disrepair, and that the landlord has had notice of the defect.

You could recover compensation for the damage to your sofa, plus a sum for inconvenience, depending on the circumstances. You will have to provide proof of the damage, the value of the sofa, and of the cost of repairing or replacing it.

**Time limits**

The time limit for you to make a claim at court in relation to the disrepair of the property is 6 years from the date when you became aware of the problem, or from the date of any damage suffered.

Please contact us to discuss how you wish to proceed. We can then provide further advice as to the options available to you.

Yours sincerely,

Sarah Parker and Ben Green

Remember that, although you may have researched the legal points extensively, your client is unlikely to be interested in the legal detail, or the process by which you formed your advice. So it is normally unnecessary to include case names or cite the law, or provide details of the Civil Procedure Rules. Your client is unlikely to want to know *how* you carried out your research, but wants you to tell him or her *what* the legal remedy is, in clearly understandable language. Clients want you to interpret the law for them, and tell them how it applies to their case.

 **7.7**   Letters to third parties

You have read about letters to your client. But what about other letters and documents?

When you write to another firm of solicitors, or other third party, you are writing on behalf of your firm, rather than as an individual. Therefore it is normal to use 'we' rather than 'I'. Make sure you are consistent throughout the letter. If you were in practice in a solicitors' firm, you would sign the letter using the name of the firm. In a clinic environment, you need to check what is appropriate.

If this is the first contact, explain that you have been instructed in this matter: 'We have been consulted by Mrs Brown in relation to the cancellation of her flight with your client on 15th January 2011.'

Start by acknowledging your last contact. This might have been a letter, or a telephone call. You might say something like, 'We write further to your letter of 1st May.' You will probably have spoken to your client to establish what response he or she wishes to make, so you could add, '... on which we have taken our client's instructions.'

For many clients, their legal case is a source of worry, stress and, in some cases, anger. It is easy to be drawn into this, but, as an advisor, it is essential to stand back and avoid expressing extreme emotions.

Similarly, correspondence you receive from your opponent, whether a solicitor or an individual acting in person, may create feelings of anger or irritation. In the majority of cases, it is more productive to deal with the facts of the case and avoid being drawn into recriminations or lengthy justifications unless this is essential to the progress of the case. Use exclamation marks sparingly.

Consider leaving the completed letter and coming back to read it again. Look at it objectively and consider how the person receiving it would view the letter. Remember that, in some cases, correspondence can be included in court bundles and read by a judge if the case proceeds to hearing. Letters should be clear, professional and deal with the legal issues.

It may be appropriate to send a draft to your client for approval. This is a matter of judgement, but if there is complex information, this can be a useful way to check this, and to ensure your client is happy with the letter. It is better to take the time to do this rather than to face an irate client if there are errors that your client could have corrected.

## Drafts

Drafts should be clearly marked – simply write 'draft' in the top right of the letter, or it may be possible to use a computer function to print the document with the word 'draft' marked on it. This is normally contained under the tab 'page layout'. If you then click 'watermark', there are a number of choices, including disclaimers such as 'draft'.

Make sure the file copies of letters distributed as drafts are also marked as draft, so that it is clear to anyone checking the client file which letters have been sent as final copies, and which ones are still in draft form.

## 'Without prejudice' letters

In most civil actions, if a party wants to reach a settlement, the appropriate step is to make a formal offer of settlement under Part 36 of the Civil Procedure Rules. However, in some situations, such as arbitration or cases on the small claims track, this is not possible. Documents marked 'without prejudice' will be privileged, even after a compromise has been reached, and are generally inadmissible. This protects litigants from having any admissions revealed to the court, where these were made in an attempt to reach settlement. However, the correspondence can be produced to prove that a binding agreement was reached, if one party fails to comply.

### 'Without prejudice save as to costs' letters

'Without prejudice save as to costs' documents are privileged, but these documents can be disclosed to the court or arbitrator once they have made their decision on liability. A 'Without prejudice save as to costs' offer letter, also known as a 'Calderbank offer' (from *Calderbank v Calderbank* [1976] Fam 93), can provide costs protection in situations where it is not possible to make a payment into court.

In these letters, you should type 'Without prejudice save as to costs' in the top right of the letter. However, if you overlook this accidentally, do not panic too much: the courts have held that the principle of 'privilege' can protect subsequent and even previous letters in the same sequence of correspondence. Strictly speaking, therefore, it is not necessary that every letter be marked 'Without prejudice' if it is clear that the communication is intended to be part of the settlement negotiations.

However, this also means that just because documents are marked 'Without prejudice', unless they are intended to be part of a genuine settlement attempt, they will not actually enjoy 'privileged' status and will not be protected from disclosure.

## **7.8** Letters of claim

The purpose of letters of claim is to ensure that potential defendants have prior notice of a claim which may be made against them, and to provide them with enough information about the nature and value of that possible claim. It also enables potential defendants to contact their insurer.

The Civil Procedure Rules (CPR) contain a number of protocols, with the intention that the defendant is provided with clear information on the allegations. This provides a clear framework, encouraging early resolution, with court action as the last resort. The protocols provide extremely useful support for the various actions covered by the CPR, and you should consult them whenever relevant. The protocols include sample letters, such as an early notification letter, a letter of claim, a letter of instruction to the expert, a special damages form and a statement of costs.

In Nicola Ridley's case, she has a claim against her landlord arising from the condition of the property, and therefore the Pre-Action Protocol for Housing Disrepair Cases applies. The Protocol provides example letters, including a letter of claim for the tenant to send to his or her landlord, although this could be easily adapted to enable it to be sent by you as the advisor.

 Writing to counsel

You may be asked to write to a barrister asking him or her to represent your client in court (brief to counsel) or to obtain a written opinion from counsel on your client's case (instructions to counsel).

Written communications with barristers remain rather formal and archaic in format, with the barrister being referred to as 'counsel' and addressed using the format, 'Counsel will note that Ms Ridley has been unable to produce the written tenancy agreement,' rather than 'You will note.' Also, you refer to yourself as 'those instructing Counsel'.

Normally you will list the attachments at the start as enclosures, which will be any relevant documents, including witness statements and court documents. It is important to make it clear what you are requesting. For example, with an opinion, make it clear which aspect of the case you require an opinion on, for example, quantum or prospects of success.

A brief requires the barrister to represent your client at a hearing, so make sure details of dates, times and venue are included and, in all cases, details of any legal aid or other funding.

Traditionally, the whole document (the brief or instructions and the supporting documents) is folded in half and tied with pink legal ribbon. A back sheet is used, which has on it the names of the parties, instructing solicitors and the court name and case number. This is folded around the brief or instructions.

If you do not follow this somewhat archaic format, there will be no adverse consequences, and no doubt over time these formalities will change, but if you have an awareness of the accepted style, you can decide how far you wish to conform to this tradition.

---

In the Nicetown County Court                                      Case number

Nicola Ridley                                      Claimant

v

Harry Atkinson                                      Defendant

**Instructions to Counsel**

Counsel will find enclosed herewith:

1  Copy Particulars of Claim
2  Copy Defence and counterclaim
3  Copy draft witness statement of Nicola Ridley
4  Copy expert report

Counsel is instructed by Jane Little, supervising solicitor, of ABC Law Clinic. As set out in the Particulars of Claim, Ms Ridley is pursuing a disrepair claim against her current landlord, Mr H Atkinson ...

---

## 7.10 Legal drafting

Each different type of claim will come with its own set of requirements as to what needs to be included within the relevant legal documents. For example, Part 16 of the Civil Procedure Rules provides that a claim form must include a statement confirming the nature of the claim, the remedy claimed, and a statement of value where the claim is for money. There are additional requirements imposed by Practice Direction 16 if the claim relates to personal injury, fatal accident or hire purchase etc.

Given the extensive rules, it is therefore impossible to provide a comprehensive guide to legal drafting in this chapter. However, some basic guidance is set out below.

### Form and content

Some legal documents require the use of a prescribed form, and so you should check carefully whether this is the case. If you are required to use a particular form, ensure it is the correct one and the most up-to-date version. This may be easier said than done. For example, there are two different claim forms currently in use at the employment tribunal.

Once you have identified the correct document, identify any specific content requirements. Failure to include prescribed information could result in the form being rejected by the court/tribunal.

### Use of precedents

Drafting an important document, such as a contract or particulars of claim, can be intimidating and time-consuming. However, you do not have to reinvent the wheel. Check whether you can locate a relevant precedent or clause from either a practitioner textbook or the Encyclopaedia of Forms and Precedents.

However, you must use precedents with caution. Check they are applicable to your client's case and do not simply copy them over unamended; you must ensure you tailor the wording to the case, as appropriate.

### Language

Contracts, statements of case, wills and so on are by their very nature formal documents. That does not mean, however, that you should default to the stereotypical lawyerly language referred to at the beginning of this chapter. That is not to say informal language is acceptable either. You need to strike a balance. Your language should be appropriately formal and legal terminology should be used. Expression should be clear and concise, as with letters.

### Checking

It can be difficult to amend statements of case which have been filed with the relevant court or tribunal, so it is good practice to have your client check the factual detail prior to filing the document.

## 7.11 Skeleton arguments

Another document you may be required to draft in respect of legal proceedings is a skeleton argument, which outlines the key points of the case. The form and content of a skeleton argument differs according to the type of case and court but, generally, there are some core similarities. For example, a skeleton argument would ordinarily set out the facts or issues in dispute and the relevant law. If you are required to draft a skeleton argument, check whether your institution has any models or precedents or, alternatively, consult a practitioner text.

## 7.12 Methods of communication

### Using email

Email, if a permitted means of communication, should be used with care. Although it is widely used in the workplace, there are issues to be aware of:

- Email communications with your client should not be used without checking that this is acceptable to the client. He or she may share a computer with other users, and there could be confidentiality issues if the emails can be easily accessed by others.
- You need to consider what address the email is sent from. Ideally there should be a central office/clinic address which is used as a mail box and checked daily for incoming and outgoing messages.
- Emailing clients or third parties from your own email address should be avoided, as it could lead to you receiving unwanted messages, even after the case has concluded, or receiving messages when you are away from the clinic.
- Emails are by their nature a quick and informal way of making contact. However, in a lawyering context, you need to treat the sending of emails in the same way as you would if sending a letter. Ensure it is properly drafted with the same conventions, layout and formalities as your letters. Have it checked in the normal way, and place a copy on your client file. Similarly, ensure that emails received are treated like incoming letters and logged in the normal way, shown to your supervisor, and a hard copy placed on file.
- Security is an issue to consider. A copy of the email could remain on the server, and/or on your computer or laptop, so ensure that consideration is given to security of any laptop, computer or USB stick.
- Beware of using track changes. Your deletions and changes can be viewed by others if they use the 'show markup' function. You may consider cutting and pasting the final version of your letter or document into a new document, which reduces the likelihood of this.

### By fax or by post?

There are situations where it may be appropriate to send letters and/or documents by fax, if they are urgent or there is a short deadline.

> **Practical tips**
>
> - It is common practice in many firms to fax a document and then send a hard copy by post, although it is worth checking this to find out the practice adopted by your clinic, as the CPR indicate that hard copies of faxes should not be provided as this duplicates the correspondence which the court has to process. This also applies to bodies such as the Criminal Injuries Compensation Authority, which request that, if faxed, the letter or document should not also be posted.
> - The letter should be marked on the top right, 'By fax and by post' or 'By fax'. This makes it clear on the file copy what method was used.
> - It is also good practice to print off a record from the fax machine to check that all pages of the document have in fact been successfully faxed to the correct location. This proof of transmission should be placed on the file with the faxed document or letter so that it can be referred to should there be any queries. However, remember that, according to the CPR, the document is not filed at court until it is delivered by the court's fax machine, which is not necessarily the time at which you sent it.
>
> So if you are dealing with an urgent case or one where the limitation is about to expire, you may consider delivering the document personally if possible, or contacting the court to ensure that your fax has arrived.

## **7.13** Summary

'Lawyers have two common failings. One is that they do not write well and the other is that they think they do.' (Carl Felsenfeld, 'The Plain English Movement in the United States' (1981–82) *Canadian Business Law Journal*, Vol 6 (from Rylance, 1994))

Solicitors could be stereotyped as aloof and elitist. It will take time to change these views, but by aiming for clarity and precision, you can make your writing style something that benefits clients, rather than baffles them.

##  Further reading

### Introductory

**Boyle, F et al,** *A Practical Guide to Lawyering Skills* **(Cavendish Publishing, 2005)**
An accessible text on legal skills, which dedicates three excellently written chapters to legal writing (Chapters 1 and 2) and drafting (Chapter 6).

**Elkington, A et al,** *Skills for Lawyers* **(CLP, 2010)**
A general skills text aimed at the Legal Practice Course market.

**Solicitors Regulation Authority Legal Practice Course Outcomes 2007**
The standards of legal writing and drafting expected by the SRA on completion of the LPC can be accessed through the link below:
www.sra.org.uk/documents/students/lpc/outcomes.pdf

**Webb, J et al,** *Lawyers' Skills 2010–11* **(Oxford University Press, 2010)**
One of the more up-to-date publications which forms part of the Legal Practice Course Guide series. A general skills text which covers legal writing and drafting.

## Intermediate

**Adler, M,** *Clarity for Lawyers: Effective Legal Writing* **(The Law Society, 2006)**
> A useful text which provides guidance on how to communicate more effectively and offers a plain language workshop to help you write clearly.

**LawWorks Student Adviser Handbook 2006**
> Appendix C of this Handbook contains additional templates and example letters including an advice letter, a general letter to third parties and a file-closing letter.

**Rose, W,** *Pleadings Without Tears: A Guide to Legal Drafting Under the Civil Procedure Rules* **(Oxford University Press, 2007)**
> Written in an engaging conversational tone, this book offers advice on drafting a variety of documents including claim forms, witness statements and skeleton arguments.

**Rylance, P,** *Legal Writing and Drafting* **(Blackstone Press, 1994)**
> Not a recent publication but still a well regarded book on the skills of writing and drafting in the legal context.

## Advanced

**Boutall, T and Blackburn, B,** *Solicitors' Guide to Good Management: Practical Checklists for the Management of Law Firms* **(The Law Society, 2001)**
> An advanced text intended for management but which contains useful guidance that you can make use of as part of your clinical and pro bono activities.

 Activities

### Activity 1: Reflect and review

Part of being a reflective practitioner student or clinician includes reflecting on your own pieces of writing and any feedback you are given. Initially, there are bound to be points that require amendment, and you may need to adapt to the 'house style'. But use these earlier comments to inform your writing. When you have written a new letter, look back at the last piece you produced. Have you repeated any of the same errors? Proofread and edit ruthlessly before asking your supervisor to check it.

### Activity 2: Pruning pays off

Take a piece of legal writing you have prepared. Look at every word and ask yourself whether that word adds anything to the letter, and consider pruning it out if the answer is no. Use a highlighter pen to highlight extraneous words, and then read through the letter again, ignoring the highlighted parts. Could you cut the unnecessary words and maintain the meaning?

### Activity 3: Letter swap

Exchange some of your written pieces with fellow clinic students or friends, and ask for constructive criticism. If they were the recipient, would they have understood what you were trying to tell them? Then try explaining your letter to them verbally. Was this clearer? Make sure the document is not subject to any duty of confidentiality.

# 8 Practical legal research

> 'Know where to find the information and how
> to use it – that's the secret of success.'
>
> Albert Einstein

## 8.1 Introduction

The above quotation is attributed to Albert Einstein by various websites, but did he actually say it? An Internet search does not elicit an authoritative source that can be trusted for this quotation, nor have any of the websites made reference to where Einstein is supposed to have said this. This highlights an important issue for all researchers when information is so readily available. You have to be sure that your information is up to date and authoritative; otherwise, it may appear sound but could ultimately lead you to the wrong conclusion. For a student or lawyer working on a case, it could mean giving the wrong advice to your client – something potentially catastrophic.

The key to being able to cope with 'real world' problems as a student or a professional is to develop practical research skills. Therefore this chapter will consider the meaning of practical legal research, the stages of research, information sources and how to use them, and how to record and present your research.

This chapter will refer to Nicola's tenancy case study (see **6.4**) to illustrate the principles and challenges of practical legal research (PLR). It involves legal problems that clinic and pro bono students regularly encounter.

Being confronted with a problem like Nicola's might seem quite scary. You might be wondering, 'How do I begin to advise on this problem? I do not remember studying any of this during my degree.' If you are thinking this, you are partly right, although you may have studied some of the background law during your land law studies. Some knowledge of basic contract law might also help, but essentially this problem and the law surrounding it may well be new to you.

You already have many of the skills necessary to understand the legal and factual issues that emerge from this problem, so do not panic. One of the best things about clinic and other pro bono work is that you will develop and add to these skills. This helps you prepare for your future career where the ability to tackle unfamiliar problems is vital to success.

What is practical legal research?

You will have already developed some legal research skills while studying law. There is an assumption made in this chapter that you are accustomed to finding and reading legislation and case law (if you need further guidance on this, please refer to the texts identified in the Further Reading section at the end of this chapter). These are key skills for academic and practical research. However, PLR requires additional skills. Nicola's tenancy problems typify some of the most important differences between academic legal research and PLR. Please read the text at **6.4** before continuing with this chapter.

### Differences between practical legal research for clients and academic research

There are several differences between PLR and academic research, which are considered below:

### Your goal is to assist your client

The first and most important difference to note is that, when working for clients, the goal is different. You are not trying to show your understanding of an area of law to a tutor. Your goal is to provide your client with advice and, as far as possible, resolve his or her problem.

**Nicola's problem**

> Providing advice means going further than being able to say, for example, that you believe Nicola's landlord will owe a repair obligation in respect of the windows. It means you first have to establish what she wants to achieve. Does she want the windows to be repaired by the landlord and/or compensation for living in a draughty flat? Or some other remedy? It will not be enough simply to tell her that the landlord should repair the windows. Her question to you will almost certainly be, 'and how are we going to make that happen?' You will need to research the remedies available and find out the procedure for compelling the landlord to repair the windows. You will also need to try to quantify how much the claim is worth. Alternatively, Nicola's main goal may be to remain in the flat and not be evicted. If this is the case, will pursuit of compensation put her position at risk?

Whenever you are carrying out PLR, keep in mind your client's goals.

### With real problems the facts are not always clear

**Nicola's problem**

> Take a look again at the excerpt from Nicola's interview (see **6.4**). You can see she is not presenting the problem as you would expect in a normal seminar scenario. In a regular problem question the facts would be clear, logically and chronologically set out, and you would know from the question whether Nicola had complained to the landlord about problems with the flat, what she had complained about and why he has threatened to evict her. Is it because she is complaining about the flat? Is there another reason? Has she complained to the landlord about her neighbour? Why complain to her landlord about what the neighbour is doing? Is her neighbour a tenant too? What sort of flats ▸

> are these? Has Nicola complained about the window to the landlord? What did he say about that? What threats has he made about evicting her? Has he taken any steps to evict her? And so on. When working for clients, you will need to develop the skill of collecting and analysing the facts. This does not just take place at the first interview. It is an ongoing process.

## There will be irrelevant facts

Clients do not filter out the red herrings in their problem for you as an academic tutor might. You have to be prepared to try to distinguish material facts from the irrelevant. You may not know these when you begin your research and need to be prepared to further refine your view as you go. For example, is Nicola's neighbour's reference to her boyfriend and martial arts material to her case? If so, in what way?

## With clients you have to assume there may be another side to the story

For a seminar, you will not often be asked to consider whether clients can prove their case. You will often, for good reason, assume that the facts presented are true. When working with clients, you have to be prepared to look for gaps in the facts, inconsistencies in the account, and what the other party says or might say about the issue.

## When working for clients the legal problem is not always clear

For a seminar you will at least know the subject. You may also be told the particular legal issues. Your tutor may well have given you directed reading and you will probably have had a lecture on the subject. Nicola's case offers no such guidance. Nicola does not know what areas of law are involved and cannot tell you. Working for her requires you to identify the legal areas and independently research them for yourself.

## With client work there may be more than one area of law involved

There is a good reason for teaching law in compartments. Imagine how confusing it would be if you were required in your first year to study contract, land and tort all together in each seminar. However, real-world problems often involve a mix of legal areas.

For example, a client has been stripped of clothing in a police station. He believes his complaint about police conduct has not been dealt with properly by the Independent Police Complaints Commission (IPCC) and he also wants compensation from the police. The possible areas of law range from tort (battery for the removal of his clothing), breach of his human rights (Article 3 of the European Convention on Human Rights (inhuman and degrading treatment) and Article 8 (right to private life)), through to public law (police powers and treatment of suspects in the police station and challenging the decision of the IPCC through judicial review) and beyond.

## With client work the research you do will not always be limited to 'the law'

You will be used to reading primary sources of law, but in real life you will often need to go further than this. In Nicola's case, there is a possibility of involving the local council for the rat problem (and possibly the windows too). Part of your research might well necessitate investigating policies and procedures to see what action the council might take.

### Solutions to problems for clients often do not involve the courts

You have to be prepared to research methods of solving clients' problems that are not simply court-based as this is often time-consuming and costly. Again, in Nicola's case, could the local council solve her rat problem for her?

### You have to advise on the best possible course of action, but there may be no one certain answer

In academic legal research there may well be no one certain answer, and when working for clients this is also often true. For example, in contentious cases, there is always the possibility that you may not be able to prove your case. Or, for example, there may be some crucial facts missing which mean you cannot decide whether a statutory rule applies. You should still attempt to give the best possible advice – qualifying it by reference to the uncertainty that exists.

 ## 8.3 The stages of practical legal research

 **Top tip**

Keeping a trail of your research is essential. You will be doing a lot of thinking and searching. Much of this will be wasted if you do not keep a record of what you are searching for and where you have searched and do not keep clearly referenced records of what you have found. You must be able to do this to present a proper research report and also to be able to retrace your steps if you need to check your understanding. Keeping a record of your research can either be done manually or on computer while you carry out your research.

### The client's goals

Start with what your client wants to achieve. You can do this by asking him or her during the interview. Remember that your client may have several goals and they might not be limited to compensation – even in contentious cases. For example, a client coming to see you about being sexually harassed at work might want to leave her job and be compensated; or stay in her job and be compensated; or she might simply want to stop the harassment; or possibly consider reporting the perpetrator to the police.

#### Nicola's problem

In Nicola's case, from the brief outline we already have, her potential goals would appear to be:

- Staying in the flat and not being evicted – highly important.
- Getting rid of, and preventing the return of, the rats – including having her neighbour clear up.
- Compensation from the landlord for the rat problem. ▶

▸
- Compensation from the neighbour for the rat problem.
- Repair of the rotten window in her flat.
- Compensation from the landlord for having to live in draughty and damp conditions including the cost of a replacement sofa.

Considering your client's goals will help focus your efforts.

## Fact analysis

As you have seen, clients will not always present you with just the relevant facts organised in a logical manner. Having identified what you believe your client's goals to be, you will need to consider the facts and organise them into a succinct summary which recognises the important (or possibly important) issues. As the problem is unfamiliar to you, it may be difficult at first to recognise facts that may be material to the case and those which have no bearing. For this reason you should be prepared to return to the record of your interview at a later stage in your research to ensure that you have recognised all of the important facts.

### Nicola's problem

Looking at Nicola's problem again, your summary might be as follows:

'Nicola has rented a flat since April 1996. She has no written tenancy agreement and pays rent monthly. One of the windows in the flat is rotten and possibly (note that you should acknowledge any issue that you are not sure of) causing damp which has also damaged her sofa and made the flat cold. Her neighbour is an alcoholic who has left rubbish around which is possibly causing a rat infestation in Nicola's flat. Her neighbour refuses to clear up and is abusive. Nicola has complained about some or all of these issues to her landlord but he appears to be threatening to evict her.'

## Legal problem identification – turning unfocused legal problems into focused legal problems

The skills you already have from your legal studies degree should mean that you are able to answer focused legal problems. However, in clinic and pro bono you will be dealing with unfocused scenarios.

### Nicola's problem

The problem with a case like Nicola's is that it has not been focused for you. At this stage, perhaps you do not know which areas of law are involved. As a start, try to identify the legal questions you will need to understand in order to begin to address her problems. Some of the questions will be very broad because you may know very little about the law in this area. Look again at the summary of Nicola's problem and the goals which have been identified. Try to think about areas of law that might be involved. It might help to break this down (see McKie, 1993: 34) into substantive and procedural law questions; the former relating to where a duty or cause of action arises, and the latter relating to how we might go about enforcing those rights.

▸

As an example, this might lead you to ask the following questions about Nicola's window problem (other questions would arise concerning her other problems):

- What appears to be the broad category of law? Property? Housing? Landlord and tenant?
- What sort of tenancy, if any, does Nicola have? Does it make a difference that it is not in writing and she pays rent monthly? Would this affect her agreement with her landlord and her rights in relation to the windows?
- Who has the duty to keep the flat in repair: the tenant or the landlord?
- If the tenant has a duty to repair, where would that originate from? Contract law? What form would the contract take? A tenancy agreement?
- If the landlord has a duty to repair the windows, where would that duty originate? Again, in contract law through the tenancy agreement? Is it possible that the state has regulated this area and that there may be legislation governing landlord and tenant obligations?
- If the landlord has a duty to repair the window, what are the available remedies?
- If damages are available, how do the courts assess these? Are there fixed tariffs or is there any case law that might be relevant? What is the procedure for making such a claim?
- If a remedy to compel the landlord to repair the window is available, how do you procedurally enforce such a claim through the courts?
- Is it possible that another agency – the local council or some other state body – might have powers and responsibilities in relation to domestic tenancies?

**Top tip**

While going through this exercise, do not be afraid to take cues from your existing knowledge. For example, you may have studied the repair obligations of a landlord or the basics of leasehold when studying land law. You might well be a tenant yourself. Your own personal knowledge of your tenancy agreement and your rights may help you identify the area of law involved.

### Searching for information – how and where to start? Use secondary sources

You have probably been warned against using Google and other search engines. In fact, with caution, these can be useful. The Internet is an incredibly powerful resource, but until online delivery becomes commonplace for all law texts, it is not usually a good idea to start with the Internet or, in fact, primary sources of law.

Usually, the best place to start is with paper copies of academic textbooks, practitioner texts and *Halsbury's Laws*. These commentaries are an essential secondary source. Searching them will help you begin to understand the parameters of the problem and to further categorise the areas of law and the issues involved. Guy Holborn calls this starting from square two and explains the process in some detail (Holborn, 2006: 19). Once you have a sufficient grasp of the basics, you will then be in a better position to start looking at the primary sources of the law – cases and legislation. If you start with the primary sources, it is very easy to become lost.

Before you can begin to search through textbooks and practitioner texts, you will need to think about how you can search such sources. You will usually do this through the index or the contents pages. Before you go to these, you will need to identify some keywords that will help you with your search.

## Keywords

Keywords are important when searching indexes and contents pages. You will need to think about the areas of law and also specific words that relate to your client's problem that may appear in the index. For example, in Nicola's case it may not be that helpful just to look up the word 'tenancy'. You will want to think about other subheadings associated with 'tenancy' concerning the areas you want to know about.

When devising keywords, think not only of the obvious vocabulary but also of synonyms for those terms. In Nicola's case you might think of the 'duty' of the landlord and 'obligation' as a synonym. Similarly you might identify 'oral' as a keyword because you are looking for types of tenancy agreement and you know this one was not in writing. It would be a good idea to use 'written' as a keyword too in case the index refers first to written tenancy agreements with a subheading of oral agreements.

If you want a more sophisticated method of identifying keywords, see the discussion in Chapter 4 of McKie (1993).

### Nicola's problem

Look again at the legal questions posed in respect of Nicola's window problem, together with her goals in respect of the windows. You might think of the following:

| Possible main heading in the index | Possible subheading(s) |
| --- | --- |
| Tenancy agreement | Types/classification<br>Oral<br>Written<br>Effect on rights to repair<br>Landlord's obligations/tenant's obligations |
| Repair | Duty/landlord/tenant<br>Tenant's rights/obligations<br>Landlord's rights/obligations<br>Damages for non-repair/disrepair<br>Court proceedings/enforcement<br>Procedure<br>Remedies |
| Disrepair | Repair/mend/fix/restore |
| Housing | Tenancies/types of tenancy<br>Oral agreements/repairs/obligations |

While searching, you should also bear in mind other facts that may be important but probably will not appear in the index (for example, the tenancy appears to have begun in 1996). As you learn more about the area, other keywords for searching will become apparent and you should add these to the list.

## Initial search using academic textbooks, practitioner texts and *Halsbury's Laws*

Note one of the most important rules when conducting research – it is rarely a good idea to rely on only one source. Try to ensure that you search for references in several sources.

### Academic textbooks

Academic textbooks can sometimes prove a useful starting point for your research. If you believe you know the area of substantive law involved, they can help you to decide the legal issues. They may even deal with the specific problems in your case. When searching academic textbooks, it is usually best to start by searching for your keywords in the contents pages and index.

However, academic textbooks rarely deal with procedural issues – how to enforce the legal right you have discovered. They are also not always aimed at common problems in legal practice but at fundamental issues of legal principle. As a result, while starting with an academic textbook can be useful, you may be better looking at practitioner texts and *Halsbury's Laws*.

Another issue to watch out for with academic texts is that they may not be published regularly. The law can change quickly, so use the most up-to-date edition and check to see how old that edition is.

 **Top tip**

It is essential to check that the law you believe you have identified is up to date. In *Hinks v Channel 4 Television Corporation* (*Lawtel*, 3 March 2000), the lawyer, who was not a defamation expert, was instructed in 1998 by his claimant client. He consulted a textbook on defamation published in 1994 which indicated that the limitation period (period in which a claim must be brought to court) was three years. He relied on this, but his client's case was struck out by the court because the limitation period was amended in such cases to one year in 1996 and he did not commence the action in time. If the lawyer had checked and updated his knowledge from the most recent sources available, this would not have happened.

### Practitioner texts

Practitioner texts are those aimed at the legal profession, focusing on certain areas of law. They guide the busy practitioner on the substantive law and/or procedure pertaining to that subject-matter. This means that there are some highly specialised texts on issues as diverse as construction contracts, stamp duty, company directors, inquests and consumer credit.

Practitioner texts assist lawyers in solving problems and giving practical advice. They are therefore quite likely to give guidance on your client's problem. In addition to the texts aimed at specialist practitioners, there are books aimed at students on the Legal Practice Course or Bar Professional Training Course. These latter texts can be a useful starting place because although they will not offer the same coverage, they are often written for the novice and so will be easier to understand. Some key practitioner texts are listed on the Companion Website, arranged by area of law.

Larger practitioner texts, such as *Harvey on Industrial Relations and Employment Law* and *Halsbury's Laws*, tend to refer to section or volume, chapter and paragraph number, rather than page number. If you bear this in mind, you should find it easier to use them.

## Updating practitioner texts

Some practitioner texts are not regularly updated, while others are updated by the publication of a supplement. You should always check the supplement to ensure that the law has not changed. Often, the supplements refer to the reference in the main volume of the text. Therefore you can ascertain whether there have been any developments by looking in the supplement for the chapter and paragraph numbers for the material you have already discovered in the main text. In the supplement, you may find amendments to the original text where there have been developments (for example by way of case law). If there are no references to the chapter and paragraph numbers then the authors of the text do not consider there have been any developments as at the date of the publication of the supplement.

## Practitioner texts online

A growing number of practitioner texts are available online. If your institution subscribes to *Westlaw*, for example, you may find in the 'Books' section useful texts such as *Archbold: Criminal Pleading, Evidence and Practice* and *Woodfall: Landlord and Tenant.* On *LexisLibrary*, for example, you may find useful texts such as *Clarke Hall and Morrison on Children* and *Butterworths Family Law Service* under the 'Commentary' tab.

Your law library is likely to have a more comprehensive set of printed resources, so continue to find your bearings using paper resources before searching electronic texts online.

### *Halsbury's Laws*

*Halsbury's Laws* is a very useful secondary resource. It is intended to be a comprehensive statement of the law. You will probably find it in your law library. It can also be accessed online if your institution subscribes to the service via *LexisLibrary*, but note that initial use of *Halsbury's Laws* is usually best done using the hardcopy resource.

If you know how to use *Halsbury's* – it does not take more than 20 minutes to learn the basics – it can be an invaluable source of information and a useful first port of call when researching unfamiliar problems.

It is published as a series of books by area of law arranged alphabetically. The bound volumes are currently being updated so that some areas of law are covered by the 4th edition and 4th edition reissue brown volumes, and others by the 5th edition black volumes.

There are also primary source collections entitled *Halsbury's,* for example *Halsbury's Statutes.* These are largely for research when you are clear about the area of law and the statute you wish to look at. It is best not to use them initially. Make sure the volumes you are looking at are *Halsbury's Laws.*

The best way to search *Halsbury's* when you are looking at an unfocused legal problem is to go to the Consolidated Index. This is contained within three separate bound volumes (A–E, F–O and P–Z). Looking again at the client who has been stripped by the police, a search under the word 'Detention' brings up a number of references until 'treatment of detained person' as a subheading is found. That leads to a reference of 11(2) (4th) 957 where the relevant law can be found.

*Halsbury's* is referenced by the volume number (11(2)), then the edition (in this case 4th) and lastly the paragraph number (957).

 **Top tip**

When looking at *Halsbury's Laws*, always read the footnotes as they often provide a greater level of explanation than the text itself.

### Updating *Halsbury's Laws*

The main volumes of *Halsbury's Laws* have been published over a number of years. To update any material found in the main volume, you must first go to the *Cumulative Supplement*. This is published yearly and accumulates all of the changes since the publication of the volume. Supplements to each volume of *Halsbury's Laws* are arranged sequentially in the *Cumulative Supplement*. In the supplement, turn to the volume number you wish to update (volume 11(2) in this case) and then turn to the paragraph number (957). Any updates to the paragraph will be noted here. If there are no entries or amendments, there have been no developments since the publication of the original volume.

However, the *Cumulative Supplement* for 2010 is only up to date to 13 November 2009. Therefore, to be sure there have been no developments since then, you need to use the *Current Service Noter-up* (currently a bound black paperback and issued monthly). Check the *Noter-up* using the same method as for the *Cumulative Supplement*.

 **Top tip**

You may be hoping that there is a less cumbersome way of updating *Halsbury's Laws* than this. There is. *Halsbury's Laws* is available online through *LexisLibrary*. However, note that it is often easier to use the paper index and paper main volumes to find the material. After that, you can easily find the same material online by reference to the volume title and paragraph number. The difference is that, at the bottom of the text, the online version is updated for you without you having to look in separate volumes.

### Nicola's problem – a worked example

In this example, you can see some of the key stages in researching the window problem that forms part of Nicola's case. This is not an exhaustive account of the research that would need to be done. A complete research report for Nicola's case is available on the Companion Website.

So far, the chapter has set out Nicola's goals, the relevant facts, the questions of law to be answered and keywords. It appears that the issue mainly concerns property and/or housing/landlord and tenant law.

Starting with the windows problem, what sort of tenancy, if any, does Nicola have? Does it make a difference that it is not in writing and she pays rent monthly? Would this affect ▶

her agreement with her landlord and her rights in relation to the windows? It seems logical to start here because the nature of her tenancy may well affect her rights and obligations.

How might you research this point? Look first at property law textbooks, for example one of the major academic works on this subject is Megarry & Wade, *The Law of Real Property*. Consulting your list of keywords, you might decide to search first under 'tenancy types'. An index search brings up a reference to 'classification'. Turning to the text, you will find references to various types of tenancy including weekly, monthly and yearly tenancies. However, if you are unfamiliar with this area of law, you might find *Megarry & Wade* to be a very dense textbook. This is an example of a situation where it might prove more fruitful to look at a practitioner text and then return to the academic text once you have more background information and can see the wood for the trees.

You may therefore decide to look for a more introductory text, which is also dedicated more to tenancies in a practical context. This might lead you to *Housing Law and Practice,* College of Law Publishing. The first few pages of this text give you a brief introduction to leaseholds and tenancies. From that, you will immediately see that there will be some further questions to ask your client to see if she has a leasehold interest in the land. For example, you will need to check that she does not occupy simply by way of a licence – so that all of the requirements for a tenancy are met. If you read further through the book, you will see that nearly all new residential tenancies, granted after 15 January 1989 are subject to the Housing Act 1988 and will be known as 'assured' or 'assured shorthold' tenancies – though there are exceptions which will need to be checked.

 **Top tip**

Once you have found reference to appropriate passages in a textbook, it is often necessary to read beyond the specific reference. For instance, you may need to go back a few pages and read other material in order to understand the specific reference.

Reading on, you will determine that Nicola has a monthly periodic tenancy, which is an assured tenancy by virtue of the Housing Act 1988. The book then deals with the ending or determination of a tenancy, which is something you will need to come back to in relation to the threats to evict your client. However, at the moment you are concentrating on Nicola's windows problem. Turning to the index again, you will then search using the 'repairs' keywords identified above. The 'repairs' keywords include disrepair. The index refers to 'landlord's obligations' and you might decide to start there. Turning to that page, you will soon realise that you need to begin at the start of the chapter, which provides a definition of disrepair. You will also note that there may be terms in the tenancy agreement imposing repair obligations (but in this case there is no written agreement). Further reading will lead to a statutory imposition of an obligation on the landlord to, amongst other things, keep in repair the structure and exterior of the dwelling house (Landlord and Tenant Act 1985, s 11). This provision applies to all periodic tenancies. You might then wonder whether the windows are part of the structure and exterior of the dwelling for the purposes of s 11. According to the textbook, windows are, but there does not appear to be a reference to a definitive case on the subject. Make a note to search for case law on the subject later. The textbook also advises that *Quick v Taff Ely* [1986]

QB 809 is a good illustration of the difficulty in some cases involving dampness. Nicola has said that the windows are causing the property to be damp. Make a note to check the case law on this and read *Quick v Taff Ely*.

You might turn next to *Halsbury's Laws*, particularly if looking for more specific guidance on the level of damages and assurance that the windows do form part of the structure and exterior for the purposes of s 11 of the Landlord and Tenant Act. By now you will have a much better idea of the subject areas, but you will still probably search *Halsbury's Laws* using the index rather than looking through the volume titles. As the keyword 'Disrepair' was an important one in respect of the previous text, you should check this in the Consolidated Index. There is no mention of it, so you should check your other keywords. At the start of the entry to 'Tenancy', the index refers also to 'Landlord and Tenant'. If you check this entry and use the subheading 'Repairs,' you are referred to 'Repairing Covenant; Repairs to Leasehold'. There are references here to volume 27(1) 416 for the landlord's statutory obligations. Referring to 27(1) 416 confirms what you already know about the landlord being under a duty to keep the exterior and structure of the dwelling house in repair. Footnote 6 refers specifically on windows to the case of *Irvine v Moran* (1990) 24 HLR 1, [1991] EGLR 261, which you should make a note to check.

 **Top tip**

Checking the case law will be a lot quicker if you have access to the online version of *Halsbury's Laws*. The online version has the same footnote and case reference of course but, as with many other cases, there is a hyperlink direct to the case itself which you can click on.

You will see that the landlord does not have an obligation to make the repairs until he has notice of them. You should make a note to consider whether he has had notice and how you might prove it.

As volume 27(1) was published in 2006, you must update it. Check the *Cumulative Supplement* under the reference 27(1) 416. There is no reference here. Check also the latest *Noter-up* for March 2010. Again, there is no reference here. It appears that there have been no developments.

## Using *Halsbury's Laws* online

This is a very useful electronic version of *Halsbury's Laws* which (if your institution subscribes) can be found in the Commentary section of *LexisLibrary*.

You can search it by keyword(s), searching the entirety of the volumes. As indicated above, you will usually be more successful in searching if you use the paper Consolidated Index in the library. In a paper index, you can cast your eye across numerous headings and subheadings and this can often help you identify the right keywords. This is more difficult online. Simply putting in a keyword or two can lead to a dispiritingly large number of 'hits'. For example, in Nicola's windows case, if you search using the terms 'disrepair' and 'damages', the search returns 86 hits, the first of which is to volume 1(2) of *Halsbury's Laws*, para 851 and has the heading, 'Fishing Mill Dams'!

You can also search *Halsbury's* on *LexisLibrary* using the 'Browse' function. This allows you to see all of the volumes of *Halsbury's* and you can look further into each volume by expanding the lists to see the headings to each paragraph.

There are advantages to using *Halsbury's* online. Any reference to another paragraph in *Halsbury's Laws* or legislation is hyperlinked. This means that you can click on the link and go straight to the next section. Any case carried by *LexisLibrary* is also hyperlinked so you can click on those cases and read them. In addition, if you find something particularly useful that you would normally photocopy from a text, you can easily save it to disk or print it off for later reference.

### Searching for information – using primary sources

Once you have a good understanding of the legal problem, you may have identified primary sources which need to be checked. Textbooks and practitioner sources do not always cover every eventuality. For example, if you were looking at the case of the client stripped naked in the police station, you would want to check the detailed provisions of the Police and Criminal Evidence Act 1984 and the Codes of Practice to ascertain when and how the police may remove the detained person's clothing.

You are also likely to want to look at case law on a subject. In Nicola's case, you found a reference to *Quick v Taff Ely*, which suggested that there can be difficulty in dampness cases. Reading the case will probably assist in understanding this issue and whether or not it is an issue in Nicola's case.

Primary sources are often easier to find and access on the Internet, and it should be easier to establish that they are up to date.

### Primary sources: legislation

As already noted, you have probably already received some training in finding and reading legislation. There is insufficient space here to comprehensively cover this topic. This section provides a basic guide to using the resources available. There are suggested textbooks at the end of this chapter if you want to brush up on your skills.

 **Top tip**

Make sure you are looking at the most up-to-date version of the legislation available. The best way to do this is to understand the source from which you have obtained the information. Is the source automatically updated, showing the latest version including the effect of any amendments? Do you need to update the information by looking at a supplementary updating resource? Or is this just simply the original version of the legislation with no resource for checking amendments?

### The main paper sources for researching legislation

#### Halsbury's Statutes

*Halsbury's Statutes* contains the amended text of every Public General Act applying to England and Wales currently in force. This multi-volume resource works in a similar way to *Halsbury's Laws*. A guide to using *Halsbury's Statutes* can be found at the front of *Halsbury's Statutes Current Statutes Service*. As with *Halsbury's Laws*, it is necessary to update by reference to regularly published updates in the *Current Statutes* and *Noter-up* services.

If you want to look for the most up-to-date statutes on paper then *Halsbury's Statutes* is probably the ideal version. It has the added virtue of listing case law relating to sections of each Act at the end of each section. In the case of Nicola's windows, it is possible to find a number of cases referred to at the end of s 11 of the Landlord and Tenant Act 1985 concerning the landlord's repairing obligations.

### Current Law Statutes Annotated

This is a series of bound volumes published for each year since 1948. The annotations can assist with issues such as the debates in Parliament on a particular section. These volumes are not updated, and so it is usually preferable to use *Halsbury's Statutes* or an appropriate database on the Internet.

### Halsbury's Statutory Instruments

This provides up-to-date information on every statutory instrument (SI) in force in England and Wales. Not all of the text of every SI is included. You can use this multi-volume service to check on the changes made to original SIs. A guide to using the service is available at the front of volume 1 of the *Halsbury's Statutory Instruments Service*.

## The main online resources for legislation

### LexisLibrary: legislation

This online resource is subscribed to by many law schools and law firms. It contains up-to-date amended text of all UK statutes and statutory instruments. It can be accessed via the Legislation tab on the *LexisLibrary* Home Page. There are helpful tutorials that guide you through finding Acts and statutory instruments.

 **Top tip**

A reminder of why client problems are usually not best tackled through primary source searches first. In Nicola's case you identified 'damages' and 'repair' as keywords. If you go straight to *LexisLibrary* and perform a search using these terms, 416 sources are found.

The advantage of using *LexisLibrary* is that you do not have to check to see if the legislation is current because the material is updated. Usually this is done in the text itself. If there have been some very recent changes that have not yet made it into the text, *LexisLibrary* will announce this with a Stop Press alert at the top of your search result.

When accessing UK statutes, you can see more than just the text of each section; the notes at the bottom will tell you if the section is in force and often provide links to subordinate legislation. For example, the section of a particular Act may give the Secretary of State power to make regulations under that section which actually contain much of the procedural detail you are looking for. A click on the link to the subordinate legislation will often identify the material in detail.

*Westlaw*

This online database contains all UK Acts of Parliament since 1267 and all statutory instruments since 1948. Again, the text is updated so that the current law can be viewed. There are notes to indicate if a section has been repealed or is current. There is a very useful function in Legislation Analysis which allows you to check on the cases citing a particular section. There are direct links to cases that *Westlaw* carries and also a list of journal articles on the relevant section.

*Lawtel*

This online service is widely subscribed to. It has all of the original full text Acts published since 1984. It has a statutory status table which contains information on amendments and repeals.

Legislation.gov.uk

This free, government website allows access to both original texts of statutes and the amended text taken from the UK Statute Law Database. However, it appears that occasionally amendments are not fully applied to the database for some time, in which case you have to undertake a rather complicated search process. This website replaces opsi.gov.uk, with which you may be familiar.

### Primary sources: case law

As already noted, this chapter does not deal with all of the issues involved in reading and finding case law. For a comprehensive analysis of this subject, see Holborn (2006). If you have a citation for the case you are looking for, you can of course look it up in the law report cited or on one of the online databases.

### Paper-based case law search sources

If you have the case name but not the citation, then for cases between 1845 and 1946 you should use *The Digest*. To find a case, you should start with the consolidated table of cases. For cases from 1947 onwards, the Current Law Case Citators, which should be in your law library, can be used to find cases.

However, it may be that you are looking for case law relating to a particular statutory provision or in relation to an aspect of common law. In terms of paper-based material, the main method of looking for case law is to use the Current Law Yearbook. This arranges references to cases by subject. However, a full search for case law by subject is far better performed online.

### Online sources for cases

You will find summarised below the main online resources for case law searching. As indicated above, it is rarely a good idea to start your research into an unfocused problem online. They are excellent tools once you have a reasonable idea of the law you are considering and have identified some of the leading cases using secondary sources.

*Westlaw*

*Westlaw* has a sophisticated search engine which allows you to search for cases by case name or subject. It is less comprehensive than *LexisLibrary* in terms of being able to give you full text case reports, but it is arguable that it is the best place to start a search for case law due to its search engine.

You can search by case name using the party names field. If you are searching by subject then use the free text field. A guide to using search terms and connectors is available on the site. This is worth reading because simply putting in a search term can lead to hundreds or thousands of hits.

When you perform a search, *Westlaw* will give you a 'Case Analysis' option as well as links to any case reports that are on the site for the case. It is a very good idea to click on 'Case Analysis' first. This provides:

- *Where the case is reported*, including a hyperlink to the report if it is available on *Westlaw*.
- *A digest of the case*. This is a very useful summary which will help you decide if the case is relevant.
- *Significant and other cases cited in the case.*
- *Cases which subsequently cited the case you have found.* This is extremely useful if you know that the case you have found is relevant to your case but you want to see how the courts have further interpreted the law in subsequent cases, or you want to see if a later case has overruled your case.
- *Legislation cited in your case.*
- *Journal articles available on Westlaw about the case, with hyperlinks.*
- *Books available on Westlaw about the case, with hyperlinks.*

---

### Nicola's problem

*Halsbury's Laws* indicated (see above) that the windows of a dwelling-house appear to be part of the structure and exterior for the purposes of s 11 of the Landlord and Tenant Act, such that the landlord will owe an obligation to Nicola to repair them. *Halsbury's* referred to the case of *Irvine v Moran*. A search using the party names on *Westlaw* leads to the case of *Irvine v Moran* itself. The case analysis and the abstract confirms that external windows do form part of the structure and exterior. You can read the full official transcript by clicking on the link.

You can then look to see which cases have cited *Irvine v Moran*. The more recent case of *Sheffield City Council v Oliver*, Lands Tribunal, 18 August 2008 (unreported) reviewed the authorities in this area and came to the conclusion that external windows will form part of the structure and exterior. There may be circumstances in which they do not, but these appear to be exceptional.

The case analysis of *Irvine v Moran* also indicates that the case has not been overruled and so you can satisfy yourself that that is the current position on the law.

---

### LexisLibrary

*LexisLibrary* contains many of the reported cases. If you are searching for a particular case, for which you have the name or citation, you can use the 'Search Cases' function (not to be confused with the 'CaseSearch' source). If you search all of the subscribed sources, this will give you both full text case reports and also a link to the case in 'CaseSearch'.

The 'CaseSearch' facility states the court in which the case was heard, a list of cases where it has been applied, distinguished, overruled, considered or followed. A 'Case History' shows the courts it was held in. It will also sometimes summarise the case for you.

*LexisLibrary* also has journal sources which you can search for articles on your case.

### Lawtel

*Lawtel* contains all major law reports since 1980 and unreported cases. While it is not as comprehensive as *Westlaw* or *LexisLibrary*, it has the advantage of having a very user-friendly summary of each case on the screen as you look at the list that your search has identified. This helps to screen out irrelevant cases quite quickly.

### BAILII (British and Irish Legal Information Institute)

This free website has judgments from all major United Kingdom and Irish courts from 1996 onwards. It does not, however, provide information as to the subsequent treatment of the case by the courts, so it is only of benefit if you want to read the full judgment. There are other free access databases, for example *EUR-Lex* (on EU law) and at www.echr.coe/int (European Court of Human Rights).

## Other secondary sources

You should by now have quite a firm grasp on the legal issues involved in your client's case. You might still be confused about the implications of the latest leading case in the area, however, or your client's case might involve a regulatory agency or local or central government. The following is a non-exhaustive list of further sources of information:

- *Legal journals* – particularly useful for comment on developments in the law or discussion of a recent case. For example, *The Journal of Legal Action Group* publishes regular updates on housing law which would be particularly useful in Nicola's case.

- *Government websites* – for example, the UK Border Agency website contains critical information as to the treatment of asylum seekers.

- *Local authority websites* – for example, in Nicola's case, the council may well have information on its pest control operations and details of how to report complaints.

- *Other official websites* – for example, the websites of the Association of Chief Police Officers and the Health and Safety Executive.

- *Other people* – often the best source of information for lawyers is either their colleagues or employees of organisations such as local government departments. Obviously, you need to consider whether you can contact such people (it would be inappropriate in a simulated activity for example).

### Summary of the stages of practical legal research

Remember that going through this process will involve constantly considering the facts of your client's case and his or her goals. You need to be prepared to retrace your steps and revisit sources as your understanding grows. You must make sure that you have thought carefully about your conclusions.

## 8.4 Preparing a practical legal research report

It is very important to record and present your research properly when working for clients for the following reasons:

- You need to be able to do this as a trainee solicitor or pupil barrister.
- You may be working on the case with fellow students, or they may work on it in future. They need to have the benefit of your hard work so that it does not have to be repeated and they can concentrate on assisting the client.
- You need an accurate record and report from your research for your own purposes. If you have to come back to it after several weeks, you may well have forgotten the minutiae of the law and the sources you used.
- Your supervisor may want to check your work for accuracy, or there may be some legal elements with which he or she is not entirely familiar.

### Research report format

There is no one way to present research, but it is recommended that you use the headings below, subject to your institution's requirements. They ensure that you go through the process fully and deal with all of the necessary information.

### The client's problem

This heading essentially sets out your attempt to analyse and identify the important facts and consider the client's goals. We have already done this in Nicola's case, above.

### Identification of problem/areas for research

Here you will be thinking about and recording what you believe the legal problems to be that you will need to research. The areas could be very broad at the outset of your research if you are unfamiliar with the area of law. In other cases they may be slightly more focused – and if you update these as you research you will find they become more and more focused and specific as your understanding grows.

### Keywords/phrases

You have already seen that identifying possible keywords and phrases will assist with index searching. You should make a record of them before you begin so that you can force yourself to spend time thinking them through and so that you have a record of words and phrases you have searched for. This can be particularly useful for online searching – to prevent you coming back and making the same search twice.

**Top tip**

Start writing your report before you start your information search. So, when you are thinking about keywords, for example, write these down as part of your report. The headings used for the report contain some important initial research prerequisites that you have looked at above in relation to Nicola's case, such as identifying keywords.

## Research report

In this section you will set out the law and apply it to the facts of your client's problem. Your research report should state the law relevant to your client's case and should also make reference to the facts of your client's case, drawing conclusions as you proceed. Stay focused on your client's goals and the facts of his or her particular case. You are not giving a general statement of the law but a specific report on how the relevant law impacts on your client's case. Remember that you are usually not only trying to advise your client about the impact of the substantive law on his or her problem. For example, being able to advise a client that his package holiday provider is liable for a failure to provide the services contracted for in the package will be only part of the solution to the client's problem. Your report will also need to focus on the procedure for obtaining redress, the forms of redress available, the likely level of any damages and how strong the client's case is by reference to the evidence available.

Try to make sure that you structure your report in a logical way. In many respects the structure will be similar to that in answering a problem question on your law course. If confronted with a general problem question on negligence in tort, for example, you would expect to deal first with duty of care issues, then breach, then causation and finally defences. The same is true for the structure of a PLR report. Try to address each legal issue in turn. Within that, of course, you may also be considering your client's goals and the facts of the case in greater detail than in an undergraduate problem answer.

Your report should make reference to all relevant primary and secondary sources for the information within the body of the report. In this way, it differs from a standard undergraduate problem answer. You would expect a standard problem answer to make reference of course to the primary sources. You would not usually expect, outside of a bibliography or reference to specific opinion from a commentator, to see reference to textbooks and practitioner sources within the body of the problem answer. However, with PLR, it is very useful to you and any other reader (supervisor or fellow student) to know exactly where the information you are using for each statement comes from. This makes it much easier to go back and read the secondary source and consider whether the report accurately summarises the law in a particular respect.

**Top tip**

If you find a particularly useful secondary source online, it can be very tempting to simply cut and paste that text into the body of a report. There are several important reasons why you should not do this. If your work is being assessed, it is likely that your report will not be sufficiently your own work (leading, at best, to a poor grade for academic merit if you have acknowledged the source and, at worst, a finding of plagiarism if you have not).

You should record all sources for the law by placing footnotes alongside your text, using your institution's preferred citation method. When referring to secondary sources, you should also make reference to the page number or section and paragraph number depending upon how that source is structured.

Again, if you make notes as you read each source and carefully record what it says and where you obtained the information, this will make writing up the report a lot easier.

### Top tip

Do not be tempted to write reports in the form of a history of your research. For instance: 'First I went to *Halsbury's Laws* which told me ...' An example of a full report on Nicola's case can be found on the Companion Website and illustrates an appropriate style.

### Additional information required

This is a crucial area when working with clients. Your research is not usually there merely to provide a once-and-for-all answer. It is extremely rare that a client can provide all of the facts in a case at a first interview. Usually there will be additional information necessary. This could be because you need further facts from the client, an opponent or a third party to establish which legal principles will apply. Perhaps the case may turn on the strength of the evidence available and you are searching for further evidence, or you require more information to establish the level of loss.

It is very important, therefore, that you list the additional information required. This will assist you in managing the case.

### Nicola's problem

In Nicola's case, the focus so far has been on her window problem. You may remember that the research indicated that, in order to be obliged to repair the windows, the landlord must have notice of the problem. Nicola's goals appear to include being compensated for having to live in a damp and draughty flat. This issue alone would give rise to the following list of further facts that you require:

- Does the landlord know about the window problem?
- How did the landlord come to know of the problem? In writing? Orally?
- What proof do we have that he has been informed?
- When was the landlord informed?
- What was the landlord's reaction to the problem? Did he refuse to take any action? If he did refuse to take action, did he give reasons for that?

### Summary

This should be a short synopsis setting out the conclusions of your research. In a contentious case, you should attempt to comment on the strength of your client's case and the likely remedies available.

## Primary sources

This section should list all of the primary sources applicable to the piece of research. For ease, the sources should be subdivided into legislation and case law. It is best to state the precise section numbers of Acts when referring to them, and when referring to case law make sure you provide the full citation.

## Secondary sources

Here you should list all of the textbooks, journal articles and practitioner texts used in your research, providing full citation details. Again categorise the different sources used for ease of reference.

### State how you have checked that the law in your report is up to date

You have read above how crucial it is that your sources are updated. Your report should explicitly record how you have done this. This includes updating practitioner texts and *Halsbury's Laws*, ensuring you use up-to-date legislation sources, and using tools such as Case Analysis on *Westlaw* to check that the important case authorities you have identified have not been overruled or distinguished.

A pro forma incorporating the above headings, which you can use for your PLR reports, is available on the Companion Website. An alternative PLR template is available in the LawWorks Student Handbook, a link to which is available on Companion Website.

**Top tips for research**

- Focus on the client's goals and being able fully to meet these.
- Think about your research before you start. Identify the facts, possible legal issues and keywords.
- Use hardcopy secondary sources first.
- Make sure all sources you use are authoritative.
- Keep a careful note of all your sources as you go.
- Apply the facts of your client's case to the law. Your client does not want a general statement on the law.
- Try to come to a reasoned conclusion that proposes action.
- Write a proper research report that is properly referenced.
- Make sure you use more than one or two sources; check information elsewhere.
- Make sure you check the law is up to date.

 **8.5** Summary

Practical legal research is performed for the purpose of providing advice and assistance to clients. It involves the skills of the legal academic coupled with application to the facts and the goal of practically solving a client's problems. If you keep these key issues in mind, you will be able to help your clients and build skills that will help you be an effective, and hopefully fulfilled, professional in practice.

## PLR flowchart

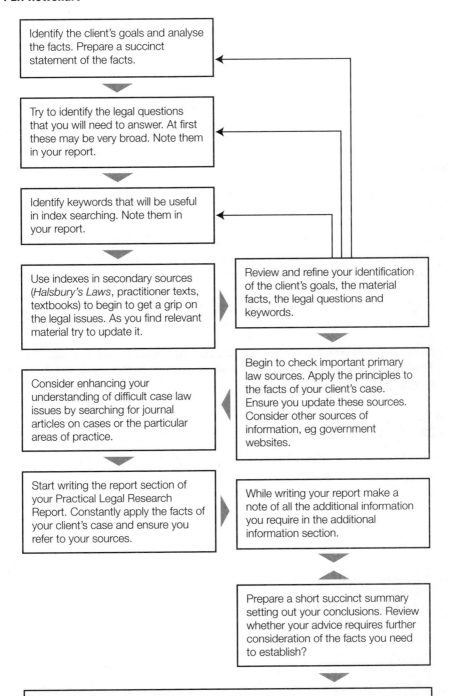

 Further reading

You will find a list of useful books that are commonly used in clinic for specific legal problems on the Companion Website. The books recommended here relate to further guidance on research.

### Introductory

Boyle, F et al, *A Practical Guide to Lawyering Skills*, 3rd edn (Cavendish Publishing, 2005)
Chapter 3 provides an introduction to legal research and identifying legal problems, whilst Chapter 4 looks at practical legal research in more detail.

### Intermediate

Webb, J et al, *Lawyers' Skills 2010–11* (Oxford University Press, 2010)
Chapter 5 contains some useful points on using legal sources and on problem identification.

### Advanced

Tunkel, V, *Legal Research* (Blackstone Press, 1992)
This book is excellent on the process of legal research and contains examples of attempts at research.

McKie, S, *Legal Research* (Cavendish Publishing, 1993)
This book has some very useful material on identifying keywords and categorising legal problems.

Holborn, G, *Butterworths Legal Research Guide*, 2nd edn (Oxford University Press, 2006)
This comprehensive text looks closely at all elements of legal research and is highly recommended.

 Activities

The activities for this chapter can be found on the Companion Website as you may wish to use electronic resources to complete the tasks.

# 9 Organising and strategising

'He who is prepared has the battle
half fought.'

Cervantes, *Don Quixote*

## 9.1 Introduction

Every day, life requires you to organise and strategise. Combining study, work and home life requires you to organise your time, think about your future goals and plan ahead. Throughout your life, you process, file and record all kinds of paperwork, from household bills to letters from your university or employer. You are required to arrange and diarise appointments with your GP, dentist, tutors and bank. Usually, how successful you are in juggling and coordinating all these tasks affects you and you alone.

During your clinic or pro bono activities, you will be dealing with real clients, just as a lawyer is required to do in practice, or acting in role during simulations that require you to perform as a lawyer would. The skills needed to complete tasks efficiently will be similar to the abilities you need to coordinate yourself every day. However, as a professional, your ability to carry out these tasks has a large impact not only on you, but more importantly on your client and your employer. Organising and strategising are therefore important parts of your clinic and pro bono activities. They are also vital skills which you need to develop for your future career. It should also be emphasised that the ability to strategise is often viewed as a very important factor in clinical or pro bono assessment where these activities are graded. Displaying impressive skills in this area can make a big difference to the overall view your supervisor has about the quality of your work.

Your clinic and pro bono activities may be your first experience of real legal work; you may have never written to a person in a professional capacity before, or worked in a law office. This chapter will therefore provide you with guidance on what is meant by organising and strategising, why they are central to your role and, most importantly, how to do them. They can be challenging skills to master, so this chapter also provides hints and tips which will assist you with your case work and pro bono projects.

## 9.2 Strategising (case management)

### What is it?

Strategising, or case management, is the method by which you progress your client's case or plan your pro bono project. In the context of casework, strategising is concerned with ensuring that you take the correct or most appropriate steps on your client's file at the correct time or within appropriate timescales. It is also about ideas. A good strategy will be reviewed regularly and new angles or possibilities investigated. You should be willing to think broadly about the issues that arise out of your client's problem and be receptive to fresh ways of analysing the case and the potential remedies available.

Every area of law is different. There are different time limits by which work needs to be completed, and each client file, type of case or clinical work has different demands. The strategy you need to engage will therefore vary depending upon the type of work you do.

To develop good case management skills, you will have to identify quickly the type of case or matter you are dealing with and the relevant issues. You will also need to be proactive in identifying practical options for your client. This can be harder than it sounds.

### Why is it important?

As stated in the introduction, the ability to strategise has benefits for a variety of people.

### For you

Two of the core duties of a solicitor are to act in the best interests of your client and to provide your client with a good standard of service (Rule 1 of the Solicitors' Code of Conduct 2007). When conducting legal work for clients, you will be expected to adhere to the Code or at least its principles. If your supervisor is a practising solicitor then his or her conduct, and therefore any work produced in his or her name, will be governed by this Code of Conduct.

When clients or organisations instruct you to do work for them, you owe them a duty of care. They are relying on you to provide good quality, accurate advice and assistance in a timely manner. Regardless of the fact that you are not a qualified lawyer, when undertaking pro bono work your organisation is holding you out as someone who is capable of accurately and correctly advising and assisting clients with their legal problem. This requires a high level of personal responsibility. It is your responsibility to ensure that your client's case or your project is handled in the correct manner and in a way which protects the client's interests.

In order to protect your client's interests, you must ensure that you do not miss or overlook anything on his or her case. As your clinic and pro bono activities may be your first substantive legal experience, you may not know what you are looking for in a case and what is actually in your client's best interests. It is therefore important that you develop good case management skills so you can quickly identify the issues and discuss them with your supervisor and fellow students. Even if you are at the stage where you do not fully understand the importance of the issues, if you are able to identify the client's goals and the key points of a case then, with supervision and guidance, you should be able to plan and progress the matter.

It is always important when handling a file that you think ahead so you know in which direction the case is going. This means that you can properly and clearly advise your client and prepare for future events. It will be impossible for you to plan and organise your time if you are clueless as to the direction or the amount of work that needs to be dedicated to each step in your case or project. Failing to time-manage may also have an impact on your other academic work or outside commitments.

If you fail to think ahead and plan out the action you need to take in the future, you may miss a deadline or limitation date. This could have grave implications on the case and therefore on you personally, as you will have to deal with a disappointed or angry client. It could also have serious consequences for your organisation or clinic, as it may be liable to pay compensation to your client if your actions were negligent.

You must give your client accurate advice and practical options to deal with his or her legal problems. By developing good case management skills, you will run the case more effectively and you will hopefully therefore be providing a high quality service. It may, however, also be important to you if your clinical or pro bono work is being assessed as part of your course or programme.

Good case management skills are transferable so, even if in the future you do not enter the legal profession, you can still put the skills to use in a variety of occupations. It may also assist you in becoming more efficient in your dealings in everyday life.

### For your clinic, organisation or supervisor

Your supervisor is placing a great deal of trust in you to pursue a client's case or undertake pro bono work for the public. Remember, ultimately it will be your supervisor who will be answerable to your client if the client is not happy with your work. Your supervisor is also a professional. As stated earlier, you may be working on a real case under your supervisor's legal practising certificate. Your supervisor will have a professional reputation to protect and therefore it will be important to him or her that you are handling the case correctly.

Legal problems can be critical to, and potentially a distressing part of, someone's life. Just because your clinic or organisation may work for free does not mean that your clients will not demand a good level of service. Your clinic or organisation may have spent many years building a good reputation in the local community, relying on repeat custom or good word of mouth. The standard of the work you produce and the service you provide to your client may impact on the work your clinic or organisation receives in the future. Maintaining a good reputation can ensure that future students receive good quality clinical work.

As stated above, failing to manage your client's case correctly and efficiently may result in a complaint or, at worst, a negligence action.

### For your client

Clients come to your clinic or organisation because they require assistance, whether that is with a legal dispute or by way of a community presentation. Your ability to strategise, plan and progress a matter impacts hugely on them. So, for example, if you are conducting a Streetlaw project, and you fail to organise your time effectively and produce your presentation on time, this could cause huge embarrassment to your client who may have advertised it to the community.

If you are conducting live cases, clients will be expecting a prompt and reliable service from you. They will want the best possible outcome to their problem and they will want it quickly. If you display good case management skills then this will be reflected in the work you produce for a client and the speed at which the claim or dispute is resolved.

Good case management skills should ensure that you avoid a complaint. If you have identified the direction in which your case is going, you will find it easy to keep your client updated, and you will be prepared for each stage in the case. As a result, there should not be long delays between the completion of each task, and your client will hopefully have no cause to find fault with the service provided.

##  Where to start

### Case planning

The first step you need to take is to identify your client's requirements, goals and objectives. At this stage, you may not know much about the type of work you are doing. However, even with limited legal knowledge when meeting your client for the first time, it should be possible to ask appropriate questions to establish why that person has come to you for assistance and what he or she wants to achieve. It is also advisable to ascertain at an early juncture what your client is willing to do to achieve those objectives. It is worth making a clear note of these goals, objectives and requirements.

When you first start doing clinical work, it is easy to get swept away in the excitement of conducting real cases for the first time. After you have taken instructions, you may discover that the client has a strong case and you know you can get him or her a good outcome. However, you client might be adamant in wanting to avoid court. He or she may be willing to accept less or nothing, rather than go to court. You must always remember that it is your client's case and not yours. It is therefore very important to establish the boundaries within which you have to work. You can advise a client as to the best option, but ultimately you must act on his or her instructions.

After you have established the goal, the next step is to establish what you need to do to achieve the goal or objectives, ensuring at the same time that you satisfy your client's personal requirements and the requirements of your clinic or organisation.

A word of warning – if you are dealing with real clients then you must be prepared for the unexpected. Clients' goals and objectives can change. This can be for a variety of reasons: they may feel more confident once you are assisting them, they may have a change of heart, or they may become disinterested in the case. You must ensure that you review their goals at various points in the case and be prepared to adapt your strategy accordingly.

## Action plans

The easiest way to case plan is to produce an action plan for your file. A written action plan is a permanent record of what you need to do. You can refer back to the plan to refresh your memory and to keep yourself on track. It is certainly useful to have an action plan when working with others on a case. It will make it easier for you to divide tasks and responsibilities. It will also ensure that you are working to the same goals and moving in the same direction. An action plan will also benefit your supervisor, who may be working on a number of cases or projects. He or she will be able to use it to refresh his or her memory and this will make supervision more efficient and effective.

Production of an action plan is not just something you will do during your clinical legal education. The Law Society has acknowledged the importance of action plans for effective case management and has produced the Lexcel Practice Management Standard. Solicitors are awarded the Lexcel Practice Management Standard if they meet certain criteria in their practice. Part of the Standard addresses the issue of case management. At point 8.2, it requires that case strategy is clear from the file and that an action plan is devised for complicated cases.

Although not all of your cases will be highly complex, learning at this early stage to develop and effectively use an action plan will improve your professional practice for the future.

Below is a simple pro forma, which you may wish to use for your case planning. Even if you choose not to use this pro forma, it would be useful to have some clear note on your file as to the steps you need to take to progress your client's case. You may even wish to develop your own pro forma that is specific to your own clinic.

---

**Action Plan**

Client Name: ....................................................................................................

Case Reference: ................................................................................................

Date: ..................................................................................................................

Names of the parties: ........................................................................................

Deadlines: ..........................................................................................................

Outcome/client goal: .........................................................................................

Steps to be taken (insert date and time estimate for completion beside each step):

..........................................................................................................................

Research to be completed: ...............................................................................

Evidence to gather and collate: ........................................................................

Important points to note: ...................................................................................

Signed ...................................          Date...................................

Full Name ...................................

Approved by Supervisor

Signed ...................................          Date ...................................

Full Name ...................................

## Who is involved?

This may seem very simple, but establishing who exactly is involved in a dispute is not always straightforward. It is important to establish from the outset the key people and organisations connected with the case. There is likely to be a delay to the progression of your case if you fail to identify the correct opponent. There may also be several people involved and, by identifying them early in the case, you will be in a better position to assess their involvement and liability as your case progresses. In essence, it will assist you in getting a clearer picture. For example, who might the parties be in Nicola's case (see p 112)? Her landlord? Her neighbour? The neighbour's boyfriend? All of them?

## Client goals

As stated earlier, the first step to case planning is to write down what your client's goal is. What does your client actually want to achieve? Does he or she want compensation? Does he or she want the return of something? You can then work backwards to ascertain what steps you need to take to obtain this goal. Establishing what action you need to take in pursuit of these objectives will involve you considering the type of work you are doing and the specific rules and time limits applicable to that work. Therefore, at this stage, you may need to undertake some initial research. Please refer to **Chapter 8** for guidance and tips on legal research.

There can be a number of ways to achieve the result your client is seeking. Perhaps a conventional route of obtaining redress is not an option to your client, possibly for financial reasons, so you may need to be creative. This is why, at the outset, it is important to establish your client's limits and what he or she is actually willing to do to achieve a resolution to the problem.

As part of your case planning, it is important that you consider and document the key steps that your clinic or office requires you to take. So, for example, if you work in a clinic running real cases, you will be required to send out a client care letter in accordance with Rule 2 of the Solicitors' Code of Conduct 2007. You will need to ensure that this is documented on your action plan.

## Deadlines

As stated earlier, the type of work you are doing will dictate the deadlines. When you are case planning, you must carefully consider whether you have any urgent time limits or deadlines to comply with. It is important that you not only make a note of these on your action plan, but also diarise and monitor them accordingly.

## Time limits

It is important, when devising your action plan, that you also estimate the date by which each step needs to be taken. So, for example, you may wish to ensure that your client care letter is sent within seven days of your first meeting with your client, or you may want your Streetlaw presentation completed within four weeks of taking instructions.

In order for you to set and meet realistic deadlines, you will need to calculate the length of time you require to complete each task. You should consider whether there are legal reasons why you will have to complete a task within a set period of time. For example, does your client have an urgent limitation date and, if so, what tasks need to be completed prior to this date? You will need to build into the time period the fact that it is likely to take you longer than a legal professional to complete each task, and that your work will probably need to be checked by someone else to ensure it is correct.

Once you have established your action plan, you will have to organise your own time effectively to ensure that you are able to complete the tasks on your action plan.

## Time management

Time management is a key skill and vitally important to good case management. When you work in a clinic or take part in pro bono activities, you are likely to be doing it alongside your other academic studies. You may also have part-time work or other commitments. Coordinating your time is essential to ensuring that your work is conducted promptly and correctly.

### Early bird or night owl?

It is important to establish when you work best. 'Some people work much better in the mornings, and others later in the day ... You will work much better at your own peak times, and as far as possible you should try and organise the more mundane and routine tasks for times when you are naturally less alert.' (Mayson, 1992: 61)

It is therefore advisable, if you have important research to complete, that you do this when you know you will be at your most alert. You can save tasks, such as ensuring all your filing is complete, to periods when you are less alert. However, this is not an excuse to fall behind with more basic, routine tasks.

### Synchronising

Working in a clinic or pro bono organisation also brings the challenge of working with other people. This can make time management difficult. It is likely you will have to work with at least one other student. You should try to ensure that you arrange times during the week when you will both be available, and set regular meetings to review and discuss your work. This is dealt with in more detail in **Chapter 5**, 'Working with your supervisor and others'.

When planning your workload, you will also have to build in time to allow your supervisor to check your work. It can sometimes be very difficult to stick to a plan, as you may not know when your work will be returned by your supervisor. It is also possible that, when the work is returned, you will have to make corrections or conduct further research. It is therefore good practice to allocate sufficient time when devising your action plan to allow for any delays. Clinical and pro bono activities provide perfect opportunities for you to develop the skills of coordinating your time around this unpredictability. If you are waiting for your supervisor to check a piece of work, use this lull to complete the next task on your list or some of your other academic work. Clinical and pro bono work is unpredictable. By completing work well in advance, the more prepared you will be to cope with busy periods in your academic year, for example in the run-up to coursework submission dates, or when your casework places more demands on you.

The most important thing is to make time for all of your work. Once you have established how long a task will take, schedule blocks of time to complete the task. Give the task your full attention and try not to jump around and switch tasks. It is also useful to remove all distractions, whether this means working apart from talkative friends or turning off your email or social networking sites.

### Diaries and 'to do' lists

Professionals rely heavily on diaries to ensure that key dates are not missed. It is therefore important that you start to use a diary. Although your clinic or organisation is likely to have a central diary to record all key information, it is still important that you have your own diary. At this stage, you are unlikely to have numerous cases with deadlines, but a diary will still be useful to coordinate your clinical or pro bono work, other academic studies and personal commitments.

Ensure you remember your duty of confidentiality. If you are using your diary for live client work, you may have to use abbreviations or leave your diary in a secure place in your clinic. You should always seek guidance from your supervisor or tutor as to your clinic or organisation's requirements for the recording and storage of confidential information.

| What to record in your diary |
| --- |
| • Appointments/interviews |
| • Deadlines |
| • Time limits |
| • Hearing dates |
| • Dates to chase replies to your letters |
| • Deadlines for completing research or for finalising certain letters |

It is useful to place double entries for urgent deadlines or limitation dates in your diary. If you place a reminder in the week before the deadline or limitation date, this will ensure you are aware that the date is approaching and give you time to check that the necessary work is complete.

You should consult your diary daily to ensure that no task or deadline is missed. It may also be useful to prioritise the entries in your diary so you complete the most urgent work at the start of the day.

'To do' lists are a very useful way to ensure that you manage your time effectively and complete work in a timely fashion. Once you have developed an action plan, you should make a list of what you need to do on a piece of paper or electronically. Your list should be detailed, so you are clear as to what exactly is expected. For example, if you have arranged an interview with your client, your diary should record the date of the interview. Your 'to do' list might look like this:

Book interview room [Immediately]

Send letter to Client confirming time/date of interview [Immediately]

Prepare interview plan [7–10 days before interview]

Send interview plan to Supervisor for checking [7 days before interview]

Make any amendments to the plan and resubmit for supervisor approval [3 days before interview]

Detailed 'to do' lists help you to appreciate exactly what needs to be done and therefore how much time you should allow yourself for each of the tasks. They can also assist you in dividing up the tasks if you are working with another student.

Once you have prepared your 'to do' list, it is important that you prioritise the tasks. It is human nature to put off the more complex or lengthy tasks, but these are probably the most important. As in your case planning, it is useful to note beside each task how long it should take you to complete. You can then be realistic as to what you can achieve in a day.

## 9.4  How to develop good case management skills

- Think ahead – from the outset of your case, prepare a timetable of what action needs to be taken, when it needs to be done, and who will do it. Make sure that your timetable is realistic and stick to it.
- Diarise key dates – have a diary system to accurately record deadlines to ensure that you do not miss any important dates.
- Establish your client's objectives – always remember that the case 'belongs' to your client.
- Work out tactics and strategies – plan the best way to achieve your client's goals.
- Think outside the box – there may be a number of ways to achieve your client's goals. Alternatively, you may face an unusual legal problem that cannot be resolved by conventional methods. Use common sense and explore your options.
- Be proactive – do not wait for a deadline. Prepare work in advance to ensure that your supervisor has opportunity to check it first. If you have spare time, think about what will happen next and be prepared. Make sure that you deal with any correspondence you receive promptly.
- Share, discuss, argue – the most productive case strategy meetings are often ones where students and the supervisor have open and frank discussions about what progress has been made, or exchange ideas about how to progress a matter when things appear to be stagnating.
- Keep your client up to date – it is important that your client is aware of what is happening on the case and the likely timescales in which you will complete the work. Clients who have their expectations managed in this way are more likely to be pleased with the service you are providing and therefore less likely to complain.

## 9.5 Organising (file management)

### What is it?

File management is the skill of organising your client files. The organisation at which you carry out your clinic work or pro bono activities is likely to have strict rules for the management of client files. This mirrors real legal practice where every firm has its own specific procedures.

File management is not limited to how an individual file looks or is organised. File management involves the opening, closing, storing and recording of client files.

### Why is it important?

In a clinical or pro bono environment, file management is important to different people for different reasons.

### For you

When you perform clinical or pro bono work as part of your studies, you are taking on a high level of responsibility. You are ultimately responsible for your client's file and are answerable to your client and your supervisor.

Under the Solicitors' Code of Conduct 2007, you owe a number of important duties to your client. One of those duties is the duty of confidentiality (Rule 4). Clients' files will contain personal information about them and their legal problems. It is therefore important that you ensure such files are safe and secure at all times.

You also have a duty to ensure that no conflict arises that would restrict your ability to act for your client. Your clinic or organisation is likely to have a system to enable you to check that no conflict arises and that you can take on the matter and assist the client.

As a student, you may begin working on a case but not have time to complete it before your studies finish. The person taking over your file will need to establish exactly what has happened on a case, what steps you have taken and what work is outstanding. It is therefore important that your file is set up in a standard way, it is in order and it is up to date.

Having a file that is in order and up to date will also assist anyone you are working with on a case. When participating in clinic or pro bono activity, you may not always be able to meet with the person who is working with you. It might be a matter of designating certain tasks to each other or, alternatively, working on the case on alternate dates. As such, it is important that you all know what is happening on the file and that it is kept in good order.

### For your clinic, organisation or supervisor

It is important to your supervisor and your clinic or organisation that you comply with the rules in place for the management of clients' cases. There will be established procedures to ensure that there is an accurate record of the files on which you are working. The clinic or organisation will also need to know when files are closed, as there are strict rules on the length of time files must be kept before they can be destroyed. If you do not follow these rules then a file could go missing or, if not correctly recorded, may be overlooked once you finish your course or module.

**For your client**

Just because you are providing free legal services as part of your course, this does not mean that your client will not expect confidential and personal information to be stored safely and securely. The case or activity may be part of your education but it is also a real legal issue. Your client will entrust you with personal documents and it is essential that he or she can rely on you to keep them safe and return them when required.

Your client is relying on you to provide a service and may at some point in the future, if you cannot assist him or her further, request that you provide a copy of the file or documents from the file. There is also a chance, if your client finds alternative assistance from another organisation or firm of solicitors, that the new representative may request a copy of your client's file. The new representative will expect to receive an organised file which contains everything needed to take the matter further. It will be embarrassing and potentially damaging for your clinic or organisation if you are unable to provide copies of all the work you have completed for your client.

## **9.6** File management systems

It is likely that your clinic or organisation has a system for the management of your cases. This system is likely to vary depending on the type, level or amount of work being done. The most important thing you can do is to learn the system which is in place and follow it.

> **Examples of elements of file management systems**
>
> - Alphabetical filing system
> - A computer database for storing client names and addresses
> - Different coloured files arranged by type of case or year of commencement
> - A marking system for the front of the file to denote key dates or whether court or tribunal proceedings have been commenced
> - Separate wallets placed on a client file for different types of documents

## **9.7** Where to start

When you first meet with your client, he or she is likely to give you documents that relate to his or her problem. It can be daunting to have to deal with this for the first time, particularly if there is a copious amount of paperwork. Your first steps are likely to involve opening a file for your client and recording all relevant information about his or her problem. Although your organisation or clinic will have a safe place for storing files, it is always advisable to take copies of your client's documents and return the originals to him or her as soon as possible. In most cases, you will be required to return original documents to your client at the end of the case anyway, so it is better to do this earlier rather than later.

When opening a new file, it is important to ensure that everything is organised. Gather all of the documents and any correspondence together and make sure that you place them in the correct location on the file. So, for example, your clinic or organisation might stipulate that all client documents should be stored in a separate wallet on the file.

Once everything is in the correct place, ensure that it is in a logical order so that the documents are easy to locate. Correspondence on a client's file runs from newest to oldest. So your first ever letter to your client is likely to be at the bottom of your file, and all subsequent letters are placed in reverse chronological order on top.

Make sure that all relevant information is on your file. This includes any work undertaken before the file was officially opened. The same principle applies if you are taking over a file from someone else. Read over the file carefully, checking that all documents are in the correct place. If anything appears to be missing, make a note of it and speak to your supervisor. For example, if your organisation or clinic has a requirement that all clients provide identification, verify that copies of the client's identification documents are on file.

If your client has too many documents to fit onto one file, do not leave them loose. Open a second file if necessary. If you open additional files then you should clearly mark on the file how many files are open for that client.

## 9.8 How to develop good file management skills

When you are conducting casework as part of your course or programme, it can be quite difficult and time-consuming to keep on top of your file management. This is because your clinical or pro bono activities are likely to be carried out alongside your other studies. You may also be working with other students and it can be difficult to manage your files effectively if more than one person is working on them at once.

Here are some tips to assist you in maintaining good file management:

- Keep on top of filing – as soon as you receive any correspondence from your client, opponent, the court or tribunal, ensure that it is immediately placed on your file. No documents should be left lying around the office or loose at the back of the file.
- Be consistent – if there is more than one person working on the file, try to approach the set-up and layout of your file the same way. So, for example, if you write letters in the font, Times New Roman 12, make sure that your partners write in the same font.
- Make sure that any time recording is done immediately – legal professionals have to record their time so that they can accurately bill their cases. Regardless of whether you are billing your clients, it is important that you accurately record the amount of time it takes to complete your work. This should be done immediately and not retrospectively. It is not a riveting task, but it needs doing. So get into this habit quickly.

- Make contemporaneous notes of the work you carry out on the file and any telephone calls or attendances with your client or other parties to the case – it is vitally important that your file contains accurate information, so when you speak to anyone connected with the case, you must immediately make an accurate note of the conversation. This note must then be placed on file. If you do not make a note contemporaneously then you may forget exactly what was said, or you may neglect to make the note at all. Furthermore, if you fail to record the work undertaken or the conversation, your supervisor and any other student working on the file will not know what has been done. This can result in work being duplicated. For example, your partner might complete a task not realising that you have already done it. Worse still, it will be embarrassing and look unprofessional if your partner calls your client to advise him or her of a development when you have already done this.
- Regularly review your file – your office or organisation may have a system in place for reviewing files. If it does, you must complete the review paperwork promptly. If it does not then regularly review your file to make sure it is in order and everything is up to date.
- Always store your file correctly and securely – your client's file should be placed within your clinic or organisation's storage system once you have finished working on the file. It is common for files to be stored alphabetically. Make sure your file is placed in the correct place for ease of retrieval.

 **Top tip**

If you are opening a new file, ensure that it is opened and correctly logged by your clinic or organisation immediately. Once a matter is closed, check all original paperwork has been returned to your client and ensure that you close your file promptly.

## 9.9 Summary

You will already organise and strategise, but you must carry out these skills in specific ways when conducting legal work. There are also various rules you need to follow. These may be practice rules, for example the Solicitors' Code of Conduct, and/or the specific rules of your clinic or organisation.

The key to good case management is to be proactive and think ahead. You are being trusted with real legal problems and your supervisor will be expecting you to take responsibility for running the case. Ascertain your client's goals and work towards them. Think outside the box and try to find the best method for achieving those goals.

You must always bear in mind that legal cases are subject to strict time limits. When planning the progression of your case, think about the time limits which are specific to your case and factor them into your time estimates.

File management is closely connected to case management. Often, when people refer to case management, they are referring to the case planning and progression of a case as well as to the physical management and organisation of client files. There are a number of professional rules which impact on file management, such as your duty to keep client details confidential. Keeping your files in good order and in an organised system will enable you to work more quickly and efficiently. You will also find case management easier.

The strategising and organisational skills that you will develop whilst undertaking your clinical work will serve you well in your future career, whether or not you continue to pursue a career in law. Use the time you have in a clinical environment to develop and improve your skills, as you may not get this time again once you have left university.

 Further reading

There are few dedicated books on case and file management in the context of legal casework. These skills are usually covered alongside various other issues, such as advocacy, in legal skills books. Texts on personal management skills are useful for hints and tips on general organisation. For more specific guidance on the legal requirements for conducting client files, see the websites of the Law Society and Solicitors Regulation Authority.

When researching what steps need to be taken in your particular case, you should refer to a specific practitioner text for the relevant area of law. For example, if dealing with an employment matter, consult a book on employment tribunal practice and procedure.

### Introductory

**Mayson, S, *Personal Management Skills* (Blackstone Press, 1992)**
   This book has one chapter dedicated to managing yourself and your practice. It gives useful, simple tips for coordinating your time.

**Webb, J et al, *Lawyers' Skills* (Oxford University Press, 2010–11)**
   Chapter 9 of this book focuses on managing your workload. It provides tips on how to organise your time and how to work effectively with others.

### Intermediate

**The Law Society**
   www.lawsociety.org.uk/documents/downloads/lexcelv4standard.pdf
   This webpage sets out the Lexcel Practice Management Standard, which is a best practice framework. Solicitors' firms who meet certain criteria are awarded the Standard by the Law Society. It is therefore interesting reading for those who want to research and/or understand what is required of a legal practice. Practice Management Standard 8 covers file and case management.

 Activities

### Activity 1: Self-test

It is important to establish how good your time management skills are. Complete the self-test questions below.

## Clinical Time Management

Think about your clinical work and read the statements below. Circle the number that applies to you. Total your score at the bottom.

| | Always | Sometimes | Never |
|---|---|---|---|
| I send work to my supervisor on time | 3 | 2 | 1 |
| My clinical work fits easily into my timetable | 3 | 2 | 1 |
| I spend time each day prioritising my tasks | 3 | 2 | 1 |
| I lose track of what work I have to complete | 1 | 2 | 3 |
| I use a diary effectively | 3 | 2 | 1 |
| I keep a list of tasks which need completing | 3 | 2 | 1 |
| I feel on top of my clinical work | 3 | 2 | 1 |
| I complete my most difficult tasks first | 3 | 2 | 1 |
| I feel overwhelmed | 1 | 2 | 3 |
| I have to rush to complete tasks on time | 1 | 2 | 3 |
| I complete my work at the time of day I am most productive | 3 | 2 | 1 |
| When I am given a task, I immediately assess how long it will take me to complete | 3 | 2 | 1 |
| I get easily distracted | 1 | 2 | 3 |
| I cope well when given an urgent task | 3 | 2 | 1 |
| I feel that there are not enough hours in the day | 1 | 2 | 3 |
| **Total** | | | |

### If you scored between 30–45
You clearly have well-developed time management skills. It is very important that you continue to use your good time management skills to effectively manage your clinical work alongside the rest of your university work. You should have no problem with this. Think carefully about the various skills you use to manage your time and continue to develop them.

### If you scored between 15–29
You are clearly on your way. Consider the various hints and tips in this chapter for improving your time management skills. Try a couple out and then take the test again to see if there is any improvement. The easiest way to instantly improve your time management skills is to remove distractions such as social networking sites or personal email and, if possible, to work in a quiet area or away from your friends.

### If you scored below 15
Time management is clearly one of your weaker skills. This could pose problems for you when undertaking clinical work. It is important that you read this chapter carefully and consider some of the additional reading on time management. It is advisable to start by drawing up a 'to do' list and prioritising your weekly tasks. Your university is likely to have guidance available which will assist you in improving your time management skills. Make use of any services and guidance on offer.

## Activity 2: Case planning

Consider Nicola's scenario (see **Chapter 6**). Using the case planning pro forma, assess the client's goals, objectives and requirements and plan how you will meet them.

## Activity 3: Prioritisation

Consider the list of tasks below and place them in order of priority:

(a) File away loose papers on the file.
(b) Place on file a copy of the client care letter which was posted today.
(c) Your client left you a message earlier today; return his or her call.
(d) Complete research on court costs so you can advise your client next week.
(e) Prepare the required work for your seminar next week.
(f) Complete some research for your dissertation which has to be submitted in five months' time.
(g) Draft particulars of claim in anticipation that your client will want to pursue court proceedings.
(h) Organise a meeting with your partner to discuss a 'revised action plan' for your case.

# 10 Advocacy

'Only lawyers and painters
can turn white to black.'

Japanese proverb

## 10.1 Introduction

This chapter will focus on the skill of advocacy in the context of the courtroom. Most law students, whether they admit it or not, aspire to be great advocates. There is just something about the notion of having a courtroom hang on your every word that has universal appeal. Unfortunately, this thinking tends to stem from the stereotypical image that the media portrays of the advocate. What you will discover in practice is that the glamorous, ambitious type of advocate that you see on the television screen bears no relation to the advocate you will actually encounter in a real courtroom. Contrary to the media image, a good advocate is not one who sets about winning a case by intimidating witnesses, banging the desk with his fists, pacing around the courtroom, arguing with the judge and belittling his opponent. The good advocate is simply a master of persuasion, one who can quietly, but confidently argue that black is white and you believe him. If you bear this in mind then you are on the right track to becoming a great advocate.

Of course, the other feeling that advocacy tends to evoke is fear. Advocacy is a skill that does not always come naturally, and the unpredictable nature of the activity, coupled with its public performance aspect, is sufficient to leave many students with a feeling of foreboding and a few sleepless nights prior to the event.

This chapter will consider the various advocacy opportunities that may arise during your time in clinic and it will also consider some practical points which may assist you if you are representing a client. If your clinic or pro bono activities do not involve advocacy then you may still wish to develop this important skill by participating in one of the many student mooting, negotiation or mock trial competitions which take place every year.

For skills relevant to public speaking and presentations, which are a common feature of Streetlaw presentations and advocacy schemes, see **Chapter 11**.

## (10.2) Advocacy in clinic

Whilst some clinics only provide clients with advice, others will undertake casework and provide representation on behalf of the client. Advocacy is an important skill in any lawyer's armoury, whether you want to be a barrister or a solicitor. Many students say that they do not want to undertake contentious work and therefore do not need to do any advocacy. However, the ability to articulate your client's case in a concise and persuasive manner is equally important in the office as it is in the courtroom.

Advocacy is not the terrifying experience that many students believe it to be at the outset and, most importantly, it is a skill that can be learned and developed over time. You will find that, with every little piece of advocacy you undertake, your confidence will increase and you will gradually become more adept. You will also learn what judges are looking for when a case is being presented and therefore build your effectiveness and confidence with every experience.

---

**Reflection**

As ever, reflection is key. Whenever a lawyer comes out of court, he or she will think about what went right and what could have been done better. The lawyer can then harness this experience to improve subsequent performances.

---

For those about to undertake their first experience, we have outlined some common issues below.

### Grasping the opportunity

It is all too easy to shy away from an offer of working on a case that will involve advocacy, as it is something that fills many students with fear and dread. This is not uncommon, but you must make an effort to seize opportunities as and when they arise. Remember that the vast majority of students looking for career openings will have nothing on their CV beyond work experience. You already have an advantage in that you are working with real clients, but having some real advocacy experience will undoubtedly set you apart. So, if the opportunity to undertake advocacy comes your way, seize it before someone else does.

### Dealing with nerves

Remember that it is normal, and in fact healthy, to experience a certain degree of nervousness before undertaking advocacy. When you are nervous, adrenaline pumps through your system and this gives you the extra energy you need to perform at your very best. Some students will experience sweaty palms and butterflies before standing up and speaking out loud, but this generally wears off once they are 'on their feet' and the advocacy is underway. Unfortunately, there are others for whom the whole experience remains a daunting ordeal, and this can have an effect on the quality of the advocacy. If you still feel you lack confidence, then do not let it show; act confidently and nobody will know the difference. A useful thing to keep telling yourself is: 'This is not about me – it is about my client.'

## Fear of making mistakes

Remember, you are still a student and are not expected to be of QC standard; everyone will start awkwardly and make mistakes along the way as it is part of the learning curve. Secondly, acknowledge that your apprehension is more than likely based on the fear of getting things wrong, or of not knowing the answer to an unexpected question, or perhaps of just not knowing when to sit or stand. This is common, and it is simply fear of the unknown.

For the first time, you will be acting like a real lawyer in a real courtroom with a real client, rather than simply practising as a student in your familiar university environment. This will involve you stepping outside of your comfort zone and it can be disconcerting. The only way to overcome this fear of the unknown is to make it familiar.

If you can, acquaint yourself with the courtroom by attending and sitting in the public gallery so that you can observe how other advocates deal with unexpected questions and also pick up on court etiquette and room layout. Make sure you understand the case and any relevant law or matters of evidence that may be applicable; make sure that you know the facts well and can quickly find your way around the case file so that you cannot be caught out if the judge asks you a question.

Thirdly, know the weaknesses in your case and anticipate the arguments of the opposition and areas where the judge may require clarification. In this way you are less likely to panic if someone raises a challenge. If you prepare your case fully then you should be ready for anything that may arise, and this should both allay your nerves and reduce the chance of you making a mistake.

## **10.3** Rights of audience

One of the biggest obstacles to a student wishing to undertake advocacy is a concept known as 'rights of audience'. This is essentially a rule which prohibits certain people from advocating in particular forums.

A litigant is entitled to represent him- or herself in any legal forum, including the Supreme Court. However, if the party is represented, the representative must have the right to appear before the court or tribunal. As a student, you will have very limited rights of audience and therefore you will only be able to represent your client in certain forums.

You will be able to represent in any forum where you do not need to hold a formal qualification, such as certain tribunals. Within the judicial system, you will not be able to represent in open court, but you will be able to appear in matters that are dealt with in 'chambers', that is, in the judge's room. This means that you can represent in small claims cases and many interim applications.

However, rights of audience are much wider within the tribunal system and therefore you will be able to represent a client in most tribunal hearings, such as in the employment, social security and Criminal Injuries Compensation tribunals. There are exceptions to this, such as immigration tribunals, where the representative should be accredited by the Office of the Immigration Services Commissioner.

## 10.4 Modes of address

It may be that you are required to conduct a hearing before a panel or a judge. You must ensure, before you get carried away with your plans for a great cross-examination, that you know how to address the people you are presenting your case to. The following is a basic guide:

| | |
|---|---|
| District judge/County court judge | Sir/Madam |
| Tribunal judge | Sir/Madam |
| Magistrates | Sir/Madam – or collectively 'Your Worships' |
| Court clerk | Madam Clerk/Mister Clerk – or, if addressing the panel, 'Your learned clerk' |
| Your opponent | My friend – or 'learned friend' if it is a barrister |

If you are appearing before a panel other than the magistrates, ensure that you always address the panel chair as Sir or Madam and that, whenever you are asked a question, you address your answer to the chair. If you are appearing at a hearing where you are unsure how to address the panel or judge, speak to your supervisor in advance; he or she will not think any less of you for asking as this is the sort of thing that will normally only be obvious to people who regularly appear in court.

## 10.5 Keeping it formal – court etiquette

You must always bear in mind that a court or tribunal appearance demands a certain level of respect and formality. Where possible, you should always try to sit in on a hearing beforehand so that you can observe some of the etiquette that takes place, such as when to sit and when to stand, how to address the court, if and when to bow, how to ask for a break in proceedings and so forth.

### Standing, sitting and bowing

It is usual for all court users to stand when the judge/panel enters the room, and you may only sit down once the judge/panel has sat down and indicated that you may be seated. Whenever you enter or leave an open court, or indeed whenever the judge/panel enters or leaves the room, you must bow (a firm nod will suffice) to the judge/panel as a gesture of respect. As a general rule, you should always stand when making an address and remain seated whilst your opponent speaks. If the judge directs a question to you, then immediately stand and remain standing as you answer; you may only sit down when the judge indicates that there is nothing further he or she wishes to ask you. At all times, remain polite and courteous to other court users as their opinions of you can often feed back to the professional panel that will hear your representations.

Tribunals are much more informal in this respect. As with a court hearing, you should stand when the judge/panel enters and leaves the room, but you remain seated when conducting your advocacy.

## Appropriate dress

It almost goes without saying that you must dress smartly, preferably in a suit. After years of dressing casually for university, you may feel a little conspicuous and uncomfortable wearing a suit, but you will feel even more conspicuous and uncomfortable if you find yourself under-dressed in a court of law. There is an expectation that you will dress smartly and conservatively, so outlandish ties, eccentric hairstyles, killer heels and plunging necklines are all to be avoided. You may also want to consider temporarily removing facial piercings. If you look professional then not only will you blend in at court, you will feel professional and hopefully act accordingly.

**10.6** Mind your language – what to say and how to say it

The best way to deliver a professional submission is to select your words carefully, and then communicate those words effectively.

## Slow down and speak up

Some students faced with a court hearing become overly self-conscious about their voice; they worry that they will dry up, or that their accent may not be understood, or that they may stumble over legal jargon. As a result, student advocates tend to talk far too quickly, with their heads down, reading from a script, in the hope that they will get through their speech quickly and without anyone having the opportunity to chip in with a tricky question. This has several undesirable consequences. First, and most importantly, your audience might not catch what you have said, and you may be asked to repeat yourself. Worse still, the judge might just let it go and render your point ineffective.

Secondly, if you speak too fast you may become breathless, or your voice could 'dry up' completely. You need to speak at a slow, measured pace and use pauses effectively. Take your lead from the judge or the clerk. If he or she is frantically scribbling down notes and obviously struggling to keep up, then you are clearly talking too fast and you are running the risk of losing him or her, so slow yourself down. The key is to talk much more slowly than you would in ordinary conversation as you are making points that need to register with the listener and have impact. If you do have a strong accent, try to speak as clearly as you can, but do not artificially change your accent as you may find yourself becoming overly concerned with maintaining your 'court voice' rather than focusing on the points you wish to make.

Try to keep your voice audible and authoritative so that your arguments sink in and carry some weight. When you speak, make sure that you sit/stand straight up and raise your head, look at your audience and let your words carry over, loud and clear. If you have referred the court to a document then give your audience time to read the document before you continue with your address; otherwise they will either fail to take in the importance of the document, or they will stop listening to you in order to read. Remember that what you have to say is important and worth listening to, so do not rush through in an effort to 'get it over with', as you will not do yourself, or your case, any justice.

**Top tip**

Let the pace of the judge's pen dictate the speed of your advocacy.

## Choose your words carefully

It is important to avoid lapsing into informal language, colloquialisms or slang as this can be seen as disrespectful. Furthermore, by using slang references, you run the risk of confusing your audience, who may not actually understand what you are trying to say. Select your words carefully and think before you speak. Do not make sweeping statements that are likely to upset or antagonise your opponent, for example, 'It is abundantly clear that this trivial claim is entirely without merit and should never have been brought before this court'. Not only will this annoy your opponent and cause him or her to fight twice as hard, it will antagonise the panel or judge and you will have to work that much harder to bring them back on side.

## Know when to move on

When addressing the panel or judge, do not be surprised if they indicate that they have already read a certain piece of information that you were about to refer to, or perhaps if they indicate that they do not need to hear any further submissions on a particular point. This is commonplace, particularly in busy courts where any short-cuts that are available need to be taken. Should you find yourself in this position, you will need to graciously acknowledge that you do not need to provide further detail with a simple, 'I am grateful for that indication' or, 'I am obliged for that Sir', and move on. Do not irritate your audience by ignoring their indication and forging ahead on the basis that you have spent hours preparing this submission so they should listen to it regardless. Not only will you be wasting your time and that of the court, you will be seriously falling out of favour with the court, which will see you as disrespectful and inflexible.

## What to do if you are asked a question you cannot answer

It is inevitable that at some point in your advocacy, you will be asked a question to which you simply have no answer. This happens to all advocates and does not mean that you are a failure. The way to deal with a difficult question is to give it serious consideration, and if this means having to buy some thinking time then feel free to say something along the lines of, 'If you would just grant me a moment Sir to consider that issue'. If, having thought carefully, you are absolutely stumped then deal with it appropriately and salvage what you can. If, for example, the judge has mentioned an authority you have not read, acknowledge that the authority may well be relevant but then refer back to a case you have found that is equally relevant and explain why. Alternatively, if the judge has exposed a weakness in your case then see if you can find some argument to suggest that, despite this weakness, you are still in a better position than your opponent. If there is no prospect of salvaging the situation then you need to graciously accept the situation with a simple, 'Thank you Sir for raising that issue. I do not see how I can take that point any further so I would like to move on if I may', and then move on to your next point.

### Keeping control of your emotions

In addition to checking your language, you will also need to restrain your emotions. This can be difficult when you are convinced that your client is telling the truth and you feel that he or she is not being believed by the court. Or, alternatively, you may find yourself being drawn into an argument with a witness you are supposed to be cross-examining. Although a certain degree of passion is admirable, emotions can be detrimental if they prevent you from doing your job properly. So, if something upsets you, deal with it professionally. For example, if a witness seems to be challenging you, remind him or her that you are the person charged with asking questions and ask the witness to restrict him- or herself to responding to your questions. If you feel that your opponent is belittling your client as he gives his or her evidence, raise an objection and ask the court to have him or her refrain from doing so. If the judge seems to be consistently rejecting your arguments, or perhaps not grasping the point that you are trying to make, then be politely assertive in your clarification and perhaps try to make the point in a slightly different way, but do not labour the point or try to beat the judge with it, as this will never work. If you have no option but to challenge the judge, then make sure that your challenge starts with the words, 'With respect ...'. This sort of deference is absolutely necessary as it shows respect for the judge's opinion but still allows you to politely advance your case.

## 10.7 Case planning

All good advocacy begins with good preparation. As a student in clinic, you are likely to have more time to prepare than a busy practitioner, so make the most of it. There are lots of advocacy manuals available and each will have its own particular method of case planning. You must choose whichever system works best for you, but, as a minimum, your case planning should cover the following:

### Know your case

The first step is always to know the facts of your case inside out and know your way around the file so that you can locate the information when you need it. The only way to get to know your case is to read, read and read again. If you are working in a pair, have your partner quiz you for details. When you truly know your case, you will be able to answer his or her questions without hesitation.

### Identify your case theory

The second step is to identify your case theory. What are you saying has happened here? Take, for example, a simple landlord and tenant case where the tenant has left without giving due notice and the landlord is now suing for damages in respect of unpaid rent and damage caused to the flat. Is your case theory that the tenant deliberately and maliciously caused the damage because the landlord had to continuously chase him for rent? Or are you acting for the tenant and your case theory is that he did not cause the damage, rather he left the property secure and someone else must have broken in and caused the damage? Or is your case theory that your client did cause some damage, but the property was already in a poor state of repair when he moved in? By establishing your case theory, you will be able to decide how best to get your story across by selecting appropriate witnesses and eliciting relevant testimony. It will also help you to draft your closing argument. **Chapter 9** provides guidance on how to conduct a case analysis, which should assist.

### Break it down

The next step is to deconstruct the case so that you can see both sides of the dispute and the evidence that will be used in support. You can do this by drawing up a table, or whatever form of diagram you choose, and then listing, first, what each side needs to prove in order to win its case, secondly, what facts each side has to support its case, thirdly, what evidence each side will call in order to prove those facts and, fourthly, what problems, if any, there may be with that evidence. It is at this stage that you need to ensure that you know your law, for example you must know the elements of the offence, or know what is required of your civil application, and make a note of each step that is required, such as filing notice, exchanging documents and meeting deadlines. If you have all of this information clearly mapped out in front of you, then there is very little chance of anything being overlooked.

### Fill the gaps

The final step is to try to fill any gaps that your case planning has identified. For example, in a shop theft case, you might realise that, although you have the act of theft caught on CCTV and a full signed confession, you may not have a 'loser's statement', which is vital to the charge. As soon as you are aware of the gaps, you can try to obtain evidence to fill them, in this case by way of a statement from the shop manager confirming that nobody had the right to steal from the shop. If, however, you are unable to fill the gaps, then at least you have identified your weak point and you can anticipate that this will be targeted by your opponent. This will enable you to take steps to mitigate the damage. For example, in a theft case, you may have a solid defence but you are aware that your client has 10 previous convictions for theft. In such a situation, the prosecution are highly likely to bring those previous convictions into play under s 101 of the Criminal Justice Act 2003 and you are unlikely to be able to stop them. What you can do, however, is steal their thunder by having your client concede his previous convictions in his examination-in-chief, and perhaps explain that he committed those thefts in order to fund a drug habit but he has since been through rehabilitation and is now reformed.

## 10.8 Preparing your submission

At some point between the case planning and the hearing, you will have to deal with the thorny issue of notes. How much of your advocacy should you commit to note form? Should you write the whole thing out verbatim, or should you make short notes, or use bullet points, or perhaps flash cards would help? The answer is that there is no set rule as to how you should prepare your submissions and questions.

By this stage in your legal education, you will have noticed that different things work for different people. You must do whatever feels right for you, but with consideration of the pitfalls involved in each option.

Although you may favour writing out every word, this has serious limitations. Yes, it will prevent you from having to think on your feet and, if well delivered, it can allow you to speak confidently, safe in the knowledge that you have thought all of this through beforehand and you know that it sounds convincing. Unfortunately, what you have written down beforehand may no longer be appropriate, for example the evidence may not have come out the way you anticipated it would, or your client has changed his instructions at the last minute. For this reason alone, you must ensure that your notes allow for some flexibility. If you must write fairly extensive notes, consider using bullet points or some other form of broken down text so that the words act more as a prompt than a script. The added advantage of this is that you do not find your eyes glued to the page, so you can more readily look up at the person you are addressing and make eye contact to reinforce those all-important points.

Another clear advantage of having bullet-pointed notes is that you will find it much easier to find your place if you are interrupted mid-flow. Interruptions are to be expected when you are conducting real-life advocacy, and you must be able to deal with the interruption and return to the point you were making without having to leaf through pages of detailed text.

As previously mentioned, it is extremely beneficial for your development as a lawyer to attend court as an observer whenever you have the opportunity to do so. No textbook will ever provide the same level of insight as that which you can glean simply by observation. Therefore, in preparation for your hearing, go on an outing to your local court or observe your supervisor in a similar hearing. This can be an extremely comforting, or equally discouraging experience, depending on the quality of advocacy you observe. You may see some advocates reading from scripts, and it can be a comfort to know that even qualified, experienced lawyers also require detailed notes. But you may also observe advocates speaking without any reference to notes, and this can be quite daunting. You must remember that, although the latter may seem more professional and impressive, it is the quality of the advocacy that counts. The lawyer who advocates 'off the cuff' may not be making as many relevant points as the nervous lawyer who is reading from a script. Similarly, although the judge/panel may look as if they have lost interest in the lawyer who is reading from a script because he or she is not particularly engaging, they might be equally unimpressed with the 'off the cuff' lawyer who keeps losing the thread and has started to ramble or become repetitive. So you can see that it is simply a case of finding what works for you and allows you to present your case as effectively as possible. Your supervisor is likely to want to approve the substance of your submission in advance, and if this is the case, check the level of detail needed.

## (10.9) Delivering a submission

Although advocacy is essentially reactive and involves you having to think on your feet, there are certain submissions that can be prepared beforehand, such as opening speeches or certain forms of application. There can be an overwhelming temptation to prepare a script for these occasions, and if that is your preferred method then it is entirely acceptable, subject to any rules imposed by your supervisor. What you must try to do though is avoid being entirely reliant upon your script, as this can result in a very boring, stilted performance. Use your script to practise what you intend to say. If you read through it a number of times, preferably out loud, you will inevitably start to become more familiar with your speech and you will memorise parts of it. This will have three main benefits. First, you can make eye contact with the judge/panel, making your speech so much more effective. Secondly, you will be able to hear how your argument comes across and fine-tune it even further. Thirdly, you will become used to speaking out loud and hearing your own voice, which will give you more confidence.

When drafting your speech, you need to focus on communicating your argument as effectively as possible. You can achieve this by ensuring that your speech is well structured. To help with this, you should 'signpost' your arguments at the start of your address, for example, 'In making this submission I have three main points to make, first ..., secondly ... and thirdly .... I will deal with each of these points in turn before responding to the issues that have been raised by my friend'. By signposting in this way, the judge can clearly see where you are going with your speech; he or she knows what to expect and can keep track of your speech rather than being left to wonder what you are going to deal with and when you are going to finish. Another advantage of signposting is that you will be able to keep yourself focused and avoid repetition.

You must also aim to keep your speech brief. Remember that your audience will have a limited attention span, and after so long they will simply switch off. So, keep it short and to the point. This is particularly so if you are addressing a judge. Remember that a judge will be familiar with the law and will not require quite so much 'story-telling' as a lay panel, so pitch your speech accordingly.

Practice makes perfect, and this is certainly true when it comes to making a speech. It is advisable to practise by standing in front of a mirror, or a video camera if you can bear it, and speaking out loud. You may feel a little embarrassed about doing this but it will pay dividends. You will become used to the sound of your voice, and you can check whether you find yourself talking too fast, too high, too softly, or perhaps you will discover that you rely heavily on making 'um' or 'er' noises. You may also notice that you sway, wave your arms about, or fidget with your pen or your hair, or repeatedly shuffle your papers. Everyone has their own nervous little habits that manifest themselves in times of stress, and it is as well that you spot them at this stage and try to control them rather than let them become a source of distraction for the panel or judge.

Once you have practised in front of a mirror, or bravely studied your videoed performance, the next step is to run through your speech in front of someone else. If you feel brave, this could be your supervisor, but otherwise you could ask your firm partner or a trusted friend. Be prepared to accept constructive criticism about your arguments and/or your personal quirks as any feedback is designed to help you further improve. You should invite the person to challenge your arguments where he or she feels it appropriate. Although this might be a little daunting, it is good preparation for the hearing, where you might find yourself repeatedly interrupted by the judge and/or your opponent. Part of the skill of advocacy is learning to cope with questions and then being able to return to your argument as seamlessly as possible.

Remember to try to appear as engaging as possible. This is not to say that you should be overly dramatic, but do try to vary the pitch of your voice and use pauses effectively so that you do not sound too monotonous. Also try to make your arguments as readily understandable as possible. Some students seem to think that indulging in lengthy rhetoric, which employs convoluted arguments and legal jargon, is the way to win favour with the judge. Indeed this could not be further from the truth. The fact that you have studied law means that you must be of reasonable intelligence; there is no need for you to try to prove this in the courtroom as this will detract from your argument.

## 10.10 Opening speeches

Although opening speeches are dealt with at the very start of a hearing and can therefore be fairly nerve-wracking, they are usually the easiest piece of advocacy to deal with. They are one of the few occasions where you can, if you feel it necessary, prepare a script, as you are unlikely to be interrupted in an opening speech and it is important that this, your first address, is both accurate and confidently delivered. In an opening speech you are essentially telling the court what you intend to achieve in the course of the hearing. If you are bringing a claim, you need to introduce yourself and your opponent, tell the court what the dispute is about, what it is that you say has happened (your case theory), what is in dispute, and indicate the evidence you intend to call to prove your case. If there are to be issues of law then, again, this should be briefly explained.

**A very simple opening in Nicola's housing case**

'Sir, this case concerns a landlord and tenant dispute. I represent Ms Ridley, the tenant, and my friend represents Mr Atkinson, the landlord of the property in question. My client has brought a claim for compensation in respect of disrepair. I shall be calling evidence from Ms Ridley, who will give evidence about the state of the property, Miss X, the cleaner in the apartment block where the rented flat was situated, who will give evidence about gradual deterioration of the property, and finally Mr Z, who carried out the repair work to the windows.'

It is important not to overstate your case in your opening speech. If you give the court very precise details about what you believe a witness will say and then the witness does not 'come up to proof,' that is, say what you expect him or her to say, then your opponent will seize upon that and suggest that you have not proved what you set out to prove.

In civil cases, it may be prudent to ask the judge whether he or she has had an opportunity to read the papers. If the judge is familiar with the case (perhaps there have been several direction hearings before the main hearing) then do not spend too much time on your opening. If the judge requires more detail, be ready to provide it. Always have spare copies of statements of case and other important documents to hand in case the judge or your opponent has lost his or her copy, or in case you need to hand a copy to a witness.

In tribunals, for example the employment tribunal, opening speeches are not used, but any preliminary issues which need bringing to the tribunal's attention should be raised at the outset.

## **10.11** Closing speeches

A closing speech is often the most important part of any hearing. This is your opportunity to explain to the court or tribunal precisely why it should find in your favour. This is not something that will just magically 'come to you' at the end of the hearing, rather it will be the culmination of all of your case planning. You should have conducted the hearing and extracted the evidence in a way that allows you to make all of the winning points that you set out to achieve. A good closing speech will not be lengthy; it will simply cover the points in a succinct and effective manner. If your closing speech turns into a long-winded ramble, then this suggests that you are simply trying to wear the court down, rather than relying on a strong case.

As part of your advocacy preparation, you will have given serious consideration to the points you will cover in closing. Obviously, you cannot write your closing speech beforehand, as much will depend upon how the evidence comes across, but you can certainly ensure that you have a basic framework set out. If you have a framework to hand, you can slot in the evidence as it unfolds. The content of your speech will vary depending on whether you are bringing the case or defending the case. If you are presenting the case then, provided you have the luxury of a closing speech (depending on the area of law, you may only be allowed an opening speech), you need to remind the court of what you set out to achieve, briefly summarise the law, demonstrate how the evidence you have called has supported your case and then explain what the court now needs to rule upon. If you are defending the case then you will be pointing out the flaws in the claimant's case, highlighting areas where the claimant has failed to make out his or her case or where the claimant's evidence is lacking or otherwise undermined, or where your case has been particularly persuasive. Whichever side you represent, you are effectively telling the court why it is that you should win your case. Whether you are bringing the case or defending the case, you should always address any relevant points of law in your closing speech and, again, this is something that you can, to an extent, plan out beforehand. If you are involved in a civil hearing then it may be appropriate for you to have pre-prepared a draft order or schedule of costs that the judge can then simply approve or otherwise amend.

Eventually, you will come to the end of your submission and, regardless of the type of hearing, you will need to conclude and sit down. This may sound like the simplest action in the world, but it is surprising the number of students who, after a beautifully crafted and well-delivered speech, awkwardly shrug their shoulders and say, 'Er, that's it', before hurriedly sitting down. You need to know your closing line off by heart so that you can sound confident and professional. All that is required is something as simple as, 'Sir, that concludes my submission unless I can be of any further assistance to the court'. The judge will then either ask you any residual questions or, alternatively, he or she will thank you or invite you to take a seat.

## 10.12 A question of ethics

When you are conducting advocacy, even as a student, you will need to bear in mind the Solicitors Regulation Authority Code of Conduct, particularly Rule 11 which specifically deals with advocacy. There are similar rules issued by the Bar Standards Board. Both codes are available on the regulatory bodies' websites. The court or tribunal will expect you to follow these rules, and you could get into serious difficulty if you do not. One of the key rules is that you must never deceive or knowingly or recklessly mislead the court, and this includes failing to mention authorities that may damage your case. It can be terribly tempting to provide a little white lie in court in order to save face or perhaps to boost a weak case. You might think that no one will ever realise your untruth and that it was done with the best interests of the client at heart. You cannot take this sort of risk, as you will inevitably be found out and the court will not be remotely interested in your justifications. If you mislead the court, you will simply lose all credibility as an advocate and you could find yourself being reported to the relevant disciplinary body; this is not a great start to your career as a lawyer.

You must also ensure that you do not lapse into giving evidence or your own opinions. All evidence must come from witnesses, so avoid saying things such as, 'I have visited the scene of the accident and it is clear to me that the road signs are inadequate'. You must allow the court to come to such conclusions itself; so you could rephrase this statement as follows: 'The court has been shown video footage of the scene of the accident and this includes footage of the road signage. The court may be of the opinion, having heard all of the evidence and having seen the footage, that the signage was inadequate'. This latter statement achieves exactly the same result as the former in that the court is being made aware that the signage was inadequate, but rather than being rudely told this by the advocate, the court has been politely invited to come to this conclusion based on the evidence it has seen and heard.

| Avoid | Appropriate |
|---|---|
| 'I believe ...' | 'It is submitted that ...' |
| 'I suggest ...' | 'It is the claimant's/defendant's case that ...' |

## 10.13 Trial

The vast majority of hearings that you may encounter as a student advocate are hearings where you are simply required to make a submission. In such a situation, the above-detailed advice on delivering speeches should suffice. Occasionally, however, you may find yourself in a small claims trial, an employment tribunal or perhaps a Criminal Injuries Compensation Appeal. In these situations, you are likely to encounter witnesses. It is therefore important that you know how to deal with witnesses, the format for giving testimony (examination-in-chief, cross-examination and re-examination) and the styles of question that can be used.

### How to handle a witness

### Be polite

You must never lose sight of the fact that witnesses are real people too. It is easy to get overly involved with the case and see them as puppets in your own case, or 'the enemy' if they are for the opponent. You cannot allow yourself to think this way as it will influence, perhaps even subconsciously, how you speak to them. Think for a moment how the witness must be feeling. You might be nervous if this is your first experience of advocacy, but at least you have had some training and the opportunity to observe hearings so that you know what to expect. In contrast, the vast majority of witnesses appear in court as a one-off and it is usually with a great deal of reluctance; they feel intimidated and unsure of what is likely to happen. Remember that you are there to ask questions that will hopefully help your case as well as undermine your opponent's case, so it makes perfect sense to treat the witness respectfully so that he or she feels more comfortable in answering your questions. The more at ease a witness is, the more likely he or she is to cooperate with you. Do not treat a witness disdainfully or rudely, as it will cause him or her either to become confrontational or to clam up completely, and this will do nothing to help your case or endear you to the court. Furthermore, it is a breach of the Rule 11 of the Solicitors' Code of Conduct to say something that is intended to insult the witness. So smile, be polite and ask simple questions that are capable of answer.

### Avoid filling the silence

This can happen in two ways: first, you want to let the witness know that you have heard his or her reply to your question, so you use a stock phrase such as 'Thank you', 'I see', 'Right then' or 'Okay' after every reply. Not only is this an irritating habit, but it is unfair to the witness who might think you are agreeing with him or her, and it can also damage your credibility as an advocate. Instead, when you receive an answer, pause briefly and then ask your next question. The second situation in which you may find yourself 'filling the silence' is when you do not receive an immediate reply. When this happens you may be tempted to say, 'Let me put that another way ...' or 'I'm sorry, perhaps I'm not being clear'. When this urge arises, fight it and remain silent; just give the witness time to answer. Only rephrase your question if the witness indicates that he or she does not understand.

## Do not repeat the answer

This is another irritating habit and the sign of an inexperienced advocate who is buying thinking time before he or she comes up with the next question. Unless you are seeking to emphasise a particularly crucial piece of evidence, do not repeat the answer that you have just been given. Aside from it being irritating, it means the court gets to hear the evidence twice, which might not be what you want, particularly if it is evidence that damages your case.

## Questioning witnesses – leading and non-leading questions

There are essentially two types of questions to use when you are questioning a witness: leading questions and non-leading questions.

A leading question will either assume a certain fact that has not as yet been adduced in evidence, or it will suggest an answer. Take for example:

'It was a black handbag that David stole, wasn't it?'

This is a leading question as it assumes two things: first, that David stole a handbag and, secondly, that the handbag was black. The advocate has essentially put these words into the mouth of the witness. This is undesirable if this is your witness (ie you have called him or her to support your client's case) because the evidence needs to come from the witness, not you. So, to avoid falling into the trap of leading questions, you need to re-frame your questions so that the facts come from the witness. This is done by asking non-leading questions. Look at the following series of questions, which elicit the same information but allow the words to come from the witness:

| | |
|---|---|
| Advocate: | 'What happened next?' |
| Witness: | 'Someone grabbed the handbag.' |
| Advocate: | 'What colour was the handbag?' |
| Witness: | 'It was black.' |
| Advocate: | 'Do you know who the person was who took the black handbag?' |
| Witness: | 'Yes, it was David.' |

Although you cannot ask leading questions of your own witness during examination-in-chief, you can sometimes obtain the permission of your opponent to lead on agreed facts up to a certain point. For example, if you were appearing in a landlord and tenant dispute, you might ask your opponent if he or she had any objection to you leading your landlord witness until you get to the issues in dispute. This means that you can quickly establish that there was a lease, the date of the lease, the parties, the agreed terms, the period of occupancy, etc, until you get to the part where, for example, it is alleged that the tenant has vacated the property having caused substantial damage to some of the rooms. If you have agreed to lead up to a certain point, be sure to warn the judge/panel, otherwise you are likely to be pulled up short.

The only other situation where you may ask leading questions of your own witness is when the witness has been ruled 'hostile'. This really should be a last resort as a hostile witness is, by very nature, unlikely to be of any use to you, regardless of the style of questioning you adopt. Remember that, for such a ruling, the witness must appear hostile to your questioning. It is not enough that he or she is just a poor or forgetful witness who is not saying what you expected him or her to say. In such a situation, you are entitled to put leading questions to the witness and, if necessary, put the witness's previous inconsistent statements to him or her.

The only time you should actively use leading questions is in cross-examination. In cross-examination, you are trying to elicit evidence that will help your own case and undermine your opponent's case. This means that you need to keep tight control of the witness, and you can do this by asking questions that have simple 'yes' or 'no' answers (for example, 'Was he tall?'), or questions that have a limited number of answers (for example, 'Was he tall or short?'), or questions that amount to statements (for example, 'He was tall, wasn't he?'). All of these examples amount to leading questions (sometimes known as 'closed questions') and they allow you to control what the witness will say.

## 10.14 Examination-in-chief

Whenever you call your client, or a witness who supports your client, to give evidence, then your job is have that person tell his or her story to the court. This is called examination-in-chief.

As part of your advocacy preparation, you will have taken a proof of evidence, or witness statement, that clearly and logically sets out the account of that particular witness. You will have provided the witness with a copy of that statement so that he or she can familiarise him- or herself with it. Remember that the Code of Conduct prevents you from coaching witnesses as to how they should give their evidence. On the day of the hearing, you will ask the witness a series of questions designed to elicit that same account. Unfortunately, you will not be able to ask leading questions, as already discussed, and this can result in the examination-in-chief being something of a test of memory as far as your witness is concerned. Good witnesses, who are telling the truth, should have no difficulty in recalling their accounts, but forgetful witnesses, or those whose statements are perhaps not entirely truthful, may struggle. You can direct good witnesses toward the day of the incident and then take them through their evidence by means of simple 'prompting' questions, for example:

Advocate: 'Did anything unusual happen on your way to work?'
Witness: 'Yes, I saw a man steal a handbag from a lady as she crossed the road.'
Advocate: 'What did you see?'
Witness: 'As they passed each other on the pedestrian crossing, he snatched the bag from her hand.'
Advocate: 'And then what?'
Witness: 'He ran off with it and she chased after him.'

You can also ask questions based on what the witness has just said; this is known as 'piggy-backing', for example:

Advocate: 'You said that you saw "a man steal a handbag". Can you describe the man in more detail?'
Witness: 'Yes, he was about six foot tall with short brown hair and glasses; he was wearing blue jeans and a black jacket.'

Advocate: 'You also said that "he snatched the bag". Can you describe the bag?'
Witness:    'Yes it was a black leather handbag.'
Advocate: 'You said that this happened "as they passed each other on the pedestrian crossing". Where was this pedestrian crossing?'
Witness:    'It was on the High Street, just opposite the newsagent.'

By using a combination of prompting questions and piggy-backing questions, you can easily take your client through his or her evidence without being accused of leading that evidence. Remember that once the evidence is safely extracted by means of a non-leading question, you are then free to ask leading questions about it, but remember to tread carefully. If, however, your witness is truly forgetful then, despite your best efforts to draw out his or her testimony, you may need to seek leave of the court to allow the witness to refresh his or her memory from his or her witness statement. The test is found in s 139 of the Criminal Justice Act 2003 (for criminal cases), but, in civil cases, the statement itself is usually relied upon as the evidence-in-chief and therefore you are unlikely to find yourself in this position.

The trickiest part of examination-in-chief can be keeping control of your witness. You will be working to your case theory and you will know exactly what you want each witness to say in order to fit in with your case theory. You must not allow a witness to go off on a tangent and talk about other issues. This can be damaging for several reasons. First, and most importantly, the witness could say something that is unexpected and potentially damaging to the case. Secondly, your inability to control a witness will be spotted by your opponent who will perceive you as inexperienced, and he or she may try to take advantage. Thirdly, you risk upsetting the court by indulging the witness in talking about matters that are not relevant to the case. Given the risks involved, it is much easier to politely interrupt your witness and bring him or her back to the point.

Another objective of examination-in-chief is to anticipate matters that your opponent is likely to raise in cross-examination. By anticipating these points and covering them in examination-in-chief, you can effectively take 'the wind out of the sails' of your opponent so that he or she has fewer points to raise in cross-examination.

## 10.15 Cross-examination

This can prove to be the most challenging, but exciting part of any contested hearing. You may have seen extracts of cross-examination on television or in films, and it is usually portrayed as highly dramatic, with witnesses crumbling under the pressure of questioning and confessing all. Unfortunately, this does not accurately reflect the reality of cross-examination and your aim should not be to destroy the witness.

In cross-examination, you need to need to focus on the following issues:

1 Challenging the account of the witness where it does not fit with your case theory
2 Putting your version of events to the witness
3 Discrediting the account of the witness
4 Obtaining evidence that supports your case

## Challenging the account of the witness and putting your version forward

These two principles are inextricably linked. The basic rule in advocacy is that you are taken to accept any evidence that you do not challenge. So, the first thing you need to do is consider whether you need to cross-examine at all. It may be that this particular witness does not say anything that damages your case. If this is the situation, then simply indicate that you have no questions for the witness and let him or her stand down. Do not try to impress your client or the judge by asking lots of pointless questions just for the sake of it, as this will give the witness an opportunity to reaffirm his or her evidence and perhaps even add to it.

If, however, the witness has given evidence which conflicts with your case theory, you will need to cross-examine and actively put forward your client's version. The reason you have to 'put your case' is to give the witness the opportunity to comment on any contradictory evidence that you will subsequently be calling. You will need to do this carefully and skilfully to avoid causing further damage. You are not likely to get very far if you constantly tell the witness that he or she is wrong or lying, or you ask questions such as, 'You say that you were nowhere near the scene when this robbery took place, but I put it to you that you were, so what do you have to say about that?'

If you are lucky, the witness will simply deny it, but he or she is far more likely to deny it and go on to give an explanation as to why he or she could not have been anywhere near the scene. This means that the witness gets a second opportunity to tell his or her story, and you have lost control of the witness. It would be far better to say, 'Three witnesses describe someone who looks like you as being present at the scene, but you do not agree with that, do you?'

All the witness can then do is say 'no'. You have clearly put your case (you think he was there despite him saying that he was not) and you can make your next move. There is no need to point out the obvious by saying that three witnesses outweigh one, as this is a comment you can work into your closing speech. If you were to make some comment about that to the witness, then he might come back with some devastating comment such as, 'Yes, but your three witnesses have clearly put their heads together, they were seen discussing their evidence in the court cafeteria this morning.'

## Discrediting the witness

At the core of all disputes are two conflicting versions of events. It is almost inevitable that part of your case will be that your opponent is wrong, mistaken or lying about a particular issue. As you present your case, you will be attempting to demonstrate to the court why it is that your opponent should not be believed. In some cases, it is entirely appropriate to bring this across by means of a direct challenge, but, more often than not, there are gentler, more subtle means of conveying your mistrust that can be equally effective.

## Conflicting evidence

The first method is to *put to the witness conflicting evidence* from his or her own previous statements or from another witness who has given similar but conflicting evidence. For example:

| | |
|---|---|
| Advocate: | 'You have said that you left the pub at 9.00pm. Is that right?' |
| Witness: | 'Yes.' |
| Advocate: | 'Are you absolutely sure about that?' |
| Witness: | 'Yes.' |
| Advocate: | 'You definitely left at 9.00pm that night?' |
| Witness: | 'Yes, I am sure of it.' |
| Advocate: | (Hand him the previous statement) 'Is that the statement that you made on (date)?' |
| Witness: | 'Yes.' |
| Advocate: | (Refer to the declaration clause) 'And in that statement you declared to tell the truth?' |
| Witness: | 'Yes.' |
| Advocate: | 'And in that statement you said that you left at 10.00pm.' |
| Witness: | 'Yes.' |
| Advocate: | 'So in your statement you said 10.00pm, and yet in your evidence you said 9.00pm. It cannot be both, so which is the lie?' |

This is quite a confrontational but extremely effective move, as it is immediately apparent that the witness has either lied in his statement or has lied when giving evidence. In his excellent book, *The Devil's Advocate*, Iain Morley QC likens this tactic to pulling a metaphorical lever to open the trapdoor on the gallows so that the witness hangs himself with his own evidence. The witness may well bluster and make excuses about being confused and mistaken, but the damage to his credibility is already done.

Alternatively, you could confront the witness with the evidence of other witnesses who have given conflicting evidence, for example:

'You have said that you left the pub at 9.00pm, yet the court has heard three witnesses who were all confident that you were still sitting in the pub at 9.30pm. Are all three of those witnesses mistaken, or is it possible that you may be slightly confused about what time you left?'

This is not quite as pointed as the previous example, but it has the same effect. You are suggesting that if he maintains his account, then he must be lying as there are witnesses that contradict him. If he backs down and concedes that maybe he got the timing wrong, then it looks as though he was lying in the first place. Either way, the witness is discredited.

### Confront the witness

The second method is to remind the witness of all of the parts of your case theory that he has accepted through his examination-in-chief and then *confront him with your version*. For example:

| | |
|---|---|
| Advocate: | 'You admitted in your evidence that you were in the city centre at the time the bag was snatched?' |
| Witness: | 'Yes, but it wasn't me who took the bag.' |
| Advocate: | 'You accepted that you were on the street in question?' |
| Witness: | 'Yes.' |
| Advocate: | 'You agree that you crossed the street to get to the newsagent?' |

| | |
|---|---|
| Witness: | 'Yes.' |
| Advocate: | 'You agree that the street was very busy with traffic at that time of day?' |
| Witness: | 'Yes, so what?' |
| Advocate: | 'You agree that you must have used the pedestrian crossing to safely cross the street?' |
| Witness: | 'Yes.' |
| Advocate: | 'And it is correct that you are six foot tall with short brown hair?' |
| Witness: | 'Yes.' |
| Advocate: | 'Then it stands to reason that you are the man that all three witnesses have described as snatching the bag from the lady on that pedestrian crossing at that time of day?' |
| Witness: | 'No, it wasn't me.' |

By asking this series of questions, you are narrowing the area of dispute and suggesting that, as your witnesses have been correct on every other point, they are also correct in their assertion that he was the bag-snatcher. Although this can be an effective method, it invariably culminates in a denial and it also involves reiterating the evidence that the witness has already given. For this reason you should use the tactic sparingly.

### Common-sense argument

The third method builds on the second method. Where you have substantial agreement as to what has taken place, but there remains disagreement on the key issue, you can apply a *common-sense argument* that results in the witness's account being incapable of belief. For example:

> 'So it must be a coincidence that on the same day, at the same time, in exactly the right place, where you accept you were, some other man who looks just like you snatched this lady's handbag and it is also a coincidence that all three witnesses mistakenly believe it was you?'

Or consider the following example:

| | |
|---|---|
| Advocate: | 'So you say you were nowhere near the scene of the bag-snatching incident and that you were at home in bed with flu?' |
| Witness: | 'Yes.' |
| Advocate: | 'Were you very sick?' |
| Witness: | 'Yes, really sick, I couldn't get out of bed.' |
| Advocate: | 'You work full time do you not?' |
| Witness: | 'Yes, I work for the council.' |
| Advocate: | 'So I take it you called in sick and you have proof of that?' |
| Witness: | 'I do not know if I rang in sick.' |
| Advocate: | 'Well you must have called in sick if you were as poorly as you say?' |
| Witness: | 'I was poorly!' |
| Advocate: | 'Even if you did not ring work, you must have telephoned someone to help. You said you couldn't even get out of bed?' |
| Witness: | 'I do not think I did call anyone.' |
| Advocate: | 'So you were severely ill with flu but did not ring your workplace or any friends or family for help?' |
| Witness: | 'That's right.' |

Advocate: 'And it is because you were apparently so sick that you could not possibly have been the man on the High Street who was responsible for this incident?'

Witness: 'That's right.'

In this series of questions, the advocate is testing the account of the witness by applying common-sense principles that will automatically strike a chord with the court. If there was any truth in his assertion that he was too sick to leave the house on the day of the bag-snatching, then common sense would dictate that he would have contacted his workplace to explain his absence or that he would have called a friend or family for assistance. The fact that he did not casts doubt over whether he was actually as sick as he alleges and allows for the possibility that perhaps he was the man on the High Street.

Do not, under any circumstances, go on to say, 'I put it to you that you were not in bed feeling ill at all. You were there, in the High Street, and you took the bag, didn't you.' You may think that such a question is full of drama and you are actively putting your case, but it is such a dangerous move. What if the witness responds, 'No, you're wrong' or, worse still, 'No, you're wrong, I was really sick and the reason why I did not ring the council or anyone else was because my wife was with me all along, so she rang in sick for me.' You can see that, by asking that last one killer question, you have lost all the points that you had just gained. If you had just stopped after the witness's final answer, you could have used all of that material in closing to remind the court how unlikely his explanation sounded, and now you have nothing. In fact, his explanation sounds entirely plausible and your case theory has been undermined.

 **Top tip**

Cross-examination should not be cross! Ensure you remain calm but persistent and always treat the witness with respect.

You will notice that, in most of the sample questions, the questions are leading questions (sometimes known as closed questions) as opposed to open questions. You are suggesting the answer so that the witness need only reply with a 'yes' or a 'no'. You are not asking 'why' questions, or 'what' questions or 'tell me about it' questions. You are not providing any opportunity for the witness to put things in his own words or provide explanations; you are controlling him at all times. This is vital if you are to extract evidence that will support your case, or if you are leading the witness into a trap. For the same reason, you should be extremely wary about asking a question if you do not know what the answer is going to be. It might be helpful, but it could be absolutely devastating to your case, so play safe with controlled, leading questions.

## Obtaining evidence to support your own case

Cross-examination is not all about attacking the witness. It may well be that the witness can give evidence that fits in with your case theory. If this is so, gently tease out that information by means of leading questions, preferably at the start of the cross-examination and before you get into any direct challenges. Store up any useful information that you can glean and refer back to it in your closing speech.

## Things to avoid in cross-examination

### Bamboozling the witness

Some students think that the key to cross-examination is to bamboozle the witness with a barrage of quick-fire questions or with a long, convoluted question that leaves the witness unable to answer simply because he or she cannot understand the question. This is to be avoided at all costs. You run the risk of confusing the witness and the court, and you could attract a hostile response from your opponent who objects to you treating his or her witness in such a way. You must ask short questions that are capable of an answer. By the same token, it is unfair to ask a question and not give the witness time to answer. You must be fair, ask one question at a time and allow the witness to respond before moving on to the next question. By treating the witness with this level of courtesy, you are much more likely to gain his or her cooperation, and the witness may find him- or herself relaxing and making concessions that he or she may not have done if you had adopted a more aggressive style of cross-examination.

### Complacency

If you find yourself putting questions to a witness in cross-examination and you are clearly gaining the upper hand, please resist the urge to add a note of sarcasm or smugness to your voice. Although this may be the mainstay of slick American courtroom dramas, it has no place in a real courtroom and will reflect badly on you. Try to keep your voice controlled and as matter-of-fact as possible. If you wish to emphasise a point, it is better done by way of eye contact with the judge/panel. If you feel that you have 'scored a point' then make a mental note and refer back to it in your closing submission. Do not smile knowingly and thank the witness for this devastating blow, as the witness might realise that he or she has slipped up and try to go on and repair the damage. Similarly, if you have managed to highlight weaknesses or inconsistencies, do not point them out to the witness: he or she might just explain them away. Instead, hang on to those weaknesses and use them in your closing speech.

### Know when to stop

As soon as you have made your point, or you feel that the witness has been shaken, leave it and move on. If you continue to press the point then not only are you badgering the witness, you are also providing him or her with an opportunity to remedy the situation.

## 10.16 Re-examination

Once your witness has been subject to cross-examination, you will have the opportunity to re-examine. This does not mean that you get a 'second chance' to reaffirm all of his or her examination-in-chief, or another chance to bring up everything that you forgot to deal with first time around. It is simply an opportunity for you to deal with any new matters that were raised by your opponent in cross-examination. It may be that your witness has said something that was particularly damaging to your case, and you now need to revisit that issue and try to repair the damage as far as you are able. Remember that, in re-examination, you are questioning your witness and you must therefore avoid leading questions. As a general rule, it is best to avoid re-examination where possible, as the need to re-examine simply highlights the fact that your opponent has drawn out damaging evidence.

## 10.17 Taking notes

You must also remember that, aside from preparing your submission to help remind you of what you intend to say, you will also have to take notes of what is said by the other advocate/judge/witness during the hearing. Of course, if you have the opportunity, it might be helpful to have a fellow student attend with you to act as note-taker so that you can focus on your advocacy, but in practice it will be you alone who has to perform both tasks, so it helps to devise a system of note-taking that works well for you. As a student, you will be used to writing lecture notes and seminar notes, and it may be that you have your own system of shorthand. Ensure that when you do take notes, you leave sufficient space to add to them, particularly when noting down testimony. A useful method is to draw a long line down the middle of the page and then jot down the questions asked on one side of the page and the witness responses on the other side so that you can easily gauge what was said. If, when noting down the testimony, you pick up on something that you might want to pursue in cross-examination, or use in your closing speech, then immediately circle it and write a couple of words alongside that will trigger the point you wish to make so that you can easily return to the issue when it is your turn to speak.

## 10.18 File notes

Related to note taking is the issue of file management. You must ensure that you can easily locate documents in your file or bundle whilst 'on your feet'. This may seem obvious, but it is not unusual to see inexperienced advocates frantically thumbing through their papers and losing track of their submission. This is not the professional image you wish to convey. If you find it helpful, flag up certain pages with post-it notes, use highlighters on the witness statements, use different coloured pieces of paper for claimant and defendant documents and so on. If, in the course of one of your speeches, you are going to refer the judge to a practitioner text or, for example, the Civil Procedure Rules, then ensure that you have flagged up the relevant pages so that you can refer to them with ease.

## 10.19 Types of hearing

Types of hearing you may encounter in your clinic and pro bono work include the following:

- Civil – any small claims court hearings, including trials, and civil case interim applications, such as applications for disclosure.
- Criminal injuries – appeal hearings against decisions of the Criminal Injuries Compensation Authority.

- Employment – case management discussions, pre-hearing reviews, substantive hearing and remedies hearing.
- Housing – hearings on matters such as non-return of deposit, disrepair and possession. There are also tribunals dealing with rent and other residential leasehold disputes.
- Welfare benefits – hearings to appeal the decision to withdraw various benefits including employment and support allowance, disability living allowance and jobseeker's allowance.

The unification of the Tribunal Service brings a very wide range of disputes before the First-tier tribunal. You may have a right to appear on behalf of clients in these types of cases. They include disputes in the following areas:

- Social security and child support
- Pensions
- Mental health
- Care standards
- Criminal Injuries Compensation
- Asylum support
- Special educational needs and disability
- VAT and duties
- Consumer credit
- Charity
- Information and data protection
- Gaming

Remember that some types of hearing these days may be conducted over the telephone or even by video link.

## 10.20 Summary

Advocacy is the one skill that divides students. You will either love it or loathe it. You clearly already know that practice makes perfect and hopefully you will have found some of the suggestions in this chapter helpful.

Whatever career you intend to pursue, you will need to have the confidence and ability to stand up and advance your argument. As we have discussed, advocacy is a skill that you can learn; it is not a skill that you are born with. It is true that some people may have more flair for it than others, but everyone is capable of standing up and presenting an argument. So, start small by getting involved in discussions and debates in your firm meetings. Once you start to feel comfortable expressing your arguments, you could tackle a presentation where you explain a point of law to the rest of your group. You could then draft a speech on one of your cases, perhaps even organise some role-play and then, when the opportunity arises, put yourself forward for some courtroom action. Once you start, you may become one of those people who loves it.

 Further reading

There are a range of publications which you can consult on advocacy, and a selection is set out below if you want to read further.

## Introductory

**Boyle, F et al, *A Practical Guide to Lawyering Skills* (Cavendish, 2005)**
    This is a very useful book to have to hand in general, as it covers a whole range of skills that will be useful during your time in clinic. The chapter on advocacy is particularly helpful. The advice is straightforward and practical, with some good sample extracts on questioning.
**Evans, K, *The Golden Rules of Advocacy* (Blackstone Press, 1993)**
    Another classic advocacy text often recommended to law students. This is a short, easy-to-read guide to advocacy with lots of useful examples. If you are serious about improving your advocacy then this is a good place to start.

## Intermediate

**Hill, D and Pope, D, *Mooting and Advocacy Skills* (Sweet & Maxwell, 2007)**
    This book guides you through the various stages of a moot from preparation through to presentation, and the advice is equally applicable to real-life hearings.
**Morley, I, *The Devil's Advocate* (Sweet & Maxwell, 2009)**
    The classic guide to what makes a good advocate. The book is aimed at anyone wanting to improve their advocacy skills, not just barristers. It is very reader-friendly and full of worked examples.
**Shaw, N, *Effective Advocacy* (Sweet & Maxwell, 1996)**
    This is a more detailed guide to advocacy, with a particular focus on advocacy in the criminal courts. There is, however, a very useful chapter on civil hearings which guides you through the various applications step by step.

## Advanced

**van den Brink-Budgen, R, *Critical Thinking for Students* (How To Books, 2004)**
    This book covers in some detail critical thinking skills and considers how to identify arguments, analysing arguments and exploring weakness, all of which will assist with planning your case tactics in relation to your submission.

 Activities

Before any court appearance you should have a dress rehearsal. It will be difficult, if not impossible, to practise in a real courtroom so you will need to improvise.

### Activity 1: Individual advocacy preparation

If you have a skills room in your law school equipped with a video camera, book out this room for an hour. If you do not have this luxury then just do this at home using the video record facility on your mobile phone. Prepare two versions of a 10-minute, formal court or tribunal submission based on one of your cases. One version should be wholly scripted. Write it out in full. The other must be written in bullet or diagram form on no more than half a side of A4. Record yourself completing the submission as if you are addressing the court or tribunal.

Then view both versions and see what differences you can spot. The scripted version is likely to be more coherent, but the unscripted one will probably be more engaging.

## Activity 2: Team advocacy preparation

Pair up with two members of your clinic and allocate the roles of advocate, witness and judge. The advocate must try to question the witness with a view to discovering what the witness did on his last holiday, or perhaps over the course of a weekend. The judge should ensure that the advocate's examination-in-chief does not include any leading questions. Once you have completed the exercise, swap roles and repeat the activity. At the end, give each other some constructive feedback.

## Activity 3: Mock advocacy

Organise a mock trial, debate or other simulation exercise. You may be able to invite a local solicitor, barrister or even judge to ensure that the exercise is realistic. Often, it is helpful to utilise the facts from your actual cases to ensure that it is as realistic as possible, subject to any confidentiality issues.

# 11 Presentations

> 'I would be loath to cast away my speech,
> for besides that it is excellently well penned,
> I have taken great pains to con it.'
>
> Viola in *Twelfth Night*, Act 1, Scene 5, Shakespeare

## 11.1 Introduction

Not everyone will have the opportunity to undertake advocacy as part of their clinical or pro bono activities, but it is much more likely that you will be asked to deliver a presentation in some shape or form. This chapter is particularly relevant if you are a member of a clinical or pro bono scheme, such as Streetlaw, which delivers presentations to external groups. Common issues associated with presentations and public speaking, such as body language, coping with nerves and so on, are covered in **Chapter 10**. If you are required to deliver group presentations, you may find it helpful to note the teamworking tips in **Chapter 5**.

Presentations in a clinic and pro bono setting, other than those to your clinical colleagues, are typically made to groups or organisations that wish to be informed about legal issues that are specifically relevant to them. For example, charities dealing with asylum seekers may want their service users educated on immigration matters including the right to accommodation and schooling. Residents' committees may want to learn about challenging rent increases or communal charges levied by their housing association, and small businesses may want advice on intellectual property or employment updates if they have members of staff. Schools may want their pupils to be educated about the youth justice system, the legality of downloading media from the Internet and so on. Undertaking such presentations is valuable for you but perhaps more importantly for the group and society, so it is important you understand how to conduct the task effectively.

### What is Streetlaw?

The idea of lawyers and law students going onto the street to educate community groups about law and legal rights is a firmly established aspect of clinic and pro bono activities. This form of experiential activity has been taking place since the early 1970s and has grown hugely in popularity and influence in subsequent decades. The umbrella organisation, Streetlaw Inc in the United States, coordinates information, guidance and resources regarding Streetlaw activities. In the United Kingdom there are a large number ▸

▸

of Streetlaw and other community engagement projects involving legal awareness-raising activities performed by law students.

There is an important distinction between Streetlaw and traditional lawyer–client relationships. Streetlaw tends to focus not on individual client problems but on more general legal issues. Moreover, Streetlaw does not normally involve the provision of legal advice as such. Rather it tries to make the audience better informed and more capable of making decisions about enforcement of legal rights. Clearly, Streetlaw presentations may give rise to individual client queries, and it is an advantage if there is the possibility of referring potential clients to further sources of advice and representation.

Streetlaw is therefore distinct from traditional lawyering which has its focus on individual client representation. It has more in common with teaching and community activism than the provision of legal services. It also fits in with modern notions of therapeutic lawyering, whereby lawyers should not simply seek to resolve conflict but should strive to create environments where people will be less likely to develop legal disputes and more likely to seek help when problems do arise. Nevertheless, it clearly utilises and develops skills that lawyers need (such as legal research and communication skills) and has a value as a pro bono activity. It also helps students develop an awareness of the political, social and economic contexts of the law. By entering the community to engage with groups about legal issues, you become less isolated and more cognisant of the wide range of real-life issues that cannot be learned from the pages of a law book.

Streetlaw's popularity is due partly to the simplicity of the model. The absence of an individual advice element to the service removes the need for indemnity insurance and means that there is no need for premises or holding of client files, with the attendant professional obligations regarding confidentiality etc. Consequently, Streetlaw programmes are relatively inexpensive to establish and operate. This also limits the scope for developing traditional legal skills and professional responsibility.

The Streetlaw audience can be as varied as the community. Examples are tenants' groups, schoolchildren, youth workers, carers, prisoners, protesters, business people, fellow students, sports clubs and charities.

Streetlaw presentations are generally prepared in consultation with the community group so that they are relevant to the audience. They generally involve an element of team presentation, audience interaction and use of visual and other aids. Students might also prepare resources related to the presentation such as leaflets, advice sheets or flow charts.

## 11.2 Analysing your audience

Whilst you will be at the front delivering the presentation, remember that it is actually not about you. The needs of your audience are central to your presentation; therefore it is essential that you profile who will be listening, and why.

### Why profile your audience?

This is an important exercise which, if done well, can render your presentation a success. Analysing your audience will ensure you produce a relevant and useful session. You can deliver an amazing piece of public speaking but no amount of flair and oratory will cover up an irrelevant or poorly pitched presentation.

## What should you profile?

You should find out who will be there and what they want to get out of the presentation. Will everyone have the same objective for attending, or are you presenting to a mixed audience? You also need to gauge the knowledge levels so you can pitch the information at the right level. Will the audience members be novices, or are you presenting to professionals, business people and so on? Another important matter to ascertain is how many people will be attending, or at the very least an estimate. This information will help you to determine the best delivery methods (a round table discussion is ill suited to a room of 100 or more people) and the most suitable visual aids. You should also clarify whether the event is formal or informal as this again will assist with matters such as room layout and dress code.

## How can you profile your audience?

The simplest way is to liaise with the organiser, coordinator or group chair. Do not be afraid of being up front about needing to find out more information about the organisation and its clients. Alternatively, there may be information available on the Internet, particularly if you are dealing with charities and special interest groups.

**11.3** Content

Having profiled your audience and established your objectives, you can begin to research and compile the content. It is vital to remind yourself as you proceed that the audience's requirements are of paramount importance – do they want to be educated, informed or advised about a particular issue; or are you promoting your institution's pro bono or clinical services?

Make sure that you select your focus at an early stage to assist with your research. For example, is the purpose of the presentation to provide an overview of social security benefits or a detailed talk on how to apply for them? Decide on the message you want to convey and ensure this is at the centre of your content.

Given that the law is such a vast area, you will no doubt find a wealth of material, perhaps an overwhelming amount, making it difficult to decide how much and what to include. Siddons (2008: 55) suggests you ask yourself what information must be covered, what facts add value and what examples to use. You may also find it helpful to divide your information into categories, such as essential, helpful, good to know and unnecessary. Adopting this approach should ensure the content is relevant and tailored to your audience. It will also prevent you from bombarding your listeners with too much information.

## 11.4 Structuring your presentation

Once you have determined your content, you can begin to organise it; it need not be overly complex – a basic beginning, middle and end will suffice. Structure is particularly important when working as a group to ensure that there is no needless repetition and that each person's part flows seamlessly from one to the next.

### In the beginning

The start of your presentation should be used to introduce the speakers and the purpose of your talk. First impressions are important, so begin confidently and try to arouse the audience's interest. Tierney (1999: 22) suggests you can engage the listener by opening with a quotation, question, statistic or an eye-catching image. Links to helpful sources can be found on the Companion Website. Having caught their attention, signpost what you intend to cover and why it is relevant – this should keep your audience poised for the next part of the presentation.

### Stuck in the middle

Use the main body of your presentation to highlight the key issues and use examples to aid comprehension. Each point should be clearly explained before moving onto the next and should follow a logical order. Remember to relate the points to the audience.

### Ending on a high note

The end of your presentation should be used to recap the crucial matters or main theme. Providing a concise summary of your message should help the audience retain the key points long after your presentation has ended. Wrap up with a warm and friendly tone and remember to thank your audience for their attention. You may want to take questions at this point, a matter which is dealt with below.

### Getting your message across

You need to think carefully about how you can convey your message effectively. You can devise a catchy title which embodies the points you want to put across and grabs the audience's attention. Leave a pause after each central theme to allow the listener time to absorb what you have said. Repeating the point is a useful tool to help the audience remember the main themes of the presentation. The repetition can be sprinkled throughout, as with Obama's 'Yes we can', or close together, as adopted in New Labour's 'Education, education, education' mantra. However, avoid overkill; excessive repetition can become tiresome for the audience.

Your message will be more easily understood if your language is clear and concise. Do not baffle your audience with jargon. Tailor your choice of words and expression to each audience.

## 11.5 Delivering your presentation

Relevant content is only one ingredient to a winning presentation; another is engaging delivery. Your delivery needs to grab and maintain the attention of your audience. After all, the presentation is for their benefit rather than yours.

### Vocals

Your voice is a key tool in successful delivery and the main points to remember are set out in the following mnemonic: VOICES – Volume, Open, Inflection, Calm, Enthusiasm and Speed.

> **Volume** – speak up and check whether everyone can hear. Ensure you maintain an appropriate volume throughout.
>
> **Open** – open your mouth to enunciate properly and avoid mumbling.
>
> **Inflection** – vary the intonation of your voice to avoid sounding monotone.
>
> **Calm** – your voice can show nerves, so keep calm.
>
> **Enthusiasm** – sound enthused about what you are saying – this should generate interest from your listeners too.
>
> **Speed** – speak at a reasonable pace. Talking either too quickly or at a snail's pace will lose the attention of your audience.

Given the importance of your voice, it is advisable to have some water to hand if you feel it is drying up, or if you get a sudden coughing fit.

### Using notes

It can be difficult to deliver a lengthy speech from memory, so it is advisable to have some notes with you to act as prompts and reminders of the key points to be covered. You might also want to consider including icons in your notes to help with your delivery. For example, a drawing or picture of an eye at the top of each page will remind you to maintain eye contact with the audience. Similarly, the image of a loudspeaker in the middle of your notes will encourage you to check that the volume of your speech has not dropped, as can sometimes happen as presentations go on.

### Timing

If you have a time limit, you must stick to it. A useful way to discipline yourself is to inform the audience at the outset how long you intend to speak for. This both encourages you to stay within the time and alerts the audience to how long they are expected to be attentive.

## 11.6  Group presentations

Not everyone enjoys delivering presentations and it is easy to assume that everyone in the group should take a speaking role in the presentation. Check whether it is a requirement that everyone presents, or can those who prefer not to speak to take responsibility for other matters, for example, preparing handouts, making travel arrangements, liaising with the organisation and so forth?

## 11.7  Rehearsals

Even the best public speakers will undertake some form of rehearsal. You should hold at least one run through, ideally two. More rehearsals may be necessary for group presentations where it can take longer to perfect seamless handovers. Practice runs are vital if the presentation is subject to a time limit. It is a good idea to video record your practice sessions so you can clearly identify which parts need further refining. Watching your performance back can also help you identify any unconscious habits you have, such as pen clicking, mumbling or overuse of hand gestures.

If at all possible, you should hold a rehearsal at the presentation venue so that you can familiarise yourself with room acoustics, equipment and so on. This also has the benefit of accurately timing travel distances and routes.

## 11.8  Visual aids

Unless you are blessed with a voice that can make listing the telephone book sound interesting, it may be prudent to employ some form of visual aid. If used correctly, these tools can attract and maintain the audience's attention.

Visuals can be an excellent way of grabbing attention and making your presentation more appealing, but they can also prevent you transmitting your message effectively. Avoid using too many different aids in one presentation.

The use of such props and visuals may be dictated by the venue and the facilities, so it is essential that, before planning your presentation, you check what equipment is available and whether any software is compatible with that of your institution.

### Common types of visual aids

### Slides (for example PowerPoint)

These are commonly used in lectures and presentations. This does not mean that they are the best or most creative option. If you plan on using slides, it is a good idea to print these out as a handout in case the equipment fails on the day.

- Pros – cheap to produce and commonly used.
- Cons – not always employed effectively and can be unimaginative.

**Top tips for the use of presentation slides**

Less is more – limit the number of slides. 10 to 15 slides should be sufficient for a 40 to 60-minute presentation.

Use a clear font – intricate fonts might look stylish but they can be hard to read. Stick to Times New Roman or Arial.

Size matters – anything less than an 18 point font will be difficult to read.

Picture perfect – beware of incorporating copyright-protected images.

## Handouts

These are a useful way of supplementing the information you provide verbally, and can therefore be used to streamline your speech to the key points, with additional information appearing on the handout. However, as with slides, they should not be too busy in appearance and the content should be clearly explained.

If you choose to use handouts, you need to think carefully about several important points:

- Who will pay for the cost of production?
- How you are going to use them effectively? Will you cross-reference page numbers during your speech?
- Will someone need to check over the content to ensure the legal points are correct?
- Do you need to include a disclaimer as to the accuracy of the information?

Another key consideration when using handouts is when to distribute them; circulating them at the outset or during the presentation can mean the audience's attention is diverted away from you. Similarly, handing them out at the end may seem like an afterthought and therefore the material might not be read by the recipient.

- Pros – the recipient can revisit the handout after the presentation.
- Cons – not always cheap to produce, particularly if using colour, and can draw the audience's attention away from the presenters.

## Videos/multimedia

The use of videos and other forms of media, such as music, can inject colour and life into a presentation.

- Pros – eye-catching and can convey messages powerfully.
- Cons – the material is very likely to be copyright-protected which may prohibit group screenings.

## 11.9 Questions

Whilst the thought of being asked questions can be unnerving, they are a positive sign that you have engaged your audience and they have listened to what you have said.

## Dealing with questions

It is helpful for both you and your audience if you make it clear at the outset whether you want to deal with questions during or at the end of the presentation. Whichever method you choose, you should always build in time for questions; so, for example, if your presentation has a slot of one hour, talk for 45–50 minutes and leave the remainder for questions.

### Dealing with questions throughout

- *Pros.* This can engender an interactive feel to the presentation and allows the audience to ask questions as and when they need matters clarifying.
- *Cons.* This can be a difficult technique if you are a novice presenter. One or two questions can soon lead to a barrage which soon takes over and detracts from the presentation. This can knock you off course and may be difficult to recover from. Furthermore, the questions may well be answered in later parts of the presentation so the risk is you will respond on the matter and may well end up repeating the point when you reach that part in your presentation. Alternatively if you decline to answer, explaining that the point will be covered by the presentation, it can seem rude or standoffish, unless you do this tactfully. Good signposting in your introduction as to what will be covered can reduce the latter type of question.

### Dealing with questions at the end

- *Pros.* If your presentation is time constrained, leaving questions to the end will help you keep within the time limit by allowing you to gauge how many questions you can field in the remaining time. Hearing the full presentation can improve the quality of questions since the audience will hopefully have understood and digested the points in context.
- *Cons.* If an audience member has a question about something covered at the beginning of your presentation, he or she may be reluctant to ask it so late in the day.

There is a third way. At the outset, you can assure the audience that there will be time at the end for questions, but that if anyone has a *burning* question during the presentation then they should feel free to ask it.

 **Top tips for dealing with questions**

- Prepare for questions – think about what the audience might ask and plan some provisional answers so you are not caught off guard. Asking a friend, who has little or no knowledge of the subject area, to listen to or read over your presentation in advance may well pre-empt questions that an audience might ask.
- Treat the questioner with respect – it can be unnerving to ask a question, particularly in front of a group, so even if the question seems inane or it has already been covered during the presentation, ensure you answer in a courteous way.
- Listen carefully to the entire question – by listening to the first few words, and not the whole question, it is easy to jump to the wrong conclusion as to what is being asked.

- If you do not understand the question, ask for clarification from the member of the audience.
- Keep answers short and sweet – responses should not involve a wholesale regurgitation of the presentation.
- Do not feel pressured to answer – if you do not know the answer, it is perfectly acceptable, in fact advisable, to defer answering until you can give a proper and correct response.

## 11.10 Confidentiality

You must plan very carefully what you can include in your presentation, as you may be dealing with confidential material and must remain within your instructions. For example, if you are delivering a presentation on an area of law which also relates to a case on which you are instructed, it may be tempting to discuss that client's case by way of example. This clearly has confidentiality ramifications. In the flow of a presentation, it is very easy to say something you should not. Similarly, think carefully about what you are able to discuss with your friends who were not party to the presentation. Presentations may not seem as formal as working on legal cases or courtroom advocacy, but they should be treated with the same degree of respect, and this involves complying with any applicable professional conduct duties.

Similarly, you need to be careful that you do not inappropriately seek confidential information from members of the audience. If you are giving a general presentation about legal rights, for example police powers of arrest, if could lead to difficulties if you seek detailed personal information about whether people in the audience have been arrested previously. At times you may need to remind people that this is not the forum for dealing with individual legal problems.

## 11.11 Practical points

Do not get so absorbed in the content of the presentation that you overlook the practical points.

### Travel

Work out how you will travel to the venue and ensure you leave more than enough time. Arrive early so you can set up the room and check equipment is working.

If money is an issue, forward-plan to find the cheapest method. If, on the other hand, the organisation is reimbursing your travel expenses, this does not justify hopping in a taxi if there is a bus that stops right outside the door.

### Feedback

If you will be delivering the same or a similar presentation to other groups, it is a good idea to obtain feedback from your audience. This can be done verbally at the end, by a follow-up call to the group leader a few days after the presentation, or by a short feedback sheet. Questions can be limited to content and relevance, but you may wish to allow comments on your performance too.

## 11.12 What if ...?

There is always the possibility that something will go wrong on the day, but planning ahead will help you cope should such eventualities arise.

### ... the car/bus/train breaks down en route?

Make sure you have the telephone number of the venue or contact person so that you can telephone ahead and advise that you may be delayed. Ideally, you will have built in sufficient time in your journey plan to make it to the venue by some other means. Take spare cash with you in case you need to buy another ticket or to cover a taxi fare.

### ... a member of the group is ill?

This is where your rehearsals will prove invaluable. Everyone gets sick from time to time. If the person is too ill to attend, quickly decide who will take over his or her part of the presentation. Try to squeeze in a mini-rehearsal before the presentation, concentrating on the parts that were to be delivered by your ill colleague. If you do not have time for a short rehearsal, go back over the earlier dry runs in your mind to remember what was said and how it was delivered. Do not make excuses to your audience that someone is ill – be professional and do not let on that you have had to make last-minute changes.

### ... the presentation has to be cancelled?

Sometimes, matters beyond your control, and/or that of the group, mean that the presentation has to be cancelled or postponed. However, that is not carte blanche for you to cancel without good reason. Where it becomes clear that the presentation is unable to go ahead, make sure all of those concerned are notified in good time. You should check with your supervisor or coordinator prior to informing the external group, as he or she may have a solution to the problem. If you need to call off at the last minute, make sure you do so by telephone to guarantee everyone concerned receives the message. If cancellation is unavoidable, try to rearrange the presentation at the earliest possible opportunity – it is useful to have the availability of your colleagues to hand so that you can do this when you call to cancel.

## 11.13 Presentation checklist

- Have you profiled your audience?
- Have you avoided unnecessary jargon?
- Does your presentation follow a logical order?
- Have you organised your visual aids?
- Have you devised a contingency plan, for example if equipment/visuals fail?

- Have you held at least one rehearsal?
- Have you reconfirmed the time/date etc with the organisation and venue?
- Have you made any necessary travel arrangements?

---

**Which skills associated with conducting presentations are transferable to routine legal practice?**

A wide range of skills, of potential value to future lawyers, is developed through presentation activity. Some examples are as follows:

- Oral communication – you need to develop the ability to covey complex legal and/or factual information in a coherent and accessible manner.
- Legal research – you will have analysed the law in some detail in order to be able to present effectively. However, you may need to go into much more detail for an individual client. See **Chapter 8** for a detailed analysis of the *practical* nature of legal research on behalf of clients.
- Teamwork – you will no doubt collaborate in producing a presentation in a similar way that you will work with others in a law firm or other advice context.
- File management – although your presentation file is likely to be simpler than a client case file, you will develop basic organisational skills.
- Working to a brief – the instructions you are given for your presentation (particularly if you develop your instructions in consultation with a community group) have some similarity to the discipline that lawyers need in ascertaining and fulfilling client instructions.
- Precision – a time-limited presentation is likely to require you to be self-disciplined so that you remove irrelevant material and focus on the important information. This is likely to assist when you come to interact with clients and lawyers in practice.

---

 Summary

Contrary to what you might think, there is no such thing as a natural born orator. Being a good public speaker is a skill like any other, which must be fine-tuned and developed. An effective presentation needs to successfully combine relevant content, engaging delivery, and mastery of props and visual aids. Given that you are likely to have to present at some stage in your career, why not perfect your skills now?

## Further reading

### Introductory

**Peel, M, *Successful Presentations in a Week* (Institute of Management, Hodder & Stoughton, 1998)**

A concise guide to the basics of public speaking, covering preparation, presentation aids, nerves and handling questions.

### Intermediate

Nicholls, A, *Mastering Public Speaking: How to prepare and deliver winning presentations and successful speeches* (How To Books, 1999)

This book sets out the golden rules of public speaking, which include making your presentation sound 'said and not read' and avoiding nerves.

Tierney, E, *101 Ways to Better Presentations* (Kogan Page, 1999)

As the title suggests, this book sets out 101 tips and strategies on how to develop your presentation skills. An accessible read which covers matters ranging from use of language and improving presence to team presentations.

### Advanced

Siddons, S, *The Complete Presentation Skills Handbook: How to Understand and Reach Your Audience for Maximum Impact and Success* (Kogan Page, 2008)

An excellent, comprehensive text which covers the various aspects of presentations including audience behaviour, the science of memory and breathing techniques. It contains useful checklists, a delegate's kit and presentation templates. An invaluable guide to all things presentation-related, attractively supplemented by diagrams and tables.

 Activities

### Activity 1: Bland to brilliant

As a group, prepare and deliver a 10-minute presentation on one of the following topics:

- Dry cleaning
- The uses of paperclips
- The properties of soil

You will note that these are not thrilling topics, so the purpose of this exercise is to turn a dull topic into an engaging presentation. Think about how you can make the subject-matter and delivery interesting in order to hold the audience's attention.

### Activity 2: Learn from the Greats

There have been many great, controversial and memorable speeches throughout history. Select a well-known speech to analyse; ask yourself what the aim of the speech was, why it is remembered, and consider the effect of the language and structure. Finally, consider what you can learn from the speech. Some famous oratories are set out below:

Winston Churchill – 'We Shall Fight on the Beaches', speech to the House of Commons, 4 June 1940

Martin Luther King – 'I Have a Dream', Washington, 28 August 1963

Barack Obama – 'Acceptance speech', Chicago, November 2008

Edward VIII – 'Abdication speech', 11 December 1936

### Activity 3: Practice makes perfect

Once you have devised a presentation, hold a rehearsal and use the assessment sheet below to evaluate it. You can conduct this exercise as a self-assessment or a peer assessment, or have a neutral person undertake marking duties.

# EVALUATION SHEET

**PRESENTER(S):**

**PRESENTATION TOPIC:**

|  | EXCELLENT | GOOD | FAIR | BORDERLINE | POOR |
|---|---|---|---|---|---|
| **STRUCTURE**<br>Introduction<br>Key points<br>Ending<br>General content<br>Use of examples |  |  |  |  |  |
| **DELIVERY**<br>Volume<br>Intonation<br>Clarity of speech<br>Appropriate language<br>Eye contact<br>Speed of delivery<br>Timing<br>Flow |  |  |  |  |  |

**VISUAL AIDS** (Circle as appropriate)

| Were visual aids used? | YES | NO |
|---|---|---|
| Did they add value to the presentation? | YES | NO |
| Number of aids | TOO MANY | JUST RIGHT  TOO FEW |

**MAIN STRENGTH(S):**

**MAIN AREA(S) FOR IMPROVEMENT:**

**ADDITIONAL COMMENTS:**

# 12 Reflection

> '*Mirror, mirror on the wall, who
> in this land is fairest of all?*'
>
> The Brothers Grimm, *Little Snow-White*

## 12.1 Introduction

You may have read the title of this chapter and thought that a reflection is something you see when you look in the mirror. Well, in the context of reflective practice you are not far off. Even if you do not yet fully understand what reflection is, the good news is you already do it, possibly without even realising. This chapter provides an overview of what is meant by 'reflection' and demonstrates how you can reflect consciously and with purpose to improve the way you learn and perform in your clinical and pro bono work.

Many clinic and pro bono courses require you to 'reflect' on the work that you do. It is often argued that reflection is what elevates clinic or pro bono activities beyond mere provision of a service or volunteering and makes the endeavour a worthwhile educational experience. The development of the 'reflective practitioner' is an aim that many clinic and pro bono courses aspire to achieve. Educational philosophers and commentators have been writing about the concept of reflection for many decades. Some authors have traced it back to Aristotle. However, it is a relatively new addition to the legal curriculum. There is an ever-growing collection of books dedicated to reflection and what it means to be a reflective practitioner. The aim of this chapter is to set out some key principles and practical advice, with a little theory thrown in for good measure.

## 12.2 What is reflection?

It is interesting to note that there is not one universally agreed definition of reflection; it means different things to different people and, as you will see below, there are numerous ways in which you can carry out the reflective process. So that you can appreciate the various definitions of reflection which have been developed, a selection are set out below:

'Serious and careful thought' (*Cambridge Advanced Learner's Dictionary*)

'Reflection is an important human activity in which people recapture their experience, think about it, mull it over and evaluate it.' (Boud, Keogh and Walker, 1985: 19)

'The act of reflecting is one which causes us to make sense of what we've learned, why we've learned it, and how that particular increment of learning took place. Moreover, reflection is about linking one increment of learning to the wider perspective of learning – heading towards seeing the bigger picture.' (Phil Race, 2002)

'Active, persistent, and careful consideration of any belief or supposed form of knowledge in the light of the grounds that support it and the further conclusions to which it leads.' (John Dewey, 1933: 9, cited in Boud, Keogh and Walker, 1985: 21)

'Reconstruction and reorganisation of experience which adds to the meaning of experience.' (John Dewey, 1944: 74, cited in Rodgers, 2002: 845)

As you have already seen, clinical legal education and pro bono involves *learning through experience*. But how do you use your *experience to learn*? At its most basic level, reflection is looking at some aspect of your performance, understanding it, and learning from it. However, reflection is complex and multifaceted. It is not simply taking an experience and learning from it; deep reflection allows you to make sense of *how* you learn.

You can learn from every experience, be it positive or negative, through the act of reflection. Without reflection, an experience is just that – something that has happened. It is the application of the reflective process that allows you to draw meaning from the experience, to appreciate and understand what you have learned (Boud, 1993: 9).

Reflection, therefore, is what turns experience into learning. Without engaging in reflection, all you have is a series of experiences which are not linked or contextualised and which have not enriched your learning or knowledge (Boud, 1993: 9).

We have an infinite number of experiences throughout our lifetime, and reflection allows us to make sense of these separate events, piecing them together as a whole, rather like a jigsaw. It is the assimilation of these different learning 'blocks' that allows you continually to learn and revise your understanding.

## Types of reflection

Donald Schön (1982) draws a distinction between two types of reflection: reflection  in action and reflection on action, as illustrated by the following example. Imagine you are interviewing a female client about a sensitive legal matter, for instance a divorce, and all of a sudden your client begins to cry. Many thoughts probably begin to race through your head – what did I say or do? How can I get her to stop crying; should I continue with the interview? In the moment, you will decide on a course of action, perhaps allowing your client a few moments to regain her composure and then continuing with the interview. Afterwards, you will no doubt revisit the interview and wonder how you could have handled the situation better or even prevented that situation arising in the first place. What you have here are two different types of reflection. The first, while you are in the process of interviewing your client, is known as *reflection in action*, the latter as *reflection on action*.

Reflection in action is a term used to describe spontaneous reflection, which is reflection that takes place when you are still 'in' the experience. In the above example, the student recognised that the interview was not going well and sought to take measures to salvage the situation. This ability to think on your feet and implement immediate changes is evidence of reflection in action.

Schön points out that much of reflection in action may be unstated or even unconscious. For example, if you drive a car, you react as if automatically to traffic signs or hazards as they arise during your journey. You are responding to stimuli, reacting to events so as to make your journey successful.

Whereas reflection *in* action is done in the moment, reflection *on* action is carried out retrospectively. It involves analysing the experience after completion in a thorough and systematic manner, identifying the catalysts for your conduct and questioning why you acted as you did, given the almost instantaneous changes that were made. Reflection on action is a complex process and the various stages involved in the procedure are explored later in this chapter (see **12.5**).

### 12.3 Why should you reflect in clinic or pro bono projects?

Law schools cannot possibly teach you every piece of law or skill that you need to survive beyond graduation. Even if they could, the law and workplace change, sometimes with frightening speed. In any event, life would be rather dull if your learning stopped after university. Reflection is something that should extend beyond your clinical and pro bono work into your professional life to ensure that your learning continues and that you can adapt to the ever-changing employment market.

In your career, you will need to adapt to situations you have not encountered before, which you will not have been 'taught' how to deal with and in which you might not 'know' how to react. Reflective practitioners can act intelligently in unfamiliar situations as they have developed reflective habits and do not jump from one experience to the next without learning from it.

The importance of lifelong learning is well recognised. Reflection ensures that you continue to develop beyond the end of your formal education in several ways. It allows you to recognise your strengths and weaknesses, identify any further areas for development and review your progress. It also strengthens your ability to think strategically about your own learning and self-development. In essence, it gives you control over your personal and professional development, transforming you into a reflective practitioner.

Furthermore, Dewey advocates that the power of reflection goes beyond our own personal development. He argues that, because an experience is essentially an interaction between you and the world, there is a change in us and our environment as a result. Therefore, through our interactions with the world, people change it and are changed by it (Rodgers, 2002: 846). This proposition is quite deep but worth giving some thought to.

If this is not reason enough then it is worth noting that time spent on reflection will almost certainly make you perform better at the tasks you complete in clinic or pro bono schemes. Striving to improve is something that everyone does and reflection is a key method of personal development and skills enhancement. The more you reflect on your performance, the better service you will provide to clients, peers and others.

It is also worth noting that, increasingly, clinic and pro bono projects use reflection as one of the means of assessing the quality of student performance (see **Chapter 13**).

## 12.4 How do you reflect?

The good news, as you have previously read, is that you already reflect. The not-so-good news is that your supervisors and lecturers cannot *make* you think or write reflectively. They can, however, provide you with guidance and encouragement, and facilitate your personal reflective journey and skills.

Very often, when reading about reflection, you will see reference to mirrors: using a mirror to look back at an event or experience and evaluate it. However, a mirror only reflects what is there on the surface. Reflection is a much deeper process: a procedure that involves scratching beneath the exterior to discover our innermost motivations, emotions and beliefs in order to scrutinise them carefully.

## 12.5 Models of reflection

Over the years, educators have tried to pin down what exactly is meant by reflection and what it involves. Various models have been developed, although there is no one universally agreed model. Some systems are fairly straightforward and others are more complex, with several stages and levels. A selection of models is reproduced and explained below. Further examples are also available via the Companion Website.

Despite the lack of consensus, you will see that there are some core similarities between the different models. You will also note that the majority of the models are cyclical, illustrating that reflection is an ongoing process, which accords with the notion of lifelong learning.

### Basic reflective process

You reflect by thinking, although it is more than just a haphazard 'mulling over', and by asking questions, lots of questions. Obvious questions, probing questions, challenging questions ... you get the idea. Whatever experience you are reflecting on, there should always be an analysis by reference to the what, where, why, when and how. Your questioning process should examine the whole experience or event. It should not just look at the experience from start to finish, but also the before and after, so that you can appreciate everything in context.

**Questions to ask when reflecting on an interview**

How did I feel prior to the interview?
Why did I feel like that?
What influenced the way I prepared for the interview?
What did I expect to happen in the interview?
What went well in the interview?
Why did this aspect of the interview go well?
Did the interview meet its purpose?
What could I have done better?
Why did I not identify this as a possible problem before the interview?
In hindsight, why did the interview meet/not meet its purpose?
What have I learned from this experience?
What behaviour/practices/habits will I adopt in future interviews?
What do I need to improve on and how am I going to do this?

You should ask various questions to help you explore your thoughts, attitudes and emotional responses to whatever event you want to reflect on. The list above is just a small sample of relevant questions. There are far too many possible questions to include here. For a substantial list, see 'Evidencing Reflection: Putting the "W" in Reflection' by Phil Race (Race, 2002). A link to this article can be found on the Companion Website.

### Three-step models

The three-step models set out below are useful formulae to refer to when you are first familiarising yourself with the concept of reflection. They set out in an accessible manner the basic stages of the reflection process: an experience, a review of that experience, and planning some change or action as a result of that learning experience.

Greenaway's reflection model

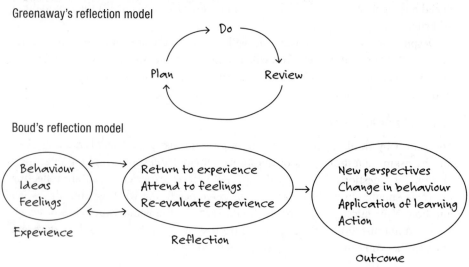

Boud's reflection model

Once you are comfortable with the basics, you should aim to develop a more profound understanding of the reflection process. The more complex models of reflection will now be explored.

## Learning cycles

Kolb and Gibbs expand on the basic models. Experience, reviewing and planning still feature, but they also explicitly include conceptualisation as part of the learning process. Gibbs' model of reflection is perhaps more accessible in the way that it is framed.

## Gibbs' reflective cycle

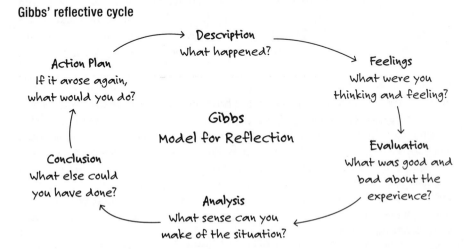

Kolb's cycle is one of the most common reflective models referred to in articles on reflection. Whilst it only involves four stages, it requires some complex and challenging thought by the person reflecting. The stages are explored later in the chapter.

## Kolb's learning cycle

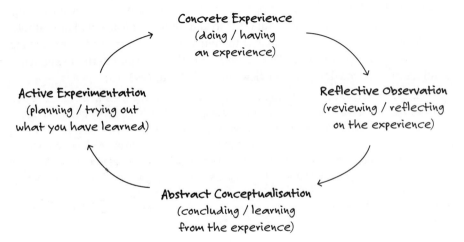

## Concrete experience (having an experience)

This stage involves having an experience, then providing an account of what happened. This might sound easy, and to some degree it is, but it involves very careful and objective scrutiny of what took place (Boud, 1993: 19). It is easy to see what you *want to see*, but the challenge of reflection is to look for the truth and see *what is actually there*. Sometimes you can miss subtle incidents or disregard what appears to be a trivial matter. However, the quality of your reflection depends on how fully and completely you recall the event. Be alert to all aspects of the experience – pay attention to every little nuance and cue. Do not disregard matters just because they do not fit with your ideals or views. Where an event has been videoed or evidenced in some format, it is relatively easy to look back over the event. If the incident has not been recorded, you should go back over the event in your mind meticulously, being careful not to gloss over anything which could be vital to your learning.

> Imagine you have just completed a difficult telephone negotiation on behalf of your client. You were trying to persuade a double-glazing firm to remove a window which your client feels is unsatisfactory and replace it with a new one. It may be tempting when you start your reflection to go straight to the result (the company has refused to complete the work) and allow this to dominate the reflection. But you need to examine each stage of the experience: preparation, strategy, commencement of the negotiation, style and tone adopted, apparent reaction of the opponent, how you responded to your opponent's attitude, implementation/adjustments to or abandonment of your strategy, unexpected matters arising, persistence, skills utilised and so on. In this way you will gather a wide range of raw material which you can begin to analyse.

## Observations and reflections (reviewing the experience)

Having described the experience, this stage requires you to take into account your emotions and behaviour. Consider what you felt during the experience. Both positive and negative feelings should be attended to. Notice also how you reacted to different aspects of the experience.

Boud and Walker (1993: 73) recognise how people influence their own learning. They argue that individuals can both develop and limit their learning. For example, when reflecting, if you are in denial as to your true feelings then you are denying yourself learning opportunities (Boud, 1993: 15). The way you interpret experience is intimately connected to how you view yourself (Boud, 1993: 15).

> In the negotiation example above, you might ask yourself how your personal knowledge of your client's plight affected you; whether you felt nervous or intimidated prior to or during the telephone conversation and, if so, what prompted this; whether you were conscious of successes or failures in your strategy during your negotiation; how you felt when it appeared you could not make progress with the negotiation; and whether you felt powerless or angry or defiant or frustrated by the negotiation.

## Formation of abstract concepts/generalisations (making sense of what you have learned)

Once you have thought about what happened and your emotional response to those events, you then need to put these into context and analyse *why* you acted and felt that way. By doing this, you should hopefully be able to see the bigger picture – it is therefore at this stage that you begin to make sense of the experience. You should evaluate *why* you thought, behaved and acted as you did. What underlying *reasons* may have caused this?

This is quite a challenging but critical stage of the reflective process. You need to realise how your previous experiences and understanding relate to and impact on your interpretation of the current experience. The work of Boud and Walker is particularly enlightening on this stage of the process.

> Returning to the negotiation example, you could reflect on what prior experience, if any, you had of negotiation-type situations and whether these enhanced or impaired your performance; how your understanding of the merits of your client's claim impacted on your conduct of the negotiation; what is it about you that made you feel emotion or anxiety; whether you controlled your nerves or emotion well during your conversation; whether different approaches to the telephone conversation might have elicited a more positive response from the opponent; what your conduct during the negotiation says about you; whether you have a conciliatory or confrontational approach to problems, and so on.

When you try to make sense of something, your ability to understand it is conditioned by what you already know and by the morals and values you hold. Therefore your personal beliefs and existing knowledge infiltrate your learning process and how you relate to each new experience (Boud, Cohen and Walker, 1985; 1993: 10). For example, imagine that, when you were a child, you and your family had been thrown out of your home, and you are now instructed to act for a landlord who wishes to evict his tenants. Your childhood experiences are likely to influence how you feel towards your client and possibly how you conduct yourself. Similarly, if you hold strong views about the sanctity of life and you are involved with a euthanasia campaign, then your views will no doubt impact on your behavioural and emotional responses. However, recognising *if* and *how* your past experiences and beliefs affect you in the present experience is the key to unlocking your learning.

At this stage, you also need to realise whether and how your understanding has changed due to the learning that has been generated from the event you have just experienced. For instance, you might realise that your previously held views are outdated or were perhaps naive. Assimilating the meaning derived from old and new experiences allows you to further your learning, knowledge and understanding.

To successfully engage with this stage of the process, you need to be open-minded and receptive to looking at things from a different perspective, approaching matters with a new way of understanding and challenging any pre-held ideas and values. Reflection therefore requires a willingness to evaluate the beliefs you hold most strongly and realise that, sometimes, your perspective can be limited by your preconceptions and limiting to your learning.

## Testing/experimentation (trying out what you have learned)

Reflection is more than just a thought process. The last stage of the procedure involves action in the form of testing out the learning which occurred in the previous step. Having made sense of your actions and emotions, you will no doubt plan what you would do differently next time, and try out this new idea when an appropriate situation arises.

> With the negotiation example, you might go back to your plan in light of your reflections and see whether changes could be made that would improve the prospects of success, either for the next case or for your next exchange with the double-glazing firm. On a very simple level, you could go through an imagined conversation in your own mind, or you could be more systematic and write down points that you would want to raise, or even try it out on a fellow student or your supervisor. Finally, of course, you could get back on the telephone and try again.

Once you have experimented with the new approach, you should reflect on this to assess its reliability or success. You can see from the Gibbs and Kolb diagrams above that reflection is a cyclical process. It is this experimentation, the trying out the new ideas, that in fact becomes the next experience, and the process begins again. In some cases, even a successful change will give rise to further ideas, perhaps even a more improved course of action. After all, there is always room for improvement. You can therefore see that reflection is a continuous refinement of your understanding and learning.

Some elements of the process are more advanced than others. The deeper aspects of reflection include understanding of cause (rather than effect) and being able to put matters into context. Additionally, you should not only reflect on the event or experience; you must also try to reflect on the learning that has taken place: what you have learned and how you have learned. For a depiction of basic and deeper reflection, see Niall Sclater's diagram, a link to which is available on the Companion Website.

It is also important to understand that reflection is not just about you or how you performed. Indeed, an over-concentration on the personal can make reflections introspective or even narcissistic. You should try to consider a wide range of influences, relationships, circumstances and consequences. Reflection on the bigger picture is extremely valuable and this is addressed later in the chapter.

## Why can reflecting be challenging?

It is probably easier to state what reflection involves than it is to *actually* reflect. Reflection is a challenging activity for a number of reasons.

- Because you cannot look up the 'answer' in a textbook or on the Internet.
- Because you have to be self-critical.

- Because you have to examine your own opinions and challenge them.
- Because you need to recognise broader issues by stepping back.

There are various factors which can affect how well you reflect. Boud et al (1993: 79) have drawn up an extensive list of barriers to effective reflection and therefore barriers to learning from experience. A selection of their list of factors is summarised below:

- Presumptions about what you can and cannot do
- Previous negative experiences
- Lack of self-awareness
- Poor preparation
- Little or no time
- Outside pressures and demands
- Little or no support from other people
- Lack of observational skills
- Unclear or unfocused intent
- Inability to break established patterns of thought and behaviour
- Inability to believe or understand it is possible to learn from experience
- Unhelpful feelings, such as lack of confidence, fear of failure or worry about how others will respond

These are real problems but not insuperable ones. Recognising that there are barriers to effective reflection is part of the process of making reflection effective. If you find yourself struggling to reflect, look at the above list and consider whether any of the listed factors apply to you. Once you have identified the barrier, you can then work to overcome it.

## **12.6** What should you reflect on?

Reflection works best if it starts from a concrete experience. In clinical and pro bono work, there is normally a vast range of experiences you can reflect on. Do not think that you need to find an extreme or dramatic event – you can reflect perfectly well on routine or even mundane activities. You can reflect on a single incident (a telephone call, a letter, an interview) or a series of events (a case, a placement or internship) – from what you did to how you felt, to how your client reacted, to why you did or did not do something ... the list is endless.

If you are working on behalf of clients, you should never be in the position of saying that you have nothing to reflect upon. The fact is that real-life creates uncertainty, which requires you to adapt and problem-solve and be creative. This provides rich opportunities for reflection.

The basic building blocks are likely to be the legal or transferable skills you are utilising when you provide a legal service to clients. The list below is not in any way comprehensive but gives you a useful starting point.

- Taking a client enquiry over the telephone
- Interviewing a client in person
- Interviewing witnesses or other participants
- Recording attendance notes
- Opening a file
- File and case management
- Client care and professional conduct matters
- Conducting factual or legal research
- Writing letters to clients and others
- Dealing with opponents
- Negotiation or other dispute resolution
- Drafting legal documents
- Dealing with courts and tribunals
- Advocacy

You can, of course, reflect on other aspects of your experience such as:

- Meetings with your supervisor/fellow students
- The office environment
- Policies and procedures adopted by your clinic/pro bono project
- Teamwork
- Interpersonal relationships
- Analysis and problem-solving
- Debates and discussions
- Level of service
- Client needs and expectations

## 12.7 When should you reflect?

The phrase 'reflective practice' indicates that it is something that should become a habit. Learning is a continual process so reflection should occur regularly.

 **Top tip:**
Timing is everything – make time to reflect deeply on your experience(s).

Reflection is a deep thought process and should not be done in a rushed manner. You should ensure that you set aside enough time to do the process justice. To help discipline yourself, try setting aside the same time each day or week to conduct some uninterrupted and leisurely reflection. Even if you do not have time immediately after an experience or event to reflect extensively, try to at least note down a few words or thoughts which will jog your memory when you get time to review the event in more depth.

## 12.8 Methods of reflection

Although reflection occurs almost exclusively in the mind, you are often required to evidence your reflection in a tangible form. This might be in written form, via a presentation or discussion, or even by using more creative methods. These different methods are explored below.

## Written reflection

There are many benefits to keeping a written record of your reflections, regardless of whether they form part of your assessment. Sometimes it can be difficult to remember what you were thinking or feeling at a particular moment in time, so it is useful to be able to look back and compare your different responses. You may notice that your views and responses differ and this can be a sign of how much learning has occurred since that particular reflection took place.

There are a variety of methods which you can use to record your written reflection including the use of blogs, diaries, journals, leaning logs and personal development portfolios (PDPs).

Strictly speaking, journals, diaries and logs are quite different things. A log, in the strictest sense, is a straightforward record of factual events (as in a ship's log). A diary can be a simple recording of the day's events or a personal account of intimate hopes, emotions and so on. A journal chronicles thoughts and feelings about particular events or aspects of life. In the educational field, diaries and journals are more commonly being used to record learning and can therefore be referred to as learning journals or reflective diaries. Given the discrepancies between the definition of a journal, diary and log, it is advisable to check with your supervisor so that you are clear exactly what is expected in terms of content if keeping a written record.

You can record your reflections using traditional pen and paper or you could opt for electronic methods, such as a reflective blog, electronic portfolio or wiki. One benefit of a blog is that you can make it public, thereby allowing your supervisor or other members of your group to read and comment on your entries. However, care needs to be taken not to breach client confidentiality if a blog is widely available. An excellent example of a blog which reflects on legal education is that of Paul Maharg (a link to his blog is available on the Companion Website).

With written journals and diaries, Moon (1999: 194; 2006: 53) suggests the use of a double-entry system, which requires a two-page layout. The left-hand page should contain your initial reflection and the right-hand page should be for secondary reflection. Secondary reflection involves revisiting your initial (or primary) reflection and reflecting again, in light of further knowledge you have acquired or the learning that has taken place since the primary reflection was recorded.

If you like the idea of keeping a diary but are not so keen on writing, consider the option of a video diary instead.

## Discussions and presentations

You can also reflect through the medium of discussions and presentations. Discussions can be a relatively easy way to engage with reflection, as you are already accustomed to talking freely and in an informal manner. Think of it as a chat where you talk about your experience and what you think or feel about it. You will have done this many times over, perhaps when chatting to a friend about a book or film.

It is not a great leap to transfer this type of conversation to your clinical or pro bono activities. You can have a reflective conversation with yourself (as an internal dialogue), with your supervisor or even in a group. It is perhaps most valuable to have a reflective debate in a group of, say, three or four. This should hopefully encourage the flow of spontaneous and lively views. The discussion can often start with one issue and quickly take a few sharp turns and diversions. It can be really interesting to see where it ends up.

Presentations are another way of reflecting in a group setting. You may be asked to present your reflective ideas either *to* a group or as *part* of a group.

Any topic or experience can be the focus of a reflective discussion or debate, and some suggestions are set out below.

---

**Skill-specific reflection**

- What are the key elements of an effective interview?
- How can you research effectively?
- What abilities are required to manage cases effectively?
- What is the most important skill in terms of legal writing?
- What skills make a good advocate?

**Reflection on wider issues**

- What is the role of a lawyer?
- What characteristics should a lawyer possess?
- What is the role of law in society?
- What problems exist with access to justice?
- What is justice and is justice always achieved?
- What is the relationship between law, morals and ethics?
- To what extent does the law reflect society's changing attitudes?
- Is the sentencing of criminals too lenient?
- Is all unlawful behaviour always 'bad'?
- To what extent does the criminal justice system rehabilitate prisoners?
- What is the role of the court system (criminal or civil)?

---

## Creative reflective methods

When first starting out, writing down your reflections may seem a daunting prospect. If so, why not start by recording your reflective thoughts using other methods which are not so dependent on the use of language? Then, once you are more comfortable with committing your reflections to paper, you can begin formalising your thoughts using the written word. Using illustrations and images for reflective work can be just as rigorous as writing reflectively because you still need to focus your mind and identify flashpoints within the experience on which to reflect. Let your creativity run wild by reflecting using pictures, drawings, collage, diagrams and posters. See **Activity 3** at the end of this chapter for an introduction to creative reflection methods, then visit the Companion Website for storyboard templates, posters and completed examples.

## Group and peer reflection

Reflection is a very personal activity. However, when you first begin your reflective practice, you may be wondering how 'well' you are doing it and if you are reflecting on the 'right sort of things.' It can often be helpful to share your thoughts with someone else to determine if you are on the right track and to develop confidence in your reflective ability.

One of the advantages of sharing your thoughts with others is that, by having to articulate your views to someone else, you can fully appreciate the strengths and gaps in your thinking (Rodgers, 2002: 856). Other advantages include:

- having the value of the experience affirmed;
- seeing things from fresh or different perspectives (other members of the group will be able to suggest alternative meanings, opinions or interpretations which can broaden your understanding); and
- receiving support to continue with reflective practice. (Rodgers, 2002: 857)

Additionally, as mentioned above, your existing knowledge and prior experiences all have a bearing on how you react and feel about an experience. Whilst you and your colleagues (or even your supervisor) may have shared the same experience, your thoughts, emotions, responses and reflection on that incident are likely to be quite different. This is due to what you personally bring to that experience and how this impacts on your subsequent reflections on it.

> If you work in pairs in your clinic or pro bono project, this provides an ideal opportunity for a small group reflection. Take letter writing as an example – you can sit together at a computer screen drafting the letter so that you have a shared experience which you can then reflect on together. Alternatively, you can both independently prepare a draft of a letter and then swap them and talk to each other about your respective approaches. This may lead to both of you making compromises as you work towards a version that you are both happy with, and it will provide you with a fruitful reflective experience. Comparing the original drafts with the final version will provide an evidence trail that will be extremely useful in understanding why you developed the letter in the way you did.

It is therefore extremely useful to reflect with others in order to understand how and why individuals respond differently to the same experience. By appreciating how different factors influence the responses of others, you can better understand how these factors affect your responses and views. It also makes you more open to challenging your views and beliefs, having been exposed to the values and opinions of colleagues. Group reflection will therefore help you appreciate how your background and previous experiences impact on your learning. For an exercise in peer reflection, see **Activity 4**.

## 12.9 Developing your reflective writing

You have read above about the different mediums that can be used to develop your reflective practice. This section focuses on the act of writing reflectively.

Recording your reflection in writing focuses the mind and forces you to articulate your thoughts and emotions. Writing is a specific form of communication, and the way you communicate is largely dictated by the intended audience. So, for example, when corresponding with clients, you should write in a way that your client will understand. With reflective writing, you are your own audience; you should therefore write freely and honestly. Having said this, if your reflections are to be shared with anybody else, ensure that there is nothing in there that is inappropriate or might cause upset or offence to the people you are working with.

While your written reflections may be shared with your supervisor or fellow students, this should not inhibit what, or how authentically, you write. If your reflection is to be shared, avoid the temptation to write what you think your supervisor wants to hear or see on the page. Your supervisor will want to read your true reflections.

Writing reflectively differs from most other styles of writing you will have undertaken. At school you will have no doubt developed your creative writing, and as part of your course you will have honed your academic writing skills. Reflective writing involves another style altogether. Stylistically it is quite informal yet structured. A common mistake when starting to write reflectively is to ramble or jump around from point to point. You have read above that reflection involves careful thought and consideration. You should ensure that your compositions reproduce on the page the rigour and quality of your thought process. To do this you will need to practise.

### Getting started

As reflective writing is something that you may not have conducted before, perhaps the hardest thing is getting started. Rather than launching into a full-blown reflective piece, it is a good idea gradually to build your writing style and technique. You might therefore want to begin by utilising drawings or pictures with short captions (see above). Moving on from this, you might want to experiment with 'streams of consciousness' or brainstorming to get your initial thoughts and emotions down on paper.

 **Top tip**
Get creative – outlets for reflection can allow you to tap in to your arty side.

A stream of consciousness, also known as free writing, is the basic act of writing down what is in your head without really thinking about it. You first need to select a topic, event or experience, then simply write down whatever comes to mind. This is best carried out using pen and paper, rather than a keyboard, so as to encourage quick and free scribbles. Write down words or short phases and avoid full sentences. The object of the exercise is to write down your thoughts quickly and then to move straight on to the next thought. As this is a free form of writing, do not worry about spelling, punctuation or even presentation. You can jot down your thoughts from left to right, down the page or even in a spiral, whatever your mind chooses. Once you have run out of ideas, sit back and read what you have written. See if you can notice any links or connections between the words and phrases. Perhaps you could even select a few of the entries on the page and explore these in more detail using the same process, or by brainstorming them.

Brainstorming diagrams visually record ideas and thoughts. They allow you to take an idea, which you then branch out and explore before moving onto the next idea or thought. The map should show links and relationships between your thoughts, ideas and opinions. Your diagrams can be enhanced by using a different colour for each separate idea or branch, and through the inclusion of images or symbols. To view an example of a reflective brainstorm, see the Companion Website. You can download software packages free of charge from the Internet, but a large piece of paper will work just as well for this type of reflection.

Never dispose of your free writing or brainstorming diagrams as it is interesting to look back on them at a later date to see how your reflective skills and depth of reflection have matured.

### Next steps

Once you are accustomed to jotting down your raw reflections, you can begin to structure your writing in a more organised and coherent way. You can develop your initial thoughts and conclusions more fully into lengthier, detailed written pieces.

Reflective writing is personal and deals with your experiences and it should therefore be phrased in the first person singular, for example: 'I felt anxious about the prospect of meeting the client for the first time.' Avoid the use of 'one', in the sense of 'one felt this or that', as this makes your writing remote and less accessible.

Reflective writing is less formal than academic writing but that is not to say it should lack structure. Your thoughts should be organised and linked logically. Whilst informal, conventions such as spelling, punctuation and grammar, sentence structure and use of paragraphs should still be observed.

### Levels of reflective writing

It is relatively easy to say what makes good written reflection, but it can be difficult to 'see' how successful you have been in converting this guidance when producing written reflections. Moon (2004: 214–16; 2006: 161–3) has produced a scale indicator that sets out the characteristics of the different levels of reflection, which can be broadly categorised as descriptive writing, moderate reflection and deep reflection. A précis of Moon's reflective framework is provided below.

Descriptive writing is a narrative account in which only the author's point of view is discussed. It contains little questioning or exploration of the issues. Ideas are not linked other than by the chronology of the event and the writing tends to lack structure or focus. Any assumptions that are identified are not explored or challenged. If reference is made to past experiences or opinions then these are not analysed or contextualised. There is no exploration of how emotions relate to behaviour or responses. The piece lacks conclusions or any suppositions are not supported by the arguments made.

Moderate reflection will contain some comparison of ideas and assumptions but, whilst these are questioned, they are not challenged in any depth and nor are they fully related to the issues. The writer explores motives and underlying rationales for particular behaviour and responses. The writing recognises the value in further exploration of ideas but fails to do this to any great extent. Alternative viewpoints or attitudes may be mentioned, but they are not explored in depth. There is a failure to recognise that views can change with time and more reflection. The conclusions drawn are not fully developed but are supported to some extent by the arguments raised.

Deep reflection is evidenced by moving away from a straightforward account of the experience towards reflective thinking and self-critique. The writing is more focused, systematic and well structured. There is evidence of the ability to stand back and evaluate the experience with appropriate questioning of assumptions and ideas. The writer refers to emotions and behaviour and demonstrates an understanding of their role in the writer's responses. External viewpoints, ideas and material are introduced and analysed. There is recognition that prior thoughts, attitudes and experiences can affect behaviour. The piece also appreciates that views can change. A conclusion is reached which draws together the ideas and recognises any limitations of the author's judgements.

Under Moon's framework, you should aim for the latter level of reflection.

Goodman (1984, cited in Palmer, 1994: 24–5) offers a similar three-stage framework. Goodman's first level of reflection is that which is largely descriptive. The second level builds on this description and shows an awareness of the relationship between values, beliefs and behaviour. The third stage acknowledges the wider influences of ethical, economic, sociological and political issues and policy which relate to the subject-matter of the reflective account. There are similarities between Moon and Goodman's frameworks, but the key difference is that, with Goodman's model, you should incorporate all three levels.

 **Top tip**

It is very important to be balanced in your self-criticism. Your supervisor will not want you to beat yourself up, nor will he or she expect to see flawless reviews. Nobody is perfect but, at the same time, everyone has strengths. Your reflections should recognise your strengths *and* weaknesses.

### Judging the quality of your written reflection

Even with the above guidance, it can still be difficult if you are new to reflection to appreciate the overall quality of your written reflective work once it is on the page. The traffic light exercise (see **Activity 5** below) uses a colour-coding system which allows you to clearly 'see' the quality of your written reflection. The colours of red, amber and green correspond to Goodman's framework. The traffic light model operates on the basis that all three of these elements are required within reflective writing.

Your reflection needs some descriptive elements to set the scene for the reader. This would fall into the red category. For instance, you need to explain what experience it is you are reflecting on, how you prepared for that experience, what you did and so on. However, a reflection which consists solely of description will clearly fall into Moon's 'descriptive' category. Once you have set the scene, you should then consider matters such as how you felt about the experience, and question why something went well or badly and what you might do differently next time. This is moving beyond description and is therefore graded amber. You will note that the reflection is still centred on your performance at this stage, and it therefore falls short of considering the wider issues; you are not yet seeing the bigger picture. It is only once you have thought beyond yourself that you hit the green stage. Reflection in this category shows an ability to see things in context. After all, your experience does not happen in isolation. There are many other relevant factors which will have impacted on your performance and your client's problem. You, in your role of law student, are just one small part of the legal system, and the legal system is part of the society in which you serve. To produce high-level reflection, you need to consider these issues which are external to, but at the same time linked to, your experience and the way in which you deal with your client's case or task.

### Worked example

Imagine that your client has approached you for legal advice about a dispute that he has. You research your client's legal position, and he does indeed have a cause of action which could provide a remedy for his problem. So, you advise your client to start legal proceedings. However, your client is not entitled to legal aid and there is no other form of funding available. As a result, he cannot pursue proceedings because he cannot afford the court fees. Clearly, this quandary involves matters of access to justice, ethics and legal policy. These issues extend beyond your lawyer–client relationship and have a broader, wider impact.

**Top tip**

Reflect on your personal experience and beyond – try to consider the wider picture.

In the example given above, you could take the opportunity to reflect beyond your own performance on a number of wider issues. For instance, should legal aid be available to all wronged parties? Has the Government gone too far in its reduction of (and in some cases withdrawal of) public funding? Should there be such a thing as court fees? Are they morally or ethically justifiable? If a party has been wronged, is it fair that that party has to pay fees to obtain legal satisfaction? If your client cannot make use of the legal system due to lack of financial means, has your client been failed by the legal system? Do the high hourly rates charged by lawyers also act as a barrier to justice? Is the role of lawyers to serve as an instrument of justice, or do lawyers actually hinder the process due to their high fees? Does the law better serve the rich than the poor? How might the public perception of the legal system be affected by these matters?

Standing back from the experience in this way allows you to recognise and appreciate how outside influences impact not just on you and your legal work, but on the legal system and society as a whole.

Reflecting on these wider issues is arguably one of the most difficult skills when first starting out. However, asking yourself 'why' after everything should help you take your reflective thoughts from red right through to green. For instance, if you are reflecting on an interview, your reflective dialogue might go something like this:

> 'I believe one reason why the interview was a success was due to the rapport I established with my client.'
>
> *But **why** is it important to have a rapport with your client?*
>
> 'Well, I want my client to feel that he can open up to me and trust me with his case.'
>
> *But **why** is it important that clients do these things?*
>
> 'If my client feels that he cannot tell me everything that's relevant to his case then I will not have full instructions and therefore cannot advise him properly; I might unwittingly give him inaccurate advice. And if my client does not trust me in the way I conduct the case then he might not pursue it further.'
>
> *But **why** is this significant?*
>
> 'Well if my client receives poor advice on this occasion (through no fault of my own), he may be reluctant to seek legal advice in the future because of the bad experience he has had in the past.'
>
> *But **why** is this important?*
>
> 'Well, it's vital that the public has confidence in lawyers as we are part of the legal system. And the legal system is there to serve the public. In some ways the profession and the system is dependent on public confidence.'

Asking 'why' at every opportunity allows you to explore whether there are any relevant wider issues and how they relate to your experience. This simple three-letter word can broaden the scope of your reflective enquiry and significantly transform the quality of your reflection.

You should note, however, that not all of your arguments can be taken through to the green level, and you certainly should not strain to do this with each and every point you have reflected on. It is important, though, to explore whether your reflection can be developed in this way.

 **Top tips for reflection**

- Just do it – do not waste time hesitating, start reflecting.
- Reflect instantaneously – reflect as soon as possible after the event.
- Be honest – write what you believe, not what you think the reader wants to hear.
- Be rigorous – do not just describe – dig deeply so that your reflection shows that you are both self-aware and learning from your experience.
- The more the merrier – reflecting with others builds confidence and provides different perspectives.
- Stick with it – it can take a little time to develop your reflective practice, but it will pay off.

## 12.10 Summary

In a nutshell, reflection is very important. It is the process by which you make sense of your experiences and learn from them. There are many stages to effective and successful reflection, and you will need to develop techniques to improve your reflective practice.

You will no doubt already reflect in your everyday life, and perhaps you also reflect to some extent in respect of your clinical and pro bono activities. Much of this reflection is likely to be on a subconscious level. To develop fully, you need to transform these implicit or internal reflections into explicit and more meaningful reflection.

The act of continuous reflection can unlock more purposeful and effective learning opportunities, extending beyond classroom teaching. It is a habit that you should apply to your professional life in order to become a reflective practitioner, which will afford you a lifetime of learning. For information on how these reflective methods may be assessed, see **Chapter 13**.

##  Further reading

There is an immense amount of material available on the subject of reflection. However, very few of these publications are aimed specifically at law students. There is some student-orientated writing on reflection in the field of healthcare, which is of general application to clinical legal work. Having read this chapter, you will now have a good grounding in reflective theory, which should allow you to appreciate the texts below regardless of whether they are framed from a teaching perspective or intended for other disciplines. An Internet search for 'reflection' or 'reflective practice' will also reveal a whole world of writing and material devoted to reflection.

### Introductory

**Hinnett, K, *Developing Reflective Practice in Legal Education* (UK Centre for Legal Education, 2002)**

> This guidance note is a great accessible introduction to reflective practice and is aimed at the legal field. You can download it free of charge from www.ukcle.ac.uk/resources/personal-development-planning/reflection/

**Race, P, *Evidencing Reflection: Putting the 'W' into Reflection* (ESCalate Learning Exchange, 2002)**

> A well written piece which sets out a raft of questions to get you started thinking reflectively. http://escalate.ac.uk/resources/reflection/

### Intermediate

**Boud, D, Keogh, R and Walker, D (eds), *Reflection: Turning Experience into Learning* (Kogan Page, 1985)**

> This is a collection of writing which considers the role reflection plays in our learning. The chapters are concise and fairly accessible. Topics covered include reflection and the development of learning skills and judging the quality of development. Their three-stage reflective model (described above) is explored in more detail at pp 20–36.

**Boud, D, Cohen, R and Walker, D (eds),** *Using Experience for Learning* **(The Society for Research into Higher Education and Open University Press, 1993)**

This text is a compilation of short works by various contributors on different aspects and personal encounters of using learning from experience. The introduction (pp 8–16) provides a good overview of the key elements of learning from experience. It addresses in an accessible way how your emotions and previous experiences impact on your learning (Chapter 5). It is quite easy to dip in and out of the book as each contributor addresses a discrete feature of experiential learning.

**Moon, J,** *Reflection in Learning and Professional Development* **(RoutledgeFalmer, 1999)**

This publication provides guidance to students and practitioners about the origins of reflection and how it can enhance learning in practice.

**Moon, J,** *A Handbook of Reflective and Experiential Learning* **(RoutledgeFalmer, 2004)**

This text analyses the theory and meaning of reflective and experiential learning, and how they relate to the process of learning. The book also provides useful ideas and advice for applying the models of learning.

**Moon, J,** *Learning Journals: a handbook for reflective practice and professional development,* **2nd edn (Routledge, 2006)**

This handbook examines the nature of learning journals and how you learn from them, in addition to providing guidance on keeping and using journals. In common with her other books, Moon provides useful exercises and activities.

**Moon, J,** *Critical Thinking: an exploration of theory and practice* **(Routledge, 2008)**

This book explores in great detail the concept of critical thinking, which is analogous to and forms part of the reflective process. It contains a number of resources and exercises which aim to develop critical thinking skills.

**Palmer, A et al,** *Reflective Practice in Nursing* **(Blackwell Science, 1994)**

You can read more about Goodman's three-stage reflective framework in this text.

**Rodgers, C, 'Defining reflection: Another look at John Dewey and reflective thinking' (2002)** *Teachers College Record,* **vol 4, no 4, pp 842–66**

If you do not fancy digesting Dewey's book, this article summarises his key concepts in a concise format. A link to the full text article is available on the Companion Website.

## Advanced

**Dewey, J,** *How We Think* **(DC Heath and Co, 1993)**

In this classic book, the godfather of reflection, John Dewey, sets out his views on how we learn. His philosophies are deep and complex, but this book has formed the basis of much of the later writings on reflection and experiential learning.

**Schön, D,** *The Reflective Practitioner: How Professionals Think in Action* **(Jossey-Bass, 1982)**

This groundbreaking text brought the two distinct types of reflection (in and on action) to the fore in the context of professionals. The book focuses on five non-legal sectors to illustrate how professionals approach problem-solving. There are a few specific references to law, and the lawyer–client relationship is covered at pp 293–4.

**Schön, D,** *Educating the Reflective Practitioner* **(San Francisco: Jossey-Bass, 1987)**

This book offers an approach for educating professionals and builds on the earlier concepts set out in 'The Reflective Practitioner'.

 Activities

## Activity 1: Self-test

It is important to evaluate the base from which you are starting, so ask yourself the following questions:

- How often do you reflect?
- What methods do you currently use to reflect?
- Who is involved with your reflection?

Once you have gauged the level of your existing reflective habits, explore how you can widen the scope of your reflective practice. For instance, if you only reflect in your head, resolve to try external reflection methods such as storyboarding or writing. If you conduct reflection alone, have a go as part of a group. If you reflect sporadically, try to be more disciplined in the frequency of your reflection.

## Activity 2: Reflection word association

Write 'REFLECTION' vertically down the page of a blank piece of paper. List as many words and phrases associated with reflection as you can for each letter. This exercise should help you judge your understanding of the various aspects and ingredients of reflection. Suggested words and phrases are available on the Companion Website.

## Activity 3: Storyboard

Select an event or experience that you would like to reflect on, for example an interview or presentation you were involved in. Use the storyboard template (available on the Companion Website) to produce a pictorial reflection of that incident. Print out the storyboard from the website and complete it by hand with drawings, collage or cut-out images from magazines. Alternatively, complete the storyboard using images from your computer's clip art function. Feel free to add captions and be as creative as you like.

## Activity 4: Mirror, mirror

You can try this exercise where you have shared an experience with someone else. This shared experience could be a jointly conducted interview, a group presentation, a hearing you observed with someone, and so on.

Reflect on the shared experience by yourself. You can do this, for example, as a short written piece or by storyboarding. Ask the other person to reflect on the same experience and ensure that he or she records his or her reflections in the same manner. Get together with the other person and share your reflections. Compare and contrast your observations and see if they mirror each other. Explore why there are similarities and, perhaps more importantly, why there are differences of opinion arising from the same experience. Question whether differently held values or beliefs are the cause of the divergent views. After your meeting, consider what you have learned from reflecting with someone else: a reflection on reflection, if you will. Repeat this with different people to take advantage of a wide range of alternative views.

## Activity 5: Reflection traffic light

Read the short reflection that follows and use the traffic light colour-coding system, set out at **12.9** and recapped below, to 'see' the quality of the reflective writing. Repeat this exercise on your own reflective compositions. The suggested traffic light colour-coding, together with annotations, is available on the Companion Website.

descriptive and sets the scene

moderate reflection, considers the perspectives of others and recognises links between thought, emotions and action

deep reflection considering the wider issues which addresses how you might act differently in the future

---

## Reflection on Advice Letter

This piece reflects on the letter of advice I drafted to Mr Smith. I had seen the client approximately 2 weeks before about an employment dispute. He'd been dismissed from his job in circumstances which, in my opinion, seemed unfair. After conducting the interview I carried out some research and the purpose of the letter was to set out his legal position.

The interview hadn't gone as well as I'd hoped. The client seemed wary of me and I put this down to him doubting my capabilities, because of my student status. Therefore, in addition to confirming his legal position, I wanted the letter to dispel any doubts the client had about me and build a better rapport with him.

I thought the best way to do this would be to impress Mr Smith with my knowledge of the law and through confident written communication. This was my first substantive piece of correspondence with the client, in fact any client, as up until this point I had only drafted routine letters confirming the dates and times of appointments etc. Due to this, I was a little unsure about how to approach the letter but I just rolled up my sleeves and cracked on with it.

I began with a summary of the problem then moved on to the advice. I set out the various elements of an unfair dismissal claim, including the requirement of employee status. I thought the client might struggle to establish that he was an 'employee' so I went into a fair amount of detail on this point. I made reference to 'mutuality of obligation' and case law which was relevant to this area. However, I became quite frustrated with the letter – the expression seemed overly complex and therefore the structure didn't have the flow I had hoped for. I tried to see if I could salvage the letter in any way but in the end I scrapped it and started again from scratch.

Before beginning my second draft I sat back and considered why the initial draft had been such a flop. I managed to identify a few reasons. Firstly, in my attempt to impress the client I had fallen into the trap of using intricate language and expression. I'd been taught in my English A Level classes to display a range of expression in my work and demonstrate my ability to use complex sentence structure. However, in the context of my advice letter this just seemed to produce flowery and over-convoluted results. If the client had been sent the original letter, rather than clarifying his legal position I think he would have been left rather confused!

▶

Also stemming from the desire to impress the client was my decision to include detailed legal references. I had spent several hours researching Mr Smith's position and by referring to the case law I thought the client would be assured that I was a competent adviser and committed to his case. But all this seemed to do was turn the letter into a legal essay!

Secondly, I concluded that I was struggling with the structure because, rather than planning the letter out, I simply started writing without giving any real thought to the content or order of the advice. So before I began my second draft, I prepared an outline structure and began writing afresh. The second draft was a much-improved attempt and after a few suggested changes from my supervisor the letter was posted to the client.

Since writing the letter I have met the client twice more and our rapport is much better. I would like to think that this is due, to some extent, to the advice letter. I've noticed that Mr Smith does not seem as wary anymore. In hindsight I may have been a little premature in assuming he was distrustful of me because of my student status. Having met him again it I think he was simply nervous about seeking legal advice – after all, it's not something people do everyday! It turned out that this is the first time in his life he has sought legal advice, which would explain why he seemed unsure. But what made me interpret his nerves as a lack of confidence in me? Perhaps the feelings I projected onto the client were in fact _my own_ inner worries. Was _I_ concerned the client would think I was incapable? Therefore did his 'uncertainty' lead me to jump to the conclusion it was about me?

I think the main reason the first letter did not achieve its objectives was due to me skewing the purpose of the letter. Clearly the purpose was to advise the client but instead I turned the letter into a vehicle to impress Mr Smith, which meant it totally missed the point. I realise that in doing this I put my own objectives first when of course, as a matter of professional conduct, I should have acted in the client's best interests. Having realised this I have subsequently ensured that I approach future work with the correct motivation and mind set.

I also realise that spending a short time planning my work before I start saves time in the long run – here a small amount of planning would have saved me a considerable amount of time as, in effect, I ended up drafting two different letters. There is no cutting corners when it comes to case work! It also made me think about a solicitor's duty to their clients when it comes to time spent on the case. It was not such a problem in this instance because I was representing the client on a pro bono basis, but what if it is a fee-paying client? Solicitors have a reputation for charging quite high fees and members of the public want to pay a fair price for the work carried out on their case. However, if their solicitor works inefficiently and charges the client accordingly, then the public may lose faith in the legal profession and look elsewhere. This is particularly important from the profession's point of view given the threat posed by the Legal Services Act.

These realisations have helped me develop my legal writing skills and also the approach I take towards my casework more generally. There are still a few areas for improvement but I am pleased with the progress I have made.

# 13 Assessment

'Success is the child of audacity'

Benjamin Disraeli, *The Rise of
Iskander*, Chapter 4 (1833)

## 13.1 Introduction

This chapter explores the issue of assessment in clinical legal education and how you can enhance your performance through effective use of feedback. It also provides information and guidance on appraisals, which you may experience as part of your clinic and pro bono activities. Even if your clinic or pro bono work is not assessed, you will find some useful information here about what makes a strong student and what is expected of you.

As assessment practices vary immensely, it is important to bear in mind that the information below is intended to provide general guidance and you should pay careful attention to the particular requirements of your institution's assessment regime.

## 13.2 Assessment – the great debate

The topic of assessment in clinic and pro bono is the subject of great debate. There are broadly two divisions: one faction believes that clinic and pro bono activities should be assessed, and the other opposes it. The different attitudes are reflected in the assorted assessment regimes which operate in clinical and pro bono schemes. Certain institutions or modules operate a grading system, others a pass/fail approach; some activities attract module credits, and some work is not assessed at all. A brief discussion of the rationale behind these conflicting views is set out below and it may enrich your understanding of why your institution has adopted a particular approach to assessment.

### Arguments in favour of assessment

Several advantages of assessing clinical activities have been identified. According to Hyams (2006: 88), the act of assessing recognises the time and effort that you invest in your work. Research has found that assessing can also serve as a motivational factor (Brustin & Chavkin, 1997: 314) and can thus engender a professional atmosphere (Brustin & Chavkin, 1997: 313).

### Arguments against assessment

Whilst there are many people in favour of assessment, you do not have to look far to find the critics. Disapproval stems from the fact that assessment *takes place*, to the fact that it involves *grading* the performance (as against a simple pass/fail). Simon Rice (2007) is a strong critic of *grading* performance and believes that students do not need assessment to be motivated. Being in a professional environment or capacity can naturally encourage you to perform better. Thus Rice (2007: 5) argues that 'the clinical experience transcends students' need for incentive'.

Furthermore, assessment in clinic tends to be continual. Therefore if clinic is a learning environment where mistakes are part of the learning process and students are forced out of their comfort zones, this raises questions about whether performance should be assessed in any shape or form. Assessing performance can also create tension between achieving a good grade and serving clients effectively.

## 13.3 Assessment – an overview

Where work is carried out as part of the curriculum, as opposed to on a voluntary or extracurricular basis, the assessment regime may be dependent on whether the module is optional or compulsory. Below is an overview of the different approaches law faculties have adopted in respect of assessment.

- You are not assessed – the quality of your performance will not be assessed and you will not be given a grade or have to achieve any particular criteria to pass, but your participation will count as part of your overall credits required for your degree or other award. There may be a requirement to show that you attended and participated.
- Assessed on a pass/fail basis – here you are required to participate in the clinic scheme and your performance will be assessed. You will not be given a grade but your performance will be judged, and if you do not meet the specified level of achievement (for example, competency) you will fail the module. Some professional course skills assessments completed in the context of a clinical activity may fall into this category.
- Assessed in line with other modules – your performance will count towards your degree progression or award in the same way as any other. This will normally mean that you will be given a percentage mark and it will count as any other module.

## 13.4 Where performance or work is not assessed

If your performance is not assessed, it is still important to take your work seriously, particularly if you are acting for real clients. The module or work might not affect your degree or course result but, nevertheless, you will be learning vital skills which can impact on your future career. As a matter of professionalism, you should afford your work the same level of respect and diligence as the assessed modules on your programme. In practice, you may find this difficult, particularly when you are preparing assignments or revising, but a certain level of self-discipline and good time management will assist.

Remember that several clinic and pro bono activities often have limited places available. If you are one of the lucky ones to have been offered a place, it can be useful to remind yourself that you are in a privileged position and should therefore give of your best at all times, assessed or not.

## 13.5 Where performance or work is assessed

Assessment in clinic and pro bono is very distinct from the traditional assessment methods with which you will be familiar. Even where the assessment method is the same, say for instance by essay, what is expected is likely to be quite different. The reason being that clinical and pro bono teaching methods and the work itself differs greatly from classroom-based activities.

In clinic and pro bono, evaluation methods tend to be more flexible and diverse to reflect the wide range of tasks and skills involved. This can be advantageous in that a broader scope of matters can be taken into account when measuring your performance. For instance, the assessment may take into consideration *how* you have approached things (the process) and not just *what* you have produced (the output or product). This often allows for non-tangible matters such as effort, enthusiasm and commitment to be evaluated, in addition to more conventional criteria.

Furthermore, a traditional examination essentially assesses your performance at a fixed point in time, whereas your performance over the entire module may be assessed in clinic (depending on the particular method of assessment). This gives you a great opportunity to achieve a good grade, provided you work well over a sustained period of time.

## 13.6 Assessment criteria

If your work is assessed, it is very likely that there will be a set of criteria in place against which you will be marked. The criteria will most probably differ from that which you are used to and you should therefore pay careful attention to them. It is impossible to state here a comprehensive list of criteria, given the various schemes in place. However, you can view example criteria and performance levels for a year-long, compulsory live client clinic module via the following link: www.northumbria.ac.uk/sd/academic/law/slonew/assessment/

You can see more examples of common assessment criteria in Brustin and Chavkin's highly regarded article, 'Testing the Grades'.

As with other modules, you should not view criteria as a checklist; you should think carefully about your level of *proficiency* in respect of each of the criteria. So examine closely not just whether you possess a certain *skill* or whether your work demonstrates a particular *attribute*, but the *level* you have demonstrated (Stuckey, R, *Best Practices for Legal Education* (CLEA, 2007) at p 238). For example, do not merely check to see whether the report or letter to your client demonstrates clarity of expression; consider whether it is satisfactory, good or excellent.

## 13.7 Assessment in live client clinics

The combination of working for real clients, in the unfamiliar context of clinic or pro bono, coupled with assessment, can understandably lead to nerves. If you ensure you focus on providing a good service for your client, a good grade should follow. Students who put too much focus on achieving a high mark place themselves under immense pressure, and this often leads to careless mistakes which students would not ordinarily make. No one can perform perfectly all of the time – so do not pressure yourself into doing so.

## 13.8 How is clinic and pro bono work assessed?

Where pro bono and clinic is assessed, various methods are employed to reflect the wide-ranging activities undertaken. You will therefore encounter much more diverse modes of assessment as compared with other modules that you are studying. Do not fall into the trap of thinking that, because the assessment methods are different, they are less valid and thus do not need to be taken seriously.

It is also important to recognise the distinction between the output and quality of work, as compared to the process and method adopted to produce the work. This difference will tend to dictate the evaluation method. For instance, a letter of advice is output (showing a *skill* – in this case your legal writing skills), whereas a piece of reflection is process (demonstrating *how* you have developed over the course of your studies).

### Types of assessment

This section provides an overview of the main ways by which your performance or work might be measured. In some cases, this may be by a combination of methods.

### Portfolios

According to Timmins (2008: 24), a portfolio 'is a collection of evidence that demonstrates learning and knowledge'. It typically contains the work you have prepared throughout your clinical and pro bono experience which demonstrates your learning and level of achievement. As contrasted with an examination or coursework, a portfolio is a useful tool which records a much wider range of skills and proficiencies.

As your portfolio builds, you can clearly see your development and growing experience. Consequently, portfolios support your learning and professional development. At the point at which it is assessed, the portfolio will show your development over a period of time. Therefore, whereas an exam provides a snapshot of your abilities at a specific point in time, a portfolio charts your development over a longer timescale – and is arguably a much fairer assessment in that respect.

**Top tip**

Collate your portfolio as you go, even if it is not due to be submitted until the end of the module. This will save time in the long run and reduce stress levels as the submission deadline approaches.

## Issues with portfolios

If you have not been assessed by means of portfolio before, you may be concerned about the following points:

*How should I organise my portfolio?*

Unless you have been given specific instructions on how to organise the content, you generally have autonomy to arrange your portfolio as you see fit. Regardless, there should be some logical order to the content. You may perhaps wish to organise the work by client or skill. Whatever you decide, ensure it has a professional presentation – you will have worked hard on conducting yourself in a professional manner, so ensure adopt the same approach with your portfolio. Contents pages and cover notes lend a polished feel to portfolios.

### Example contents page – ordered by skills

---

**Portfolio Contents**

1 Contribution Statement
2 Reflective Work
3 Appraisal Form
4 Written Communication
   a. Letters to clients
   b. Letters to opponents
   c. Letters to third parties
5 Drafting
   a. Claim forms
   b. Witness statements
   c. Skeleton arguments
6 Research
   a. PLR on substantive law
   b. PLR on quantum
   c. PLR on court procedure
7 Case Management
   a. Case chronologies
   b. Action plans
   c. Case analysis
   d. File reviews
8 Miscellaneous
   a. Minutes from meetings
   b. Notes on feedback

---

*What if I have worked collaboratively?*

Many clinic and pro bono activities involve working on projects in partnership with other students or as part of a team. You might think that this is incompatible with the notion of individually assessed portfolios. However, your assessor will be well aware that work has been carried out in collaboration with other students and will bear this in mind when marking.

There are some steps you can, and should, take to demonstrate your contribution to the work. Marking each and every document in your file with your relative contribution level can be time-consuming; therefore the simplest method is to place a cover note at the front of your file confirming how the work has been prepared. For example, it might state 'all work in this file has been prepared on a 50/50 basis unless otherwise indicated'. You should then clearly mark documents which have been completed by you alone or on a different contribution basis accordingly. You can do this in various ways, but initialling the document and noting 100% alongside should suffice in the case of a document which you have completed individually. Another straightforward method is to print documents which you have completed by yourself on a coloured piece of paper so that they are easily identifiable. Whatever method you opt for, ensure the contribution statement is clear.

You might also want to bear in mind the advice in **Chapter 5** which encourages the division of work, thus allowing you to show off your skills in isolation from your partner.

 **Top tips for portfolios**

- Avoid the 'kitchen sink' approach – choose your content carefully. The key is quality, not quantity, so avoid 'padding out' your portfolio with documents that do not add value or demonstrate your development. Classic examples of 'padding' documents are series of attendance notes stating 'called client, no response, will call them back' or bulky print-outs from legal databases which you have consulted when conducting your research. If you have autonomy regarding what goes into your portfolio, consider carefully which pieces best highlight your skills and development.

- If your portfolio contains items which your supervisor has not seen previously, for example action plans which you have prepared using your own initiative, make sure these are clearly brought to your supervisor's attention. You can do this by tagging such items with post-it notes or sticky tabs. This should ensure you are given credit for 'unseen' work.

- Make sure all of your hard work and effort are not let down by sloppy or careless presentation. Feel free to use subject dividers, numbered pages and so on to display your work at its best.

## Case studies or reports

These methods tend to assess your understanding and analysis of a legal issue or aspects of a case which you have conducted. Invariably, you will be required to show awareness of any professional or ethical issues raised by the case and practical limitations which affected your conduct of the file. Other approaches to case studies and reports include providing an outline of the facts of the case, details of your research and the methodology adopted in conducting the case or project.

## Essays

Essays in clinical and pro bono environments differ from traditional essays, not least because the subject-matter tends to be very different. However, general conventions such as clear structure and presentation still apply. You may be asked to critique a particular point of law encountered in your case work or project and this will often involve a discussion of background detail and your adopted approach. As with case studies and reports, you should demonstrate good levels of critique and an awareness of any external influencing factors.

## Live/recorded performances, including presentations

This mode tends to be used to assess a particular skill, rather than knowledge, for example interviewing or advocacy. It will involve your assessor observing a live performance or a recording of a live performance. Make sure you achieve your potential by focusing on the performance itself, not on the fact that it is going to be assessed. Typical assessment criteria for this form of assessment include style, structure, audibility, timing and so on.

## Specific task

You may be assessed by one or more task, such as a preparing a letter of advice, research report, interview or attendance note. If you have conducted the tasks previously, make sure you review any feedback and comments that you received on your earlier work.

## Log

You may be required to keep a record of any activities undertaken. This may, or may not, require supporting evidence, such as letters or slides from a presentation.

## Reflection

This is a very common method utilised to assess *how* you have developed and to what extent you are proficient in various matters. Reflection can be assessed in various formats including journals, logs, diaries and essays.

Good reflection requires a high level of self-awareness and the ability to think broadly. What is expected in your reflective pieces is not always clear, but a suggested assessment grid showing excellent, good and satisfactory levels of reflection can be found in Zubizarreta, J, *The Learning Portfolio: Reflective Practice for Improving Student Learning* (Jossey-Bass, 2009). Jennifer Moon also sets out the characteristics of different depths of reflection in her book on learning journals (Moon, 1999; 2004). See **Chapter 12** for further guidance on reflection.

## Attendance/participation

Your attendance levels may be taken into account when calculating your grade. If this is the case, it is important to attend all of the required sessions. If you are unable to attend, you should inform your supervisor in advance and explain why you are unable to attend. Merely turning up may not be sufficient as often the assessment depends on how well you have contributed to the sessions.

## **13.9** Common concerns about assessment

It is only natural to be apprehensive when you are unfamiliar with the assessment method. A few common concerns are explored below.

### How will I be marked fairly and consistently?

Typical assessment methods in non-clinical environments tend to involve everyone sitting the same exam or attempting an identical coursework question. Where students work on different types of cases or activities under different supervisors, you may be worried that marking cannot be fair or consistent. Variable factors such as these do not render an assessment regime unreliable or unfair. As is the case with all other assessed work, there will be a moderation process to ensure the marking is consistent. In most cases, your supervisor will have monitored your work closely and he or she is therefore in an excellent position to grade your work, as contrasted with anonymous marking which can sometimes be employed in respect of course-work and exams.

### I have only worked on a few files, but other students have had numerous cases

This concern is very common and it is quite simple to address; it is a matter of qual-ity not quantity. Just because a student has had a greater number of cases does not mean that he or she will have performed well. If you only have one or two cases to conduct, you should ensure that you make the most of the opportunities which those cases present. For example, if your case seems to have stalled, rather than sitting back you could complete a case review to check whether you can identify any new avenues, or you could prepare work which will be required once it is back on track. This sort of proactive attitude and initiative will impress your supervisor and can enhance your grade.

### I am working in a pair – how can I make sure my supervisor sees *my* strengths?

You have already read about the benefits of working with others and the importance of teamwork. However, you may be worried that your supervisor cannot distinguish your performance from that of your partner, and this concern is heightened when it comes to assessment. **Chapter 5** has several suggestions of how you can work apart yet together so that your supervisor is able to credit your strengths (and weaknesses) when it comes to assessment.

### I am working in a pair and feel my weaker partner is getting credit for my work

Rest assured that your supervisor is likely to have several years experience of teach-ing and can often instinctively spot individuals who are riding on the success of another student. However, if you do not want to leave anything to chance, you could have a quiet word with your supervisor, but ideally you should try to resolve the matter with your partner without the need for supervisor intervention.

## 13.10 What makes a good clinic/pro bono student?

This is the niggling question that is secretly harboured by every student entering a clinical or pro bono environment. Up until this stage in your legal education, the goal was simple: you attended lectures, sat the assessment and hoped for good marks. By contrast, in a law clinic, your supervisor will be monitoring you closely, sometimes for an extensive period of time, and it may feel as though you are constantly being assessed. Although this may feel a little uncomfortable, it is exactly what happens in the working environment. When you find yourself working in an office, your boss will not simply judge you by your report or your letters; it is fair to say that he or she will be looking at these 'results', but he or she will also be scrutinising your method. By the same token, your supervisor will be assessing your work by means of checking letters, interview plans, attendance notes and so forth, but he or she is also looking 'behind the scenes' to see how you work.

So what is your supervisor looking for? To get an indication of this, you should scrutinise the criteria against which you will be judged. These should clearly indicate what areas are to be assessed, such as your level of autonomy, your time keeping, your ability to correctly identify legal principles, your ability to get things right at first draft, and so on. If you arm yourself with this information from the outset, you will know what to aim for.

There are, of course, certain additional fundamental skills and traits that all supervisors look for that are perhaps not so obvious. These are outlined below.

### Independence

You might be thinking, 'Independence? But I thought I had to run everything by my supervisor.' This is very true, but there is a difference between being *led* by your supervisor and being *guided* by your supervisor. The difference lies in how you approach your supervisor with questions and ideas.

Each supervisor will have his or her own particular preference as to how you should contact him or her with questions. Some supervisors will allocate certain periods during the week when you are free to approach them, others favour emails or phone calls, and others may have an open-door policy. Your supervisor will let you know his or her preference, usually during your early meetings.

How you go about asking appropriate questions is a matter of striking the right balance between enthusiasm and independence. Your clinic or pro bono experience is likely to prove a steep learning curve. At the start of the year, you will undoubtedly want to double-check every single point with your supervisor, but as time passes and you become more confident, you will find yourself asking fewer questions. To an extent, your supervisor will be looking for this increasing sense of autonomy and independence, but it is important to remember that, however confident you feel, you must continue to have your work checked by your supervisor, particularly if the work will be going out in his or her name.

When you need to approach your supervisor, try not to bombard him or her with repeated, ad hoc queries. If you have a problematic case that you have lots of questions about, ask if you can meet up with your supervisor for a discussion, rather than drip-feeding questions over several days. If you do have a specific question to ask your supervisor, try to think about the possible solutions before you put the question. In this way, you are showing your supervisor that you have not simply asked a question because you cannot be bothered to look up the answer yourself. This is the difference between being led and being guided.

For example, consider saying, 'This is the problem [explain the problem] ... I do not understand A, B, C ... I think I need to do X, Y, Z ... Is that right?' You can see that this sounds so much better than, 'This is the problem [explain the problem] ... I do not understand A, B, C ... Can you tell me what to do next?' The first scenario shows that you have taken the initiative to fully think through the problem and propose a solution upon which you seek guidance, whereas the second question is a plea to have the solution handed to you. It is clear which will impress your supervisor the most.

---

**What do you look for?**

'Reliability and dedication are the key things which impress me. The ability to be creative and to think outside the box.' (Caroline, Clinical Supervisor)

---

When you do find yourself needing to discuss your case with your supervisor, make sure that you jot down any questions or ideas you may have and take them along to the meeting. This will ensure that nothing gets overlooked and it will help you to advance your ideas and proposed solutions clearly without forgetting anything important.

You will find it useful to keep a notebook with you whenever you are working so that you can jot down ideas, questions and, crucially, whatever your supervisor says, taking an accurate record there and then. This has two major benefits. First, it saves you the embarrassment of not being able to remember what was said and then having to go and ask a second time. Secondly, it instils confidence in your supervisor that you are listening and taking on board what he or she has to say. This is a good practice to get into, and, after all, you would not dream of going into a seminar or a lecture without something to make notes on, so do not treat a meeting with your supervisor any differently.

### Being proactive

From day one of your clinical experience, you may be told not to provide any advice or take any steps without first consulting your supervisor. This is simply to avoid any allegation of negligence which could damage your supervisor's practising certificate or institution's reputation. That is not to say that you are not actively encouraged to be proactive with your cases.

**What makes a good student?**

'Being proactive – looking at what the next steps are, coming to me with suggestions rather than expecting me to spoon feed. Going above and beyond, volunteering to do extra things.' (Carol, Clinical Supervisor)

There will be times when your workload is fairly quiet; perhaps you are waiting for a hearing, or things seem to have ground to a halt, or your client is not responding to your letters. This is when you should take the opportunity to re-examine your case or project to ascertain what can be done to move it along. Perhaps you can find some new angle on your case, a novel ground of appeal, or a fresh line of enquiry that has previously been overlooked. This will then generate an opportunity to conduct some further research. It could involve an interview with your client, or it might necessitate a consultation with your supervisor. This is the important skill of being proactive. Proactivity shows your supervisor that you are enthusiastic and committed to your client, as opposed to simply waiting and reacting to the next letter or phone call that comes in.

## Setting deadlines

This is linked to being proactive. Some matters by their very nature generate their own deadlines, for example civil litigation or employment cases, but some cases are much more open-ended. Occasionally you will encounter a client who wishes to know if he or she can challenge a decision, or perhaps a conviction, and you are already outside of the official deadline for filing any form of appeal. In such cases it is important not to let the matter drift. It is often the case that students will embark on such a case with lots of enthusiasm, but, without a deadline to work toward, their enthusiasm will wane and the natural inclination is to deal with more exciting cases, or more pressing deadlines, such as coursework and dissertations. This situation requires a certain level of self-discipline to keep the case moving along.

**What do you look for?**

'Someone who is genuinely interested in what they are doing. These students will naturally work harder at their files and take an active role in progressing them as they are genuinely keen to experience new things and move the case forward for the client.' (Joanne, Clinical Supervisor)

You should speak to your supervisor and agree deadlines for researching the case, formulating advice, checking that advice and, finally, delivering the advice. This sort of planning is essential to inspire confidence in your client and your supervisor. It is also a good habit to get into as a lot of your work as a lawyer will involve routinely chasing up cases and moving them along without being prompted by anyone else.

When you are working toward deadlines, it is important to remember to build in sufficient time to allow your supervisor to check your work and to allow you to make any necessary amendments. This is particularly important when you are approaching client interactions, such as interviews or hearings, where you need to be confident in your position.

A final word on setting deadlines: be realistic. You are unlikely to be working exclusively on your clinic or pro bono activities and there will be other subjects competing for your time and attention. It is therefore much better to create a realistic deadline rather than enthusiastically agreeing a short deadline and then not being able to keep to it.

### Keeping files in order

It might seem to be stating the obvious that files should be kept in good order, but it is helpful to appreciate why this is so. First, you are likely to be working on the case with another student. It is only fair to your colleague that the file is kept in good order, or you run the risk of miscommunication and duplication of work. Secondly, your supervisor is likely to undertake spot-checks on your files, and if they are not in good order then that will not create a good impression and could lead him or her to think that you may be as careless with your advice as you are with your files. Thirdly, this is a good habit to get into for practice as most firms are subject to audits and inspections, often at very short notice, and there is therefore a legitimate expectation that the files will be in order. Finally, you should take some pride in your files. A well-ordered file not only reflects positively on you personally; it also makes life so much easier when you can lay your hands on documents as and when you need them.

### Learning from mistakes

Remember that the skills you are trying to learn do not magically develop overnight; they are achieved through a process of trial and error. Your abilities will improve and work should be returned to you with fewer amendments, but you must be patient.

**What do you look for?**

'The ability to learn from mistakes – only making the same mistake once or twice is a good sign.' (Philip, Clinical Supervisor)

When you receive amended work, do not assume that your supervisor has deliberately found fault in an attempt to diminish your efforts. Your supervisor is obliged to ensure that the work is of the required standard, and you should be looking to see where and why amendments have been made so that you can try to avoid making the same mistake in future.

### Effort

When real people are involved, the stakes are automatically higher, and a 'do just enough to get by' approach cannot and will not be tolerated. You need to go the extra mile. If you have so far adopted a bare minimum approach to your studies, you will find clinic extremely testing, and this is likely to put you on a collision course with your supervisor and colleagues.

Having said that, the vast majority of students who choose to study clinical modules or participate in pro bono activities tend to be highly motivated.

## 13.11 Appraisals

You may be subject to an appraisal as part of your clinical and pro bono activities or whilst on placement.

### What is the purpose of an appraisal?

An appraisal is an opportunity to provide feedback and have your performance evaluated. It can also be used to identify areas for improvement, targets and objectives. It is a misconception that an appraisal is a chance for your supervisor to 'have a go at you'. It should be an objective and constructive discussion.

The purpose of the appraisal does, however, largely depend on when it takes place. For example, an appraisal which occurs at the end of your clinical or pro bono experience will review your performance, whereas one which takes place mid-way through may also set objectives for going forward.

If you do not have an appraisal system, there is no harm asking your supervisor if he or she would conduct an informal appraisal with you.

### What are you appraised against?

Generally, you will be appraised against one or more of the following:

- any assessment criteria in operation;
- clinic standards (for example, adherence to any policies your clinic has in place);
- professional standards (for example the Code of Conduct);
- supervisor expectations.

### Dealing with a 'negative' appraisal

Sometimes appraisals do not always go as well as you might hope. It is natural to view this negatively. However, remember that an appraisal is designed to identify poorer aspects of your performance and suggest ways of improving, as well as feeding back on your strengths. This should actually be viewed as a positive experience. Whatever you might think, supervisors do not enjoy giving poor performance reviews to people with whom they work closely. Remember that any constructive criticism will usually be aimed at your behaviour or actions and not you personally. This should help you to understand and accept the comments more readily.

### Why might you be underperforming?

In most cases, underperformance stems from students being unfamiliar with the different way in which clinic works and the expectations that are linked to this. However, there can be more deep-seated reasons behind poor performance. Once the issue(s) are identified, action can then be taken to address these and work on improving standards. McKirchy (1998: 82) suggests common reasons for poor performance:

- You do not know or understand *what* you need to do, or what is expected of you – this can feel very disorientating but there is always someone to guide you. Try first to figure it out for yourself; it may just be blind panic making you feel like this. Sit down and brainstorm or read any material with which you have been provided. If this does not help, see your supervisor and ask for some advice.

- You understand *what* you need to do and what is expected of you, but not *how* to do it – this can be common as you may be undertaking tasks for the first time and may be approaching work from a different perspective. There will undoubtedly be a book or similar resource which will provide guidance on the practical matters. If you cannot find the answer yourself, see your supervisor for assistance.

- You do not know *why* something needs to be done and therefore you lack motivation to do it – if you cannot work out the rationale behind a task, ask. It is unlikely that you will have been told to do something for the sake of it, so, no matter how menial it might seem, there will be value to what you are doing.

- You are worried about making mistakes or failing and therefore adopt a tentative approach – this is a common fear, even among confident students, because the nature of clinical and pro bono work is quite different from what you may have encountered elsewhere on your course. Have confidence in your abilities and seek support where necessary from your colleagues or supervisor.

- Personal problems are affecting your performance – if this is the case, it is best to speak to a member of staff rather than suffer in silence.

- Your priorities lie elsewhere – this can be a particular problem if your clinic/pro bono work is not assessed. Find some way of motivating yourself to do the work to a good standard and think about the benefits this type of work can have on your future career.

 **Top tips for appraisals**

- Leave yourself sufficient time to prepare – successful appraisals require preparation by the appraiser and appraisee. Think carefully about what you would like to say and complete any appraisal documentation well in advance.

- Review your performance against the assessment criteria – you may be asked, 'How do you think you are doing?' as an opening question, so you need to be prepared to have some points at the ready.

- Right to respond – appraisals are a two-way conversation, so make sure you respond to comments as appropriate. Ensure your remarks are considered and not defensive rebuttals.

- If you do not agree with or do not understand the comments – it helps to have concrete examples so you understand your appraiser's point of view. If you are not provided with instances of when you did this, that or the other, ask. Similarly, if you are not told why the appraiser has formed a particular view, politely request explanation.

- Listen carefully to what is being said – this means the positives and the negatives.

- Be open to constructive criticism.

## 13.12 Feedback

You have read above about some of the standards and qualities you should look to display. However, you are not expected to be the finished article when you begin, or indeed finish, your clinic or pro bono activities. So how do you improve? One way is through practice, but perhaps the most valuable resource is feedback. This section explores the purpose and uses of feedback and how it can help you excel in your clinic and pro bono work.

### Purpose of feedback

As with appraisals, feedback is designed to recognise what has been done well, identify strengths and areas for improvement, and provide guidance which will help you in future.

Clinic and pro bono is an environment which tends to allow for continuous and detailed individual feedback. Your work is reviewed regularly and often it will take several attempts before something is approved. At each juncture you will receive feedback, whether you realise it or not.

### Forms of feedback

It is important to recognise that feedback can be provided in many formats and is not always clearly labelled 'feedback.' If you can identify the forms of feedback and realise when you are receiving it, this will put you at an advantage.

#### In writing

Written feedback can be supplied in various ways and is not restricted to feedback sheets. The absence of the heading 'feedback' on a document does not necessarily mean that the comments should not be regarded as feedback.

- Handwritten comments on drafts of work – if you cannot read them, make sure you ask your supervisor. Do not be shy about asking him or her to decipher a segment of scrawl – he or she is likely to be more embarrassed that you could not read it, than you are of having to ask.
- Word-processed or handwritten memos/feedback sheets – perhaps the most recognisable form of feedback, particularly when given by means of feedback sheet.
- Email – your supervisor may not be able to meet with you on each occasion feedback is called for and may choose to provide comments via email. Email is extremely accessible and forms part of our everyday life. However, that does not mean that feedback via email should be treated any less seriously than feedback provided by any other means (Race, 2005: 122) or not considered as feedback at all. Make sure you print out emailed feedback so it does not get 'lost' in your inbox.

#### Verbal

Written feedback can be viewed over and over and thus can have benefits over verbal feedback. If you are given verbal feedback, you should make a note of it so that you can review it as required. It is important to listen to all of the feedback before digesting it – otherwise you may start analysing the first point and the rest of the feedback is lost on you (Race, 2005: 120). Another advantage of oral feedback is that you may have the opportunity to discuss it there and then with the provider, which is not always possible with written feedback.

Verbal, as with written, feedback can take many different forms:

- One-on-one – guidance may be given face-to-face, by telephone and so on. When receiving verbal feedback in this manner, it is useful to gauge your supervisor's tone and body language (Race, 2005: 119). A smile or stern look will often be used to reinforce the spoken comments.
- In groups – your supervisor might give feedback to the whole group. This might seem embarrassing regardless of whether the feedback is positive or constructive, so why might your supervisor do it? Positive feedback given to an individual when the rest of the group is present can encourage other members to perform well, as they may want to be the next recipient of praise. Constructive feedback given to a group may act as a helpful reminder that members of the team are not alone in making mistakes (Race, 2005: 121). This latter type of feedback is not an exercise in public humiliation, and your supervisor will tend to provide such feedback where the error in question has been committed by more than one member of the group.

### Using feedback

Feedback is intended to help you improve your performance, but this is only achieved if you actually use it. Store all of your feedback in one place so you can refer to it in order to improve future performance. A notebook or ring binder file will suffice. You could store it electronically, but this can be time-consuming if feedback is handwritten and needs typing up. If feedback is given verbally, it is good practice to make a note of this contemporaneously. You can then store your notes with the written feedback.

You should consult your feedback file regularly. For example, if you received comments on a draft letter or research report, before you begin your next letter or research report, consult your previous feedback to ensure you note and take on board any previous remarks.

### Barriers to using and receiving feedback

All feedback is helpful, but certain factors can affect how well you receive and use it:

- Do not be offended – the purpose of feedback is to help improve your performance; it is not a criticism of you as an individual. Reflect on what has been said and plan how you can improve in the future.
- Do not focus solely on the negative – equal attention should be given to what you have done well and areas in need of improvement.
- Recognise the difference between effort and output – it can be disheartening to be told that something is not up to scratch when you have exerted a great deal of effort in completing the task. Failing to appreciate that effort and output are

not always correlative can result in you devaluing the feedback provided and therefore means you cannot use it effectively.

 **Top tips for succeeding in clinic**

- Be enthusiastic – but do not be overly confident or reckless, both of which are a cause for concern for supervisors.
- Act professionally – how you behave reflects on your institution, not just on you as an individual.
- Put your client first – if you are dealing with real clients, you should always remember that their needs and problems are often greater than your own.
- Respect your supervisor – you do not have to like your supervisor, but you should at least be able to work with one another in a professional and mature fashion.
- Enjoy the experience – it will be challenging and hard work, but these are the aspects which ultimately make clinic and pro bono so rewarding.

## **13.13** Summary

You will develop and acquire numerous skills and qualities during your experience regardless of whether your work is assessed. You can only truly capitalise on this learning opportunity by being open to feedback and employing it effectively. You also need to readjust your perceptions in terms of assessment methods. If you can manage this, you will be well on your way to realising potential and should excel on the assessment front.

 Further reading

### Introductory

Bee, R and Bee, F, *Constructive Feedback* (**Institute of Personnel and Development, 1996**)
> This book provides useful guidance on how to receive and use feedback. An easy-to-read and very accessible text.

Eggert, MA, *The Managing Your Appraisal Pocketbook* (**Alresford Press Ltd, 1996**)
> A short and easy read, which will allow you to quickly grasp the basic appraisal principles.

### Intermediate

Gillen, T, *The Appraisal Discussion* (**Institute of Personnel and Development, 1995**)
> Aimed primarily at the appraiser; nevertheless, you can still glean some useful guidance from this text.

Hind, D and Moss, W, *Employability Skills* (**Business Education Publishers, 2005**)
> A good text which explores various key employability skills.

Hyams, R, 'Student assessment in the clinical environment – **what can we learn from the US experience?'** *International Journal of Clinical Legal Education,* **December 2006, 77–95**
> This article sets out key arguments in favour of assessment and considers the best way to assess clinical work.

McKirchy, K, *Powerful Performance Appraisals: How to Set Expectations and Work Together to Improve Performance* (**National Press Publications, 1998**)
> This practical guide to appraisals is a valuable general tool for personal development.

**Moon, J, *Learning Journals: A Handbook for Reflective Practice and Professional Development*, 2nd edn (RoutledgeFalmer, 2006)**

This book encapsulates everything you need to know about learning journals. Pages 161–3 are particularly helpful in setting out the levels of reflection against which you can judge the quality of your written reflection.

**Rice, S, 'Assessing – But Not Grading', Clinical Legal Education Macquarie Law Working Paper No 2007-16**

The Working Paper, which contains interesting perspective on assessment of clinical work, can be downloaded at www.law.mq.edu.au/research/working_papers.htm.

**Timmins, F, *Making Sense of Portfolios: A Guide for Nursing Students* (Open University Press, 2008)**

Healthcare professionals have been using portfolios much longer than law students, so you can learn a good deal from this text. The most helpful chapters are perhaps Chapters 5 and 6, which deal with the content and structure of portfolios.

### Advanced

**Brustin, S and Chavkin, D, 'Testing the Grades: Evaluating Grading Models in Clinical Legal Education' (Spring 1997) 3 Clinical L Rev 299–336**

A comprehensive article which explores assessment and reviews the pros and cons of grading. You can view evaluation criteria from two different clinics at Appendix A (p 329) and Appendix B (p 333).

**Klenowski, V, *Developing Portfolios for Learning and Assessment: Processes and Principles* (RoutledgeFalmer, 2002)**

An informative text if you want to discover more about the educational theories which underpin portfolios. At p 94 you can find a useful grid of an example grade descriptor used to assess portfolios.

**Murray, V and Nelson, T, 'Assessment – Are Grade Descriptors the Way Forward' [2009] IJCLE 48**

**Race, P et al, *500 Tips on Assessment*, 2nd edn (RoutledgeFalmer, 2005)**

This book is aimed at educators but will provide you with an understanding of the rationale behind and uses of assessment methods, together with their pros and cons.

 Activities

### Activity 1: Functioning feedback

Ask yourself the following questions to determine how well you use the feedback you receive:

1 Do I recognise when I am receiving feedback?
2 Do I get defensive when I receive 'negative' feedback?
3 Do I concentrate equally on positive and constructive feedback?
4 Do I review feedback before attempting new tasks?
5 Do I feel able to discuss feedback openly with the feedback provider?

### Activity 2: Self-appraisal

Look carefully at your institution's assessment criteria for your clinical and pro bono work. Conduct a careful self-appraisal against the criteria. It may help to grade your work and skills using a scale of 1–10 where 1 is poor and 10 is excellent. Note any marks below 5 and plan how you can improve in these areas, using the action plan template below.

| Area/skill | Mark out of 10 | Particular concerns | Techniques to improve |
|---|---|---|---|
| Letter writing | | Use of jargon and poor structure, occasional typos | Use spell-checker, take a break before reviewing work |
| | | | |
| | | | |

# 14 Clinic, pro bono and your career

> 'Pro bono experience is a clear winner with recruiters and will always make you stand out in a competitive job market.'
>
> Janice Morris, Careers Adviser

## 14.1 Introduction

You have read in earlier chapters how pro bono and clinic can have a positive effect on the lives of those people you assist and the wider community. It clearly also has benefits for you and your future career.

This chapter focuses on how to make the most of your clinical and pro bono experiences in the recruitment process. Given the vast amount of information available, this chapter is not intended to replace your wider reading on careers, but rather to demonstrate how you can sell the valuable skills and experience acquired from your clinical and pro bono work when applying for jobs. Within this section you will find guidance on how to enhance your applications and effectively incorporate clinic and pro bono in interview situations. It also briefly sets out some of the career opportunities that are available to you with your legal qualifications.

## 14.2 Employability

Entry into graduate careers, particularly law, can be extremely competitive and challenging. You can no longer walk into your dream job just because you have a degree. Employers demand more of candidates and are devising increasingly robust recruitment processes due to the overwhelming number of applications they receive. Additionally, reports suggest that graduates are not fully equipped with the skills or experience needed for the world of work (see, for example, the Lambert Review and Leitch Review of Skills, 2006).

Your pro bono and clinical activities can set you apart from other applicants, making you an attractive candidate for whichever job you apply for. However, in order to stand out from the crowd, you need to know how to market the valuable skills and experience you have acquired.

'The clinical experience really does make the big step onto the career ladder that little bit smaller by introducing you at an early stage to the fundamental workings of a law office.' (Danny, Trainee Solicitor)

## **14.3** The importance of clinic and pro bono to your future career

It is quite possible that once you are firmly on the career ladder, your pro bono activities will continue. Many large organisations have corporate social responsibility policies which involve 'giving back' to the community in which they operate. Law firms often have Pro Bono Co-ordinators, and a 2007 survey found that 65% of solicitors in private practice had conducted pro bono work at some stage during their legal career (Law Society, The Pro Bono Work of Solicitors (2007)). LawWorks has almost 100 member organisations, including Clifford Chance, Eversheds, Vodafone and BT, providing pro bono assistance. The fact that you have already shown a commitment to pro bono work in some shape or form certainly provides you with a talking point at interview.

## **14.4** Transferable skills development

All of the skills that you develop through your clinic or pro bono activities will be useful for your future career, regardless of whether you plan to practise law. Before starting your applications, it is vital to think carefully about what skill set you possess and how you can evidence this. Many students often do not fully appreciate the variety of skills they have acquired, and outlined below are some of the abilities you are likely to develop. Whilst the skills are discussed in the context of clinic and pro bono, they are transferable to non-legal employment and are considered in more detail in other chapters.

### Communication

When preparing your applications, it is important to sell both your written and verbal communication skills, as you will perfect both to high levels through your clinic and pro bono work.

### Written communication

During your course, you will hone your written communication skills largely through essays and exams. However, in your clinic and pro bono work, it is very likely that you will encounter several other types of written forms, all of which require a slightly different kind of approach. For example, letters to clients demand straightforward, accessible language that is not necessarily present in your essay writing. Correspondence with an opponent calls for a formal yet polite tone, and statements of case should be concise and adhere to appropriate drafting etiquette. These fine distinctions mean you will acquire more sophisticated and strongly developed written communication techniques than those who have not experienced the same range of written tasks. Having an understanding of requisite tone, content and style will ensure you can tackle almost any type of written assignment in your future career. Written skills are set out in more detail in **Chapter 7**.

### Verbal communication

In the same way that your written correspondence is tailored to the intended recipient, your verbal communication will be similarly customised to your audience. You will speak to your supervisor, colleague and clients in very different ways and will therefore develop varied oral communication techniques. The ability to communicate clearly with your target group is vital for achieving successful outcomes and good working relationships.

### Research

You have seen in **Chapter 8** that one of the key skills you will develop during your course is the ability to explore unfamiliar and new areas of law. The ability to locate relevant sources of information in relation to an area of which you know nothing, or very little, means you can approach any task your employer allocates to you with confidence, regardless of whether you have studied the topic as part of your course.

### Problem-solving/analytical ability

Linked to your research skills is the capacity to analyse facts and provide viable solutions to problems. Almost every job or task has challenges and issues which need to be resolved. During your clinic and pro bono activities, you will no doubt encounter challenges or hurdles that require you to analyse the issues, identify possible solutions and demonstrate a flexible approach to problem-solving.

### Decision-making skills

You make choices on a day-to-day basis, but in clinic and pro bono your decisions affect others and therefore need careful consideration. You will develop the ability to think strategically, weighing up the benefits and risks of proposed options in order to reach informed, balanced and objective decisions.

### Teamwork/interpersonal skills/leadership

Every job requires some degree of teamwork skills. In your clinic and pro bono activities you will potentially be working with a variety of people in order to achieve shared goals. Good teamwork requires an ability to listen to and respect the views of others, an element of compromise and focus on the objective to be achieved. The ability to interact with individuals from varied backgrounds is vital to working together effectively. In your working life, you may have to work alongside individuals you dislike, but your polished interpersonal skills should allow you to overcome any difficulties and engender an effective, professional relationship. **Chapter 5** considers these skills in more detail.

## Advocacy/public speaking

As part of your clinic and pro bono activities, you may have the opportunity to appear before a court or tribunal, or experience some form of public speaking, perhaps through an advocacy scheme. Businesses often have to deliver presentations when tendering for contracts and regularly give team talks. Therefore, the ability to form and deliver structured, persuasive arguments will be helpful in your future career. You can read about these skills in more depth in **Chapters 10** and **11**.

## Initiative/proactivity

Casework, in particular, can involve working to tight deadlines, and you will therefore develop strategies to progress your files to ensure you are well prepared to meet any deadlines which are imposed. Being proactive, rather than reactive, and using your initiative are vital to managing a varied and extensive workload. These skills are examined in more detail in **Chapter 9**.

## Prioritising and time management/organisational skills

Balancing your academic studies with your clinic module or pro bono activities requires excellent organisational skills. You will become skilled in managing your work, planning your time and prioritising your tasks. **Chapter 9** contains helpful hints on how best to perfect these skills, and success in the workplace is linked to the ability to effectively juggle competing duties within your workload.

> 'My time in clinic was without a doubt the most invaluable element of my university experience in terms of laying down the foundations of a career within the legal profession. The clinical experience has given me the confidence and legal skills necessary to carry out my current role as a paralegal. I was immediately capable of managing my own case load and sticking to deadlines under pressure, making the transition from university to the world of work considerably easier having had such previous hands-on experience.' (Carolyn, paralegal)

## Commercial awareness

You will be able to appreciate how commercial issues and developments affect an organisation and its clients. By experiencing real-life tasks outside of the lecture theatre, you begin to develop commercial awareness and business acumen. You acquire an understanding of what it takes to run a successful enterprise. As part of your pro bono or clinic work, you may be involved in fundraising, managing budgets or marketing. If you have worked in a citizens advice bureau or law clinic, you will be conscious of the cuts to legal funding and the financial constraints on organisations working in this sector. Businesses, first and foremost, need to be profitable, and the ability to make decisions with a proper appreciation of the commercial issues is a skill sought by every organisation, even charities and not-for-profit groups.

## 14.5 Using your experience in the application process

Having read about the skills you can develop in your clinic and pro bono activities, it is vitally important that your applications fully reflect your abilities. Below is an overview of the main written application methods employed by organisations in the recruitment process, with examples of how best to exhibit your skills and experience. The advice is relevant to applications for vacation placements, internships or full-time employment.

## 14.6 Application forms

For the vast majority of large organisations, the first stage in the recruitment process is the completion of an application form. Many forms are now completed online rather than by hand. Regardless of the completion method, there are several rules to remember when preparing applications. First, research the organisation and sector in detail – find out the scope of services it provides, the typical client's profile, details of recent developments, the skills the firm looks for in its employees and so on. Once you have found this information, use your findings to plan answers that are specifically tailored to the organisation. Your application needs to convince the recruitment team that you are genuinely interested in working for their establishment – well-researched, bespoke answers clearly demonstrate this. Generic applications are very unlikely to result in an invitation to the next stage of the recruitment process, so make sure you spend sufficient time on your research to enable you to produce a strong application.

Compare the two answers below and see how effective a well-researched answer can be:

Q. Why do you want to work for us?

Answer A

I am keen to join your firm so I can work on high profile cases and assist your commercial clients. I believe this will involve challenging and stimulating work and I look forward to contributing to the firm's ongoing success.

Answer B

I am keen to join your firm so that I can work on high profile matters, such as your recent case of Litigant v Litigant, and assist your multinational commercial clients, including Big Corporate Entity Ltd. I believe this will involve challenging and stimulating work and I look forward to contributing to the firm's continued success, which has been recognised by your recent win at the Excellence Awards.

It is important also to recognise that application forms serve a dual purpose; primarily they allow prospective employers to check you have the requisite qualifications and experience, and secondly they test your written communication skills. It is therefore important that you apply the written communication skills from your clinic and pro bono activities to help get you off to a good start. Many employers set a word limit on answers so it is vital that your responses are concise.

**Top tips for strong applications**

- Go beyond the usual level of research. A quick glance at the firm's website is not sufficient. Large firms and organisations frequently publicise their latest deals or products. Use this to your advantage by incorporating such information within your application. This will demonstrate that you are seriously interested in the firm. For example, has the firm recently taken on any new clients or high-profile projects? Has it recruited any well-known experts in a particular field? Has it opened a new office or expanded its service provision? Has it received any industry awards?

- Spend time on your application. Yes, it can seem like a protracted process, but what are a few hours if it results in your ideal job?

- Remember it is quality, not quantity. It may feel like job-hunting is a lottery, but your odds of securing an offer of work are likely to be higher if you submit a few well-prepared applications rather than numerous half-hearted forms. It is easy to state you excel at this, that or the other, but employers are looking for proof of the skills you claim to have. Therefore you must ensure that you provide supporting examples that evidence your skills and attributes.

- There will often be an 'additional information' section on the form, which can be used to explain any gaps in study or employment or any personal circumstances that may have affected your results. However, do not use this section to restate what you have already said elsewhere on the form.

- Proofread your application, or perhaps ask someone else to look over it to check it makes sense. Ideally you should obtain feedback from a careers advisor or tutor before submitting your application to ensure your potential is accurately reflected on the form. Employers often have hundreds, sometimes thousands of applications to sift through, and typos, poor spelling and grammatical errors are one of the surest ways to consign your application to the reject pile.

- Remember to keep a copy of your application. If you get invited to an interview, it is useful to remind yourself of what you included on the form.

**Checklist**

✔ Have you spell-checked and proofread your application at least twice?

✔ Have you effectively made use of your research when answering the questions?

✔ Have you provided examples to back up your answers?

✔ Have you answered all aspects of the questions?

##  CVs

CVs used to be the main application method, but due to technological advances and increasing numbers of applications, most organisations tend to use some kind of prescribed form. However, CVs are still in use, so it is important to know how to draft a convincing CV which properly showcases your clinic and pro bono work.

There are different styles of CV you can adopt when looking for employment, so the first stage is to decide which style suits you best. There are two main categories – the chronological CV and the skills-based CV.

- Chronological – the traditional style of CV which sets out skills and experience in chronological order, as the name suggests.
- Skills-based – this type of CV can be effectively used when your skills meet the organisation's requirements more so than your employment history. It is also a good style if your qualifications are not particularly strong but you have an abundance of skills or work experience.

Regardless of the style you opt for, there are some rules of thumb that you should always follow when drafting your CV.

---

- Your CV does not need to be headed CV or Curriculum Vitae – it should be clear from glancing at the document what it is. Use your name as the heading instead. Recruiters will have to sift through numerous CVs, so make sure your name stands out. Use a sufficiently large font for the heading – 18 point is perfectly acceptable for standard fonts such as Times New Roman and Arial.
- Your CV should not exceed two pages in length – employers are too busy to read long, rambling documents.
- Use clear subheadings to separate the different sections of your CV. The key areas to be covered are personal details, education, employment and work experience, interests and referees.
- Highlight your skills and qualities via your work experience and employment. Do not simply confirm for whom you worked and in what capacity – state what skills and abilities you developed in the role.
- Use an appropriate font – you are applying for a job, so your CV should look professional. Times New Roman and Arial are sensible choices. Ornate and child-like fonts should be avoided.
- Be concise – you have not got the space to waffle if you are going to stay within the two-page limit.
- Do not overcomplicate the layout – you want the reader to easily digest the information, so do not distract from the content by overusing headings, underlining, italics, bold font, bullet points and so on.
- Referees – two referees will suffice. Ideally one should be academic and the other a current or previous employer. In terms of your academic referee, you may be fortunate to be able to choose from a variety of staff members, for example your guidance or seminar tutor. However, more often than not your supervisor or pro bono coordinator will be best placed to comment on your skills and abilities having seen you in a work-like environment. Whoever you choose to act as your referees, as a matter of courtesy, ensure that you ask their permission first.

---

 **Top tips for drafting a winning CV**

- For a CV with a professional appearance, use a template. CV pro formas and templates are readily available on word-processing packages and careers websites.
- Use the page layout effectively to maximise the content – bullet points can be effective to highlight key points, but they can also take up a fair amount of space, as can listing things down the page. Use the width of the page effectively to ensure you adhere to the two-page limit.

- Ensure you are consistent. If using different styles, fonts or text effects for different categories of headings or subheadings, ensure this is applied consistently. If your education section is ordered date followed by institution, use the same order for your employment and work experience sections. This level of attention to detail will not go unnoticed and helps with the professional presentation of the document.

- Make sure your contact details are up to date – it is sensible to provide a term-time and permanent address and be clear when you will be available at those residences.

- Space is at a premium, so ensure the content is relevant to the role for which you are applying. For example, if the vacancy is a postgraduate position, do you need to list each and every part-time job you have ever had? Be selective and carefully edit the content as appropriate.

- For legal CVs, make sure you clearly distinguish your law-related employment and work experience first, and separate it from your non-legal experience. The most effective way to achieve this is by having a subheading for each.

- Stand out from the crowd using the interests section of your CV. Standard inclusions are reading, travel, music, socialising and so on. Now is the time to own up to any unusual hobbies which might make your application memorable. If your interests do not go beyond the norm, maximise their impact by providing additional details such as what skills you have developed from that particular hobby.

**Checklist**

☑ Have you chosen a style which best suits your profile?
☑ Is the content tailored to the particular organisation?
☑ Have you effectively highlighted your skills?
☑ Have you selected the most appropriate referees?

Below are extracts from two CVs showing how you might sell your clinic and pro bono activities. The full CVs can be viewed on the Companion Website.

---

# JULIA BLOGGS

**EDUCATION**

**Academy Law School 2009–2010**
**Legal Practice Course    Commendation**

| *Stage 1* | *Stage 2* |
|---|---|
| Business Law and Practice 62% | Commercial Dispute Resolution 71% |
| Civil and Criminal Litigation 64% | Advanced Criminal Practice 73% |
| Property Law and Practice 65% | Housing Law and Practice 68% |
| Skills: Competent | |

*Student Law Centre*
As part of my LPC I conducted voluntary casework in the law school's award winning Student Law Centre, working on several employment matters. I have

---

experience of interviewing, drafting legal documents, undertaking research, providing clear and succinct advice, and Employment Tribunal advocacy. I also have experience of negotiating settlements on behalf of clients via ACAS.

I researched diverse areas of employment law and I therefore have a broad understanding of the field. I have undertaken various aspects of case management and trial preparation including disclosure and inspection and compilation of trial bundle.

My experience has made me proficient at decision making and managing clients' expectations. I am skilled at managing files and working to deadlines. I am able to work independently but also enjoy working as part of a team.

# ADAM SMITH

## RELEVANT SKILLS

### Communication

- As a volunteer advocate with the Citizen Advocacy Scheme I communicate with vulnerable adults with learning difficulties and liaise with relevant service groups on their behalf.
- In my role of Team Leader I hold regular team meetings and communicate targets and objectives.
- I prepared monthly reports for the Student Law Society Executive.

### Presentation Skills

- Delivered presentation to 6th form students on legalities of downloading from the internet as part of a Streetlaw programme. Feedback from the audience was positive and my group was invited to deliver subsequent presentations to other year groups.

### Leadership

- Led a team of 6 students in managing and organising a Streetlaw presentation to secondary school children. Involved setting deadlines and delegating tasks.
- Awarded Duke of Edinburgh Gold Award which demonstrates leadership and motivation.

## WORK EXPERIENCE

**2009–Present      Citizen Advocacy Scheme      Volunteer Advocate**

Advocate for vulnerable adults in my local community. Assist clients in making complaints and advise them of their rights.

## 14.8 Covering letters

Covering letters are not as commonly used as they were in the past since many organisations now have online application systems in place. They are usually required where application is via a CV, although you may choose to attach a covering letter to your application form. The purpose of the letter is to highlight the key points within your CV or application. You can also use it to explain any personal circumstances affecting your academic grades, much in the same way as the additional information section on an application form might be utilised.

As a guide, your covering letter should address why you want to work in that role/sector, why you want to work for that particular organisation, and what skills, experience and qualities you possess which make you well suited to both the job and that employer.

As with CVs, there are some basic conventions you should follow when preparing a covering letter.

**Top tips for effective covering letters**

- Your letter should be no longer than one page.
- Use decent quality A4 paper – no coloured paper.
- It should be addressed to a named person – if you are not sure to whom the letter should be addressed, telephone to find out.
- Make it clear what role you are applying for and state what enclosures you are providing (CV or application form). You may want to insert a heading below the salutation stating the job title for the avoidance of doubt.
- As with application forms, the content should be tailored to the organisation.
- Keep your paragraphs concise and to the point – two or three paragraphs will suffice.
- End the letter positively, for example by giving dates when you will be available for interview.

**Checklist**

✔ Have you addressed your letter to a specific named person?
✔ Have you clearly aligned your skills and experience to what the employer is looking for?
✔ Have you used the correct mode of salutation?
✔ Have you ended the letter positively?
✔ Have you checked whether the letter should be typed or handwritten?
✔ If handwritten, is your letter legible?

## 14.9 Assessment centres

Assessment centres, also known as assessment days, are a common feature of modern recruitment processes. Essentially they are an additional stage to further shortlist applicants prior to interview. Assessment centres involve a group of potential recruits participating in a series of activities and vary in length from half a day to several days. The format and content is varied, but typical exercises which you may encounter can include the following:

Julia Bloggs
1 Highgate Mill
Bradford
BD13 2SF

Law and Order LLP
Drake Street
Bradford
BD1 1JA

1st July 2010

Dear Mr Brogan,

**Training Contract Application**

I wish to apply for a training contract to commence in 2011, as advertised on your website, and enclose my CV for your consideration.

I have been interested in practising law for five years as it is provides a stimulating and challenging career. I look forward to the prospect of tackling real legal problems and using my sound knowledge of the law to resolve clients' disputes.

Having undertaken an enjoyable work placement with you last year, I am excited at the possibility of joining your firm. I am keen to work in your immigration, crime and prison law departments, areas in which your firm has a formidable reputation, as recognised by Legal 500. I am keen to become an experienced solicitor and believe the firm's training contract will help me realise my potential through your unique in house coaching programme. It is my aim to work in a high street practice specialising in crime as I have a strong interest in this area, as evidenced by my chosen dissertation topic and previous work experience. I believe I will be able to make a valuable contribution to your organisation, assisting with complex Crown Court cases, such as R v Khan, on which your firm was recently instructed.

You will see from my CV that I possess a good balance of skills, experience and qualities, which I feel make me a strong candidate for the role. In particular, I have developed excellent client care skills and the ability to proactively manage files through casework conducted within the Student Law Centre. The centre conducts cases for vulnerable members of society on a pro bono basis; therefore I have an acute understanding of the needs of your client base and the challenges of working on publicly funded cases. My employment has further developed teamwork and interpersonal skills, time management and organisational abilities, which will benefit your firm in my capacity of trainee solicitor.

I look forward to your response and meeting to discuss my credentials in more detail.

Yours sincerely,

Julia Bloggs

### Case studies/role plays

These will generally test your analytical ability, problem-solving and decision-making skills and can often form the basis of a group activity or discussion. For example, you might be asked to devise a new marketing strategy for an organisation, advise on an appropriate restructure or evaluate a proposed takeover.

### Group activities

These are designed to test your teamwork and interpersonal skills. It is important to participate fully and listen to the other members of your team yet not dominate the group. There may well be different views or approaches so there may have to be some element of compromise.

### In tray exercises

Your time management and organisation skills are put to the test as you work through an in tray full of memos, reports, letters and so on. Skim-read the documents to ensure you action them according to priority.

### Presentations/debates/discussions

These are designed to test your communication and presentation skills. Make sure your presentation is clear, well structured and engaging. If there is a time limit, make sure you stick to it. Debates and discussions should not descend into a free-for-all. Ensure you make valuable contributions as it is a case of quality, not quantity.

### Psychometric testing/personality questionnaires

These activities can test a range of abilities including logical thinking, numeracy, verbal reasoning and personality traits.

### Written tasks/aptitude tests

It is often common for the day to include a written exercise or test.

### Preparing for assessment centres

There is a vast amount of material available which will help you prepare. First, check the firm's website as this may contain details about the assessment centre – if it does not, the graduate recruitment team may be able to tell you what type of exercises are used. Use the Internet to read up on the different types of activities and what each task is designed to test.

For more detail on assessment centres see graduate careers sites, for example targetjobs.co.uk. Various online tests are also available, so set some time aside to practise your skills prior to the real thing. Do not forget that your careers service is likely to hold information and resources on assessment centres.

 **Top tips for assessment centres**

- Do your research before the day – having an idea of what you may be asked to do should reduce the fear of the unknown.

- Enjoy the experience – this should help you relax and perform well.
- Be an active participant but avoid dominating the group.
- Apply the skills you have developed through your clinic and pro bono work – your problem-solving, logical thinking, teamwork and communication skills will prove invaluable.

## 14.10 Interviews

Having sailed through the application stage and possibly an assessment day, you have just one more hurdle to overcome – the interview. This section aims to provide you with some general information about interview techniques and will demonstrate how you can use your clinic and pro bono activities to impress in interviews.

Many recruiters do not realise the high quality and extensive pro bono work that universities and colleges undertake. So it is very important to spell out exactly what your experience involved at an appropriate point during the interview. Ideally you will have already referred to it in your application or CV, but now is your chance to provide specifics. When detailing your skills and activities, be sure to highlight *your* contribution. This is particularly important if you have worked as a team. Where appropriate, try to use, 'I did, I was responsible for', and so on instead of, 'We did this, and we did that.'

> 'I found my clinical experience to be of great benefit when applying for jobs after university. Clinical experience gives you an opportunity in job interviews to talk about the development of your legal skills from a real account. I am certain that my clinical experience helped to give me the edge in securing my current job.' (Rich, CAB Adviser)

### Preparing for interviews

Preparation is key to a successful performance. Plan everything from what outfit you will wear to what questions you want to ask. Arrange how you are going to get to the interview to ensure you will arrive at least 10 minutes early. Prepare some outline answers to questions which are likely to come up. Your answers should be specific and concise without sounding rehearsed.

### Top tips for succeeding at interview

- Be confident – you have reached the interview stage because you are a strong potential candidate. Focus on this positive to help reduce any nerves or concerns.
- Re-read your application – it is highly likely that you will be asked to expand on some of the more interesting features of your application, so it is advisable to read over it before your interview.
- Often, several weeks or even months may have passed between submitting your application and the interview. Research and read up on any developments in the industry and check to see if the organisation has been in the news recently. This will allow you to demonstrate a genuine interest in the company and your commercial awareness.

- Do not use the same example more than twice to support your answers if possible. Draw on the full breadth of your experiences to demonstrate what a well-rounded person you are. If your experiences are limited, try to vary the way in which you refer to them.

- Find out who will be conducting the interview and look them up on the firm's website. This will hopefully put you at ease as to who will be quizzing you, but it can also be useful to forge a connection during the interview. For example, you will usually be given the opportunity to ask questions. You could perhaps ask, 'I know that you work in X department/section/area of specialism. Would you be able to tell me what a typical day in this department/section/area of specialism involves?'

- Avoid asking questions to which the answer could have easily been found on the website. Questions about salary are generally taboo and should normally be avoided.

- If being interviewed by a panel, ensure you make eye contact with everyone, not just the person asking the question.

## Interview questions

The questions you will be asked at interview naturally differ according to the role. You will often find that the questions also depend on the type of organisation you have applied to. For example, innovative firms sometimes ask unusual questions to test your creativity and ability to think on the spot. Some jobs involve being interviewed more than once, so questions will also vary depending on what stage of the interview process you have reached.

As part of your interview preparation, you should consider what questions you may be asked and prepare some answers. However, as well prepared and rehearsed as you might be, it is absolutely essential that you deliver your answers in a natural manner in the interview itself.

All of the questions below have been asked by law firms, and similar questions are more than likely to be asked by other types of organisation in the appropriate context.

### Typical interview questions

- *Why did you decide to become a lawyer?*
  It is easy to imagine what it might be like to work as a lawyer, but it can be difficult to answer this question persuasively if you do not have any real experience of the job. Here is where your clinic and pro bono experience can prove invaluable. You can answer this question in full knowledge that you have essentially been working as a lawyer when conducting your casework. You can therefore use this experience to show that your career aspirations have been consolidated with actual experience.

- *What skills do you think are needed to become a lawyer?*

- *What are a few of your key qualities that make you suited to a career as a lawyer?*
  These two questions essentially require the same answer. You need to show an understanding of the necessary skills and evidence how you have demonstrated

these skills. As above, you can draw heavily on your clinic and pro bono experiences for this question.

- *Why should we offer you the job over the other candidates who have applied?*
This question is essentially asking you to explain what sets you aside from the other shortlisted candidates. You can take it for granted that the other candidates will all meet any academic criteria which the organisation has set, so this question is a great opportunity to really sell your clinic and pro bono experience, which not everyone will have. For example, you can confidently say you have a proven track record in advising clients or managing files or public speaking and so on.

- *What is your biggest achievement to date?*
Your clinic and pro bono experience lends itself well to answering this question. The example you provide does not have to be stunning or unique; the skill is in explaining why you consider it to be an achievement. Your answer might cover negotiating a settlement for a client, successfully appealing a decision, having a pro bono activity recognised by an award and so on. You can then highlight how your skills and attributes contributed to the successful outcome.

- *What are your strengths and weaknesses?*
This is a tricky question which is almost guaranteed to be asked. Often your clinic and pro bono work allows you to discover a great deal about yourself. You may have made some surprising discoveries due to the challenging work it involves. You should therefore have an excellent appreciation of your strengths and weaknesses. Select a few strengths and back them up with appropriate examples. In relation to weaknesses, the secret is to spin any weakness into a positive. Alternatively, you can mention a weakness that you had in the past but explain how you have managed to overcome it.

- *How would you provide an excellent service to our clients?*
It is highly likely that your clinic and pro bono activities have a client at their heart. Your standards and actions will be determined by that client's best interests. You therefore have a proven track record in client and customer care. The numerous skills you have developed can be effectively used as evidence of how you can provide a service which exceeds expectations. You may even have an example of when a client provided positive feedback which can be particularly useful in proving your high levels of service.

- *How do you cope under pressure? What strategies do you have?*
Balancing your studies with your clinical and pro bono work can be challenging, particularly if you also hold down a job. As mentioned above, you will develop various skills which allow you to work under pressure, including proactivity, time management and forward planning. You will probably have at least one example to draw on from your experiences. Perhaps you have worked to a tight deadline, a presentation might have been brought forward unexpectedly, or maybe you have had to step in to do something at short notice. What did you do in those situations? Due to your proactivity, had you already foreseen or

planned for the particular eventuality? Were you able to reorganise your workload so you could focus on the priority? Did good teamwork get you through?

- *Give an example of when you have worked well as part of a team.*
  Your clinic and pro bono experiences will no doubt have involved some teamwork. You may have worked on a file together, worked as part of a team within a CAB or on placement, or perhaps you delivered a Streetlaw presentation as part of a group. When answering this question, ensure you highlight *your* contribution to the team. For example, you may have established team targets, devised a marketing strategy, motivated others or delegated tasks.

- *How would you suggest that we market our firm?*
  Law clinics and Streetlaw projects are generally reliant on word of mouth and goodwill. As part of your clinic or pro bono activities, you may have helped promote your organisation or pro bono scheme. This may have involved leafleting, campaigning or promotions. As such, you will have some knowledge of general marketing techniques which you can then widen to answer this question effectively. This question also requires some research into the particular sector in which the organisation operates and an understanding of the firm's services and client base.

- *What is a professional?*
  There is no right answer to this question, but your response might refer to integrity, high standards and so forth, with supporting examples of how you have demonstrated professionalism.

### Non-standard questions

Non-standard questions are designed to test your reasoning skills and put you under pressure. The collection of questions below is also designed to reveal something about your personality. Therefore think carefully, not so much about what your answer is, but what it subconsciously reveals about you. It is perhaps best to stay clear of vacuous personalities and individuals who have demonstrated any kind of questionable behaviour in favour of well-respected leaders or high achievers.

- *If you could speak to one figurehead from the past, who would it be any why?*
- *What person, dead or alive, has inspired you and why?*
- *Who do you most admire aside from your parents?*
- *If you could be a movie star, what genre of film would you appear in and why?*
- *What book has inspired you the most? Why was this?*

## 14.11 What career options do you have as a law graduate/ postgraduate?

A legal qualification is an excellent stepping stone into any career. The skills developed through your course are easily transferable to almost any type of employment, legal or otherwise. As more than 50% of law students enter non-legal careers, this section lists a wide range of job opportunities in the legal sector and beyond. As stated at the outset, this chapter is intended to supplement, rather than replace your wider careers research. Therefore, details on the varied roles are not provided, but you can visit the Companion Website for links to different organisations where you can find much more comprehensive information.

> 'My experience in clinic vastly enhanced my skill set and gave me the confidence to set up a business. Learning from textbooks may lay the ground work but that is incomparable to the experience of dealing with real people and their cases.' (Darren, Law Graduate)

## Within law

There are several main roles within the legal profession, most notably that of solicitor and barrister. However, these are not the only career paths to follow. Other opportunities include: paralegal, licensed conveyancer, legal executive, notary, barristers' clerk, legal secretary, patent or trade mark attorney, advice worker, caseworker and law cost draftsman.

---

**Practising as a solicitor**

There are over 145,000 solicitors in England and Wales, the vast majority of whom work in private practice.

In the last decade the number of female solicitors has increased by almost 90% with over 50,000 female solicitors in England and Wales.

The percentage of solicitors from ethnic minority groups has risen by 10%.

In the last 10 years the number of solicitors working outside of private practice has increased by over 95%.

Source: The Law Society, *Key Facts: the Solicitors' Profession*

**At the Bar**

The number of self-employed barristers totals in excess of 12,200.

The number of employed barristers is approximately 3,000.

31% of self-employed barristers are women.

Almost 40% of counsel called to the Bar in 2008 were black or of ethnic minority origin.

Since 2000 the gender ratio of those called to the Bar has been approximately 50:50.

Source: The Bar Council, www.barcouncil.org.uk/about/statistics/

---

## Law related

If you are interested in the law but feel you want a career which is not strictly law based, there are a whole range of opportunities including employment within: the Probation Service, Youth Justice Board, Police, Prison Service, Law Commission, Government Legal Service, Home Office, Court Service, Victim Support, Health and Safety Executive and Trading Standards.

You can work in human resources, legal publishing, legal recruitment, for lobbying groups and charities (for example, Liberty and Amnesty International), as a tax adviser, environmental health officer, court usher, court clerk, bailiff or research assistant.

### Non-legal employment

Typical career opportunities for law graduates include careers in tax and accountancy, banking, management and politics. The Civil Service offers a range of employment which is suited to law graduates. You may be interested in joining a graduate scheme, particularly if you have an interest in business and management. Law graduates are suited to almost any type of job because of the transferable skills developed.

> 'The experience of clinic has been an invaluable aid within my career as an auditor. The interpersonal skills developed are without a doubt the most beneficial skills I developed at university. Studying for exams and writing essays may help you acquire a vast knowledge, but without the ability to communicate such knowledge to clients in a professional manner such knowledge is wasted.' (Steph, Auditor)

### Other options

If you are not ready to commit to a particular career route or want to develop further skills before entering the workplace, you may want to consider taking a year out. A gap year can involve working in paid employment, travelling or undertaking voluntary work, all of which will boost your skills set and experience. For more detail on gap year opportunities, there are several useful websites including www.gapwork. com.

> 'My clinical experience has proved very beneficial to my education and career. It provided "hands-on" training and gave students a chance to "test the water" in a safe environment before venturing into the real world. I have recently taken up a position in the finance industry in New York, working in Regulatory Affairs & Compliance. I cannot stress how important my prior experience has been in this position. I do not think I would be where I am today if it wasn't for clinic.' (Mared, BVC Graduate and Mountbatten Intern)

 Further reading

There is a huge volume of careers-related material available, which can make it difficult to know where to start. Your institution's careers service is likely to have a range of resources and guides to various professions and aspects of the recruitment process, and this should be your first port of call. Below is a selection of some key careers publications. You can find a much more detailed list of resources and organisations on the Companion Website, including links to key organisations.

## Introductory

*Applications, CVs and Covering Letters* (AGCAS, 2009)

This accessible guide sets out everything you need to know about effective applications. It deals with the key application methods and provides sample CVs and covering letters. It also provides advice on how to answer common application form questions. Your careers centre may stock a hard copy booklet, but if not you can access an online version via www.prospects.ac.uk.

*Going for Interviews* (AGCAS, 2009)

This booklet provides a concise overview of the types of interview you might encounter, how to prepare for interviews, and advice on performance techniques. If you cannot obtain a copy of the booklet from your careers service, it can be downloaded at www.prospects.ac.uk.

## Intermediate

**LawCareers.Net (www.lawcareers.net/)**

Provides information about entry into the legal profession, but it is a particularly good site for finding out those all-important application deadlines.

**Prospects (www.prospects.ac.uk)**

As you would expect, the UK's official graduate careers website is a one-stop shop for all your career needs. It provides interactive advice and email alerts as well as comprehensive information on job sectors and applications.

**Prospects Directory**

This directory offers an excellent overview of the graduate recruitment market including graduate and company profiles, guidance on the application process and a section on alternative options which includes self-employment, further study and working overseas.

**TARGETjobs**

This publication produces a range of magazines on various sectors, and the website hosts information on over 30 key career areas. You can also download template CVs from the website at http://targetjobs.co.uk/.

**TARGETjobsLaw**

A comprehensive guide to the legal sector which is published annually. In addition to recruiter information, this magazine contains advice on entry into the profession, student and employee profiles and top tips on applications and work experience. There is also a supplementary publication covering legal work experience. See www.targetjobs.co.uk/law.

*The Training Contract and Pupillage Handbook* (The Law Society)

An annual publication which details the firms and chambers offering places for the training stage of your legal career. A comprehensive guide which is highly recommended for students intending to practise law.

## Advanced

**Baruch, Y,** *Managing Careers Theory and Practice* (Pearson Education Ltd, 2004)

An accessible and interactive text which covers the theories underpinning career choices and models which assist with career planning and management. The book includes several tests which you can use to assess your suitability for different jobs based on your personality. Chapters 2 and 3 are particularly useful.

**Trends in the Solicitors' Profession – Annual Statistical Report (Strategic Research Unit, The Law Society)**

Provides a comprehensive and up-to-date analysis of the composition and trends in the legal profession. See www.lawsociety.org.uk/aboutlawsociety/whatwedo/researchandtrends/statisticalreport.law.

For a much more concise overview of specific aspects of the profession, the Law Society also publishes a range of factsheets on issues such as solicitors' working hours, trainee solicitors' pay, and job satisfaction, which can be accessed at www.lawsociety.org.uk/aboutlawsociety/whatwedo/researchandtrends/factsheets.law.

**The Pro Bono Work of Solicitors 2007 (Strategic Research Unit, The Law Society)**

This report details the pro bono activities undertaken by the solicitors' profession. See www.lawsociety.org.uk/secure/file/180124/e:/teamsite-deployed/documents/templatedata/Publications/Research%20Publications/Documents/pro_bono_report_v7.pdf.

 Activities

### Activity 1: Skills inventory

Draw up a list of the skills and attributes you have acquired or developed specifically from your clinic or pro bono activities. For each skill, give an example of how and when you have demonstrated that skill or attribute. Once you have completed your list, identify any key skills which are missing, then devise an action plan of how you can acquire those skills.

### Activity 2: CV

*If you already have a CV* – once you have read the information above, take another look at your CV and consider whether there are any ways you could improve it. Is the full extent of your clinic or pro bono experience highlighted effectively? Could you improve the appearance by using a template? Recruiters have to be ruthless when deciding whom to shortlist – so take this opportunity to make sure your CV is up to scratch.

*If you do not yet have a CV* – it is always helpful to have an up-to-date CV to hand just in case any jobs or placements are advertised at the last minute. Re-read the key tips above and take a look at the sample CVs on the Companion Website. Decide which style suits you best and begin preparing your CV. Then follow the instructions set out above in 'If you already have a CV'.

### Activity 3: A question of communication

Prepare an answer to the following question based on your clinic or pro bono experience. Your answer should not exceed 250 words.

*'Give an example of a time when you have been required to communicate complex information to someone. How did you approach this and what was the outcome?'*

# 15 Resources

In addition to the Further Reading set out at the end of each chapter, the general resources listed below may be of use. You can find further links and suggested texts on the Companion Website about specific areas of law which may be useful for your casework. Additional resources linked to specific chapters and examples of pro bono activities which you can become involved with can also be located on the Companion Website.

## Books

**Brayne, H et al, *Clinical Legal Education: Active Learning in Your Law School* (Blackstone Press, 1998)**
Currently out of print but your library may contain a copy. This book provides an overview of the pros of clinical legal education with anecdotes from the authors' own experiences.

**Maharg, P, *Transforming Legal Education: Learning and Teaching the Law in the Early Twenty-First Century* (Ashgate Publishing, 2007)**
This book is a wide-ranging critique of existing theory and practice in legal education, focusing particularly on the value of technology, simulation and transactional learning.

**Burridge, R et al, *Effective Learning and Teaching in Law* (Routledge, 2002)**
A practical guide to legal education including chapters on experiential learning and ethics.

**Solicitors' Code of Conduct 2007 (Law Society)**
Available in hardcopy but also online at www.sra.org.uk/code-of-conduct.page.

## Journals

**Clinical Law Review (Clinical L Rev) (ISSN: 1079-1159)**
This is a journal published by New York University School of Law. It addresses issues of lawyering theory and clinical legal education and is jointly sponsored by the Association of American Law Schools, the Clinical Legal Education Association, and New York University School of Law.
www.law.nyu.edu/journals/clinicallawreview/index.htm

**International Journal of Clinical Legal Education (IJCLE) (ISSN: 1467-1069)**
Published by Northumbria University, this journal features articles, practice notes and reviews relating to all aspects of clinical legal education. Volumes can be found on

HeinOnline. More information about the annual conference which complements the journal can be found at www.northumbria.ac.uk/sd/academic/law/entunit/conferences/.

**International Journal of the Legal Profession (ISSN: 0969-5958)**
With three issues per year, this journal includes articles on matters such as work practices, skills and ethics in the context of the legal profession.

**Journal of Legal Education (ISSN: 0022-2208)**
This US journal, published quarterly, contains articles dealing with various aspects of legal education and the profession.

**Journal of the Legal Profession**
Another US journal which deals with legal ethics and other matters affecting the legal profession.

**Legal Ethics (Hart Publishing)**
An international journal dedicated to legal ethics.

**The Law Teacher (ISSN: 0306-9400)**
Produced three times a year, this is the journal of the Association of Law Teachers, which contains articles that address issues centred on legal education.

## Academic/regulatory

**Bar Council** www.barcouncil.org.uk

**Bar Library (Northern Ireland)** www.barlibrary.com

**Bar Standards Board** www.barstandardsboard.org.uk

**Faculty of Advocates (Scotland)** www.advocates.org.uk

**Higher Education Funding Council for England** www.hefce.ac.uk/

**The Institute of Legal Executives** www.ilex.org.uk

**Joint Statement on the Academic Stage of Legal Education (Joint Academic Stage Board, 2002)** www.sra.org.uk/students/academic-stage.page

**Junior Lawyers Division (England and Wales)** www.juniorlawyers.lawsociety.org.uk

**Law Library of Ireland** www.lawlibrary.ie

**The Law Society (England and Wales)** www.lawsociety.org.uk

**Law Society of Ireland** www.lawsociety.ie

**The Law Society of Northern Ireland** www.lawsoc-ni.org

**The Law Society of Scotland** www.lawscot.org.uk

**Quality Assurance Agency Subject Benchmarks for Law** www.qaa.ac.uk/academicinfrastructure/benchmark/honours/law.asp

**Solicitors Regulation Authority** www.sra.org.uk

## UKCLE clinic resources

The UK Centre for Legal Education (UKCLE) is the Higher Education Academy's subject centre for law. UKCLE supports law students and teachers to improve the learning experience. Its website (www.ukcle.ac.uk/resources/trns/clinic/index.html) holds many useful resources and articles on pro bono. UKCLE also produces 'Directions in Legal Education', a biannual newsletter which often features items related to clinical legal education. The Autumn 2010 edition contains interesting articles on the Student Pro Bono Awards, the benefits of extracurricular pro bono activities and Streetlaw. See www.ukcle.ac.uk/resources/directions/.

## Pro bono organisations

### Access to Justice Foundation
This foundation receives and distributes financial resources to support pro bono providers. The website contains a useful guide to pro bono costs orders.
www.accesstojusticefoundation.org.uk/

### Bar Pro Bono Unit
This organisation matches volunteer barristers and individuals who need pro bono representation.
www.barprobono.org.uk/

### The Clinical Legal Education Organisation
This organisation has established model standards for live client clinics. They recognise that individual institutions will have their own specific ideas and requirements, but these are intended to provide a 'benchmark for those active in or setting up clinics, and reflect the wide experience of those already running clinics both in the UK and abroad'.
www.ukcle.ac.uk/resources/clinic/index.html

### Free Representation Unit (FRU)
With over 30 years' experience, FRU provides pro bono assistance and representation via its team of trained law students and junior advocates.
www.thefru.org.uk/

### ILEX Pro Bono Forum
The ILEX Pro Bono Forum works with pro bono providers on various national and international pro bono projects.
www.ilex.org.uk/about_ilex/pro_bono.aspx

### LawWorks
This charity aims to provide free legal help to those who cannot afford to pay for it and who are unable to access legal aid. LawWorks also provides assistance to law schools wanting to establish pro bono projects and has a useful resources section on the website. It also hosts a student conference and recognises pro bono activity through the LawWorks and Attorney General Student Awards.
www.lawworks.org.uk/

### National Pro Bono Centre
A newly established centre housing LawWorks, the Bar Pro Bono Unit and the ILEX Pro Bono Forum.
www.nationalprobonocentre.org.uk/

### ProBonoUK
A national website devoted to pro bono issues
http://www.probonouk.net/

## Pro bono projects/access to justice organisations

### Advocates for International Development (A4ID) www.a4id.org/
### Amicus
Amicus is a charity which provides legal assistance to those on death row in the USA. Internships and casework opportunities are available to students.
www.amicus-alj.org/

### Amnesty International www.amnesty.org.uk

### Citizens Advice www.citizensadvice.org.uk

### Fair Trials International www.fairtrials.net/

### Global Alliance for Justice Education (GAJE) www.gaje.org/

**The Howard League for Penal Reform**

Established in 1866, the Howard League for Penal Reform is the oldest penal reform charity in the UK. There are nationwide student groups which campaign, fundraise and raise awareness of penal reform issues.

www.howardleague.org/

**Innocence Network UK**

This organisation is involved with casework and research in instances of wrongful conviction and has links across the UK.

www.innocencenetwork.org.uk/

**JUSTICE** www.justice.org.uk/

**Law Centres Federation** www.lawcentres.org.uk/

**Legal Action Group** www.lag.org.uk

**Liberty** www.liberty-human-rights.org.uk

**Public Interest Law Institute (PILI)** www.pili.org/

**Streetlaw**

Originating in the USA, Streetlaw projects educate the public about various legal issues. The Street Law Inc website provides information on the international Streetlaw programmes in operation and various related publications.

www.streetlaw.org/

# Index